FROM CULT TO CULTURE

Cultural Memory
　　　in
　　the
　Present

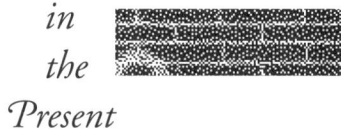

Mieke Bal and Hent de Vries, Editors

FROM CULT TO CULTURE

Fragments Toward a Critique of Historical Reason

Jacob Taubes

*Edited by Charlotte Elisheva Fonrobert
and Amir Engel, with an Introduction
by Aleida Assmann, Jan Assmann,
and Wolf-Daniel Hartwich*

STANFORD UNIVERSITY PRESS
STANFORD, CALIFORNIA

Stanford University Press
Stanford, California

English translation © 2010 by the Board of Trustees of the
Leland Stanford Junior University. All rights reserved.

From Cult to Culture was originally published in German in 1996 under the title *Vom Kult zur Kultur: Bausteine zu einer Kritik der historischen Vernunft* © 1996, Wilhelm Fink Verlag.

Preface © 2010 by the Board of Trustees of the
Leland Stanford Junior University. All rights reserved.

No part of this book may be reproduced or transmitted in any form or by any means, electronic or mechanical, including photocopying and recording, or in any information storage or retrieval system without the prior written permission of Stanford University Press.

Printed in the United States of America on acid-free, archival-quality paper.

Library of Congress Cataloging-in-Publication Data

Taubes, Jacob.
 [Vom Kult zur Kultur. English]
 From cult to culture : fragments toward a critique of historical reason / Jacob Taubes ; edited by Charlotte Elisheva Fonrobert and Amir Engel ; with an introduction by Aleida Assmann, Jan Assmann, and Wolf-Daniel Hartwich.
  p. cm. — (Cultural memory in the present)
 "From Cult to Culture was originally published in German in 1996 under the title Vom Kult zur Kultur."
 A collection of essays from 1953–1983.
 Includes bibliographical references and index.
 ISBN 978-0-8047-3983-2 (cloth : alk. paper)
 ISBN 978-0-8047-3984-9 (pbk. : alk. paper)
  1. Philosophical theology. I. Fonrobert, Charlotte Elisheva II. Engel, Amir. III. Title. IV. Series: Cultural memory in the present.
BT40.T2813 2010
210—dc22

2009013192

Contents

Acknowledgments — ix

Preface to the English Edition
Charlotte Fonrobert and Amir Engel — xi

Introduction to the German Edition
Aleida Assmann, Jan Assmann,
and Wolf-Daniel Hartwich — xviii

PART I. LAW, HISTORY, MESSIANISM

1. The Price of Messianism (1983) — 3
2. Martin Buber and the Philosophy of History (1963) — 10
3. Nachman Krochmal and Modern Historicism (1963) — 28
4. The Issue Between Judaism and Christianity: Facing Up to the Unresolvable Difference (1953) — 45

PART II. WORLD ALIENATION: GNOSTICISM AND ITS CONSEQUENCES

5. The Dogmatic Myth of Gnosticism (1971) — 61
6. The Justification of Ugliness in Early Christian Tradition (1968) — 76
7. Notes on Surrealism (1966) — 98
8. From the Adverb "Nothing" to the Substantive "Nothing": Deliberations on Heidegger's Question Concerning Nothing (1975) — 124

viii   *Contents*

   9 The Iron Cage and the Exodus from It, or the
Dispute over Marcion, Then and Now (1984)   137

10 The Demystification of Theology: Toward a
Portrait of Overbeck (1966)   147

PART III. THEOLOGY AFTER THE COPERNICAN TURN

11 Dialectic and Analogy (1954)   165

12 Theodicy and Theology: A Philosophical Analysis
of Karl Barth's Dialectical Theology (1954)   177

13 On the Nature of the Theological Method:
Some Reflections on the Methodological
Principles of Tillich's Theology (1954)   195

14 Notes on an Ontological Interpretation
of Theology (1949)   214

15 Theology and Political Theory (1955)   222

PART IV. RELIGION AND CULTURE

16 From Cult to Culture (1954)   235

17 Culture and Ideology (1969)   248

18 Four Ages of Reason (1956)   268

19 The Intellectuals and the University (1963)   282

20 On the Current State of Polytheism (1983)   302

21 Psychoanalysis and Philosophy: Notes on a
Philosophical Interpretation of the
Psychoanalytic Method (1963)   315

22 Religion and the Future of Psychoanalysis (1957)   334

Notes   *343*

Index of Names   *391*

Acknowledgments

This volume has been many years in the making. It began a few years ago with the previous editor of the humanities at Stanford University Press, Helen Tartar, with whom we acquired the rights to the English edition from Wilhelm Fink Verlag, the German publisher of *Vom Kult zur Kultur*. I came to participate in the project when Dana Hollander was preparing the translation of Taubes's lectures on Paul for the Cultural Memory in the Present series at Stanford University Press, based on Jan and Aleida Assmann's posthumous edition of those lectures.[1] Dana had solicited my advice for the rabbinic material that Taubes draws on in his Paul lectures. But, as it so often happens, life took a few detours before we returned to the project. I therefore wish to thank first and foremost Emily-Jane Cohen, the current editor of the humanities at Stanford University Press for her relentless encouragement to finish this English edition of Taubes's essays. Her expertise in French also helped us to parse out some of the French texts that Taubes quotes freely and extensively.

We also thank Hent de Vries for enabling the English trilogy of Taubes's books to appear with Stanford University Press in his and Mieke Bal's series on Cultural Memory in the Present.[2]

In the process of reinvolving myself with the project, I was fortunate to be able to enlist the participation of Amir Engel. Without Amir's dedication, this work would not have come to be. He has been a great *chevruta* for mastering this challenge. I have also had many discussions with my friend and colleague Eugene Sheppard at Brandeis University whose deep interest in Taubes's work convinced me of the importance of this English edition. During the course of the preparation of this volume I have also been fortunate to know Jerry Z. Muller, who is currently working on an intellectual biography of Taubes. I owe Jerry thanks for his encouragement.

We are particularly grateful to the two translators who helped us prepare this manuscript, Mara H. Benjamin and William Rauscher. While many of the essays in this volume did appear in English originally or in print after their German publication, there were ten that remained to be translated.

Finally, I would like to thank my colleague and friend Vered Shemtov, whose unending support in every respect made this work possible.

This volume is truly the fruit of collaborative effort.

CH. F.

I have been fascinated by Jacob Taubes's work for many years. However, it is one thing to read his works and quite another to edit and prepare them for publication in English. I was humbled by the experience. I am delighted to thank the people who allowed me to be in this position. I thank Amir Eshel for his support and trust, Assaf Sharon for his attentiveness and critical mind, and Bill Prinzmetal for helping me to escape when that was necessary. I thank Ayelet Landau, without whom this project and many other (also more mundane) projects would be worthless. Finally I would like to thank Charlotte Fonrobert, who shared with me her knowledge, passion, and friendship. Without her dedication and trust this project would have been unimaginable.

A. E.

Preface to the English Edition

1. Jacob Taubes's Work

The English edition of the edited collection of essays *Vom Kult zur Kultur: Bausteine zu einer Kritik der historischen Vernunft* (ed. Aleida Assmann and Jan Assmann, and Wolf-Daniel Hartwich and Winfried Menninghaus [Munich: Wilhelm Fink Verlag], 1996) is first and foremost an opportunity to acquaint oneself with the work of Jacob Taubes. Taubes was an outstanding intellectual figure of the kind that is rare to meet in the Anglophone intellectual world. He did not publish much during his lifetime, other than in essay form, and much of his intellectual influence was due to his charismatic teaching and interdisciplinary initiatives. It is quite possible that these very characteristics made him what he was: a leading intellectual figure in Germany.

The essays collected in this volume might seem simultaneously familiar and foreign. They are familiar because in them Taubes discusses issues and thinkers at the core of many endeavors in the humanities that inform the way we now think and assign meaning. Paul, Marx, Heidegger, philosophy of history, Gnosticism, and politics are just a sampling of topics taken up in these essays. Yet as erudite and observant as Taubes was and as familiar as his topics are, these essays differ dramatically from the kind of essays we are accustomed to anticipate from scholars of his stature. Taubes makes bold and sweeping claims about topics that most would not even venture to comment on. He rarely refers to secondary material, and his referencing is sporadic and somewhat careless, but his engagement with the primary texts is personal and demanding. Thus, many of his observations are not precise in a scholarly way, at least not in the narrow sense of the word. Most importantly, Taubes does not ever blunt his critique or mask his attacks, which are always personal and poignant. To be sure, his is a very unusual form of scholarly discussion.

Thus, even if the questions Taubes raises are familiar and widely debated, his style of argumentation is foreign, especially in the American academic context. It is the uniqueness of Taubes's rhetorical style that we would like to comment on in this preface to the English edition of the collection of his essays, as the introduction to the German edition (translated for this volume) takes on the task of providing a commentary on his thoughts. Taubes's style is not only a matter of personal disposition but also essential for understanding his project.

Taubes does not think in isolation. Even if all the essays gathered in this volume are overtly penned by him, one could argue that all his literary production is a result of a collective effort of some sort. Practically all the essays present an attempt to answer, critique, or question an already existing position or idea. Many times, he writes a direct attack on another intellectual and his ideas. Of course, this is not an entirely unique approach. Most scholars respond to and argue with other thinkers. Writing is always an argument and an attempt to join an existing conversation of living and dead thinkers who already made their point. But in Taubes's work discussion has a particular prominence. For Taubes the discussion itself does not merely serve heuristic purposes; rather, it is the fundamental form of social interaction and intellectual production. This is true in the most rudimentary as well as in the most profound sense.

Practically all of Taubes's publications are the product of conferences, interdisciplinary research groups or workshops, and edited volumes of collected essays, which he organized, to which he was invited, and for which he produced his contributions. As rich and suggestive as it might be, Taubes's legacy is therefore mostly a series of responses, rebuttals, and deliberate provocations. Many of the essays collected here, as the editors of the original German language volume indicate,[1] are the product of two research groups that met more or less regularly during the 1970s and early 1980s.[2] One obvious example is the essay "Notes on Surrealism," which consists of some introductory remarks by Taubes and an edited protocol of the subsequent discussion. The editors of *Vom Kult zur Kultur* chose to publish that protocol along with Taubes's brief essay,[3] so we integrated it here as well. Other examples are not as obvious and essentially resemble most other scholarly essays. But these are the exceptions. It ought to be mentioned, therefore, that the context of the framing debate is a helpful tool in the attempt to grapple with Taubes's essays. Much of the introduction to the German edition is devoted to describing the discussions; therefore, we will not attempt to do the same in this preface. The reader is, in any case, advised to keep in mind that Taubes is, more often than not, addressing a specific audience with specific positions on the debated questions. Thus the discussion that informs Taubes's essays is indeed a discussion in the most literal and rudimentary sense.

But the discussion in which Taubes takes part *kata sarka* only mirrors the more abstract discussion that informs the structure of Taubes's essays and his argumentation. Discussion is not only a physical reality but also an idea about the essence of the intellectual project. In the foremost sense it is this approach that propels Taubes's method. That is, for Taubes discussion is a form of thought, and it is foregrounded also in the content of the essays and not only in the circumstances of their production. The editors of the German edition write in their introduction:

The form of hermeneutics he cultivated drew from authors such as Nietzsche, Freud, Benjamin, and above all Carl Schmitt. The rule of thumb of this hermeneutic reads: "Against whom is this text written?" or "What key sentence was this text written to 'conceal?'"[4]

Taubes reads the sources, therefore, not as finite texts with finite ideas. They are for him palimpsests, which can barely conceal already existing conversations, debates, and discussions. The texts that Taubes discusses themselves also try to make a point on the background of an already given argument and in an already given historical moment. Taubes considers these texts primarily as an axis. For him—in true Talmudic fashion—each primary source is, first and foremost, a moment in time and a position in a debate. This might help explain the footnotes, or the lack thereof. It also explains why Taubes's claims move between and encompass far-flung historical circumstances, ideas, thinkers, and approaches. In this environment, where every text is an axis around which events, ideas, ideal, other texts, and foreign circumstances turn, it is difficult to do close reading and to insist on philological finitudes.

If this indeed describes Taubes's method, it must also bear some significance on the outcome, on Taubes's written text. If indeed Taubes understands texts as axes, then it should be significant not only to the texts Taubes reads but also to the texts he writes. Taubes is not only debating with his contemporaries. With these essays, he inserts himself into the argument and becomes, himself, part of the ongoing discussions, which, at least to a certain degree and again in good Talmudic fashion, transcend time and space. It would seem, therefore, that understanding Taubes requires familiarity with the themes and problems he debates. While this is obviously helpful, more crucial still is a familiarity with this way of thinking. The debate is not simply the engine of the discussion, nor is it merely an opportunity to talk, nor just the motivation that structures the method. The debate is, more importantly, the essence of the intellectual work in the first place. For Taubes, the discussion is the reason to undertake a study and is its real end. Thereby the dead letter comes alive again.

It is perhaps for this reason that Taubes's polemic is so sharp and poignant. Surely, being polemical as he was is also a matter of personality. But there is more to it than idiosyncratic character. Taubes's tone and style leave no one untouched. They demand an answer and a strong one, if possible. This brings us back to the point: more than anything else, Taubes's approach is a battle against complacency and indifference. His attacks compel and force a reply. A discussion thus ensues, topics are debated, and questions that seem to be buried in the past become important, meaningful, and alive. Of course, scholarship in whichever disciplinary guise is the prerequisite. But it is called upon only insofar as it is important; that is, insofar as people are willing to argue about it.

Criticism and negation are the building blocks of Jacob Taubes's work. He aims to refute commonly asserted ideas, argue with them, and quite literally reverse their directionality. Taubes's work attempts to think critically and anew about even the most well-established truths and questions, including their institutional setting. It proves that such an undertaking is possible and that the great texts, those that connect to important conversations and dramatic moments in history, still require rereading and attention. It demonstrates, furthermore, that such a rereading can reveal the drama of the texts' conception and shows that the tension that brought them into being still desires resolution. Indeed, Taubes's essays demonstrate that the revolutionary power of ideas does not entirely dissipate and that it still abides in revolutionary texts.

The intellectual endeavor is, for Taubes, not merely a professional or even primarily a scholarly endeavor, but rather something very personal. It should be so. For, if ideas matter, if texts still contain the energy of their inception, and history really brings about change, then the debate about them is not merely a matter of erudition and publication is not only a matter of formality.

It should come as no surprise that Taubes's name is tied to a number of intellectual and political controversies. As Mark Lilla recently noted, "Frequent the intellectual circles of any of these cities [intellectual centers in Europe and the United States . . .] and you will discover that everyone of a certain age has a Taubes story."[5] No one has yet collected these stories or written Jacob Taubes's biography.[6] As intriguing as his biographical stories are, we leave them to the biographers. Here, it should suffice to say that the biographical stories can be read as bearing more than strictly personal significance. At the same time, the style of work, its method, reason, and motivation should not be understood merely as professional. So, it is not only Taubes's ideas and positions on different issues that matter, nor even his labor of putting art in a religious context, religion in a historical context, and ideas in a social context, as has now again become so fashionable in the era of interdisciplinarity in the humanities. It is also the brilliant effort to mesh the personal and the professional, the historical and textual, the heuristic and the scholarly.

2. The Genealogy of the English Edition of *Vom Kult zur Kultur*

By now the German volume *Vom Kult zur Kultur* has attained somewhat of a canonical status in the oeuvre produced by Jacob Taubes. The credit goes to Aleida and Jan Assmann as well as Wolf-Daniel Hartwich, all of them Taubes's students, and to Winfried Menninghaus who assembled and selected the widely scattered essays that were to serve as a testament to Taubes's intellectual work. Without that volume, the impact Taubes has had on the intellectual life specifically in West Germany, but more broadly on the humanities, would hardly have become as visible as it has in recent years.

True, the broader reception of Taubes's work in recent years is due primarily to his lectures on Paul and to his creative and critical engagement with Carl Schmitt. It was perhaps Taubes's insistence that Paul needed to be taken seriously as an intellectual figure that helped spark the interest in Paul in the current intellectual scene, such as that exhibited by Giorgio Agamben[7] and Alain Badiou.[8] However, in Germany there has been a much broader recognition of the influence of Taubes on shaping not only the academic scene and the minds of many of his students but also on public intellectual life as well.[9] In addition, Agamben helped spread the gospel of Taubes to Italy,[10] where some of his work has been translated and discussed.

It seems therefore that an English edition of Taubes's essays is long overdue, not only to complete the trilogy of Taubes's books in English, *The Political Theology of Paul, Occidental Eschatology,* and now *From Cult to Culture*, and not only for reasons of intellectual history. Rather, Taubes himself—after having completed his doctoral degree and dissertation, which was the *Abendländische Eschatologie,* in Switzerland—started his academic career in the United States, at some of the major universities on the East Coast: Harvard, Columbia, and Princeton. Indeed, many of the essays assembled here, especially the early ones, were published originally in English in American journals and anthologies. For instance, the entire third section of *Vom Kult zur Kultur*, that is, all five essays on theology assembled there (Chapters 11–15), were published in English during Taubes's sojourn at American universities in the 1950s, as were a few essays in the fourth section. In addition, the essays on Jewish thought in the first section (Chapters 1–4) were also published originally in English, not only the early ones, but—we may surmise—because much of contemporary intellectual Jewish discussion is carried out in English.[11] The fact that the majority of the essays were originally published in English therefore allows us to consider this volume an English edition rather than merely a translation of *Vom Kult zur Kultur*, even as we follow the German volume.

It goes without saying that where an English original existed we adapted that version for our purposes rather than translating back from the German translations in *Vom Kult zur Kultur*. At times, therefore, the English versions that appear here are not entirely identical to their German translation in *Vom Kult zur Kultur*. As to the essays that appeared originally in German we translated them for this volume, and we are grateful to our translators Mara H. Benjamin and William Rauscher. We list their names at the end of the essays for which they prepared the initial translations. Translating Taubes is a difficult and at times impossible task, especially when trying to preserve the tone of the original. The difficulty is increased by the fact that the essays cover an incredibly broad range of subjects and intellectuals, many of whom have not been translated themselves, such as some of the work by Hans Blumenberg and Odo Marquard, to name only the most prominent. This means that often we faced the difficulty of translating the creative philosophical German of these writers into intelligible English, as Taubes quotes liberally from his interlocutors.

We discuss the provenance of each of the essays in our endnotes, in order to supplement the more general discussion in the introduction to the German volume. Further, we decided to leave Taubes's essays intact in their original form, that is, with the endnotes that he supplied (or not), in order to preserve his style. For the purposes of this volume, we sought to supply more detailed bibliographical information, and in some cases clarifications, recorded in the endnotes for each of the essays. This labor presented us with problems that at times seemed insurmountable. Often, Taubes supplies no reference to the source. Or, the endnotes lack some information that made tracing Taubes's reference very difficult, let alone those cases where Taubes quotes his sources inaccurately. Wherever possible we render Taubes's quotations directly from the existing English translations, with the corresponding reference. Where texts are not translated into English or where the source could not be traced, we translated the quotations ourselves and kept Taubes's reference in place.

All of this is to say that as much as we tried to achieve precision, this volume is not a critical edition of Taubes's essays. Alas, that aspect of the endeavor of scholarship was of only minor importance to Taubes himself. With that said, we hope that this volume will allow Taubes to continue to ignite discussion and debate on the very stage where he commenced his intellectual path.

CHARLOTTE FONROBERT AND AMIR ENGEL
STANFORD, KISLEV 5769

Introduction to the German Edition

Jacob Taubes's essays collected in this volume range from 1953 to 1983. Since there is no other monograph from Taubes after his *Occidental Eschatology* (1947), it is the task of these essays to represent Taubes's thinking across a span of thirty years. The project of editing a collection of essays represents a challenge similar to that of the volume of lectures on Saint Paul. There, it was a matter of constituting an unwritten text from an oral discourse, while here it concerns the reconstruction of a life's work out of scattered essays. That this important twentieth-century work appears only in essay form is not accidental. This circumstance resulted from the fact that Taubes constitutionally lived in a state of constant physical, psychic, and spiritual unrest, and he had little affinity for the sedentary lifestyle of a professorial scholar. Moreover, the work's essentially polemic character causes it to be documented in fragmentary literary form only. The Taubesian energy of thinking is kindled by conflict, and so, behind every text stands a specific controversy and a concrete adversary, even though they are not always foregrounded. First and foremost, therefore, the editors are faced with the task of illuminating these polemical contexts, in which a rudimentary effort will be undertaken to reconstruct the circumstances and the controversies, which are by now mostly forgotten.

These essays emerge from various time periods and far-flung intellectual contexts (Harvard, Columbia, Berlin, and Jerusalem), and to this day they remain captivating, extraordinarily dense, original, and inexhaustibly inspiring. This certainly has something to do with the particular form of hermeneutics Taubes practiced for more than two decades, holding the chair at the Freie Universität in Berlin and the Institute for Hermeneutics. His hermeneutics does not, as that of Gadamer, draw upon the Protestant theology of the Reformation and the historicism of the nineteenth century, nor does it go back to the rabbinical tradition that he, in contrast to so many deconstructivist sympathizers of Judaism, as an ordained rabbi knew in extreme detail and valued highly. The form of hermeneutics he cultivated drew from authors such as Nietzsche, Freud, Benjamin, and above all Carl Schmitt. The rule of thumb of this hermeneutic approach reads: "Against whom is this text written?" or "What key issue was this text written to conceal?" It is the matter of a hermeneutic on the trail of the implicit and marginal because it assumes that that which is disguised governs a text more than that which is articulated. It further assumes that the trace of a decisive truth proceeds diagonally toward an encoded communication. He shares with Carl Schmitt a critical sense for that hidden affinity, which binds the sharpest antagonists together. This sort of affinity linked Taubes equally to the Catholic Schmitt and Erik Peterson as well as to the representatives of the so-called dialectical theologies (Overbeck, Barth, Bonhoeffer). Essential elements of his thinking—for example, the negation of the concepts of "religion" or "culture"—stem from those Protestant thinkers.

Viewed together, Taubes's essays delineate a genealogy of modern religiosity. In order to make this subject of a life's fragmented work visible within a prismatic constellation of texts, a selection and thematic arrangement of the present material appears more sensible than a comprehensive chronological arrangement, which ultimately would have to encompass more than sixty texts. In the present arrangement, the numerous relations to the fundamental thoughts behind the two focal points of his work, the *Occidental Eschatology* (of the twenty-two-year-old Taubes) and the lectures on Paul (by the sixty-three-year-old Taubes), become distinct. In this retrospective, the "red thread," or perhaps better said, the motor of restlessness that powered his thinking throughout the decades is clearly visible. This motor is Gnosticism. Gnosticism is, for Taubes, a liminal form of thought and life, which keeps close to the border in order to be able to transgress them. In his thinking, the border does not have the function of keeping two domains apart from one another, but to do the opposite, to play them against each other or to blend them into one another. Taubes thinks from the borders. His point of view is thus one of an exposed outsider, with an advanced position. He writes on themes of theology and the history of religio-historical themes as a philosopher, on philosophical ones as a theologian and a scholar of religious studies, on Christianity as a Jew, on Jewish themes as a Paulinist, and on themes of culture and politics as a Gnostic and apocalypticist. His genius consists in casting light on what has in each case been suppressed, and in accounting for all the costs that were thus incurred. Yet, the border determines not only his method of hermeneutic border crossing but also his objects of inquiry. Every essay deals with boundary demarcations and Copernican turns.

Consider the boundary between "Cult" and "Culture," which is discussed in the early essay on Oskar Goldberg. We have chosen the title of this essay as the title for the volume because it casts light *pars pro toto* on the vector of Taubes's contributions. "From Cult to Culture"—that sounds like an evolutionary expression akin to "From Mythos to Logos." It should, however, not be understood as such. The decisive figure for Taubes's thought is not the evolutionary process, but rather the "Copernican turn." This expression occurs throughout Taubes, in both a literal and metaphorical sense. Copernican turns are transition points where it is made clear that irreconcilable positions must remain bound to one another. If the expression "from cult to culture" is understood in the sense of a Copernican turn, its dialectical tension becomes visible.

In his book *Die Wirklichkeit der Hebräer* (1925) Oskar Goldberg put forth an uncompromising archaism: his motto was "back to cult." Taubes, however, knew that there was no return to before the Copernican turn. Against this Goldbergian archaism he opposed the Kleistian insight that the return to paradise can never be found by forgetting, but rather by eating a second time from the tree of knowledge. One can never go back beyond a stage in the history of consciousness once it has been left behind. One can, however, through an excess of reflection and knowledge, remain conscious of boundaries and of that which they have excluded, and in theoretical reconstruction, envision it as an alternative to the given conditions. In light of such alternatives, the absolute tyranny of the world as a given is overcome. This outlines the program of these essays: they probe a realm beyond the border in order to be able to critically illuminate the present. To use the terminology of this essay, they thematize "cult" in order to play it against "culture." Even if one cannot return to cult, it can still be rendered potent as a critical perspective on culture in philosophical and historical reflection over and against culture. Cult can be used as an

Archimedean point to hoist the world of culture off its safe, complacent hinges: it is made accessible to freedom and negativity. Through the "antagonistic power" (H. Marcuse) of cult, the petrified forms of culture are forced open, preventing culture from becoming a steel cage.

The concept of cult, as Goldberg and Taubes use it, is equivalent to "myth." They signify a bygone stage of consciousness that depends on the principle of the here and now. For a given, precisely circumscribed "here and now" cult mediates real presence of the holy on the backdrop of its ordinary state of withdrawal. The holy is present and accessible, but not always, everywhere, and for everyone. The mode of its exceptional presence is determined through the normal circumstances of its distance and concealment. The cult concentrates and monopolizes forms of manifestation for the otherwise absent and unapproachable. In contrast, culture is to be determined as the project of creating a sphere of assured supply and satisfaction of needs based on the principle of "everything, always, and everywhere." Happiness and justice are the central values by which the goals as well as the means of culture are circumscribed.

Considered in this light, cult and culture confront one another as irreconcilable opposites. The thought of withdrawal is unbearable to culture as a project of constant supply. It strives for a homogenous and correspondingly diffuse and diluted propagation of meaning on which human life is dependent. The signature of a culture understood in these terms is, in the terminology of Herbert Marcuse, a "one-dimensional" world. Like Marcuse and Benjamin, Taubes is also in search of resources for alterity, dissimilarity, the unaccountable, of "air from other planets." Unlike Taubes, Benjamin, Marcuse, Adorno, and today most decidedly George Steiner draw the antagonistic force of their cultural critique not from the source of cult but from that of art, which in place of "cult" moved to a position external to culture toward the end of the nineteenth century and which made "air from other planets" into its program.[1] They defend the "here and now" of art that cannot be translated into the simultaneity and ubiquity of culture without losing its substance—its "aura." Jacob Taubes belongs to this line of cultural criticism, which is fed by Jewish tradition and nurtured by Kant, Hegel, and Marx, and he stands out as one of the few who did not participate in this turn to aesthetics, but rather still argues from the standpoint of "cult." Thus Oskar Goldberg, in full recognition of his fallacies, is interesting for Taubes. In Taubes's reading, critical theory achieves a new actuality because it "passes through the needle's eye of the theological."[2]

The sites and sources of such opposing forces, the antagonistic perspective of his critique, were in the first place theology and the philosophy of history. For Taubes, theology describes the external horizon of alterity, which in negation and alienation took a stand against culture as the sphere of familiarity and whose antagonistic force he intends to strengthen in a time in which Christian, particularly Protestant, theology in its conventional understanding has long since been incorporated into culture as one of its domains among others. Taubes struggles against this liberal theology, and even though his guarantors here are Kierkegaard, Overbeck, and Barth, he also draws from Jewish sources. In Taubes's understanding, theology is a product of crisis, arising out of crisis of cult and of myth. The antagonistic force of cult is recognized by theology under the conditions of crisis; that in any case is its task, which it forgot often enough. Taubes does not belong to those who believe in an evolution of consciousness in the sense of progressive rationalization. "Mythic energies" do not disappear with the decline of myth, and they "cannot be ignored without danger to society."

Another border—or is it the same one in another light?—intensified for the sake of resistance against facticity and the deployment of antagonistic energy is that between nature and history. Nature for Taubes is blind necessity, compulsion, causality, and natural law—he finds a similar concept of nature in Oskar Goldberg. Greek philosophy stood under the spell of nature glorified as cosmos. The great turn occurred with Descartes: here the human dimension, the spirit, is rendered accessible and as *res cogitans* opposed to Nature as *res extensa*. This occurred in the philosophy of the subject at the expense of the social dimension, which entirely disappeared. Hegels's concept of spirit, which Taubes circumscribes with the concepts of freedom, action, and negativity, catches a glimpse of the social dimension by way of the category of action. The proprium of the spirit is its radical historicity. History liberated from the constraints of necessity and from the course of nature: what was, can end. Everything historical is relative. Marx extends these trajectories into the political, Freud into the psychological realm. Taubes also saw in Freud a liberator who undertook the task of forcing open the compulsive constraints and restraints of human "nature" through a radical historicization of the individual. What as "nature" had turned into steel and robbed of human dimension is carried over as "history" into the human dimensions of language, of discursive unfolding, hope, and transformation.

Taubes's notorious antiliberalism, which often brought him into precarious proximity to Carl Schmitt and other conservative antiliberals, stood under the sign of this antagonistic energy. Taubes detested liberalism on the grounds that it did not recognize the very demarcations which for him made the world inhabitable at all. This also applies for the boundary between Judaism and Christianity, whose supposedly clear course, to the dismay of Jews and Christians, he repeatedly obfuscated. Early Christianity turned into Utopia to him, a brief historical phase in which the religions had not yet broken away from one another and the oppositions had not yet become lethal, but rather they channeled every force into an unheard-of escalation of internal tension. The border between Judaism and Christianity can be crossed from the perspective of the radical Gnostics, for whom all further distinctions became irrelevant.

What George Spencer Brown establishes as the first "law of construction"—"draw a distinction"—is for Taubes a law of freedom. All these distinctions have their final ground in the fundamentally Jewish distinction between "this world" and "the world to come," which Taubes accentuated in a serious and at the same time playful tone when he says, "You have to excuse me, I can't live in just one world!" The insistence on this border in all its transformations and modifications sharpened his view of the occult history of spirituality in secular modernity. He is not to be counted among thinkers like Max Weber and Hans Blumenberg who hold the project of secularization to be desirable and capable of completion. For Taubes, Gnosticism is the form in which the virulence of religion's revolutionary potential remains undiminished both after and as a result of the end of its confessional and institutional manifestations. Thus he might decode the traces of a religiosity in the modern world that is not only repressed and ever returning but above all unacknowledged and displaced. A particularly vivid example of this is the controversy with Blumenberg over the implications of surrealist aesthetics.

Taubes's thinking must be seen in the context of the reinvention of Judaism in the twentieth century. Today we see more clearly that the Jewish way to emancipation as indexed in the nineteenth century does not point toward a historically irreversible end-station, but rather that the phase of emancipation can be followed by a phase of postemancipation, a de-emancipation. It has become just as clear that the violent disruption of Jewish tradition through persecution, expulsion, and annihilation in the Holocaust actuates new forms of recomposition and reconstruction. Looking for a way from the periphery back to the center, these movements found the kernel of Judaism in various forms: Rosenzweig found it in liturgical existentalism, Buber in the Chasidic movement, Scholem in the kabbalah, Taubes, with the help of Paul, in a spiritualized Judaism. Taubes reconstructed Judaism not out of the sources of Jewish mysticism, but rather out of the Jewish/early-Christian apocalypticism that absorbed the explosive content of Gnosticism. After an encounter with Eric Voegelin, the latter was said to have remarked to a friend with every indication of horror: "Today I met a Gnostic in the flesh!" Taubes understood "Gnosticism" as a tradition of breaking with tradition, which sets on fire the cages of the world that are otherwise frozen in their immanence.

I. Law, History, Messianism

The essays in this section revolve around a concept of history that sets up the historical dimension of human existence as alternative and antithetical to everything that as "nature" or "law" in the form of the given and factual takes on the appearance of being beyond interrogation or annulment. We have placed Taubes's latest essay at the beginning in order to open the volume with a bang: "The Price of Messianism"[3] is perhaps the most radical critique that Gershom Scholem encountered during his lifetime. Taubes had submitted the lecture to the 1979 Jewish World Congress in Jerusalem, and it was rejected by the Congress' leadership, an unheard-of occurrence. For Taubes this congress meant the first return to the holy city after twenty-five years of banishment—as one might well call it in light of his fall out with Scholem. Thus it is anything but accidental that he wanted to connect with or rather stage this return as an attack on Scholem. After a minor alteration in the title, the lecture was finally accepted and presented. Members of the audience report that Taubes carried out the following discussion in six different languages (German, English, French, Hebrew, Yiddish, and Polish).[4]

Scholem had put forth, in two essays, the thesis that Jewish messianism amounts to an exit from history because it puts off the yearning for justice to the world to come and transforms the antagonistic force of critique and change into an attitude of passive expectation and hope. This is what Scholem regards as the price that Judaism has had to pay for messianism on a psycho-economic scale. The price of messianism is the retreat from history into the stand-by mode of hoping and waiting. History is for those whose time has come. That Taubes could not acquiesce without contestation to this thesis should be immediately clear. For him, messianism concentrates and forms antagonistic forces, instead of paralyzing them, and always transposed them into revolutionary action. Messianism provides a basis not for retreat, but rather for an entry into history and an exodus from the natural world of the cosmos and its political order integrated into it.

Thus it is even more astounding that Taubes waited until 1979 to formulate his opposition, and until 1982 (that is, until Scholem's death) to publish it. In 1966 he was still in agreement with Scholem's theses when what was at stake was a discussion of Max Weber's diagnosis of Judaism as a "pariah people" from a Jewish perspective.[5] In his essay, the Jewish people's outsider position, interpreted by Weber as "pariah," is connected by Taubes with reference to Scholem with messianism, which provided a basis for the abnegation of historical, that is, political action. The 1982 essay adjusts this position, which seems skewed from Taubes's own perspective and is thus to be read as a criticism not only of Scholem but of Weber as well. The outsiderdom of the Jewish people cannot be compared to the position of the pariah. The principle of hope, which promises future reincarnations to the pariah and thereby affirms the existing caste-order, turns the Jewish messianism into an antagonistic force that radically puts into question the given order by historicizing it. For Taubes, an unbroken line runs from here to Hegel and Marx.

This line is drawn out in the essay on "Martin Buber and the Philosophy of History." This essay is at the same time an example that Taubes was as much invested in the intensification of differences as in the deconstruction of conventional dualisms. This primarily concerns the conventional dualisms that dominate the differentiation between Judaism and Christianity, and particularly between Jewish and Christian messianisms. Scholem had determined this difference as the distinction between interiority and exteriority. Jewish messianism awaits the redemption in the public sphere of history, Christian in the inner sphere of the individual soul. In contrast, Taubes holds that the process of interiorization is part of the logic of messianism as such, regardless of its religious identity. Every expectation for redemption turns inward if the redemption fails to appear on the social stage of history.

Buber, by contrast, drew a completely different distinction with which to oppose Jewish and Christian messianisms: the distinction between "alternation" [*Alternativik*] and "predestination" [*Vorbestimmung*]. Jewish messianism relies on the principle of alternation, by which Buber understands a historical image that is fundamentally open. The course of history is not predested; repentance (Hebrew: *teshuva*) is always possible, also on God's side. *Techuva* means human penitence and divine forgiveness simultaneously. Paul, by contrast, represents a closed image of history: in God's divine plan, everything is presaged, and history is a secret unveiled in the course of time. The law is historicized as a station on an established course: it is given so that sin, and with it, forgiveness, can grow. The God of Paul turns back, following Buber, just as little as the Spirit of Hegel does. Buber sees the roots of Hegelian philosophy of history with its irreversible evolutionism in Pauline, not Jewish, messianism.

Taubes demonstrates the Jewish roots of the Pauline view of history. If this proprium lies in the notion of a divine plan, then Deutero-Isaiah was the first Paulinian. Paul stands entirely in the tradition of Deutero-Isaiah: "Guilt is healed and lies behind us." Here it is not a matter of Jewish and Christian, but rather of prophecy and apocalypse, both of which are manifestations of Jewish tradition. The comparison of confession, "alternation," and "predestination" do not represent a sustainable distinction. Additionally, if the course of history is predetermined, human understanding is not. Here is no necessity. Prophetic alternation does not overturn into a Pauline-Christological end of history, but rather takes on an internalized, spiritual form. Gnosticism is the knowledge of the new to be attained by the individual but within the frame of the community. In this interiorized form, the prophetic alternation constitutes one of the fundamental themes of apocalyptic literature and Western intellectual history. Here, according to Taubes, lie the roots of Hegelian philosophy of history, which he labels "historical futurism."

For Taubes, Hegel and his philosophy of history constitute the Copernican turn from ancient to modern philosophy, from metaphysics to history. Up to that point philosophy had been under the spell of the question of Being, of the timelessly true, enduring, and valid, but now the question of Becoming, of the "historical conditionality behind all our experience," moves to the forefront. In light of such an appraisal the question concerning the roots of historicism attains central significance. The answer to this question, which Taubes provides in his Buber essay, lies wholly in line with his *Occidental Eschatology* from 1947. It is that much more surprising, therefore, that in his essay on Nachman Krochmal,[6] Taubes answers this same question in a completely different way. We have chosen this essay because it illustrates the complexity of Taubesian thinking: he was able to consider the same issue in manifold perspectives.[7] This essay poses the question of the roots and origins of historicism, and here he gives a completely different answer than one would expect following the Buber essay. Neither the Jewish prophetic nor apocalyptic messianism is invoked, but rather—and one is tempted to add, by contrast—the Neoplatonic doctrine of emanation. In this theory, the path is already paved for a radical temporalization of reality, later to be explicitly unfolded by the Hegelian philosophy of history. Here Judaism is thus in its rabbinical, law-centered form as eminently antimessianic and ahistorical. Law and history here constitute an opposing pair. Historical thinking has no place within the horizon of the law. With the collapse of the messianic movements of the seventeenth and eighteenth centuries, the historical-philosophical impulses in Judaism went nearly extinct. There is no path leading from the Sabbatian theology of history—and here Taubes contradicts Scholem and Rothenstreich—to Hegel. The central philosophical traditions of Judaism, from Maimonides to Mendelssohn, were in any case based on the halachic order of thinking and were impenetrable for historical experience. Halacha and the rabbinical Judaism based on it form a temporal construction of its own kind, in which history has no place.[8]

Nachman Krochmal, whom Taubes evokes as the guarantor for his thesis on the Neoplatonic origin of the philosophy of history, was a contemporary of Hegel and a reader of his work. His central category, "spirit," was taken up from Hegel. Krochmal's work is, however, more than an adaptation of Hegel for the Jewish reader: it makes use of Hegelian conceptualization in order to articulate a new antimetaphysic and historiosophic philosophy on the basis of certain Jewish traditions. These traditions, however, which Krochmal describes in long and significant excurses, are all versions and transformations of Neoplatonic metaphysics: Alexandrinian philosophy, Gnosticism, Ibn Ezra's philosophy, and kabbalah. If Krochmal was able to render the Jewish tradition of Neoplatonism as useful for his reception of Hegelian philosophy of history, it appears obvious that Hegel as well drew from Neoplatonic sources—especially since it is well known that he protested against the disregard of Neoplatonic philosophy and instigated a new edition of Proclos's writings. Taubes sees the common denominator of the philosophy of history and Neoplatonism in the doctrine of emanation, which he understands as the temporalization and dynamicization of ontology: Being as process. The cosmos appears here not as the essence of an atemporal-eternal order, but rather as a process of development. In this doctrine Hegel and Krochmal were able to find an ontological context for their concept of spirit: "The turn to historiosophy is nothing other than a horizontal projection of the ontologically dynamic position: only on the foundation of Neoplatonic ontology can the equation of ontology and chronology become insightful."

In the same way as the Krochmal essay, the early essay from 1953 on the "Difference Between Judaism and Christianity"[9] makes the concept of law central and gives it the status of a defining, fundamental category. Not strict monotheism, not the aniconic reverence of the divine, but the recognition of the law constitutes the deciding touchstone and determining force of Judaism. Whoever annuls the law abandons Judaism. But even the annulment of the law, that is, antinomianism, is an inner-Jewish phenomenon in the form of negation. Christianity is part of a series of other inner-Jewish phenomena of crisis, which the history of Judaism has never been in want of. This history obtains its vitality from the tension of self-negation. Mysticism, ecstasy, and interiority ("heart") are phenomena of an inner-Judaic countermovement against which rabbinical Judaism established itself. This rabbinical core of Jewish identity stands and falls with the law, with the construction of an external public realm of representation, of legally defining and legally effective representation, and with the everyday sobriety of justice. This core, circumscribed with the concept of halacha, was in the course of history able to integrate the rationalistic philosophy of Maimonides as well as the wild mystic-mythological speculations of the Lurianic kabbalah, the magical ritualism of Jacob Halevi of Marvege, and the ecstatic prophecy of Abraham Abulafia because they did not destroy halacha, but strengthened it instead. By contrast, the antinomian movements, which wanted to annul the law, were condemned as heresies because they held that the messianic time had arrived and considered "belief" in the Messiah to be more salvific than observance of the law. As Christianity is only one among many inner-Judaic heresies, it is neither a problem nor a mysterium for Judaism. In Judaism there is no "Christian question."

In this construction of Judaism and Christianity, the antagonistic configuration of "cult" and "culture" can easily be detected. In the context of emancipation and assimilation, Christianity appears in the role of culture. "Emancipation opened the gates to Western culture for the Jewish community; yet this culture is based on Christian presuppositions and is marked by Christian symbols." Thus Judaism's liberal tendencies, which attempt to reform and to transform Jewish symbols, that is, the *mitzvot* of halacha in the context of modern culture, place the core of Judaism in question. Whoever considers the *mitzvot* to be only traditional "ritual and ceremony," that is, externalities that are more important than their meaning, exposes himself to a Pauline critique of law, which speaks of the "yoke of the law" and of "blind justice." In this way the antagonistic force is gambled away that Judaism derives from the justice of the law, which kept it alive for centuries and which "alone finally could put the arbitrariness of love in question."

The opposition between "law" and "belief" has of course a Christian history as well. The church fathers described the significant difference between Judaism and Christianity with the conceptual pair of *lex* and *fides*. From the Christian perspective, the law is understood as being ethnically as well as historically conditioned and bounded: it is valid only for the Jewish people and only for the time of proto-messianic expectation, which is finished upon the arrival of the Messiah. Christianity contrasts the ethnic character of the law with the universal validity of redemption through faith, and the law's collective character with the individual significance of pronouncement of faith, the creed. The law is devalued as "external" in contrast to the "internal" liberating belief. This sufficiently well-known story of Christianity's impact interests Taubes only insofar as it is seized by modern Jewish thinkers like Rosenzweig, Buber, Schoeps, and Herberg. Martin Buber takes up the antithesis of interiority and exteriority and turns it against Christianity.[10] The more original mode of belief belongs to Judaism, in which there exists a relationship of trust in God, while the Christian mode of holding external beliefs for true represents a degenerate form of belief. With their soteriological division of tasks between a Jewish covenant with God and a Christian mission to the Gentiles, Rosenzweig, Schoeps, and Herberg dismiss the exclusivist religious claims to validity of both prophetic religions together with their polemical frontlines.[11]

Taubes's contribution to this discussion consists of the demonstration that the opposition between law and belief, which from the Christian perspective divides Judaism and Christianity, arose on the horizons of Judaism and has an inner-Judaic history. In the religious experience of Judaism, messianism constitutes the counterpole to the law, out of whose latent antinomistic character Taubes explains the polemical tension between law and belief. While Christianity must diligently serve this antithesis in order to legitimate itself against Judaism, Judaism can assess or dismiss Christianity as one of its many messianic heresies, which in the course of its history produced its own antagonistic dynamic.

II. World Alienation: Gnosticism and Its Consequences

Taubes's preoccupation with Gnosticism arises out of two different impulses. First, Gnosticism interests him historically, as a manifestation of the (late) ancient history of religion, which, parallel to his understanding of Christianity, he regards as deriving from the inner crises and tensions of Judaism. Second, however, and far beyond any historical interest, Gnosticism determines his own religious experience and philosophy; he sees in Gnosticism a highly relevant theology, probably the only one that can cope with the death of God in the catastrophic events of the twentieth century.[12]

Introduction to the German Edition   xxxi

Almost all the essays collected here are based on Taubes's contributions to the Bad Homburger research group called "Poetics and Hermeneutics," or to a "secession group" that emerged from it and that was constituted by Taubes and Odo Marquard in the early 1980s around the theme of "Theory of Religion and Political Theory."[13] In Poetics and Hermeneutics, a group of leading young scholars from philosophy and literature studies came together at the beginning of the 1960s with the then-revolutionary demand for an interdisciplinary reorientation of their fields. Taubes, a founding member of the circle, represented a position as a philosopher and historian of religion, which stood in a productive polemic tension first and foremost with the philosopher Hans Blumenberg and the theologian Wolfhart Pannenberg.

The essay on the dogmatic myth of Gnosticism[14] is particularly aimed at Hans Blumenberg, who provided the circle's colloquium on myth with a seventy-page essay from which his monumental work *Arbeit am Mythos* (1979) subsequently emerged. There he draws a sharp boundary between "archaic myth," on the one hand, and its "late horizon," on the other, in which myth after its disempowerment enters into a history of literary and allegorical reception by way of Greek philosophy, historiography, and natural science. The aesthetically liberated play with myth replaces the terror of a superhuman presence of the holy as it is experienced in cult. Blumenberg contrasts this humane form of religion with Christian dogmatism, which imposes a new dictate of the holy over human life.

Greek Enlightenment is represented by Blumenberg as a "Copernican turn," which forever parts from myth as a binding form of knowledge in Western thought. Taubes revises and contradicts this in two points. First, he makes clear that it is not only Greek philosophy and Christian dogmatism that first liquidated myth. Rather, the prophetic monotheism of Israel was just as significant. If there is a Copernican turn here, and this Taubes affirms, then Israel plays as decisive a role as Greece does. Second and above all, he highlights the "dogmatic myth" of Gnosticism as a genuine form of mythic thought and representation that combines logic and myth, dogmaticism, and narrative. Myth, far from meeting its end in allegory, is here born out of its spirit. Dogmatic myth does not revert back beyond logos; rather, it surpasses it as it becomes the medium of an exclusive divine knowledge.

According to Taubes, Gnosticism carries out a restitution of the mythical view of the world in the religious context of Israelite monotheism. The basis of this procedure is the "romantic yearning" of humans for unity with numinous nature and cultic community. Taubes's interpretation of Gnosticism thus takes on two historical models—the Jewish kabbalah and aesthetic modernity—whose exciting analogies and differences he works out despite the chronological distance.

The mythological systems of the kabbalah, which Gershom Scholem similarly interpreted as Jewish Gnosticism, rebel against the transcendence of God. The distance between God and humankind in the Neoplatonic tradition is bridged by numinous mediators that emanate from divine origin.

The perception of God's distance intensifies through the historical experience of the expulsion of Jews from Spain and influences Isaac Luria's myth that before creation, God drew back into himself (tsimtsum) and shattered the vessels (kelipot) that were intended to preserve divine power in the world.

From here Taubes draws connections with the protest of poets in the nineteenth century against the modern demystification of the world, which is brought to bear on biblical monotheism. Thus Schiller writes already in the first edition of *The Gods of Greece* (1788): "To enrich one, this world of gods must die out." In the realm of art, a resurrection of the "beautiful world" of myth is possible. In the modus of fictionality, the artwork takes on the mediating function between divine and human, ideal and life.[15]

Taubes paradigmatically identifies analogy and difference between Gnosticism and modernity in his *Notes on Surrealism* from 1966. Proceeding from Hans Jonas's description of the Gnostic world-experience as "alienation" and "worldlessness," Taubes draws a parallel between the worldviews of late antiquity and modern science, both of which are marked by an all encompassing determinism. Man experiences nature as fate, from which he can be freed only by the belief that his actual self is not of this world, but rather communes with a distant God and redeemer. The Gnostic myths, like surrealist poetry, express an attitude of anarchic indifference to the laws of nature and society.

Between ancient Gnosticism and surrealism however lies also a

Introduction to the German Edition   xxxiii

"Copernican turn" in worldview. While the Gnostic could still envisage the goal of his flight from the world as the space beyond the Ptolemaic worldview, such a topography is meaningless in the infinite universe of modernity. The "beyond" which, following Taubes, is indicated by the "sur" in "surrealism," and is only representable in the hermetic form of the artwork, which is no longer concretely tied to the world.

The theological premises of Taubes's aesthetic position become clear in the subsequent controversy with Blumenberg, who regards surrealism as the consequence of the modern rationalization process, which fulfills the desires of Greek enlightenment. The "legitimacy" of modernity was thus founded precisely on overcoming the Gnostic tendencies of medieval religiosity. The free, subjective dominion of the modern artist over his work, which according to Blumenberg's analysis is expressed by the "sur" in "surrealist," demonstrates modern civilization's dominance over nature.

Against this Taubes singles out the culture-critical potential of the aesthetic avant-garde that it shares with cultic, apocalyptic, and Gnostic religiosity.

As the self-referentiality of the artwork, allegory survives the cosmos of Greek antiquity and Christian Middle Ages in which everything that exits is meaningfully ordered and symbolically interconnected, as in the mythic worldview. Taubes strengthens allegory as a religious and ethical form of thought to such a degree, as he positions himself against its devaluation in the Protestant tradition. That is to say, reformation theology and the humanistic hermeneutic set the original text against the "mystical" interpretation, which had made the iconicity of biblical and ancient tradition into the medium of new religious experience.[16]

Taubes sees allegory, much like Walter Benjamin, as the medium of cultural memory, which defies the ideological presuppositions of its respective epoch, whereby the Gnostic mind-set of world-overcoming—Benjamin speaks of "mortification"—provides the impetus. This we read in *The Origin of German Tragic Drama*: "Allegory is precisely what preserved [the world of ancient gods]. For an appreciation of the transience of things, and the concern to rescue them for eternity, is one of the strongest impulses in allegory."[17]

A further important point of reference for Taubes's theory of religion was Friedrich Nietzsche's conception of the "transvaluation of all values" as a Copernican turn within a culture's axiological universe. In *Beyond Good and Evil* Nietzsche thus grouped the Jewish and Christian religions together and set them in opposition to the Greco-Roman sphere of values. The "slave revolt of morality" against aristocratic culture began with the prophets and culminated in Paul. Max Weber took up the keywords "ressentiment" and "chandala" from Nietzsche when he depicted Judaism as a "pariah people." For Taubes, in contrast, importance lay in the differentiated interpretation of early Christianity which Nietzsche developed in the "Antichrist."

The revolution in values, which is connected with Jesus, orients itself primarily against the axiological universe of Judaism. Following paragraph 27 of the "Antichrist," the ethos of Jesus is "the Jewish instinct once again—in other words, the priest-instinct, which no longer tolerates the priest as reality." The Jesus movement is understood in this instance as a religious revolution, which, by the means of consciousness inversion, breaks away from paralyzed understanding of belief, value, and morality within the Jewish world.[18] The Judaism of the Second Temple also was a "visible religion," which in the space of architectural, ritual, and social visibility developed a great measure for aesthetics, that is, beauty, appearance, order, and rank. Against the "visible religion" of the Hellenized as well as the Pharisaic Judaisms, the Jesus movement became a religion of "unsightliness" in the form of a "paradoxical intervention," as it in later times was practiced by the "fools in Christ." The essay on the "justification of ugliness in early Christian tradition"[19] targets this aspect of Christianity and highlights the aesthetic aspects of this transvaluation of all values staged by Jesus, which must appear to the "Jews as a nuisance and to the pagans as a folly" (I Cor. 1:23).

In his analysis of the letters to the Corinthians, Taubes discovers the central significance of the Gnostic mythologeme of the hidden redeemer for Paul's Christology. If the world results from the fall of the original divine being into the evil world of matter, the redeemer must also become a sinner in order to liberate it. This conversion of form by the Messiah from the sovereignty of the heavenly world to the ugliness of the flesh, which the Christian aesthetic depends on, has a political dimension as well. The ancient cult of sovereignty represents the ruler in divine beauty.

Here Taubes indicates a subversive strategy similar to his later lectures on the "Political Theology of Paul," where he explains the apparent spirit of subservience that in Romans 13 declares authority as god-given by reference to the mentality of an underground rebel society that speculates on the coming overthrow of the Imperium Romanum by its Redeemer. Jesus Christ was likewise represented in art in complementary forms as Martyr and Imperator.

The essay "From the Adverb 'Nothing' to the Substantive 'Nothing'"[20] grapples with a completely different Copernican turn. It deals with the turn to Western philosophy and science inaugurated by Parmenides. With this turn, a ban is imposed on the concept of "Nothing" and a discursive universe opened in which "Nothing," which is excluded once and for all, can no longer be meaningfully thematized. Taubes interprets Heidegger's inaugural address in Freiburg as an attempt at anamnetic deconstruction that aims to move back to the beginnings in order to be able to peer behind the primordial course-setting and newly unfold the question of being in an anti-Parmenidean sense, which includes "Nothing." The philosophical critique that Heidegger received especially from Carnap and Tugendhat moves within Parmenidean bounds of discourse and can therefore only dismiss the discussion about "Nothing" as meaningless. Taubes's reappraisal of the Heideggerian texts finds a completely different ground: the theological and mystical teaching of the creatio ex nihilo. Heidegger accused theology of not noticing the conceptual paradox of creation from nothing. How can God create something that is not contained in his own essence? Taubes shows that medieval theology consciously strove toward this conclusion in order to protect the biblical message of creation from the pantheistic obliteration of the distinction between creator and creation. "Creation out of nothing" is a polemical formula.

Negative theology in the mystic traditions of Islamic Gnosticism, Jewish kabbalah, and Christian mysticism since Johannes Scotus Eriugene transgresses this thought, however, as it makes the Nothing that God creates precisely the epitome of his own essence. "The Nothing which conditions creation is He Himself." In a few brief strokes Taubes traces the Christian tradition from Böhme to Schelling and clarifies its proximity to Heidegger, even if he himself does not promote the mystic tradition. For Heidegger, the scene of encounter with the Nothing is not ecstasy, but ex-istence, which meets it "in anxiety," "which it opens onto the Nothing in its ownmost sense of disclosure" (Heidegger).[21]

The study "The Dispute about Marcion, Then and Now" comprises the introduction to the volume *Religionstheorie und Politische Theologie II*, which under the title of "Gnosticism and Politics" undertook a new inspection of the ancient Gnostic movements as well as an orientation of the present in light of the controversy on Gnosticism between Erik Voegelin and Hans Blumenberg.[22] Marcion is a key figure for Taubes because he embodies most distinctly the timeless, transhistorical actuality of Gnosticism. Martin Buber had previously placed Marcion in parallel with Simone Weil. In Marcion, "the secret question" (M. Buber) of Judaism takes on a discrete form. He embodies not so much an attack from outside, but rather a departure from within. He represents a uniquely Jewish as well as idiosyncratic force of negation, or antithesis that is turned against Judaism itself, without therefore turning into an "anti-Semite." Marcion intensified the opposition between creation and revelation, nature and history, to the extreme, as far as the renunciation of creation and the rejection of the creator. For Marcion, the God of the Old Testament is the creator-God; the God of the gospel, however, is an entirely different God, far removed from the world whom the Old Testament knows nothing about and whom humankind first experienced through Christ. Thus he advocates the removal of the Old Testament from the canon. In this, one can of course recognize a prefiguration of anti-Semitic impulses and arguments. Since he identified the God of the Old Testament with the creator-God, he argues for the removal of the Hebrew Bible from the canon. However, it appears to Taubes more meaningful to connect Marcion to the impulses and arguments of Judaism itself. It can be added here that creation theology does not at all play a central or commanding role in the Hebrew Bible and that the "God of the Old Testament" reveals himself not as the creation of heaven and earth, but rather as the liberator from Egypt. In Yahweh's self-presentation as "I am that" or "will be," every reference to the world is refused. In this religious "primal scene" the seeds of Marconite semantics are sown. From this perspective, the liberation from Egypt prefigures the liberation from the world as a whole. For Taubes, a clear line runs from prophecy to apocalypticism and from apocalypticism to Gnosticism. Apocalypticism is the answer to the case "when prophecy fails," and Gnosticism emerges "when apocalypse fails." Marcion's position stands within the perspective of what Taubes in his Paul lectures named "messianic logic."

The study about Franz Overbeck does not stem from the context of the discussions in Bad Homburg and operates on a somewhat different plane from the confrontation with dialectical theology. It is a loving reconstruction of Overbeck's positions by means of citations. Following Karl Löwith, Taubes is interested in Overbeck as an intellectual kin.[23] The antithesis between "cult" (in the sense of religion) and "culture" found its most intense expression in Overbeck's polemical writings. Overbeck's critique of liberal cultural Protestantism of the Wihelmine era was, for Taubes, spoken from the heart. What Overbeck had to say about Adolf von Harnack was tantamount, in Taubes's eyes, to an "execution," referring to a comparison with Eusebius of Caesarea: Harnack and Eusebius—both "hairstylists of the Kaiser's theological wig." Overbeck identified Christianity with his Gnostic and apocalyptic impulses of radical world-negation. Every compromise with the world, from the Constantinian turn to cultural Protestantism, was a betrayal. In this appraisal of Christianity, Overbeck and Taubes were in agreement. Protestant theology, particularly Rudolf Bultmann and his program of demythologization, relegated Gnosticism in its varying modalities to pre-Christian, pagan religions—which Bultmann interprets through the categories of Existenz-philosophy—in order to oppose it to Pauline Christianity. In contrast Taubes insists on the genetic and systematic connection between Judaism, Christianity, and Gnosticism; thus, he not only falls back on Overbeck but also anticipates many positions of recent theological research.[24]

III. Theology After the Copernican Turn

Most of Taubes's theological (in the narrow sense) or theological-critical essays come from the mid-1950s, when as a fellow of the Rockefeller Foundation he returned to the United States from Jerusalem with a project on philosophy and political theology and stayed at Harvard. The three most important essays appeared together in volume 34 (1954) of the *Journal of Religion*. They confronted the American scene practically for the first time with a modern form of negative theology based on Nietzsche's dictum of the death of God and became, as Thomas J. J. Althizer remarks in his collection on *Readings in the Death of God Theology*, "almost a kind of sacred text for many young theologians."[25] These essays are concerned with theology but from the standpoint of philosophy, particularly the philosophy of history.[26]

The essay "Dialectic and Analogy"[27] deals with the Copernican turn in a literal sense. It shows how cosmology and theology reciprocally condition one another. Medieval theology, which is based on the analogy between God and world, creator and creation, stands and falls with a universe divided vertically into heaven and earth, supernatural and natural. All earthly order and hierarchy represents this cosmic order. In the Copernican world this distinction collapses, and the theology of analogy thus loses its truth, clearing the field for theologies that place God and world in dialectical relation. Here ultimately only two possibilities remain: the pantheistic and the theistic option. The dialectic of identity comprises the foundation of the pantheistic tradition, which leads from Spinoza and Lessing to German idealism and to Hegel's dialectic of synthesis. The dialectic of alienation leads to a radical interiorization of heaven and leads from Luther and Pascal to Kierkegaard and Karl Barth's dialectic of antithesis (cf. Theodicy and Theology). Just as the Ptolemaic worldview and its theology of analogy emphasize the eternity of God, so is the God of the Copernican worldview and dialectical theology a dynamic "God in motion." From here trajectories can be identified that lead back beyond the Copernican turn. The theology of the post-Copernican worldview has forerunners in various mystical movements that likewise proceed from a becoming of God in the interiority of the human heart. Joachim of Fiores's historical-theological design is also based on a historicization of God. Both currents intermix in the pantheism of German idealism.

"Theodicy and Theology: A Philosophical Analysis of Karl Barth's Dialectical Theology" directly follows "Dialectic and Analogy."[28] If the latter traced the most significant line of development from the Middle Ages to Karl Barth, the former now indicates a metamorphosis within Barth's dialectic itself. Here Taubes distinguishes between three phases: the "expressionistic phase" of the first edition of Romans commentary; the "critical" phase of the second edition, with its negative dialectic inspired by Kierkegaard; and the orthodox, systematic phase of the *Kirchliche Dog-*

matik. A base stock of questions, concepts, and categories is shared by all three phases as is a strong yet implicit Hegelianism. Barth writes—with the claim to surpass Hegel—just like Hegel targeted theology with the claim to surpass it.

The conceptual pairs of diremption and alienation as well as the reconciliation and redemption constitute the fundamental cord in Barth and in Hegel. The first phase of Barthian thinking is aimed at redemption, the second at diremption, and the third at reconciliation. In this third phase Barth comes closest to Hegel, and like him ends up in a theodicy that is an apology for the world. That the world is not out of joint, but coherent, constitutes the fundamental presupposition of both Hegel's thought and that of the late Barth. The coherence of the world reveals itself to Barth not in sacred scripture but rather in the music of Wolfgang Amadeus Mozart, which is elevated to the status of a holy text. If the world—so the argument must be understood—were completely devoid of divinity, so out of joint and cut off from God, then the phenomenon of Mozart would not have been possible. Curiously, Taubes refers to this argument without commentary or criticism. Must dialectical theology, which can only recognize the ungodliness of the world, in the end relinquish theodicy to art, similar to Adorno, whose philosophy of negative dialectic leads to redemption in the mode of the "as if," and in which music likewise plays a soteriological role? Or does Mozart's music, and it alone, transcend the realm of art and become holy, that is, a revelatory text, which precisely by playing the fugue of "co-ordination" renders the reconstituted world audible? In the *musica mundana*, the spheric harmony of the Ptolemaic worldview will be restituted in the allegorical mode of aesthetic appearance.

Taubes's typology of the forms for the theological-philosophical dialectic exhibits a certain analogy to those Gnostic systems that represent the preferred object of his investigations. Marcionite Gnosticism corresponds to a negative dialectic (Kierkegaard and Barth II) that opposes God as the "wholly other" to the world. Lurianic Gnosticism corresponds to a dialectic of reconciliation between God and world that heals a break in divine essence itself (*tikkun*). Taubes points to Origen and Lessing, however, as positions that Barth was familiar with.

Taubes's occupation with Barth and Tillich, whom he discusses in the third essay,[29] has an autobiographical dimension. In his student days in Zurich, Taubes studied also in Basel with Hans Urs von Balthasar, the companion and antipode of Karl Barth, and underwent an initiation into theological discourse that had a lifelong impact on his thought.[30] He studied with Tillich in New York in 1949, where he had gone in 1947 after he concluded his doctorate degree in order to take a position at the Jewish Theological Seminary. In the same year, the essay by the then twenty-six-year-old, "Notes on the Ontological Interpretation of Theology,"[31] appeared; it merges the themes unfolded in the studies on Barth and Tillich. Like the essay on Barth, the study on Tillich begins with a conceptual determination of theology as a discourse of crisis, loss of meaning, and alienation. Theology begins where meaning is obfuscated and the "original symbols" no longer "speak through themselves." Theology is essentially commentary. This conceptual determination incidentally fully corresponds to Scholem's roughly contemporary Eranos lecture on "Revelation and Tradition as Religious Categories in Judaism."[32]

While theology compensates for alienation and translates the original symbols, which became incomprehensible, into each respective contemporary situation, it prolongs (as every compensation does) the condition of alienation. "As doctrine, theology eternalizes the alienation of humankind which it originally wanted to annul."

The situation of theology in the post-Christian era can be compared to that of Gnosticism, which wanted to preserve archaic myths under the conditions of Jewish monotheism and thus make them into allegories of worldlessness and the withdrawal of God. When Barth and Tillich thus emphatically invoke sacred scripture and ecclesiastic creed in order to distance themselves from bourgeois secularism, they cannot turn their backs on the "death of God."

Taubes raises the same objection against Tillich's dialectical theology that he leveled against the late Barth: the reproach of immanentism. As in Hegel, in Barth and Tillich "supernatural symbols are translated into immanent categories." With Tillich, this immanentism takes the form of a "Dionysian theology," which as such reveals itself in a symbolism of depth, a "transcendence from downward." Out of Gnostic-romantic yearning for universal unity, Tillich bends the Bible's transcendental thought of God into "Being itself," from whose originary ground the alienated being of the old Adam is to renew itself.

Against a "philosophical theology from Origen to Hegel" and thus to Barth and Tillich, Taubes brings to bear the superior truth of religious experience. True theology cannot help but compensate for the "disappearance of the original power of symbols" by increasing labors of reflection, but it is wrong to interpret these efforts as progress and achievement and to "make a virtue out of necessity."

Following Taubes, "the function of negation is decisive for the dialectical method." Thus for him the intensification, not the mediation of differences, is central. Both Barth and Tillich submit, each in his own manner, to the pull toward the mediation of contradictions, to reconciliation. The spirit can however develop its emancipatory force and expedite the construction of human reality only in the act of negation. In Taubes's view any form of mediation and reconciliation is regressive.

A philosophical theology that takes into account the intellectual-historical conditions of modernity must, according to Taubes, abandon the positivistic administration of articles of fate and think God as "Nothing" that is juxtaposed with all material and spiritual goods of this world and can revolutionize them.

Thomas J. J. Althizer, who made this study part of his collection *Towards a New Christianity: Readings in the Death of God Theology*, positions it deliberately together with a brilliant essay by Susan A. Taubes on "The Absent God," which in view of writings by Simone Weil develops the concept of a "religious atheism" and works out the "Gnostic characteristics" of this position.[33] One could not better characterize Taubes's own position as his onetime wife and companion did in regard to Simone Weil.

IV. Religion and Culture: Toward an Archaeology of Modernity

If there is one thing that protects as well as prevents a human from becoming aware of the truth about herself and her existence, it is culture. Culture reconciles her with the uncanniness of her existence in a strange and hostile world. Within this strange world, culture creates a sphere of familiarity and domesticity. However, by making the world hospitable, it impedes the person from remembering the constitutive estrangement from the world. It allows her to forget that she has nothing at stake in this world. The task of religion is to remind her of the alternative to that which is given to her. In this Gnostic reading, religion and culture are opposites. Thus religion is secured from the indictment as "opium for the people," as this verdict is now passed on to culture. In this impulse, a "discontent of civilization" expresses itself, which is opposite to that of Freud. Religion is the only authority, which can tear a person from his forgetfulness and forelornness in the world, completely aside from the question as to whether there is a God. It is imperative to hold on to religion under any circumstance, even under the conditions of the "death of God," that is, atheism, if we want at all to escape the totality of the *one* world into which we have been thrown by our existence.

In this Gnostic "culture-clastic" and world-negating impulse that drove him his entire life, Taubes found unusual and fundamentally different intellectual companions, who themselves never took notice of one another. Among these is Oskar Goldberg, whom Thomas Mann memorialized in the forms of Semuel (Joseph and his Brothers) and (above all) Chaim Breisacher (Doctor Faustus).[34] Taubes met Goldberg at the home of his father, Zurich's chief rabbi Zvi Taubes. The first publication on kabbalah by Taubes, then only eighteen years old, hearkened back to this encounter.[35] Goldberg took the mythical world at its word. If the myth tells that the Red Sea divided when the people of Israel marched through it, then it was divided. We have no reason, on the basis of our knowledge of the "rules of nature," to dismiss the myth and correct it. The myth breaks the laws of nature, assuming that it is strong enough. A myth is strong when it shapes the "reality" of a "people." The Hebrews were such a people that they could implement their myth and move mountains. Goldberg advances a collective constructivism: "myth as a way of world making." If one disregards—which is surely difficult—the "völkisch" undertones that already repelled Thomas Mann and that make the reading of Goldberg's *The Reality of the Hebrews* almost unbearable for us today then much of this is forward-looking and provides new access to mythology. In his readings of the Goldbergian opus Taubes succeeds in the difficult feat of skirting the obvious "reductio ad Hitlerum" and highlighting the explosive constructivist and cultural-critical aspects of this equally abstruse and fascinating text.

What unmistakably divides Goldberg's text and Taubes's readings, however, is the experience of fascism. When Goldberg affirms that from a broad perspective culture undermined and ultimately destroyed cult, Taubes delineates in opposition that it is the archaicizing return to cult orchestrated by fascism that has destroyed culture. In a very detailed and careful manner Taubes extracts the image of Oskar Goldberg as the model for Chaim Breisacher, but to anyone familiar with Taubes's concerns it is evident from the beginning that Goldberg interests him for reasons completely different than literary history. The connection to Thomas Mann is simply a hook by which to bring this forgotten, strange, and once influential and engaged voice again back into memory. If anyone it is Taubes who understood the art of hermeneutics as reconstructing a position within the conditions of its own time and its specific options and alternatives, independent from a present that always claims to know better.

As fantastic and strange as it might appear today not only to understand but to reestablish in all seriousness the mythical world as a reality sui generis, Taubes, in full recognition of the oddity of the undertaking, saw therein, above all, the radicality of negation and the overcoming of facticity and that which is taken as nature. For Goldberg, the mythical world of the gods was the counterworld to that of the reality of causality and natural law. With the invention of causality or necessity, the gods disappear. Goldberg wanted nothing less than to mobilize the antagonistic force of cult against the natural or natural-scientific reality, that is, to work miracles. This revolutionary and constructivist impulse had to impress Taubes. In Goldberg's resolution to bring about the other world by means of experimentation, Taubes perhaps recognized a spark of Jacob Frank's messianic heresy. While he of course could only do little with Goldberg's radical archaism and his experimental mythology, Goldberg remained a companion in his efforts to summon counterforces against everything that in the names of nature or culture had solidified into a "steel cage" that confined human freedom.

Interestingly, in his essay Taubes does not waste one word on Goldberg's glaring ahistoricism, which completely abandons a textual-critical analysis of the Pentateuch and instead understands it in toto as an archaic and *as such* sacred text. In such an ahistorical and holistic reading, which places the Pentateuch as a whole at Mt. Sinai and thus in the late Bronze Age, those textual levels that biblical criticism interpretation identifies as "priestly writings" and thus as a late postexilic stage turn into a founding stone of the Hebrew Bible. This concerns above all the law and all the cultic injunctions that it gathers. The historical sequence delineated by Protestant biblical criticism runs: first prophets, then law. The actual kernel of Israelite religion is composed of prophetic monotheism. In its ritualistic labyrinth, the law represents a reductive nationalistic contraction that revokes the universalist impulse of prophetic monotheism. Wellhausen was not the first to realize this: it appears in marginal form in Strabon and other Hellenistic historiographers when they deal with Moses.[36] In the text's self-presentation and in its orthodox understanding, with which the medical physician Goldberg unconditionally associates himself, this sequence is precisely inverted: first comes the law, then its prophetic interpretation. Prophets surface in a time of crisis. In Goldberg's eyes, they are a sign of degeneration. Real religion is always a religion of the tribe, and the real god is essentially tribal; universalistic monotheism is a philosophy that has given up the God of Israel in favor of an abstract religio-philosophical idea. God needs the tribe in order to manifest himself, just as the tribe can develop strength and endure in a world full of competing powers only through the God, which it, to a certain extent, created. A God is only as strong, and a "reality" is only as powerful, as the tribe that carries both. Israel and Egypt as well were both capable of this. Babylon represents the counterpart, which for Goldberg represents the epitome of a mixed culture, or as one would say today, a multicultural society. Multicultural societies are by virtue of their syncretistic structure no longer capable of a life in myth, of the formation of a religion and thus of an independent reality that could resist the tyranny of natural law; they have gone astray down the precipitous slope of "culture."

The fact that Taubes was neither capable nor disposed toward reproducing such an anachronistic textual understanding can only be deducted from the letters drawn on by Voigt. One could, from the standpoint of a historical-critical method, dismiss Goldberg's entire book as hogwash. In contrast, Taubes pursues a different path of interest: he strives in a very cautious manner to reclaim from the Goldbergian critique of civilization elements of a Holocaust-theology. What Goldberg wants to depict is the history of God's displacement. Taubes takes up this point and calls attention to the way in which many of the tendencies of such an expulsion became manifest between 1925, the publication date of the *Reality of the Hebrews*, and 1945. For Goldberg, culture signifies the erection of a counterreality against the God who abrogates the laws of nature. From the standpoint of cult, "culture" and "nature" are companions. Taubes as well maintained throughout his life a negative concept of nature, which for him was equivalent to causality, that is, to the steel cage of a relentless necessity. If a statement from "Culture and Ideology" is to be readapted in this context, for Taubes religion signifies "construction, overcoming of nature and emancipation from the horror of violence which returns eternally in cycle."[37] Culture, by contrast, is for Taubes a form of desensitization against the horror of violence, and in 1954 that means against the scandal of the Holocaust, a carrying-on as if nothing had happened, an obscurement of dark forces and monstrous truths: culture as concealment and compromise with the forces of this world.

Goldberg's tribal-mystique is unmistakably fueled by romantic roots, particularly Herder, and it is difficult not to dismiss these motifs as being in line with the spirit of the 1920s and 1930s, that is, as proto-fascist. The sympathy Taubes musters for this book can only be understood if the kabbalistic tradition of the incompleteness of God is kept in mind. There, one finds the notion that the collective labors of Israel in the realization of the law constitute a necessary support for the realization of an "incomplete" God in the world to come.

Behind the somewhat pale title "Culture and Ideology"[38] a fulminating critique of Weber and Gehlen is hidden. Both are reproached for having mythologized the imaginary and constructivist character of reality in which humankind lives and its fundamental freedom within this reality as "fate" (Weber) or as having naturalized it as biological necessity (Gehlen). Both positions are characterized as regressive. There is here in each case one single statement with which Taubes unhinges first Weber and then Gehlen. It is worthwhile to single out these statements. For Weber it reads, "When the talk is of fate, the one who knows should name names," specifically, the one who knows that "collectives are nothing but the opportunity for particular forms of specific actions to take place, actions of specific individual people. Nothing else." With this Weber himself described most clearly the circumstances that his own "mythological talk of fate" romanticizes. With Gehlen it is a matter of the continuation of a quote that puts it into a completely different light: "With great intention," Gehlen says, "humans are at any rate burned and consumed by their own creation and not by raw nature such as animals. Institutions are the great orders and fates which protect, absorb and outlive us, and into which humankind enters with open eyes. Humans are burned and consumed not only in Auschwitz and Hiroshima; rather the sacrifical ritual is permanent." The mere mention of Auschwitz and Hiroshima is enough to expose the "great intention" as well as the thoughtlessness of Gehlen's statement. It is not a matter of acquiescing to fate, but of indicting a crime. Taubes reproaches Weber and Gehlen not for their diagnoses, but for their complicity with history.[39] They present this history as an inescapable tragedy or as a natural-historical process, and if Marx intended to ironically expose this concept, they deploy it with unrestricted affirmation: "The darkness of nature finally rules."

What Taubes offers in contrast is a historical philosophy of liberation inspired by Hegel, Marx, Benjamin, and Adorno. History is the process of humankind's critical self-liberation. History, not nature, is the human dimension, and history means "emancipation and construction." Taubes develops a theory of the phases of emancipation, which he presents in detail under the title "The Four Ages of Reason." The first phase is the emancipation from religion. The critique of religion remains the model for all further stages of emancipation: the political follows the theological, the economic follows the political, followed by technological emancipation.[40] The business of the spirit is critique, not complicity with the existing condition. If Gehlen could envision a society of termites that imagine themselves to be made up of free subjects, Taubes by contrast envisions a society of free spirits that imagine themselves to be termites. Because the spirit, one is inclined to say with Milton, "is its own place, and in itself / Can make a Heav'n of Hell, a Hell of Heav'n."

The essay "Intellectuals and the University"[41] carries out these thoughts in a grand historical line that begins in the twelfth century with Joachim of Fiore. The third age, the time of the spirit that he sees arising, is supposed to manifest itself in a new form of community in which those fulfilled in the spirit can get along without church authority. Shortly afterward, *studium* constitutes itself as a third autonomous authority next to the *imperium* and *sacerdotium*, in the shape of the developing universities.

Introduction to the German Edition xlvii

The *intelligentia spiritualis* enacted by Joachim actualized itself not monkishly, but scientifically. It had to consistently defend itself for centuries in forever-changing constellations. Taubes connects the dots from here to McCarthy's anticommunist witch hunt, to the case of Oppenheimer and to Heidegger's Freiburg Rector address. The case of Heidegger precisely shows that "intellectuals can indeed tear the veil, but they can also weave it." If the scientificized (*verwissenschaftlichte*) society reverts to terror or immaturity, this is not due, as Taubes emphasizes in this essay as well, to "some blind or extraterrestrial fate. Because fate, which rules this reversal, is a social nexus of blindness which it remains the task of enlightenment to penetrate."

In history understood as liberation, the move from mythos to logos also has its place.[42] "When the mythic spell was broken, it awakened in humankind what we since Ezekiel have called 'soul': his ego." Taubes singles out the eighteenth chapter of the book of Ezekiel in order to mark another Copernican turn, namely, the epoch-making exit out of mythic consciousness. In place of the mythical nexus of guilt and sin in the chain of generations, Ezekiel places responsibility on the individual soul. "Behold, all souls are mine; as the soul of the father, so also the soul of the son is mine: the soul that sinneth, it shall die." This statement indicates the break with the mythical horizon and the advent of a new era, of the ego, of the soul, of subjectivity and individual responsibility. With the exodus from mythical collectivity, humanity fashions itself a "new heart and a new spirit." The return to myth, invoked by Odo Marquard with his "Praise of Polytheism," reverses this history and amounts to and signifies a "suspension of the ethical" and the "dissolution of the ego." Myth is to be had only at the cost of the subject.

If Taubes's two essays on myth, "The Dogmatic Myth of Gnosticism" (1971) and "On the Conjunction of Polytheism" (1983) are placed next to one another, the result is an astounding set of contexts. The first essay was directed against Blumenberg and his antithesis of mythos and dogma: Gnostic myth serves Taubes as an example of a connection between the seemingly incommensurate. The second essay, directed against Marquard, sets up its own antithesis, between mythos and "soul." Gnostic myth is nothing other than what Thomas Mann, taking up suggestions from the religious scholar H. H. Schaeder, so felicitously called a "novel of the soul." Its subject is the history of the soul. What Taubes asserts and demands in contrast to Odo Marquard's "difficulties with the philosophy of history" is, in his words, a "critique of historical reason." In these pages he summarizes the project that lies at the base of all his historico-philosophical labors and thus as well determines the framework of the essays published here.

The study on *Psychoanalysis and Philosophy* was originally a radio presentation broadcast on December 11, 1963, in the third installment of Radio Free Berlin's series *The New Virgil*. It places Hegel and Freud next to each other in a revealing exchange of reciprocal illumination. The common denominator is constituted by the concept of memory: "The Spirit, which recalls its history, is freed from the burden of the past." Psychoanalysis has consistently been criticized for exchanging "understanding with causal explanation" because it does not take place, like all understanding, in a "reciprocity of communication" (Karl Jaspers). As Taubes makes clear, the opposite is the case. Freud's concern is precisely to break free of causal explanations and to understand symptoms consistently as symbols, as signs in the frame of communicative intention. "Healing means here: that the shattered context of meaning in one's communication is reestablished." It works only if the patient collaborates in the process of understanding. Only his understanding frees him from the bondage of his symptoms. The patient must "recognize" the truth; it cannot be merely "read into him, without him being able to read it himself."

This figure of overcoming physiological compulsions through a dialectical understanding, that by and large is memory and recognition, is directly associated with Hegel. Both psychoanalysis and Hegel's dialectic "as methods are historical through and through," "their fundamental design is historical." For psychoanalysis "the human is essentially historical because he remembers. Memory introduces the historical element into human life, beyond the biological processes of growing, maturing, and dying."

In Hegel as well the concept of truth is a progressive revelation, and for him this disclosure occurs "in communication between a consciousness and its other, in language." In this context Hegel speaks not only of "doubt," but downright of "despair." Meaning and consciousness are not identical neither for Hegel nor for Marx, and Freud because there is such a thing as false consciousness. The process of reaching consciousness takes place in negation, and here the dialectical character of psychoanalysis is disclosed. The step to higher awareness occurs in the dialectical "recognition" of a repressed truth. "By means of the symbol of negation, thinking liberates itself from the bounds of repression and enriches itself with contents which for its accomplishment it cannot do without" (Freud).

"Religion and the Future of Psychoanalysis"[43] engages Freud's implicit concept of religion and his contribution to the history of religion. Freud was a well-known atheist and viewed religion as an "illusion" and an Ur-neurosis of humankind. One must, however, make a distinction here. The concept of religion, according to its literal meaning in Latin, refers to a state institution, to the state apparatus, by means of which worldly sovereignty can enter into relation with otherworldly forces. Biblical literature does not know this concept. Here something entirely different is at stake: redemption. As the concept of "religion" was applied to Judaism and Christianity, "Rome became triumphant over hope and redemption." Freud's explicit concept of religion corresponded to that of Romans. A different, implicit concept, however, lies at the base of his theoretical writings. They show an "insight into the unrelinquishable role of religion in the genealogy of guilt." Freud belongs alongside Augustine and Paul to the group of the great theologians of the original sin. According to Taubes, Freud himself saw it this way and "conceived of his work, theory, and therapy in analogy to the message that Paul preached to the gentiles." This thought, which remained to be developed in the last incomplete chapter of his posthumously published Heidelberg Paul lectures, represents the subject of this essay, which on this point can fittingly complement the book on Paul.

The essay culminates in a statement that deserves to be underlined: "Guilt cannot be overcome, it can only be recognized." In context, this means that for this guilt there is no reconciliation. On this point Freud and Taubes agree, in that Taubes's theological writings consistently denounced all religious theologemes of reconciliation in dialectical theology. This statement, however, also allows a reading that throws light on the German-Jewish relation and the German relationship with its Nazi past. What the German side advocates is reconciliation. The Jewish side demands recognition. What we must learn is the insight into the bitter fact that this guilt cannot be overcome, that the claim to reconciliation must be dropped, that what is required is recognition, that this recognition constitutes an ongoing work of memory entirely in the sense of a recognition of repressed truths. This is the task required of us. Memory is the secret not of reconciliation but of redemption.

ALEIDA ASSMANN, JAN ASSMANN, AND WOLF-DANIEL HARTWICH
TRANSLATED WITH THE ASSISTANCE OF WILLIAM RAUSCHER

PART I

LAW, HISTORY, MESSIANISM

1

The Price of Messianism[1]

I[2]

I intend to examine the inner dynamics of the messianic idea in Judaism. This entails reconsidering Gershom Scholem's theses on messianism.[3]

For there can be no doubt that Gershom Scholem has made a substantial contribution toward our understanding of messianism, shaping all our further scientific pursuit of the subject. Almost single-handedly he has provided us with the materials of the life of the Messiah Sabbatai Zevi and charted the consequences of his destiny as they affected Jewish history in the seventeenth and eighteenth centuries. The Sabbatian movement was all but unknown to the general scientific study of religion until Scholem's *Eranos* lecture of 1959, "Toward an Understanding of the Messianic Idea in Judaism." It is the leading essay in the book, *The Messianic Idea in Judaism*, New York 1971 (from which I quote by referring to pages only). Probably Scholem's most mature statement on the subject, it includes a psycho-economic calculation of the price of messianism in Jewish history.[4] This will be picked up toward the end of my communication and challenged outright.

It should be obvious that there is no historic investigation *tel quel*, but that all is entwined with the interpretation of the material unfolded. I would like to argue that the historic material presented by Gershom Scholem allows for a different reading, one that presupposes a more inflected theoretical frame of reference than that which guides his inquiry toward an understanding of the messianic idea in Judaism. His criterion of the interiorization of the messianic experience is a case in point.

In an introductory statement delivered with the voice of authority, Scholem maintains that Judaism "in all its forms and manifestations subscribes to a concept of redemption which takes place 'publicly.'" Christianity, by contrast, "conceives of redemption as an event in the spiritual and unseen realm." Jewish redemption occurs "on the stage of history and within the community"; Christian redemption takes place "in the private world of each individual." It is reflected in the soul of man, where it effects an inner transformation "which need not correspond to anything outside" (p. 1). The messianic turn toward inwardness is considered by Scholem as a "flight," an attempt to "escape verification of the messianic claim" on the stage of history.

Scholem's method of dividing the messianic cake seems to me not to derive from historic analysis. It is not an insight into the inner dynamics of the messianic idea when actualized in a concrete historical setting, but rather a hangover from the classic Jewish-Christian controversy of the Middle Ages. I tend to believe that such a static opposition between Jewish and Christian notions of redemption obfuscates the dynamics inherent in the messianic idea itself. For consider the dialectics in the messianic experience of a group at the moment when prophecy of redemption fails. The "world" does not disintegrate, but the hope of redemption crumbles. If, however, the messianic community, because of its inward certainty, does not falter, the messianic experience is bound to turn inward; redemption is bound to be conceived as an event in the spiritual realm, reflected in the human soul. Interiorization is not a dividing line between "Judaism" and "Christianity"; it signifies a crisis within Jewish eschatology itself—in Pauline Christianity as well as in the Sabbatian movement of the seventeenth century. How else can redemption be defined after the Messiah has failed to redeem the external world except by turning inward?

In Jewish terms, the reality of the external world is not visible in natural laws (*hilkhot olam*), but is represented by the Torah or divine law (*halakha*). A crisis relating to the validity of the structures of the world therefore translates itself "Jewishly" into the question of the validity of the law. Contrary to Scholem, I would argue that the strategy of Paul toward abrogation of the law was not dictated by pragmatic reasons, a surrender to an "impulse from the outside" (p. 57), but followed strictly from his "immanent logic" after acceptance of a Messiah justly crucified in consequence of the law. *Tant pis* for the law, Paul argues, and he has thus to develop his messianic theology in a "downright antinomian" fashion, culminating in the statement that the crucified Messiah is "the end of the law" (Romans 10:4). The crisis of interiorization also forces Paul to distinguish between a Jew who is "externally" a Jew, and one who is "internally" a Jew (Romans 2:28)—the term "Christian" does not yet exist for him. The crisis is an inner Jewish event. The crisis of eschatology becomes for Paul a crisis of conscience.

Turning the messianic experience inward, Paul opens the door toward the introspective conscience of the West. Hitler's evil genius perceived "conscience" as a "Jewish invention." It is the "invention" of Paul in the crisis of a messianic redemption that failed to take place publicly in the realm of history but is reflected in the soul of the community of "believers." Conscience is by no means "a nonexistent pure inwardness" (p. 2). It is inward, but exists in constant tension with the world, forcing us to construct casuistries to bridge the gap between it and the realm of the world.

The materials that Scholem has assembled and interpreted show beyond a shadow of a doubt that the symbols most alien to classic Judaism, such as the incarnation or the divinization of the Messiah, come to the fore in consequence of the inner logic in the messianic experience. W. D. Davies, who has analyzed the study of Paulinism since Albert Schweitzer, has also drawn the lines from Schweitzer's eschatological interpretation of early Christianity to Scholem's analysis of Sabbatai Zevi (*Journal of Biblical Literature*, 1976),[5] but he did not dare to challenge any of Scholem's theses. Removing the roadblock of interiorization that Scholem has erected to preserve in a dogmatic fashion an "essential" difference between the "-isms"—Judaism and Christianism—a more coherent reading of the inner logic of the messianic idea becomes possible. Internalization, or opening the inward realm, belongs essentially to the career of that "idea," if such an idea should have a career at all in an unredeemed world and not lead "in each of its manifestations *ad absurdum*" (p. 35).

The horns of the dilemma cannot be escaped. Either messianism is nonsense, and dangerous nonsense at that, but the historic study of messianism is a scientific pursuit, and in the case of Scholem itself scientific research at its best; or messianism, and not only the historic research of the "messianic idea," is meaningful inasmuch as it discloses a significant facet of human experience.

II[6]

Hegel once observed than an event becomes historically valid when it repeats itself. Marx added a cryptic remark to this statement: the first time the event occurs it is a tragedy, the second time, a comedy or a bloody parody.[7] As far as I can see, the messianic idea ran its full course in the history of Judaism in two messianic movements only: in early Christianity and in the Sabbatian movement of the seventeenth century. This is not as accidental as it might seem at first sight. The first occurs just before rabbinic Judaism has begun to mold the fantasy and the reality of the Jewish people, that is, before the destruction of the Second Temple, before Jamnia and Usha. The second comes to the fore at the time when rabbinic Judaism in its classic form begins to disintegrate—for rabbinic Judaism consistently opposed messianic movements. During the sixteen hundred years of the hegemony of rabbinic Judaism, we witness only the sporadic and always ephemeral emergence of Messiahs who leave no traces except in historiography. They rise and die with the Messiahs themselves, thus subjecting the messianic claim to verification in its most primitive, that is, "empirical," categories (p. 2), to quote Scholem's verification-principle of the messianic idea.

The only movements to continue are those where the life of the Messiah is interpreted, where outrage upon normal messianic expectation—death or apostasy—is "interpreted" for the community of "believers." It is the interpretation that makes the messianic music. The Messiah is merely the theme of a symphony written by bold spirits like Paul of Tarsus and Nathan of Gaza. Of Sabbatai Zevi, Scholem writes, "That just such a man could become a central figure of this movement is one of the greatest enigmas posed by Jewish history" (p. 59). Recourse to enigma is obviously the ruin of all historic reflection. I propose the opposite strategy, that is, to start from the so-called enigma and ask whether it is not consistent with the inner logic of the messianic idea that the Messiah lives on in the symbolic transformation of the "scandal" of his earthly life. It is in the interpretative context that the messianic message is to be found, not in the life-history of a person, which is as opaque as all earthly events usually are.

Enigma generates enigma: Scholem has advanced a rather strange thesis, striking but without any historical foundation, concerning the "dialectical" nexus between Sabbatian messianism and the rise of the *Aufklärung*[8] in Jewish history. The death of a Frankist adventurer at the guillotine of the French Revolution does not secure a link between Sabbatian messianism and the *Aufklärung*.[9] The link is too weak to sustain a dialectical turn from the one to the other. But I suggest that it is possible to chart intelligibly the rise of *Aufklärung* in Jewish history if the process is reversed. Both Lurianic kabbalah as the "matrix" of the Sabbatian movement that developed the cosmogonic myth of "exile," and Sabbatian messianism as a consequence of Lurianic kabbalah, were successful mythic responses of the Jewish community to the Marranic crisis.

On the contrary, the success of Lurianic kabbalah and of Sabbatian messianism was responsible for delaying the rise of the *Aufklärung* in Jewish history as it knocked on its door in the persons of Marranos like Uriel da Costa and Spinoza. The Marranic experience was a constitutive step toward neutralizing the demarcation between the established religious bodies of Judaism, Christianity, and Islam. Lurianic kabbalah and Sabbatian messianism recycled the Marranic crisis of the religious consciousness in mythic terms. In the ideology of the apostate Messiah rings a melody that was expounded nonmythically in the radical critique of religion advanced by dissident Marranos. Cardozo and Spinoza were more than chronological contemporaries. But even in its state of decomposition, Sabbatian messianism was no catalyst of the *Aufklärung*. The success of the mythic response to the Marranic crisis of consciousness was one reason for the delay of the *Aufklärung* in Jewish history, which after the mythic response had driven itself *ad absurdum* entered with a vengeance into the Jewish realm.

III[10]

Last but not least, we should consider the psycho-economic argument attempted by Scholem in evaluating the "price of messianism" to

Jewish history. It is not easy to establish this price list. Consider the last sentence of his justly famous essay on "The Neutralization of the Messianic Element in Early Hassidism": "But let us not forget that while Hassidism brought about an unheard-of intensity and intimacy of religious life, it had to pay dearly [sic] for its success. It conquered the realm of inwardness but it abdicated in the realm of messianism" (p. 202).[11] If, indeed, "every individual is the Redeemer, the Messiah of his own little world . . . then messianism as an actual historic force is liquidated, it has lost its apocalyptic fire, its sense of imminent catastrophe" (ibid.). But given that messianism in its Sabbatian form led into the abyss, why not "pay" that price gladly? Scholem here opposes the conquest of the realm of inwardness to messianic hope, whereas, historically speaking, it is only via the realm of inwardness that the absurd and catastrophic consequences of the messianic idea are to be avoided. May not Hassidism be understood as the viable mythic response whereby Lurianic kabbalah overcame the disastrous apocalyptic consequences manifested in the Sabbatian comedy of the community of the apostate Messiah, especially in its sinister version of the community of Jacob Frank that overtook East European Jewry in the eighteenth century? Scholem resists seeing internalization as a legitimate consequence in the career of the messianic idea itself.

One word more by way of conclusion regarding Scholem's general assessment of "the price demanded by messianism, the price which the Jewish people have had to pay out of its own substance for this idea" (p. 35). I quote the key sentence of his reasoning verbatim: "The magnitude of the messianic idea corresponds to the endless powerlessness in Jewish history during all the centuries of exile, when it was unprepared to come forward onto the plane of world history" (p. 35). I venture to say that this calculus does not stand up to historical scrutiny. It is not the messianic idea that subjugated us to "a life lived in deferment." Every endeavor to actualize the messianic idea was an attempt to jump into history, however mythically derailed the attempt may have been. It is simply not the case that messianic fantasy and the formation of historical reality stand at opposite poles. Consider the millenarian expectations of the Puritan community in New England. Arriving at the Bay of Massachusetts to create a New Zion, they founded in the end the United States of America. If Jewish history in exile was "a life lived in deferment," this life in suspension was due to the rabbinic hegemony. Retreat from history was rather the rabbinic stance, the outlook that set itself against all messianic lay movements and cursed all messianic discharge a priori with the stigma of "pseudo messianic." Living in the "four yards of Halacha,"[12] rabbinic Judaism developed during centuries of exile an extraordinary stability of its structures. From the *Mishna* of Yehuda Hanassi to the *Mishna Berura* of the Ḥafetz Ḥayim, the community of the "holy people" continued to live in history "as if nothing happened." For all practical purposes, we existed outside history. Only those who jumped on messianic bandwagons, religious or secular, giving themselves entirely to their cause, burned themselves out in taking the messianic risk.

When in our generation Zionists set out on "the utopian retreat to Zion," rabbinic authorities looked askance at the enterprise on the whole and were frightened by the "overtones of messianism that have accompanied the modern Jewish readiness for irrevocable action in the concrete realm" (p. 35) of history. The messianic claim "has virtually been conjured up" (36) out of the horror and destruction of European Jewry and has allowed wild apocalyptic fantasy to take over political reality in the state of Israel. If the messianic idea in Judaism is not interiorized, it can turn the "landscape of redemption" (p. 35) into a blazing apocalypse. If one is to enter irrevocably into history, it is imperative to beware of the illusion that redemption (even the beginnings of redemption, *athalta di geula*![13]) happens on the stage of history. For every attempt to bring about redemption on the level of history without a transfiguration of the messianic idea leads straight into the abyss. The historian can do no more than set the record straight. But doing so, he can pose a problem and signal a danger in the present spiritual and political situation of the Jewish people.

2

Martin Buber and the Philosophy of History[1]

I

Interpreters of history since Hegel have tended to regard the arena of world history as the high court of justice against which there is no further appeal. In the succession of ruling empires the eye of the Hegelian philosopher discerns a meaningful pattern and brings order into the crisscross of events. But at what price is this pattern of meaning, this order in the succession of events, achieved? By what criterion are order and meaning established in the course of history? The suspicion arises that Hegelian philosophy of history proceeds by a mystification, turning the *post hoc* into a *propter hoc*. The succession of events is explained and justified by the success of the stronger who through victory closes the alternatives of a specific historical situation and forces the course of history in one direction.

Is the eye of the philosopher or historian who reads meaning into history not dazzled by the success of the victor? Since the rulers of any time are the legitimate heirs of all those who have ever conquered before, the chain of succession of the periods of history reads as an apology of the ensuing successes throughout the ages. The booty carried along in the triumphal procession of the ages settles down as the heritage or tradition of man. History is written by the verdict of the victor, so that the silent suffering of the conquered does not enter into its annals.

The triumph of the successive powers in the course of history becomes all the more the last judgment when the principalities of the world claim to draw the legitimacy of their power from divine authority. Then, indeed, every soul becomes subject to the higher powers of the magistrate. "For there is no authority but of God" (Romans 13:1).[2] If the powers that be are said to be ordained by God, then whoever resists the powers resists divine ordinances. Therefore, the first great Christian interpreter of history warns that those who resist the authorities call upon themselves divine judgment and damnation. It is against such an apotheosis of history that Martin Buber feels called upon to protest. The dilemma, but also the crux of his historical thinking, is prescribed by the apparently contradictory task of taking the course of history seriously and yet brushing history against its grain.

II

Hegel's philosophy of history by elevating the course of history to the high court of justice destroys, according to Buber, the dialogical meaning of history. It liquidates both the question that a particular situation has in store for man and the answer he has in all freedom to give to the questions posed by the situation. All human decisions are turned by Hegel into sham struggles. Buber traces the root of Hegel's monological concept of history to the Christian, especially to Paul's concept of history as a history of salvation. In short: in order to oppose Hegel's philosophy of history Buber has first to strike at Paul's theology of history.[3]

Since Paul nowhere in his epistles summarizes his theocentric[4] conception of history Buber must piece together Paul's theology of history from scattered statements. Paul considers the drama of history as the "mystery" predetermined by God, kept hidden before the aeons and generations. But with the coming of the risen[5] Messiah the mystery has "now" become manifest and should be disclosed and proclaimed by the apostle as the "good news"[6] to the nations. This mystery was hidden in particular from those who were assigned the principal roles in the drama of history. For had they known this mystery then the princes of this world, whose leader Paul calls on occasion the god of this aeon,[7] would not have fallen into the trap of crucifying the "Lord of Glory." The Crucifixion of the Messiah by the powers and principalities[8] (represented by the authorities of the Synhedrion and Pontius Pilate) is a ruse of divine providence whereby the powers help to promote their own overthrow and thus accomplish, surely against their will, the end of history.

But not only in the last stage of the drama of history does the ruse of God work through the principalities and powers toward the redemption of man. Even the gift of the law to Israel, which occupies a significant and indeed central position in Paul's mind, the purpose of which is the redemption of man and the world[9]—even this law serves to multiply transgression so that grace can hereafter abound. The Messiah is "delivered up" to the rulers of this aeon in the concealing "form of a slave" and is delivered unto death according to the law, thus canceling the bond that stood in the law against man. The Messiah sets aside the claim of the law "nailing it to the Cross."[10] In his death on the cross the Messiah disarms the principalities and powers and makes a public example of them.[11]

This divine law, Paul intimates, has not been ordained by God Himself but was mediated, through angelic powers. They employ the law, which is in itself holy to make men self-righteous so that he may become completely subject to them. The law, contrary to the original designation that was announced to Israel, is no longer something that gives life and no longer effects, as was intended, the justification of man, but brings about sin and wrath. "God, whom Paul speaks of as the God of Israel, gave them the Law in order to cause them to be frustrated by the fact of it being incapable of fulfillment."[12] The law was not given in order to be fulfilled but rather to call forth sin—and thus prepare the way for man's redemption. Everything is predetermined in this drama of redemption. Paul's process of history "no longer cares about the men and the generations of men which it affects, but uses them and uses them up for higher ends."[13] In the modern period, Buber remarks at the conclusion of his analysis of Paul's theology of history, the philosopher Hegel has torn up the Pauline conception of history from its root in the actuality of faith and transplanted it into a dialectic in which "Reason" by its "ruse" forces the historical process unwittingly toward its perfection.

III

Paul's theology of history develops in the context of the apocalyptic messianic experience. This experience as we know it from "the apocalyptic writings of Jewish and Jewish-Christian coinage in the age of late

Hellenism and its decline"[14] grows, however, out of Hebrew prophetism.[15] Therefore Buber feels compelled to stress the difference between the apocalyptic and prophetic experience of history. Buber's typology, concerning the prophetic and apocalyptic spirit, is fundamental for his understanding of history.

Common to both is faith in the one Lord of the past, present, and future history of all existing beings; both views are certain of His will to grant salvation to His creation. But how this will manifest itself in the pregnant moment in which the speaker speaks, what relation this moment bears to coming events, what share in this relation falls to men . . . at these points the prophetic and the apocalyptic messages essentially diverge.[16]

The prophet announces "what God is working"[17] in two different ways. The one speaks in terms of an open alternative. But even if those to whom the prophet appeals persistently resist the call and he no longer proclaims the alternative, but announces the approaching catastrophe as inevitable—even in this threat the undertone of an alternative is still audible. The divine call and man's response are related in the Hebrew text by a correspondence of the key term of prophetic language: *teshuva*, the turn. Man's turning as well as the divine response

are often designated by the same verb, a verb that can signify to turn back as well as to turn away, but also to return and to turn toward someone, and this fullness of meaning was taken advantage of in the texts.[18]

The prophetic message preserves, according to Buber, the dialogical intercourse between the divine and the human from all temptation to encyst the mystery of history in a dogmatic fashion as in the Pauline message of the crucified Messiah.[19] The mystery of history rests for the prophets in man's power of actually choosing between the ways. Only a being who has the power to choose between alternatives

is suited to be God's partner in the dialogue of history. The future is not fixed, for God wants man to come to Him with full freedom to return to Him even out of a plight of extreme hopelessness, and then to be really with Him.[20]

Man is created to be a center of surprise in creation and therefore factual change of direction can take place toward salvation as well as toward disaster, starting in each hour, no matter how late.

The apocalyptic message stands[21] in direct antithesis to the prophetic experience of history. Nowhere in the text of the apocalyptic writers does Buber discern the experience of history actually open to alternatives.

> Everything here is predetermined, all human decisions only sham struggles. The future does not come to pass. The future is already present in heaven, as it were, present from the beginning.[22]

This future can therefore also be "disclosed" (*apo-kalypsis*) to the ecstatic visionary, and he, in turn, can "disclose" it to others in letters or pamphlets. The apocalyptic

> though he knows, of course, of the struggle in the soul of man, accords to this struggle no elemental significance. There exists for him no possibility of a change in the direction of historical destiny that could proceed from man.[23]

In short: The apocalyptic no longer knows an historical future in the real sense. The present aeon hurries to an end, and ultimately the proper (and paradoxical) subject of the apocalyptic is a future that is no longer in time. The consummation of history that the apocalyptic expects has no longer an historical character.[24] "Man cannot achieve this future, but he also has nothing more to achieve."[25]

IV

Buber's analysis of the historical categories of prophecy and apocalyptic[26] is heavily charged with language rooted in the existentialist protest against Hegel's philosophy of history. In order to understand some of the presuppositions of this protest it is imperative that we turn to the perplexities of modern philosophy of history.[27] Philosophy of history was born in a time of crisis, in response to the birth pangs of modern society in the time of the French Revolution. A new consciousness of time broke through in the revolutionary age. Time became an urgent concern of philosophy, more urgent than ever before in its history.

The problem of history came first into focus in the romantic nostalgia for passed possibilities. Since the traditions were rapidly exhausted, this nostalgia had to feed on a progressive erosion of past traditions. But soon it became obvious that philosophy of history could also be used as an algebra of revolution: the passed possibilities of history had to be surpassed in the future. The loss of tradition made a search for a new basis of human existence imperative. Hegel's philosophy of history is still midway between the romantic and the revolutionary version of modem philosophy of history. His philosophy of history is no longer philosophy as a theory or contemplation of eternal ideas in the Platonic sense, but as philosophy as a theory of action. Nevertheless, Hegel's philosophy of history is still philosophy in the classic sense and therefore, necessarily, theory of *past* action: that is, the understanding of the essence, beginning, middle, and end of history. The course of history as a whole could, according to Hegel, only be the object of philosophic analysis if history does not extend into an unknown future. Therefore Hegel had to "close" history with the advent of the French Revolution and the empire of Napoleon (or later with the Prussian state).

The students of Hegel, however, considered "the spirit of time" no longer as a measure of insight into past history only, but also as a guide for *future* action. Philosophy of history thus became for Hegel's disciples a theory of action: past, present, *and* future. Philosophy of history becomes messianic prophecy[28] in the historic futurism of the Young-Hegelians as the latent messianic element of Hegel's philosophy of history broke through and gained currency in two major versions: in the social-universal gospel, and in the national-universal gospel of redemption. A social class or an ethnic-national group was singled out to be the carrier of the universal message of redemption. This messianic carrier was destined to "realize" the heavenly city on earth.

Marxism is only the best-known version of the historic futurism current in the nineteenth century. In the Marxist drama of redemption the class of the proletariat functions as the redeemer of society. The proletarian class being actually deprived of all human dignity is summoned in this hour to act as the servant of humanity. But the messianic role in the drama of history could also be assigned to other groups: Kireyevski, Bakunin, Belinsky, Dostoyevsky, and Count Cieszkowski interpreted the role of the Slavic nations in messianic terms. Like Marx they are rebellious disciples of Hegel. Hegel, they argued with Marx, still belonged to the philosophers of the old dispensation who "interpreted" but did not "change" the world. The key terms that express this new sense of history and philosophy: the charged use of terms like "realization" or "action" (versus idle, irresponsible "contemplation," or "theory"), of the adjective "concrete" (versus "abstract," which was the damning accusation against the entire thought and life experience of the West since Descartes or since Plato and Thales), of symbols like "I and Thou" or "the relation between men" (versus the neutral or neutralizing concept of spirit in Hegel's philosophy)—these and other peculiar uses were current in the language of the left-wing disciples of Hegel who stood in open revolt but also (and perhaps therefore) in total dependence on the master.

In this context of social and national messianic ideologies current in the circles of the left-wing Hegelians we find also Moses Hess who couches the experience of the dispersed Jewry awakening to its national destiny in the language of historical messianism. Buber himself points to Moses Hess as one of his forerunners. This hint is more than merely a bibliographic footnote. In 1904 already, in a survey on the origins of Zionism, Buber draws attention to Moses Hess, who (as Buber sees it) anticipated the coming generation of Zionists. Hess grasped that the living seed of the future of Jewish life rested exclusively in the Jewish masses of the East; he perceived the regeneration of the heart as the first task of the coming revolutions, and he also recognized the significance of Hasidism as a paradigm for the Jewish historic movement of the future.[29]

In this early note, sketching the role of Moses Hess in the development of Zionism, Buber, indeed, anticipates in outline his own lifework: a theory of Jewish national humanism[30] out of the sources of the messianic experience latent in Jewish life and religion. The relation between Moses Hess and Buber is not simply a matter of filiation of ideas; rather, it points to a structural kinship: Hess anticipates Buber in his strictures against the Marxian chiliasm (and was therefore "liquidated" by Marx and Engels in the last version of the *Communist Manifesto*); in his stress on the individual (which Hess develops in a short brochure on the *Philosophy of Action*, influenced by Feuerbach and Bruno Bauer); in his theory of nationalism that assigns to different nations and peoples different modes of experience and tasks for historical realization; in his critique of Christianity that seeks the salvation of the individual in a realm not of this world; in his stress on the messianism of the prophets and the rabbis that seeks the perfection of man in the actual life of the social community.

This congruence in structure between Moses Hess and Martin Buber goes beyond a general tendency in sketching the historical development of mankind. The parallelism touches the very core of their symbolic language and shows that the symbols and criteria of contemporary existentialism in general and of Martin Buber's dialogical philosophy of history in particular have been forged in the generation after Hegel. What was controversial in the small circle of intellectuals on the margin of bourgeois society and of the academic institutions in the 1930s, 1940s, and 1950s has become in our century[31] the general temper of continental thought and experience. The generation of the Young-Hegelians forged in their controversies the symbols that became the signals for the revolutionary, socialist, and nationalist movements[32] of the twentieth century.

If, therefore, Buber aims his arrows against the apotheosis of history current in Marxism and in the German variety of existentialism, he only continues the argument of Moses Hess. Marxist theory of history, Buber contends, has erroneously been related to the messianism of the prophets. In the Marxist

announcement of an obligatory leap of the human world out of the aeon of necessity into that of freedom the apocalyptic principle alone holds sway. Here in place of the power superior to the world that effects transition, an immanent dialectic has appeared. Yet in a mysterious manner *its* goal, too, is the perfection, even the salvation of the world. In its modern shape, too, apocalyptic knows nothing of an inner transformation of man that proceeds the transformation of the world.[33]

Apocalyptic, old or new, by linking the events of history in a scheme of necessity passes over and obliterates the efficacy of individual resolutions and actions.

The shadow of Hegel, according to Buber, also looms over German existentialism. As

for Hegel world history is the absolute process in which the spirit attains the consciousness of itself; so for Heidegger historical existence is the illumination of being itself; in neither is there room for a suprahistorical reality that sees history and judges it.[34]

In the ontological affirmation of history, inaugurated by Hegel and unfolded by Heidegger, historical time is absolutized. Then it can happen, Buber remarks (in view of Heidegger's inaugural address as rector of the University of Freiburg in the fateful year 1933), that in the midst of current

18   LAW, HISTORY, MESSIANISM

historical events the time-bound thinker ascribes to the powers that be the character of an absolute. Thus the goblin called success may occupy for a while the divine seat of judgment.

V

Martin Buber's critique of philosophy of history[35] remains, however, entangled in the realm of history. He cannot take an Archimedean point outside of the process of history and, like Indian sages or Greek philosophers, declare history as an illusion or dismiss it as a tale told by an idiot surely not worthy of the attention of philosophers. His protest against the judgment of history does not lead him to an escape from history, but rather to dissent in the midst of history against the actual course Western history has taken. His protest against the judgment of history is itself philosophy of history, or perhaps formulated more sharply: in Buber's critique of Paul's history of salvation and of Hegel's dialectic of reason in history messianism is pitched against eschatology,[36] one version of messianic hope is put over and against another version of messianic consummation.

Messianic futurism is, according to Buber, rooted sociologically and psychologically in the Jewish experience, and therefore the early Buber can call messianism—in a totally mythic-immanent fashion—"the most deeply original idea of Judaism."[37] In the later writings of Buber (after the First World War) the mystic-immanent[38] interpretation of messianism gives way to a more religious-transcendent view. God is no longer chained to the social and psychic setup of Jewish experience, but He forges the recalcitrant clans into a unit in the encounter at Sinai. And in response to this encounter the tribes recognize YHWH as King over Israel and dare the expectation that He will be King over all the nations.

The origins of messianism are now traced by Buber back to the primitive charismatic theocracy in early Israel. But even in this later period (which comprises Buber's monumental works on *Moses*, on the *Kingship of God*, and on *The Prophetic Faith*) the basic symbols of the early period are carried over and overshadow the free and utterly sovereign will of God in His calling of Israel. Ezekiel in his great review of Israel's history (ch. 16) surely did not find much of a natural context for the divine action in and through Israel. Buber's statement about the prophetic theologem on history (even as late as in "Prophecy, Apocalyptic, and the Historical Hour" [1954]) still stresses man's action as an agent of redemption so as to recall the revolutionary activities interpretation of messianism of the early days. In the prophetic message I hear, however, first and foremost overwhelmingly announced that God is God and not man and that His ways are not to be measured with the yardstick of man. Even the experience of the covenant does not erase for the prophets the inscrutable and hidden God as the prime agent in history.[39]

In this perspective the difference between prophecy and apocalyptic loses much of its weight. Perhaps it is characteristic that when speaking of prophecy Buber speaks of "the prophets in the ages of the kings of Judah and Israel"[40] while I pointed to Ezekiel—and Buber himself has to admit that the other great prophet of the Babylonian exile is an exception to his concept of prophecy. But what crucial exception does Deutero-Isaiah present! What use is a typology concerning the prophetic and apocalyptic experience of history if Deutero-Isaiah, whom Buber rightly calls "the originator of a theology of world-history,"[41] has to be exempt from the rule?

Among the prophets he was the man who had to announce world history and to herald it as divinely predestined. In place of the dialogue between God and people he brings the comfort of the One preparing redemption to those He wants to redeem; God speaks here as not only having foreknown but also having foretold what now takes place in history—the revolutionary changes in the life of the nations and the liberation of Israel consummated in it. There is no longer room here for our alternative: the future is spoken of as being established from the beginning.[42]

This transformation of the prophetic perspective has been made possible, according to Buber, by the unheard-of new character of the historical situation:

Here for the first time a prophet had to proclaim an atonement fulfilled through the suffering of the people. The guilt is atoned for; a new day begins. During this time in which history holds its breath, the alternative is silent.[43]

If, however, Buber puts the emphasis on the alternatives in the *course* of history as the fundamental criterion to distinguish between prophecy and apocalyptic, then the message of Deutero-Isaiah must be transferred, much against Buber's original intention, into the opening chapter of the apocalyptic experience of history.

Considering the message of Deutero-Isaiah we must agree with Buber that the future is spoken of as being established from the beginning and that there is no longer room in his prophecy for an alternative in the course of history.[44] But in Deutero-Isaiah as well as in all other apocalyptic literature, ancient or modern, a set of alternatives arises on an entirely new level that carries an appeal to the individual and to the communities of no less if not more dramatic intensity than the message of the prophets in the ages of the kings of Judah and Israel. The apocalyptic seer confronts us with the alternative whether we perceive the change, the new beginning in history, or whether we are blind to the new day that is actually dawning. This new alternative is surely of such dramatic tension that it divides believers and unbelievers into children of light and children of darkness—a symbolism constantly recurring in the apocalyptic literature since Deutero-Isaiah until the latest version of Marxist chiliasm.[45]

It is out of the spirit of this new set of alternatives that the apocalyptic congregations throughout history have gained an intense stimulus to action. The brazen necessity in the course of history—as all historians can attest—has not in the slightest paralyzed the efficacy of individual or communal resolutions and actions, but rather strengthened the will of the apocalyptic messianists to overcome all obstacles on the way to the consummation of history. The apocalyptic "must" does not imply the kind of necessity characteristic of the neutral "must" usually ascribed to the laws of nature, but rather is coined in the strongest anticipation of the end of history in the actuality of faith.[46]

VI

Buber has justly pointed to essential Gnostic features in Paul's vision of God and human: the relation between the divine and the human is mediated in Paul's mind by derivative powers, which, ruling the world, work against the primal divine power to ensnare man; the ambiguous function and character of the law; the divine ruse in overcoming the rulers and emancipating man from them—but Paul could rightly consider his version of the history of salvation in line with the theology of history of Deutero-Isaiah, and Paul indeed, makes heavy use of the suffering servant, the central symbol of Deutero-Isaiah's theology of history, in his description of the role of the crucified Messiah in the drama of redemption.

As the anonymous prophet proclaims an atonement fulfilled through the suffering of the people, so Paul proclaims an atonement fulfilled through the suffering of the crucified Messiah. Both—so we can extend the parallel further—proclaim that "the guilt is atoned for, a new day begins." For both one can say—what Buber only admits for Deutero-Isaiah (still dividing him sharply from the apocalyptic and Gnostic experience)—that during "this time in which history holds its breath, the alternative is silent." In the interpretation of the legacy of Deutero-Isaiah's theology of history Buber could have, it seems to me, struck at the heart of Paul's theology of history, thus meeting his great antagonist face to face. Buber does not come to terms with Paul's theology of history in his theoretical treatment of the problem of history. Nevertheless, throughout his work, in the historical studies of biblical as well as Hasidic literature, Buber is guided by an "open" messianic interpretation of Deutero-Isaiah's *theologem* on the servant that contests implicitly (by unfolding the motif of the suffering servant throughout the history of Jewish faith) the Christological encystment of the messianic secret in Pauline Christianity.

The figure of the Messiah was, according to Buber, twice transformed in the course of the pre-Christian period, and both times under the pressure of crises. First, the role of the Messiah originated in the actual historic context of Israelite history, as seen in the prophetic perspective: The king is the Messiah, the anointed one, who—in the perspective of the prophets—is thereby entrusted the task of realizing the divine will in Israel. As the kings fail to fulfill the expectation the prophets reply with the prediction about the coming of one who will fulfill the task. With the destruction of the commonwealth, the old political messianic hope loses ground. It is not destroyed, but transformed in quite an unprecedented form by the anonymous prophet of the exilic community. The messianic task in its actual form was divided by him into two: the task of the political restoration is assigned to a foreign prince, to Cyrus, while the actual commission to establish the righteous community is assigned to the "servant of YHWH." The commission to him embraces two functions, which are divided among different persons, who, however, represent two manifestations of the same figure. The first function of the servant is suffering. The servant "takes" upon himself the burden of the sins of the "many." He who is without guilt exculpates them and thereby makes possible the speedy breakthrough of redemption. This preparatory function of the servant is his messianic secret occurring in his present concealed form as a prophet in Israel. The second function of the servant, the messianic fulfillment, is reserved for another public appearance: it is the messianic fulfillment. Then Israel and the nations of the world will recognize how and through whom the preparation took place. Essential to this understanding of the mystery of the servant is that the one appointed for his messianic vocation remains like an arrow in the quiver until he is drawn out.

But even in this vision of Deutero-Isaiah the messianic servant is presented as a human being and not as a heavenly one. This changes with the second crisis in the postexilic period: in the Syrian Hellenistic persecution of the community of Israel.

People tend then not merely to despair of the saving achievement of the King, but of that of earthly man in general. The world can no longer be redeemed by the world.[47]

First in the book of Daniel and then more definitely in the book of Enoch, the servant takes on heavenly features. Not the person but the form of the redeemer becomes preexistent. But from this level of experience only one step has to be taken to conceive of the Messiah as a heavenly being who came down to the world, sojourned in it, left it, ascended to heaven, and now enters upon the dominion of the world.

Against this tendency toward the deification of the servant that the Christological interpretation of the suffering servant entails, Buber insists on the continuous function of the suffering servant throughout history. Already the prophet, according to Buber (who upholds the Masoretic text), speaks "curiously enough" about his deaths—in the plural. The messianic secret in the message of the prophet unfolds in a series of servants, a series at the beginning of which the speaker sees himself. Whosoever accomplishes in Israel the active suffering "in the name of Israel" (Buber draws out the implications of the vision of Deutero-Isaiah), he is Israel as servant. And Buber sees the traces of the figure "of the suffering Messiah that appeared from generation to generation and goes from martyrdom and death to martyrdom and death" throughout the history of Israel.[48]

In the chronicle *For the Sake of Heaven* [German title: *Gog und Magog*—Ch. F.] the "mystery of history" leaves the realm of theoretical dispute and doctrine and reaches into the depth of the actuality of faith. It is a chronicle on "Gog and Magog," on the "messianic secret," and therefore the figure of the synoptic Jesus looms in the background. Reproached for changing some features of Jacob Isaak of Pshysha (called among Hasidim "the holy Yehudi" or shorter "the Yehudi" (= simply "the Jew")) under the sway of a Christianizing tendency, Buber rises to a final clarity in his answer: Whatever in this chronicle the Yehudi may have in common with Jesus of Nazareth derives not from a tendency of the biographer but from the common source that nourished their lives.[49] It is the reality opened up by Deutero-Isaiah's vision of a series of "successive servants." The life of Jesus cannot be understood unless we recognize that he stood in the shadow of the image of the servant as seen by Deutero-Isaiah. But he emerged from the hiddenness of the quiver, while others remained within it.

At this juncture the history of the messianic expectation breaks asunder. When his end is in sight, Jesus breaks the restraint imposed on the bearers of the messianic secret; he breaks the seal of this secret, imagining and declaring himself in his own person as the one who will be removed and afterward sent again to fulfill his office. By breaking the seal of the messianic secret he provided the opportunity for the mythical elements lying ready in time of Hellenistic decadence to crystallize in a new image of God: the binitarian God-image. The messianic passion for the cause of God turns into a passion for the cause of Jesus.

The breaking of the seal of the messianic secret led to the deification of one of the suffering servants in the series of the successive servants. For Buber, however, the course of messianic history *remains* a mystery and a secret: the arrow in the quiver is not its own master.

It is necessary to visualize the hand that first sharpens the arrow and then slips it into the darkness of the quiver and the arrow that huddles in the darkness.[50]

The mystery of history unfolds in the historical chronicle around two characters that, like master and disciple, really represent one destiny: Jaacob Yitzchak, the seer of Lublin; and his disciple Jaacob Yitzchak, called simply "the Yehudi," the "Jew." Note, both master and disciple carry the same name: *nomen est omen*. Both come out of the same root: the hope and passion of redemption. But Jacob Isaak, the "seer," the apocalyptic who looks and "sees" into the mystery of redemption, filled with ceaseless waiting for the hour of redemption finally tries to "grasp" the mystery by initiating and performing secret rites with the purpose of converting the Napoleonic wars into the premessianic final battle of Gog and Magog. While the apocalyptic seer "forced the end," the Yehudi, the seer's most loyal disciple, kept clear from all theurgic magic. He did not wish to hasten the end, but rather to prepare man for the end.

In language already dangerously near to the theurgic mystique of Marxism, the seer expounds the "dialectic" of the apocalyptic mystery of history:

Redemption is no ready-made gift of God handed down from heaven to earth. The body of this world must travel as in birth and reach the very edge of death before redemption can be born. . . . We must wait for the hour in which the sign will be given to us to influence them (the conflicts of the world) in the depths of the mystery.[51]

The Yehudi and other disciples sense that the master has lost the path of faith. For truly redemption does depend on man. Not on his power, however, but on this repentance.

Rightly do our sages say that all periods set for the coming of the Messiah have passed by and that his coming depends wholly on our repentance and return. . . . At times in a walking dream I see the Messiah lift the ram's horn to his lips. Yet he blows no blast. What does he await? Not that we practice incantations over mysterious forces, but simply that the erring children return to our Father.[52]

The seer, however continued with his theurgic Gnostic enterprise by fanning the flames of the great conflagration since he was convinced that "the men of Israel will not repent. And yet will the Redeemer come."

Trapped in his magic enterprise he looked for a messenger to go up to the heavens and bring him down the "secret" of redemption. He proposed to his disciple that he "should die and bring him a message from heaven."[53] The Yehudi did not waver even from this request and obeyed as a true devotee of his master. He did not refuse to give his life even though he resisted the task of the master to force the end, for "If one is permitted to bring a message from the world of truth, it is bound to be a message of truth."[54]

In the days between the Day of Atonement and the feast of Tabernacles the "passion story" of the Yehudi begins. Shortly before his death he speaks to his disciple Rabbi Bunam about

> the three hours of Gog and Magog and before the coming of the Messiah.... They will be much more difficult to endure than all the tumult and thunder and ... only he who endures them will see the Messiah. But all the conflicts of Gog and Magog arise out of these evil forces which have not been overcome in the conflict against the Gogs and Magogs who dwell in human hearts. And those three hours mirror what each one of us must endure after all the conflicts in the solitariness of his soul.[55]

In this chronicle we catch a glimpse into Buber's foundations. Surely not his entire spiritual substance originates in the faith of the Hasidim, but his striving is the continuation of the Hasidic striving: a messianic inspiration without employing in general the form of eschatological actuality. Paradoxically expressed: it is a messianism of continuity.[56]

The messianism of continuity that Buber not merely formulates as a paradox of faith but as a program of action is beset by a fundamental perplexity. The arrow that remains in the quiver and huddles in its darkness lacks (like the "beautiful soul" of which Hegel speaks in most telling passages in his *Phenomenology of the Spirit*) the power to externalize itself, the power to transform itself into an enduring existence.

> It lives in dread of staining the radiance of its inner being by action and existence. And to preserve the purity of its heart it flies from contact with the actuality and steadfastly perseveres in a state of self-willed impotence to a self that is pared away to the last point of abstraction.[57]

In this transparent state of purity it becomes a sorrow-laden "beautiful soul" that wastes away. Whether Jesus or the Yehudi: the effect is the same. Both collide with the stronger fate of the unredeemed world. Their relation to the world is entirely passive. Thus the beautiful souls conscious of this contradiction seek destruction, thirst for death, or run into madness. The call for "realization" and "action" that fill the pages of Buber's writings remains a gesture so long as it is not admitted that in the process of realization and action man's original purity of intention must be transformed and sullied by the complexity of the recalcitrant reality.

Buber's philosophy of history is torn asunder by two conflicting motives. Consider first Buber's romantic nostalgia in his relentless search for the states of immediate charismatic experience in history in which the original state of communion between men is becoming historic actuality. These enthusiastic moments in history in which human life is lived in the immediacy of an unalienated encounter between persons serve for Buber as paradigms for man's existence in history. In the perspective of these paradigms Buber judges the course of human history as a process of decay or of reification. The original spiritual impetus is slowed down or even paralyzed by the impersonal institutions that transform the personal charisma of the early stage into a routine that is sanctified by the authority vested in the institutions themselves.[58] Whether Buber describes the fate of early Israel from the stage of a primitive theocracy in the desert in which Yahweh reigned as King and leader of the tribes to the hereditary monarchy of the Davidic house that mediates the divine charisma in the organized state or whether he describes the fate of the early Christian community charting the development from the Galilean circle of disciples in the presence of Jesus to the sacramental church adoring Christ as a mediator between the divine and the human, or whether he sketches the fate of the Hassidic community from the early state of free teachers to the later state of shamanlike Zadikim following each other by the law of hereditary succession, the story Buber is telling follows repeatedly the same scheme of corruption of the status of personal charisma by the powers of institutions that try to capture the power of the spirit in impersonal vessels.[59]

Consider, however, finally Buber's continuous call for "realization" of the demand of the spirit in the midst of the historical realities and you realize that the destiny of the primitive theocracy in early Israel as well as the destiny of the early Christian or early Hassidic communities is not an arbitrary fate. Does not the momentous charismatic experience in the early (archaic or primitive) stage of a communion "necessarily" crystallize in the course of history in institutions that grant to the life of the spirit the cohesion of the generations? If the human spirit is only anxious to preserve its state of original purity, living in the dread of staining the radiance of its inner being by action and existence, then it condemns itself to a state of self-willed impotence. If the enthusiastic moments in history should not evaporate into thin air, then the critical question must focus on the transfer of the enthusiastic undivided state of communion into the very fabric of institutions that guarantee the cohesion of the generations. Buber, the historian, cannot deny that in spite of all corruption and degeneration a continuous transfer of the paradigm of an eschatological community into various historical configurations occurred throughout Western history of the last millennium.[60] Every new significant version of messianic hope, every new pursuit of the millennium has forged new forms of fellowship between men giving endurance and cohesion to the fabric of social institutions.

Surely the suspicion against Hegel's philosophy of history is valid insofar as Hegel takes the success of the victor as a criterion for meaning in history. For, indeed, the suffering of the conquered may in his endurance show better the stuff history is made of.

> Thus the world is like an oilpress: under pressure. If you are the dregs of the oil, you are carried away through the sewer; if you are genuine oil you will remain in the vessel. But to be under the pressure is inevitable. Observe the dregs, observe the oil. Pressure takes place ever in the world, as for instance, through famine, war, want, inflation, indigence, mortality, rape, avarice. . . . We have found men who grumble under these pressures. . . . Thus speak the dregs of the oil which run away through the sewer; their color is black because they blaspheme: they lack splendour. The oil has splendour. For here another sort of man is under the same pressure and friction which polishes him—for is it not the very friction which refines him.[61]

History, we would have to say against Buber's critique of philosophy of history, is constituted by both elements: it originates in the ecstatic moments and is shaped by the routine everyday. Surely the routine has to be judged in the light of the paradigm of the ecstatic moments. But the ecstatic moments have to be judged whether they are closed in themselves or whether they carry consequences creating social time and social space, dividing the periods of history into a before and after.

3

Nachman Krochmal and Modern Historicism[1]

I

Since the end of the eighteenth century a new style of philosophy has come to the fore, which has transformed all our modes of historic experience and sensibility. The new style affects, perhaps even liquidates the theological or juridical dogmatic thought patterns of the past. The historic sense or historic consciousness is not merely a tool of our historic scientific investigation, a specific technique of inquiry into historic data, but a new philosophy that invades all forms of experience and denies or rejects nature as the norm. This new sense for the historical conditioning of all our experience antiquates all previous philosophy, previous theology, as well as previous historiography.

The genesis of historicism is still an unexplored avenue. Friedrich Meinecke, the teacher of Franz Rosenzweig, published in 1936 a work in two volumes on the origin of historicism.[2] But Meinecke did not come to grips with the problem stated in the title. In tracing a line from Shaftesbury and Leibniz to Herder and Goethe, he analyzed the genesis and the development of concepts like human creativity or individuality. A genealogy of the historic consciousness, however, that bypasses Hegel and his school seems, to say the least, incomplete.

In a more penetrating way our problem was confronted by Ernst Troeltsch in his *Der Historismus and seine Probleme*,[3] a book not at all superseded by the current dogmatic fashions in philosophy, theology, or political science. Troeltsch was not unaware of the dangers and perplexities involved in the new historicist philosophy, but it seemed to him, nevertheless, futile to open up again the battle between the ancients and the moderns. The return to a dogmatic method in theology, or the return to old doctrines of natural law in philosophy or to old theories of natural right in political science, may be and, indeed, has been argued with great skill, but no amount of argument can rebuild the theological and cosmological premises on which the ancient and medieval philosophy rest. (It may be ingenious to argue for a Ptolemaic worldview several hundred years after Copernicus, but Galileo's quip remains pertinent: "And nevertheless she moves." For Troeltsch, as well as for us, it is more relevant to discuss the consequences entailed in the "Copernican turn," in the new historic sense of philosophy and theology.)

This modern historicism—if we may use the multivalent term also in this sense—rendered obsolete the tradition of a *philosophia perennis* that interpreted reality in general and human existence in particular in terms of a *lex naturae*. The new style of philosophy called into doubt not simply a juridical doctrine of natural right or of natural law, but also eroded the concept of nature as conceived by classic philosophy and carried on by medieval scholasticism. In the light of the new historic sense, also the historiography of the ancients until the period of the Enlightenment looks rather unhistorical, for classic historiography tells history as a series of *exempla* of the perennial virtues and vices of man. Writing or telling history as stories of examples presupposed the notion of a permanent and fixed nature of man. History was for the ancients less philosophical than poetry because the ratio of accidental factors was greater in a historic rather than in a poetic account.

Taking the clue from Troeltsch, from Karl Loewith, and others who have put together at least fragments toward a genealogy of our new historic consciousness, we may say with some degree of certainty that the origins of the new style in philosophy and history are to be traced back to the apocalyptic Christian theology of history—or more sharply: the historic sense of "new philosophers," to use Krochmal's coinage, is a theology *cachée*. One need merely mention the Tübingen Seminary to understand what idealistic philosophy of history at bottom is: a secularized version of Christian theology of history.

It is not within the scope of this investigation to retrace the steps from early Christian theology of history to the philosophy of history of the new philosophers of the eighteenth and nineteenth centuries. It should suffice if we focus our analysis on one of its key terms, viz. that of "absolute spirit," a term that governs also the argument and the rhetoric of Nachman Krochmal.

In one sentence of the preface to his *Phenomenology of the Spirit*, Hegel summarizes the program of the new philosophers: "In my view—a view which the developed exposition of the system itself can alone justify—everything depends on grasping and expressing the ultimate truth not as *Substance* but as *Subject* as well."[4] This sentence seems significant, for it contains Hegel's critique of classical ontology, the critique of the philosophy of Plato and Aristotle, and may well serve as a guide to understand the "transcendental" Copernican turn of the new philosophy of Kant and Hegel.

Classic philosophy, Hegel argues, developed its categories by interpreting reality as substance or by unfolding the concept of nature. If I ask, What is the "nature" of man? What is the "nature" of the world? What is the "nature" of the gods? I always ask for the same underlying *nature*. Even meta*physical* categories are still physical in their root; they are governed by a norm of *physis* or nature. This is the case also in a Christian theology that distinguished between the natural and the super*natural* realms, and, thus, conceived of the super*natural* in naturalistic terms. The new philosophers tend to break away from the ontological frame of classical philosophy. The universal category of the new philosophy is not *physis* or nature, but spirit. Its ontology must unfold in an entirely new frame. The categories of the new philosophy are transcendental and not metaphysical. They do not take nature as a norm but the production of man: history. Human creativity is placed above nature.

At the end of the passage in which Hegel states in a nutshell the program of the new philosophers, Hegel returns to the theme of the relation between substance and subject: "That the truth is realized only in the form of system, that Substance is essentially Subject is expressed in the idea that represents the Absolute as Spirit [*Geist*]—the grandest conception of all, and one which is due to modern times and its religion."[5] The absolute as spirit—this again is a statement to oppose classic ontology. Hegel does not seek the key for the interpretation of reality in the cosmos, in an eternal nature, but in the spirit that reveals itself in the historic action of man, in history. When Hegel summarizes his philosophy in the sentence "Substance is essentially Subject," or represents "the Absolute as Spirit," he is remembering the Christian origins of the Copernican turn from nature to history. Spirit is for Hegel a modern term, "one which is due to modern times and its religion."

Yet Hegel, who stresses the Christian origins of this term, when he uses it as the title for the sixth chapter of his *Phenomenology*, does not deal with a kingdom that is not of this world, nor with the history of salvation as a historic course (*procursus*) of the City of God or of the church, but rather presents the development of secular history, the history of the *saeculum* from the Greek city-state to the French Revolution and the empire of Napoleon. The realm of the spirit is the secular history. The temporal realm itself, which Christian religion had separated for centuries from the spiritual realm, is for Hegel the reality of the spirit.

II

We have to keep this Copernican turn from ancient to modern philosophy in mind when we inquire into the premises of Nachman Krochmal's program. I have stressed the Christian origins of the concept of spirit, and I think that our analysis of the passage in the preface of Hegel's *Phenomenology of the Spirit* will bear out the specific Christian lineage of this concept, which is of crucial importance for the new philosophers. Krochmal did not haggle with the "new philosophers" like some of the apologists of the nineteenth century. Krochmal took his stand entirely within the premises of the new philosophy.

Our first question must therefore be: Can the transformation of Christian theology of history into a philosophy of history be repeated in the frame of the Jewish tradition? It is true (at least as we, the heirs of the nineteenth-century historiography, can see it) that history is the inner form for the recital of acts of divine revelation in scripture. It should, however, be remembered that there are ahistorical strata of Wisdom literature in scripture to which less or no attention is paid today in the vogue of the various theologies of history. Even with respect to the history of the covenants, it must be said that since rabbinic times an ahistorical mode of exegesis of scripture prevails in the synagogue. Contrary to the general consensus, it seems to me that the rabbinic tradition, on the whole, neutralizes the historical realm and stresses Torah, both the written as well as the oral law, as a perennial law. The exegesis of the law jumps over the historic shadow and interprets the entire tradition as Mosaic or at least as of equal relevance or dignity with the Mosaic law. When rabbinical exegesis deals with historic data, it incorporates them as exempla into a perennial frame: the fathers already kept the commandments; King David or King Hezekiah fulfilled every iota of the law. Through the law of the Torah a contemporaneity is established in history which for the rabbinic tradition relegates the historic process to irrelevancy. There is no evolution from the absolute event of Sinai onward. The act of revelation is in an emphatic sense the center of history drawing all peripheral events toward itself. I do not think that the doctrine of the rabbis can be called *"geschichtsbejahend"* (affirming history) and contrasted with the doctrine of the apocalyptic writers that Professor Glatzer calls *"geschichtsverneinend"* (negating history)[6] except in the sense that the realm of creation is not negated in rabbinic doctrine. For if we ask which of the two doctrines develops a sense for history as a process unfolding in stages, then, it seems to me, that the apocalyptic doctrine is at the origin of what we call the historic sense or the historic consciousness.[7]

The sectarians could easily use covenantal language and develop categories such as the Old and the New Israel, the Old and the New Covenant, and thus provide, or at least prepare, for the Copernican turn from the metaphysical to the historical ontological categories. The conservative element of rabbinic tradition was and is not as hospitable to such extreme historicizing of the Divine acts. The messianic stance was to be kept in check by the overriding interest to conserve or to preserve the law and to build a fence around it. Maimonides, the philosopher and codifier of the law and of the entire halachic tradition, strikes at the root of the historic sense when he conceives of the messianic era in strictly halachic terms and describes the advent of the King Messiah as an opportunity to fulfill the commandments without hindrance by the Gentile nations. (While he rejects, or at least brackets, most apocalyptic law of the rabbinic tradition, he insists on the literal truth of the statement: "There is no difference between this world and the days of the Messiah but the servitude of Israel under the realms [of the non-Jews].")

Surely, as an underground the historic sense persisted in the apocalyptic and mystical traditions. But recent brilliant investigations of the mystic tradition[8] should not tempt us to lose a sense of proportion and to forget that the rabbinic tradition persisted in its suspicion against apocalyptic speculation throughout the ages. Jewish philosophy, with the exception of perhaps Yehuda Halevi, was on the whole free of the historic perspective. We find very little that would suggest the historic pattern of divine acts of revelation as an issue in the discussion of the Jewish philosophers of the Middle Ages. One could go even further and state that in the concern for the authority of the law these philosophers responded to a central theme of primary interest in classical philosophy. The union between the classic philosophy and the Jewish jurists of the halacha was not entirely accidental: the categories of the rabbinic jurists are both static and closed to the historic experience that the apocalyptic mood was able to articulate.

When in the seventeenth century apocalypticists were breaking through to the surface and were able to sway even some of the rabbinic authorities of the time, the catastrophe of the new messianism left a trauma that caused an almost complete amnesia of the historical sense or the historical consciousness in the interpretation of Judaism.[9] When Judaism and Christianity enter into the era of the Enlightenment, it is Gotthold Ephraim Lessing who interprets the Christian tradition in terms of a philosophic chiliasm, while Moses Mendelssohn in his *Jerusalem* devoids Judaism not only of all theoretical import but also of all historic sense. The odds against a Jewish philosophy of history in the period of Enlightenment seem overwhelming. Thus, the program of Krochmal is all the more astonishing and deserving of credit in the history of Jewish philosophy at the turn from the ancient and medieval to the modern phase. The late Julius Guttmann devoted some eight lines to Krochmal in his *Die Philosophie des Judentums*, and even the chapter in the enlarged Hebrew version does not bring Krochmal's significance into focus.[10] It was only Nathan Rotenstreich[11] who in his various studies of modern Jewish thought gave Krochmal a relevant place in the shift from the medieval to modern Jewish philosophy.[12]

III

Krochmal's key concept is that of the "spirit." There can be no doubt that philologically as well as structurally this key concept of Krochmal's is Hegelian in style. For what is new in this concept is the historiosophic inflection that remains foreign to the older philosophic usage of the term. Krochmal's philosophy is a philosophy of the spirit, and because it is a philosophy of the spirit it is a philosophy of history. The sixth chapter of his *Guide to the Perplexed of [the] Time*,[13] which is subtitled "The Sign of the Spiritual and its Meaning," seems of strategic importance for an understanding of Krochmal's program. The spirit is all persuasive, even in the crudest forms of superstition or idolatry: all positive religions are manifestations of the same spirit that works toward self-reflective understanding of itself. "In the spirit, substance is not one thing, consciousness another, and self-consciousness a third one, but the substance and epiphany of the spirit is principally nothing else but to become conscious of itself and to reveal the spirit to itself in one act."[14]

For the purpose of our analysis we stress the importance of chapter VI, and not of chapter XVI, which is a short and very telling recapitulation of Hegel's *Logic*. In view of the central architectonic position of chapter VI in the opus, Guttmann's suggestion of a chronological development in Krochmal's thought loses much of its cogency. Such a suggestion is after all nothing but an admission that the important parts of Krochmal's philosophy do not square with his working hypothesis. The central terms "spirit" and "absolute spirit" would be dulled if the specific historiosophic connotation were removed. Guttman, at least, was aware of the problem, whereas most of the interpreters think that one can borrow key terms from one philosopher and get away with it. If we reject the suggestion of a gradual development of Krochmal's thought as a guide for interpretation of his opus, we are obliged to interpret his work in a more systematic fashion.

In the light of the historiosophical connotation of the key terms "spirit" or "absolute spirit," we must ask: What is the function of the long and elaborate chapters on Alexandrian philosophy, on Ibn Ezra, or on the kabbalah?[15] If it is true that the new style of philosophy destroys the classic metaphysics, then the recapitulation of the essentials of the Neoplatonic metaphysics needs some justification in this work. Is Krochmal simply an eclectic, summarizing different views that do not fit together? Or is there a principle of selection at work and a systematic purpose that guides Krochmal's review of ancient and medieval philosophy and theology? In what relation do these summaries stand to the summary of Hegel's *Logic* in chapter XVI? Is it at all credible that, as Guttmann suggests, Krochmal tended in the later years of his affliction[16] toward a Hegelian view that does not inform his earlier studies?

The first thing to remember is that the summaries of Alexandrian philosophy, of kabbalah and Gnosticism, and of Ibn Ezra's philosophy cover various versions of Neoplatonic metaphysics. Let us further recall that it was Hegel who protested against the general neglect of Neoplatonic philosophy in theology; that he showed an unusual interest in the systematic structure of Neoplatonic philosophy and encouraged Cousin, his French disciple,[17] in his edition of Proclus. Is there any relation between Neoplatonic metaphysics and the modern historiosophic school?

The theory of emanation actually may provide the setting for an ontology of history. It can be used to speak about history as a process. Surely, this was not the original intention of the Neoplatonic theory of emanation, but it is this new twist that interests Hegel. Hegel as well as Krochmal, I would suggest, tried to gain an ontological context for their historiosophic concept of the spirit. It is one of the fundamental insights of Hegel and of Krochmal that the dynamic element in Neoplatonic metaphysics actually may help to inaugurate the new, the modern style of philosophy, where movement is no longer an ephemeral element as in ancient classic philosophy but occurs in Being itself. Being is movement and thus, in an emphatic sense, may be called historical. All levels of Being are only in the Neoplatonic scheme a way of Being-to-itself. The different levels of Being emanating from the highest Being, the absolute Spirit, are transitional stages of Being on its way back to itself. The direction of Being, or Being alienated from itself and returning to itself, may serve as the ontological ground for historiosophic speculation. Being is a universal process of alienation or emanation and reintegration, and the historiosophic twist is nothing but a horizontal projection of the ontological dynamic stance: only on the basis of Neoplatonic ontology can the equation between ontology and chronology that guides Hegel's as well as Krochmal's philosophy become intelligible.

Being itself is "historical," a form of movement or process. In the light of this departure of Neoplatonic ontology from classic ontology, all the differences between the various versions of Neoplatonic doctrines of emanation become insignificant. In the light of this new ontological stance, also Christian or Gnostic versions of the drama of redemption become simply subsumed as specifically religious orchestrations of a fundamental theme. Krochmal need not shy away from Hegel's concept of "spirit" or "absolute spirit" since its roots are not primarily in the Christian eschatological drama. The Christian eschatological drama itself is ontologically intelligible only in a context where Being is interpreted as movement or as history. Christian eschatology is *one* version of the eschatology of Being, a version that was of no interest to Krochmal. In medieval Jewish philosophy the historic element that is latent in Neoplatonic theology was not able to come to the fore since it was primarily *metaphysically* oriented. It is Krochmal who, as far as I can see, gives to the Neoplatonic ontology the new turn in Jewish philosophy. He does this in order to provide a base for his philosophy of history.

Only in the light of a rigorous and detailed interpretation of Krochmal's notion of Spirit as contained in the sixth chapter of his work may we hope to understand the relation between chapter VI on the spirit and chapter VII on "The Nations and Their Gods." Chapter VI concludes the philosophic part, and chapter VII opens the historiosophic part. These parts, however, remain unconnected, if we do not assume that the intention of the introductory philosophic chapters was to prepare the way for the historiosophic chapters in which at first the history of the nation is divided from the history of the people of Israel, and then for long stretches the history of Israel is sketched. In the first part Krochmal tried to establish philosophy as history or to fuse ontology and chronology, and in the second part Krochmal tries to establish history in a philosophic way.

Only if we take the Neoplatonic source of Krochmal's historiosophic schema seriously does the division between the nations and Israel in his opus become intelligible. For it is at this point that his chart of the historical process differs from Hegel's chart.

In our introductory remarks on Hegel's premises, we directed attention to Hegel's transformation of the Christian history of salvation into a secular history of salvation. It is this total transformation of the linear history of salvation into the secular realm that allows Hegel to use for world history the same straight line that Christianity reserved for the history of the *civitas Dei*. Augustine, the first Christian theologian of history, had divided sharply between the one purposeful *procursus*, the one purposeful course from beginning to end in the history of the city of God, the pilgrimage or *peregrinatio* of the church in the world, and the vicious circles of the nations of the world whose history repeat the same cycle and "run riot in an endless variety of sottish pleasure."

We are tempted to ask: Why did Krochmal in distinguishing the history of the nations from the history of the people of Israel not proceed in the manner of Augustine? The history of the nations moves in cycles, whereas the history of the people of Israel is a linear history of progress, a *procursus* toward redemption.

While the Augustinian division between the history of salvation and world history, between *Heilsgeschichte* and *Weltgeschichte*, would have provided the schema to guarantee the special status of Israel as a community of the elect, it did not provide Krochmal with the tools to take care of the specifically Jewish form of experience: that the community of the elect is not a community of the elect outside the course of world history, but rather a people subject to the laws of nations. While the people of Israel as a community of the elect is separated from the history of the nations, it is also the history of a people and not the pilgrimage of a church on earth. It is, I suggest, the specific Jewish experience of the history of salvation, of *Heilsgeschichte,* as a history of a people, that forces Krochmal to chart the history of Israel as a sequence or as a progression of cycles.

As a history of a people, the history of Israel is subject to the cycle of flourishing and decay. Israel is a part of the natural order and therefore goes through the natural cycle of flourishing and decay. The Absolute Spirit guarantees, however, the progress or the *procursus* of the history of Israel through the medium of the natural order and its cycles.

The order of the nations is also spiritual, but it is a "particular" spirit that dwells in the various nations. Spirit did not yet come to itself in the history of the nations. Nature is spirit, but spirit estranged from itself and not yet arrived at itself.

This is the case for all the nations where the spiritual in them is particularistic and therefore limited and destined to destruction. But in our nation, even in regard to the materiality and its sensuous externality, we are subjected to the aforementioned order of nature. Nevertheless, it is as the [the sages] said, "When they were exiled to Babylon, the *Shechinah* went into exile with them. When they were exiled to Elam, the *Shechinah* went into exile with them."[18] The general spirit in our midst protects us and saves us from the law governing all changeable things. We found it right to remember the times that have passed over us from the period of the blossoming forth of this nation to this day in order to show clearly how the order of these three phases [of the natural cycle] was repeated and tripled for us, and how when the time was ripe for disintegration, annihilation, and destruction, a new and vivifying spirit was renewed in us, and when we fell, how we always arose again, and were fortified, and the Lord our God did not forsake us.[19]

The passage is characteristic for Krochmal's philosophy of the spirit in general and his philosophy of history in particular. The national spirits are lower on the echelon of Being or Spirit, and therefore they are also on the horizontal axis more limited and perishable. Ontology and chronology are intertwined. As in Hegel, the personalistic and nonpersonal metaphors of the divine or spiritual are used indiscriminately. It remains moot whether the process of history is conceived as acts of Divine Providence or whether the spirit is an impersonal form. (The ambiguity is not quite as rich as in Hegel's philosophy where the concept of spirit itself contains a personalistic and a nonpersonal element due to the specific Christian use of the term "spirit," or at least due to the Latin translation of the Greek *hypostasis* as *persona*.) Krochmal translates personalistic, biblical, and midrashic language[20] into the language of the spirit: the concept of spirit has a nonpersonalistic ring in his language but is balanced by continuous references to the personalistic language of tradition.

For Krochmal, the ideal order of the spirit is, however, not merely an eternity beyond time: the ideal order of the spirit is an order in time, is historical. Since the ideal order of the spirit "dwells" in the natural order of Israel, in the history of the people of Israel, it passes through the natural cycle of blossoming forth or growth and disintegration or destruction, but goes beyond it. Krochmal speaks in this introductory passage as well as in other passages about three cycles and no more. The phases of the historical cycle have been duplicated and tripled in the history of the Jewish people. And this insistence by Krochmal on three and only three cycles leads us to ask: Does Krochmal see the history of the people of Israel as achieved and fulfilled in the progress of the three cycles, or is he hospitable to an indefinite number of cycles in the course of Jewish history? Does Krochmal share with Hegel the sense of the end of history? Simon Rawidowicz, who has published the definitive edition of Krochmal's opus, considers the sequence of cycles an open end. It is not closed with the termination of the third cycle, and Rawidowicz goes so far as to discover a fourth cycle or even a fifth in Krochmal's terse and strict sentences. Yet no amount of exegesis can overcome the fact that Krochmal speaks only of three cycles and that the third cycle ends with the Chmielnicki pogroms around 1650.

The question cannot be pushed aside. Does history or a certain type of history come to an end with the third cycle? The same question has to be asked in confronting Hegel's philosophy of history. Obviously in the case of Hegel the end of time does not mean the halt of physical time. For Hegel, the end of time contains the thesis that "now"—with the advent of the age of Enlightenment and the French Revolution—the "system of science" is accomplished and the historic process is fulfilled. The end of time means for Hegel that consciousness had become self-consciousness, that the Spirit has come into its own and has become manifest.

I suggest that Krochmal's philosophy of history lends itself to the very same interpretation. With the period of Enlightenment the spirit becomes manifest and comes into its own, and in this spiritual sense history has come to an end. I am not making the suggestion merely on structural grounds, but I will try to combine the structural reasoning with some philological explication of the text.

Krochmal in an important passage on page 255 summarizes his thesis about the unphilosophic midrashic language of the ancients, and concludes:

Therefore it was not necessary and perhaps not even within the range of the possible for the ancients to remove all dross of the strange stories in the Talmud, and it remained as it was until the depth of the last days,[21] the time in which we live, when the enlightened believer[22] will well understand that according to its character and condition the damage of hiding [the true unmythic interpretation] is greater perhaps than would have been the damage of making public [the true unmythic interpretation] in former days.

Krochmal calls his own time—and not only here—*acharit ha-yamim*, "the end of days," a term with unmistakably eschatological undertones.[23] He furthermore claims for his time—again not only in this passage—that in it the truth can be no longer concealed and kept secret. Enlightenment has become public and can no longer be reserved for the initiates.

Krochmal is aware that modern *Aufklärung* differs in kind from the enlightenment of the past. In the Middle Ages enlightenment was the preserve of an élite. This division of humankind into élite and masses is founded on the classic notion that the way to truth is a difficult and arduous one. Humankind lives in the cave, and the philosopher has to be forced to return to the cave. Outside the cave the philosopher would be alone, without support and security, no better than a wild animal. Inside the cave he has to take care that its twilight should not entirely darken the light that he transmits to some initiates. The enlightenment of the Middle Ages is esoteric. The enlightenment of the modern period appeals to the masses; it has a utopian cast; everybody is to be reached. In a very definite sense the frontier between philosophy and religion, which remains fundamental to medieval philosophy, is blurred. Philosophy itself becomes catholic and religious in its claim. The enlightenment of the moderns is exoteric.

While Krochmal divides the history of the people of Israel into only three cycles that do not reach beyond the middle of the seventeenth century, he nevertheless chronicles the story "to this day" (p. 40)—for his work is the sign of the new age. The philosophy of the "new philosophers" is like the owl of Minerva that starts its flight in the dusk. History has come to an end in order that philosophy of history may become possible.

IV

In Krochmal's philosophy of history the liquidating forces contained in the historic consciousness are still concealed. Krochmal's philosophy of history constructs an internal history of the spirit seen from the terminal station of the Enlightenment. Krochmal still tries to persuade us of the living meaning of the texts of scripture and tradition that he himself had put into a definite historic context. His philosophy of history is on the borderline between a theodicy, a theology of history evolved inside the circle of a living religion, and a historical investigation developed at a distance from the living tradition.

The fragments of his work were sent to and published by Leopold Zunz, one of the founding fathers of the historical school of *Wissenschaft des Judentums*. In the historical school the mystical veil of Krochmal's philosophy of history was torn asunder, and the liquidating factors hidden in the historical enterprise became manifest. Moritz Steinschneider, another of the founding fathers of the *Wissenschaft des Judentums*, once summarized the intention of the historical school: "We only have the duty to prepare an honorable funeral for the remnants of Judaism."[24] In Krochmal's philosophy of history the end of Jewish history could still be conceived in speculative terms. The historical school, however, took the end as an empirical datum that legitimized its task to collect the remnants of an already dead tradition.

It may not at first be intelligible why the Jewish historical school should differ in its purpose and intent from the German romantic school where the negative or destructive implications entailed in the historical consciousness did not come to the fore. The Jewish historical school, however, did not deal simply with the past of a folk tradition or of a nation, a tradition that developed organically, but with a past of a religion that claimed absolute authority. By putting the absolute transhistorical religious tradition into the historic context, the antitheological bias of the Jewish historical school was bound to assert itself.

It is often overlooked but nevertheless fundamental for the understanding of the developments of historic studies since the seventeenth century that the historic consciousness, while heir to the tradition of the historic religions, Judaism and Christianity, acts as a critical, even as a liquidating, agent for the tradition of historical religions. It is not accidental that Spinoza in his philosophic critique of biblical revelation uses the tool of historical criticism to establish the distance between the present and the claims of scripture. Insofar as the history of the people of Israel was charted as a "spiritual" history (at the expense of earth-bound national features), as the history of a religious consciousness, the work of the historical school was undermining the absolute consciousness of the religious tradition. Even Zunz's program of 1825 to deal with the history of the Jewish people as a history of a people, had an antitheological edge. The transfer of the romantic historic categories to the understanding of the history of the Jewish people entailed the suggestion that the religious history of the Jewish people was a matter of the past beyond resurrection.

For Krochmal, the concept of the spirit is still a concrete notion and a criterion of life. Spirit alone guarantees the life of the nations in general, and of the Jewish people in particular. But it cannot be denied that the criterion of the spiritual acts even in Krochmal's philosophy of history as well as in his historic investigations as a censor that suppresses several levels of Jewish historic life. What Hegel did to Christianity, Krochmal did to Judaism. Religious life throughout history was reduced to a merely spiritual history. When a generation later the ideologists of Reform Judaism conceived the history of the Jewish people as a spiritual history, nothing remained but a history of a ghost of the prophetic principle or of ethical ideals. Modern Jewish studies were for generations active in propagating this idealized image of Jewish history. With a retreat of the Jewish people to its national base toward the end of the nineteenth century and the beginning of the twentieth, Krochmal's philosophy of history comes into focus as a philosophy of the historic cycles, the flourishing and the decay, of the nations. No attention is paid to his concept of history as a linear progression of the spirit through the cycles, to be exact, through the three cycles. In the upswing, real or imaginary, of a new cycle, Krochmal was taken to be a herald of a new renaissance of the spirit. Zionist interpreters take such a renaissance to follow logically from Krochmal's system and construct a fourth or even a fifth cycle, drawing outlines supposedly jotted down in Krochmal's sentences.

I think that such interpretations have neither structurally nor philologically a basis in the opus of Krochmal, for Krochmal was less interested in an indefinite series of cycles than in the progression of the cycles toward a definite end: a spiritualized version of the eschatological end of history.

The new historiography that orchestrates the revival of the Jewish national consciousness opened a new perspective on the past. As a national body, the history of the Jewish people was no longer to be treated as a spiritual homunculus. The new historiography could face up to the lowly side of Jewish existence without constant apology to a Christian censor.

It has also rewritten Jewish history in the light of its new experience and sometimes arrived at new idyllic phantasmagorias, but more important, this new national consciousness and its historiography have transformed the religious tradition into history of the "genius" of the people.

The transfer of revelation and a religious tradition from a realm separated from human creativity to a realm of human spirit, reason, and imagination, is, however, not merely the work of the historiography in the period of national renaissance. It is characteristic for both phases of Jewish historiography since the period of the Enlightenment, viz. the historiography of the *Aufklärung* as well as of the romantic national renaissance. It starts already in Krochmal's philosophy of history. Krochmal perhaps tried the impossible to convince us of the metaphysical status of Israel by the aid of a sixth sense of history after the five metaphysical and religious senses had failed to fulfill the task.

In pondering the function and the merit of modern Jewish philosophy we are saddled with an unsurpassable ambiguity that is hard to face up to: in the turn from ancient and medieval cosmologic philosophy to historical philosophy of the moderns (and the philosophy of history is only the most obvious innovation of modern philosophy, since the historic sense really structures the ontological categories of the new philosophers)—in this turn canons of interpretation were developed that seem more in tune with the language of biblical revelation. The covenantal language of scripture is echoed in the historiosophic language of the new philosophers. But creation-revelation-redemption in the covenantal language of scripture are acts of God, the creator of heaven and earth, the giver of the law, the Redeemer of man and the world. The cosmological form of classic and medieval philosophy may be Greek and foreign to what is considered today peculiar to the Hebrew historical sense. But classic and medieval philosophy preserved the manifest or external sense of the religious symbols that is relevant to the legitimacy or cogency of the religious language. Through the shift from the cosmological to the historical philosophy, or with the rise of the new historic sense, the reality index of religious language was profoundly affected. What were once fixed points in the constellation became part and parcel of the finite and ephemeral human historic endeavor.

The critique of historical reasoning is still an unfulfilled task. We are aware that the historic sense may also be a disease and a danger to our experience of life: you take life in too easy a fashion if you take it only in an historical manner. Krochmal's philosophy of history as well as Hegel's philosophy of history pose as the cure to the perplexities of the modem mind; they may actually be the disease itself, or at least an index for the degree of our perplexity. But expelled from the paradise of a transhistorical existence, we cannot regain our innocence except through the hard and arduous journey on the road of history itself.

4

The Issue Between Judaism and Christianity:[1] Facing Up to the Unresolvable Difference

For all the current popularity of the term "Judeo-Christian" tradition, the differences between the Jewish and Christian religions are not at all resolved. They are basic, and their consequences still influence every moment of our lives. True, the immediate and more pressing issues in Jewish-Christian relations are social and political, but this does not justify postponing an examination of the fundamental issue, which is theological and from which all the social and political questions spring originally.

So long as a clear awareness existed of the basic theological differences between Judaism and Christianity there was no great need to argue the matter explicitly. But in the last twenty years it has become fashionable to gloss over and distort these differences. Now we need to restate them. Nor need we be afraid to. There is warrant for believing that, even in the sphere of the "practical," we have more to gain by defining and understanding the issues involved than by obscuring them and pretending they do not exist.

For centuries the controversy between Jewish religion and Christian dogma had for its frame the historical victory of the Christian church. All that the church required of the synagogue was that she admit her defeat. If necessary, the church could always appeal to the secular arm of the state to end the argument.

The magic spell of Christianity's historical success remains, though the church no longer uses the sword to decide her dispute with the synagogue, and this spell still constrains the Jewish-Christian dialogues of our time. Its influence can be seen in the exchange of letters between Franz Rosenzweig and Eugen Rosenstock, in the dialogue between the Protestant theologian Karl Ludwig Schmidt and Martin Buber, and in the dispute between the Christian ideologue of anti-Semitism, Hans Blüher, and the Prussian Jew Hans Joachim Schoeps. The fact that the history of the nations unfolded under the triumph of the cross (though only in the West) has for Franz Rosenzweig and Hans Joachim Schoeps, as to lesser degree for Martin Buber, a weight and relevance that seem to me to be fatal to any claim that might be made for their thought as *Jewish* theology.

A sober analysis of the Jewish-Christian controversy must set aside the argument from history, which embodies a dangerous temptation to take what *is* for what *ought to be*. After all, how can history "decide" in matters of theology? And, especially, what can historical success prove for a religion like Christianity that claims to be not of this world and heralds the end of history?

Nor is this a time for the Christian church to use the argument from history. From the viewpoint of worldly success, do we not stand on the threshold of a post-Christian era, when Christian symbols and dogmas have begun to look as antiquated as the Old Testament seemed in the Christian era? Indeed, looking at the present spiritual situation, it is most probable that the age to come will shape its religious forms in a way equally remote from both Jewish and Christian patterns. Be that as it may, the historical argument is certainly two-edged. There is a good deal of irony in the fact that, whereas Christian theologians today steer clear of the "proof" from history (warned off by such a critic as Nietzsche's friend, Franz Overbeck), Jewish thinkers like Hans Joachim Schoeps and Will Herberg have become so spellbound by Christianity's historical success that they try to give it a "theological" justification.

The issue between the Christian and Jewish religions starts from the Christian side. According to Christian doctrine, the Jewish people are an integral part of the Christian history of salvation. The synagogue is, in the eyes of the early church fathers, the shadow of the body of the church. Christian theology views the history of mankind as a progressive covenant between God and man. The covenant begins with Adam and manifests itself in different stages: from Noah to Abraham, from Abraham to Moses, from Moses to David, from David to the son of David "who is the Christ." In the ultimate sacrifice of Jesus of Nazareth who is the Christ, the covenant is made final. The last step in the covenant between God and man, according to Christian theology, is the incarnation of God in the Son of man. The history of Israel prefigures the story of redemption; the events recorded in the Old Testament do not contain their ultimate meaning in themselves, but point beyond themselves: the death of Abel, the sacrifice of Isaac, the kingdom of David, the temple in Jerusalem prefigure the life and death of Jesus the Christ, as well as the history of the church.

The Jewish people, however, not only "prefigure" the story of redemption, but are an active "figure" in the drama of salvation. The fundamental statement in the Gospel according to St. John—"for salvation is of the Jews"—does not, according to Christian theology, refer to past history or to the mere "racial"[2] fact that Jesus the Christ and his first disciples were of Jewish origin; it points rather to the essential role of Israel in that drama of salvation, which the first theologian of the Christian community described in his Epistle to the Romans: Has Israel stumbled that it should fall? Paul denies this, interpreting the refusal of the Jewish community to accept Jesus as the Christ as part of the universal drama of redemption: Israel's rejection of Jesus made it possible for salvation to come to the Gentile nations. Israel became an enemy of Jesus Christ, writes Paul to the Christian community in Rome, "*for your sakes.*"[3]

In other words, Paul can call the Jewish destiny a mystery because the role of the Jewish people is mysteriously interwoven with the role of the redeemer in the Christian drama of redemption. The Jewish synagogue refuses Jesus as the Christ, but this refusal is essential to universal redemption. The dark and mysterious "necessity," according to Paul, of the Jewish people in the drama of redemption affords no reason for Gentile self-gratulation or for condemnation of Israel. The Gentile nations should remember that the Jewish people are the natural branches of the tree of redemption, whose "root" is Israel's history. The Gentile nations were grafted onto the tree of redemption "contrary to nature," and shall be cut off if they fail in their faith in Christ. Let the Jews only not persist in their refusal of Jesus as the Christ, and how much more shall they, who are the natural branches of the tree of redemption, adorn and make part of it.

However, the key sentence, "for salvation is of the Jews," must be read in the context of the Johannine Gospel's violent attack on the synagogue. (Some serious writers on the Johannine Gospel, such as Rudolf Bultmann, the German theologian, think the clause is a gloss, since it does not accord with that dominant tendency of the Gospel which has led some Protestant commentators to call it the most anti-Jewish pamphlet ever to have appeared.) The Johannine Christ denies that Jews and Christians have one father in God; the Jews, in refusing to acknowledge Jesus as the Christ, serve the "Devil." They do not know God the Father since they do not acknowledge the divine Son in Jesus.

But *from the Jewish point of view*, the division of the divinity into "Father" and "Son" splits the divine essence; it was, and is, regarded by the synagogue quite simply as blasphemy. The doctrine of the synagogue and the Gospel according to St. John both "agree" as to what they regard as the basic point at issue, the heart of the argument, even if they arrive at opposite conclusions.

To sum up the Christian argument then: the Jewish people have a definite role in the Christian drama of salvation. Israel's history is the "root" of the tree of redemption, Israel serving in its denial of Jesus as the Christ as a negative but necessary element in the process of salvation.

If one accepts my description of the Christian "economy of salvation," I think that my statement of the basic Jewish premise can be readily understood: the Christian religion in general, and the body of the Christian church in particular, is of no *religious* relevance to the Jewish faith. There is a Jewish "mystery" for the church, but there is no Christian "mystery" for the synagogue. Christian history can have no religious significance of any kind for the Jewish creed; nor can the division of historical time into "BC" and "AD" be recognized by the synagogue. More than that, it cannot even be recognized as something which, though meaningless for the Jewish people, represents truth for the rest of the world.

This basic Jewish premise was obscured when Franz Rosenzweig, introducing a new "theological" notion into Jewish thought, interpreted the coming of Jesus as having a messianic significance for the Gentile nations, but not for the Jewish people. Rosenzweig based his theological tour de force on a bold reading of a fundamental *logion* of the Johannine Christ: "I am the way . . . no man cometh unto the Father, but by me" (14:6).[4] The history of the nations is, according to Rosenzweig, the "way" to the divine fulfillment, and this "way" to the Father leads for the Gentiles through Jesus the Christ. No man "cometh," as Rosenzweig emphasized, into the divine covenant but through the Son of God—except the Jewish nation whom God "elected" from its very beginning to make a covenant with.

The election of Israel—which is a Christian article of faith, too—implies that Israel does not march along the eternal way of history, but stands in the eternal presence of the covenant with God. The life of Israel in the divine covenant is the eternal life. Till the end of history, so argues Rosenzweig, the "eternal life" (the transhistorical destiny of Israel) and the "eternal way" (the historical destiny of the Gentile nations in Jesus Christ) are divided. Only at the end of days, when the Son of God shall deliver up the "Kingdom" to God and lay aside all his power and authority, shall the eternal life and the eternal way come together; Israel shall cease to be the holy nation living in the eternal divine presence only when Christ shall cease to rule over the eternal way of the nations.

The Christian church, says Rosenzweig, must understand that it is the essence of the mystery of salvation that the Jews shall remain separate so long as Christ does not deliver up his authority to God the Father. Through Paul, the church became the church of the nations. According to Rosenzweig, it is both anachronistic and contradictory for the church to wish to see the Jews converted: anachronistic, because it implies a return to the pre-Pauline situation; contradictory, because Christian eschatology places the conversion of the Jews at the end of time, beyond history.

I do not deny the grandeur of Rosenzweig's interpretation. Yet it seems to me a dubious thing to make Rosenzweig's highly doubtful reading of a *Christian* text the basis for the doctrine of the synagogue. What Rosenzweig is expressing here is his own spiritual biography: *his* return to Judaism started from a point on the borderline between the two faiths, when he was just about to cross over to the church. However much personal validity Rosenzweig's interpretation may have, it is theologically irrelevant. It is only too obvious that his "theological" arguments do violence to the spirit of the Gospel according to St. John, and that Jesus of the Fourth Gospel offers the weakest possible basis for the view he advances.

Rosenzweig's dichotomy between nations that are on the "way" through Jesus the Christ and "come" into the divine covenant, and a Jewish people that "are" already in the divine covenant, contradicts the whole Johannine scheme of salvation. John denies the Jewish people any knowledge of God, insisting that only through the Son could the Jews have known the Father (8:19). Moreover, the same sentence that calls Jesus Christ the "way" (which is the basis of Rosenzweig's speculation about the division between the "eternal way" and the "eternal life") also calls Christ the life: "Jesus saith unto him, I am the way, and the truth, and the life. . . . " I do not understand how Jesus can be conceded to be the Christ in Rosenzweig's halfway fashion: How can Jesus be the Messiah come to redeem the nations, but not the Jewish people? Rosenzweig categorically denies that Jesus has any messianic significance for the Jewish people, and he denies even the significance for the Jewish people of messianic redemption in general (since Israel exists outside the messianic dialectic of history), but under the spell of the success of the church in the Western world, he raises Christianity's mundane history, in the fashion of his master Hegel, to the level of the divine.

Even as speculation, Rosenzweig's argument has a glaring weakness: Islam.[5] He treats Islam, which made its appearance centuries after the advent of Christianity, in exactly the same way as such Protestant scholars of the New Testament era as Schuerer and Weber treated the period of "late Judaism" in the time of Jesus—that is, as an irritating supererogation. A thorough analysis would show that Rosenzweig was a captive of the Protestant vocabulary, the only difference being that where the Protestant scholars say "rabbinic theology," he says the Islamic religion. Since Islam hardly counts as a social factor in the West, and there was no group to take up the cudgels on its behalf, Rosenzweig's caricature of Islam could pass. Will Herberg, accepting Rosenzweig's view of Islam, calls it a "kind of Jewish-Christian heresy."[6] This summary disposal of a world religion follows readily enough from Mr. Herberg's (highly private) conception of a Jewish-Christian "orthodoxy." Yet Islam, because it claims only the title of *prophet* for Mohammed, is much more the complement (less heretical!) of Judaism than is Christianity.

I shouldn't have criticized Rosenzweig on this point if his example had not given the lead to other Jewish writers. Hans Joachim Schoeps states that, from a Jewish point of view, "perhaps [?] no Gentile can come to God the Father otherwise than through Jesus Christ." Will Herberg is convinced that it is sound Jewish doctrine to assert that Israel can bring the world to God only (!) through Christianity.[7] I cannot help asking: Who informed Mr. Schoeps and Mr. Herberg that the Gentile nations have no way but the Christian one to salvation? Israel can acknowledge *prophets* to the nations and of the nations. But to posit an event that has messianic significance for the Gentiles yet does not touch Israel is absurd and "arranges" a rapprochement between Christians and Jews somewhat too neatly.

On the Christian side again, I cannot see what justifies Rosenzweig's and Schoeps's assumption that Paul's Epistle to the Romans—especially chapters 9 to 11, which are the basis for my description of the Christian attitude toward the Jews—constitutes no Christian dogma, but is rather Paul's subjective opinion. Karl Barth bases his remarkable description of the Jews in the light of Christian dogma entirely on these chapters of the Epistle to the Romans, and the Catholic Church declared as early as 1236 that even though she held her arms affectionately out to every convert, she embraced Jewish converts "with even greater affection"—basing this attitude on Paul's likening of the Jews to the natural branches of the tree of redemption.

It remains a puzzle that Franz Rosenzweig, who more than anyone before him appreciated the theological relevance of the realm of liturgy, should have overlooked the special place assigned in it to Israel. On Good Friday the Catholic Church prays that all mankind may receive the fruit of redemption. The church prays for the church, the Pope, the bishops, and the holy nation of the church; she prays for the government (of the medieval empire), for the pagans, and for all heretics and schismatics. The church also prays for the Jews—but how? "We pray also for the perfidious[8] Jews [*pro perfidis Judaeis*], that the Lord our God may lift the veil from their heart so that they may acknowledge Jesus Christ our Lord." More significant than the prayer itself (which already applies the ominous theological adjective, "perfidious," to the Jews) is the ritual accompanying—or rather not accompanying—it. In all other prayers the deacon exhorts the community: *Oremus. Flectamus genua* (let us kneel and pray). But when the prayer for the Jews is reached, a gloss remarks: "No Amen. At this point the deacon omits calling the community to their knees lest the memory of the shameful genuflections with which the Jews mocked the Savior at this hour be renewed."

Eugen Rosenstock, in his discussion with Franz Rosenzweig, declared that it was no longer a Christian dogma that the Jewish people were "obdurate." But this must be regarded as a personal opinion, since the church continues to pray for an end to Jewish obduracy and for the redemption of the Jews from their darkness (*a suis tenebris*).

In their exchange of letters both Rosenzweig and Rosenstock presented marginal attitudes rather than the classic positions of church and synagogue; nor did they express theological doctrine. Both were preparing the way to a post-Christian existence for themselves, since the era of the Christian church, Catholic and Protestant, had come to an end for them in Hegel's philosophy and Nietzsche's prophecy.

The dispute between Karl Ludwig Schmidt and Martin Buber is more central. The Protestant theologian insists that the "only relevant question" is Israel's obdurate rejection of Jesus as the Christ, and he asks whether the destruction of the temple was not its consequence—a consequence that deprived the Jewish people of a spiritual center. Schmidt, in accordance with the whole Christian tradition, establishes a "theological" relation of crime and punishment between the Crucifixion and the destruction of the temple. The nearly forty years that elapsed between the Crucifixion (33 CE) and the destruction of the Second Temple (70 CE) are "symbolically" seen as years of trial, similar to the forty years' wanderings in the wilderness.

Martin Buber, answering from "inside" the Jewish consciousness, states that the Jewish people do not feel themselves to be "rejected" by God. In an enigmatic phrase he admits that for Israel the Christology of Christianity is "surely a relevant event between above and below," but he insists that Israel experiences the earthly reality as unredeemed by a Messiah and cannot admit such a cesura in history as Jesus, as the Christ, represents. Moreover, since no divine revelation can exhaust the divine essence, Israel cannot allow that there should ever have been an ultimate incarnation of the divine in human flesh.

Buber's description of Jewish experience and doctrine is excellent, but it seems to me that he is vague when it comes to dealing with the concrete question asked by the Protestant theologian: Did the Jewry of the Diaspora lose its spiritual center after the destruction of the temple? The answer to this question is simple but fundamental: not the temple but the Torah was, and is, the spiritual center of Jewry. The Jewish people did not come to life with the laying of the first stone of the temple, but with the giving of the law to Israel in the covenant of Sinai. It is clear, however, that Martin Buber was not at all prepared to give this answer, since he has always emphasized the Agadic or mythical element of the Jewish tradition, as against the tradition of the law.

It is perhaps no paradox that Paul, a Pharisee and son of a Pharisee, who claimed to have studied under Gamaliel and to have excelled in his zeal for the law and tradition—that this same Paul was better prepared than modern Jewish apologists to define the basic issue dividing Judaism and Christianity. That issue is the law. All the premises of Paul's theology were "Jewish" and even "Pharisaic," but from these he drew heretical conclusions: thus from the possibly legitimate Jewish premise that the Messiah would usher in the end of the law, he drew the heretical conclusions of Christianity, holding that the Messiah had already come and that the law was superseded: "For Christ is the end of the law for righteousness to every one that believeth" (Rom. 10:4). But the basis of the Jewish religion since Ezra has been the Torah, the law, or better still—halacha, the "way" of the law in a man's life. All theological speculations are secondary to this.

The recent insistence on a rigid monotheism as the defining characteristic of Jewish religious life is contradicted by a fact that contemporary Jewish thinkers tend to overlook: the centuries-long predominance of the Lurianic kabbalah in Judaism. The kabbalah developed theogonic speculations that can only be compared to the Gnostic (and pagan) mythologies. The mythical union of the divine King and Queen, the Adam-Kadmon speculation, the mythology of the Ten Sefirot, which are not attributes but essentially different manifestations of the divine, challenge every historian of religion who presumes to judge what is Jewish and not Jewish by the criterion of a "rigid monotheism." The Jewish religion could not have withstood the outburst of kabbalistic mythologizing if its fundamental and defining characteristic were a rigid monotheism. As it was, it was able to absorb the kabbalah's insights and to draw added power from them.

The kabbalistic mythologies did not shatter the structure of Jewish life; on the contrary, they strengthened it in time of crisis by their enhancing of the prestige of halacha. Halacha, which is the conduct of life according to the *mitzvot*, they did not understand as a pedagogical system (as in the period of medieval enlightenment), but as a way to achieve sacramental union with the divine. The bulk of the *mitzvot* became a *corpus mysticism* reflecting the divine and cosmic order in the human realm; in this way they attained an importance they never had before in Jewish history—and in any case, the Jewish vision of God is far too rich and various to be reduced to an abstract monotheism. Challenges not to Judaism's monotheism, but to the validity and interpretation of the law, shake the Jewish religion and community to their foundations. Any messianic claim represents such a challenge because it claims to have ushered in an age in which the law is superseded.

It is hasty to conclude, as so many do, that because halacha shapes the classical pattern of Jewish life, Judaism is purely "legalistic." Halacha is a structure in which a considerable variety of religious experience is integrated. The language of halacha is capable of expressing such contraries as rationalist philosophy (Saadia and Maimonides) and, mystical mythology (Moses de Leon and Isaac Luria), ecstatic prophetism (Abulafia), and magical ritualism (Jacob Halevi of Marvege). Yet halacha is not an empty vessel into which any sort of contents can be poured. It has its limit in the divine law, and messianism in any form must necessarily transgress that limit. It is true that Christian orthodoxy in interpreting itself tries to set up limits against heresies that would discard the Decalogue. But Judaism is bound to insist that Paulinian doctrine still remains destructive of the law, and therefore at this point, too, Judaism must reject Christianity's interpretation of itself. Paul, when he was Saul, would have been the first to admit this, and indeed he persecuted the early Christian community on the very ground that it was setting aside the law. Judaism never traveled the road to Damascus, and it cannot, without committing suicide, change Saul's judgment.

Christian history, Jesus's claim to the title of Messiah, and Paul's theology of Christ as the end of the law, are not at all "unique events" for Judaism, but things that have recurred in the Jewish pattern of religious existence. Christian history, as I have said, constitutes no "mystery" for the Jewish religion. Christianity represents a crisis that is "typical" in Jewish history and expresses a typical Jewish "heresy": antinomian messianism—the belief that with the coming of the Messiah, not observance of the law, but faith in him is required for salvation.

So far as we can judge, rabbinic tradition has always regarded Jesus' messianic claim and Paul's theology as heretical antinomianism. Maimonides, in his Code, specifically lists Jesus with other heretics who sought to persuade Israel to abandon the law. No statement as to the messianic significance of Jesus for the Gentile nations can be got from any Jewish halacha.

Gershom Scholem, in his study of Sabbatian messianism,[9] makes an arresting comparison that enables us to see the beginnings of Christianity in a new light. Sabbatai Zevi's appearance, quickening all the latent hopes of the seventeenth-century Jewish ghetto, precipitated the most tragic messianic episode in modern Jewish history. The fact is that the new messianic community of the Sabbatians, like that of the early Christians, centered around a catastrophic event that, like the death of Jesus, could only be overcome and transcended by the "paradox of faith." For the Sabbatians, this paradox was Sabbatai Zevi's conversion to Islam. His apostasy shook the community of his followers to its foundations, yet became the motor of the Sabbatian "paradox of faith."

The tragic paradox of a dying Messiah and of an apostate savior was interpreted in the light of the prophetic vision of the "suffering servant." "In both cases," writes Scholem, "a certain mystical attitude of belief crystallized round an historical event that drew its strength, in turn, from the very fact of its paradoxicality. Both movements began by adopting an attitude of intense expectation toward the *Parousia*, the advent or return of the savior, be it from heaven or from the realm of impurity. In both cases the destruction of the old values in the cataclysm of redemption led to an outburst of antinomian tendencies, partly moderate and veiled, partly radical and violent; in both cases you get a new conception of belief as the realization of the new message of salvation . . . in both cases, finally, you get in the end a theology with some kind of Trinity and with God incarnated in the person of the savior."[10] These striking parallels between Sabbatianism and early Christianity cannot be attributed to the influence or imitation of Christian prototypes, since the Sabbatian heresy arose in the Islamic ghetto. Both Sabbatianism and early Christianity were independent expressions of crises into which the Jewish community was plunged when believers in an arrived Messiah were summoned by their theologians to strike off the shackles of the law, that harsh schoolmaster whom the redemption was to render obsolete.

If, then, the issue between the Christian religion and the Jewish community revolves around the law, I would hold that the Jewish argument cannot ultimately be given in midrashic—or rather pseudo-midrashic—terms. The counterpart to Christian dogma is not a Jewish dogma affirming certain articles of faith concerning the nature of the Divinity and its manifestations. Christian theology is based on Christology, which means that all things, human and divine, achieve relevance only as they relate to Jesus the Christ. Judaism, based on the law, grants relevance to all things, human and divine, only as they relate to halacha. It is the weakness of all modern—and not only modern—Jewish theology that it fails to name halacha, the law, as its alpha and omega. The Jewish religion has been in a crisis since the time of the Emancipation because it lost its center when halacha lost its central place and cogency for Jewish thought and conduct.

The moment halacha ceases to be the determining force in Jewish life, the door is opened to all the disguised anti-halachic (antinomian) and Christian assumptions current in modern secularized Christian society. Judaism ceases to be a matter of principle and remains only one of tradition. Religious revivals that do not reckon with halacha as the vital essence of Judaism degenerate into so much romantic nostalgia and only hasten the end of Judaism. A few months ago I attended services at an Orthodox *shul.* The rabbi, product of a modern yeshiva, gave me a cordial greeting and "explained" (during the reading of the Torah!) that "ceremonies" and "rituals" are only "external" and not "so important" as would seem at first sight. He surely did not realize that by translating *mitzvot* by "ceremonies" and "ritual" he had surrendered to the Paulinian criticism of the law.

Halacha is inevitably eclipsed in an age that can envisage religion only in terms of man's "private" experience, as a (poetic) dialogue between man's lonely soul and the lone God. But such a religion of the heart, even of the "pure" heart, remains disembodied—and who but the elect can lay claim to purity of heart? Halacha is based essentially on the principle of representation: the intention of man's heart and soul has to be presented and represented in his daily life. Consequently, halacha must become "external" and "juridical"; it must deal with the minutiae of life, for only in the detail of life is a presentation of the covenant between God and man possible. Halacha is the "path" of man's life on which he can "walk" before God. Against the ecstasy and delirium of man's soul, halacha emphasizes the rational and everyday sobriety of justice. Halacha is the law because justice is the ultimate principle. Ecstatic or pseudo-ecstatic religiosity, however, sees only dead legalism and external ceremonialism in the sobriety of justice, just as anarchy can conceive of law and order only as tyranny and oppression.

Emancipation opened the doors of Western civilization to the Jewish community. But that civilization rests on Christian presuppositions and is shaped by Christian symbols. The civil calendar is the same as the Christian calendar; the initials "BC" and "AD" express a fundamental Christian article of faith. I am aware that the civil calendar is losing its Christian character, that its Christian initials are being transformed into mere technical signs. But though the Christian meaning of the calendar may be suppressed, it can never become obsolete. The Christian calendar has withstood a number of attempts to replace it with a secular calendar; the French Revolution in the eighteenth century and the Italian fascists and the Russian communists in our own century tried to do so and failed. We therefore do right to keep in mind the Christian foundation upon which our civil society rests.

This is not all. By the very language we use decisions are made that limit and define our spiritual horizons. The Jewish holy scriptures are called the "Old Testament" in English. The term "Old Testament," however, implies the basic Christian claim that the "old" covenant has been superseded by the "new." But it is a Jewish article of faith that the law never becomes antiquated, that the covenant of Sinai is as valid today as it has always been. Even to call the Torah "law" already implies that pejorative meaning Paul ascribed to the Mosaic law in his violent critique of it.

The antinomian critique made by a secular society that is nevertheless Christian in its presuppositions is reinforced by the critique of the law that was made within the Jewish community; the modern Jewish stress on redemption through belief, rather than through a way of life conforming to divinely ordained law, reached its peak in Abraham Geiger's criticism of rabbinic law. It is an established fact that the last stage of the Sabbatian heresy ushered in the first stage of Jewish reform. Is it at all surprising that, in these circumstances, the Jewish side in the Jewish-Christian controversy cannot argue today from the center of Jewish faith and experience? The inner crisis of the Jewish religion determines the character of its controversy with the Christian one. If halacha is no longer valid as the divine and human way of life, if halacha, in a caricature of "reconstruction," is reduced to a mere bundle of customs and folkways, where shall the Jewish argument get the strength to stand up against the Pauline rejection of the law?

Modern Jewish thinking is in large part a prisoner of this antinomianism, which pervades modern thought in general; in the world today the principle of law is reduced to a juridical device and the "pathological inclination of love" (Kant) is exalted over against the "blind principle" of justice. The pseudo-Agadic stress in modern Jewish religious thinking on the "romance" of Hasidism, or the romance of a mythologized East European Jewry in general, is in the end no obstacle to the Christianizing of the Jewish people. For what greater "romance" can there be than the incarnation of God in flesh? Only the principle of halacha offers a check to "romance" between God and man by making the sobriety of justice the foundation of man's life. The controversy between the Jewish and Christian religions points to the perennial conflict between the principle of law and the principle of love. The "yoke of the law" is challenged by the enthusiasm of love. But the "justice of the law" may, in the end, be the only challenge to the arbitrariness of love.

PART II

WORLD ALIENTATION:
GNOSTICISM AND ITS CONSEQUENCES

5

The Dogmatic Myth of Gnosticism[1]

I

Dogmatic myth is a particular form in which the mythic appears in its late horizon.[2] To grasp it as such, however, means encountering difficulties because the emblematization of allegorical representation, *which moves the experiences and religious principles of the post-Homeric age back into primordial times* (J. H. Voss), has been discredited since the Enlightenment. A method that allows for the *intentional and discrete* transformation of a mythologeme *into the expression of a concept* (Schopenhauer) could not persist in the face of the judgment of classical aesthetics.[3] Even the theological scholarship of the last century adopted the contemptuous judgment of classical aesthetics about allegorical interpretation without considering that in the end the methodology of all theological exegesis is allegorical.

In Winckelmannian spirit, yet by means of a more sober historiography, Hans Blumenberg attempts to extricate "mythology including the history of its reception" from a network of categories in which the mythic—not only myth in its original form, but distinctly in its later horizons as well—remains in some way or another tied to the dogmatic doctrine proper to all theology. Hans Blumenberg's categories for describing myth and its reception "are categories of contrast to theology and to the metaphysics that has entered it or that it has left behind."[4] A line of demarcation is drawn between a dogmatic and mythic tradition that prohibits any transition between the two. The consequences of such an approach are far-reaching. The form of allegorical hermeneutic[5] inaugurated by Greek philosophy and Christian apologetics is repudiated. The judgment about the allegorical form of representation is unambiguous: it has "misunderstood" myth.[6]

It appears to me mistaken to want to assess the form of allegorical hermeneutic from the perspective of the original alone, that is, of archaic mythology. Allegory as exegesis of archaic myth might indeed imply such a judgment. However, allegorical interpretation is not exhausted in the exegesis of myth; instead, it becomes a vehicle for a new understanding of reality that is differentiated from archaic myth. Allegory is a form of translation. It translates mythic forms, names, and the destinies of mythic narrative into concepts. In allegorical interpretation, however, the mythic template gains a new content.

The testimony of allegory is ambiguous. It is a monument to the triumph of a demythologized consciousness over mythic consciousness. At the same time, however, it demonstrates the power of mythic tradition because myth remains fundamental in all its overhauled and translated allegorical transformations. If the demythologized consciousness of Greek philosophy had been able to cast the divine fables and hero sagas from its memory, no allegorical myth-interpretation would ever have emerged. An unbroken remainder of mythic content is the presupposition of any such interpretation. Philosophical allegory attempts to ban this remainder. Yet precisely through the philosophical interpretation of Greek myths, the ground of antiquity was prepared for a new understanding of reality. The rhetorical forms developed in philosophical mythic allegories achieve a new index in late antiquity. In late antiquity, the hierarchies of meaning in allegorical forms of representation reflect the hierarchies of being. It is the congruence between the hierarchies of being and the hierarchies of meaning that gives shape to the presuppositions of allegorical form of representation since late antiquity. From then on, the allegorical method is no longer merely a literary principle; it also shapes the content of late ancient consciousness. It acts not only as the rationalizing exegesis of archaic myth, but itself turns into the form of representation of a "new" myth.

In late ancient gnosticism, a new form of myth emerges that I would like to refer to as dogmatic myth, especially in view of the demarcating

The Dogmatic Myth of Gnosticism 63

line that Hans Blumenberg draws between dogmatic and mythic tradition. As inexhaustible as the variations of the Gnostic mythologemes are and as liberally as the Gnostic narrative handles the predetermined images of ancient mythologemes and philosophemes, and as confusingly rich as its allusions and intimations resonate with ancient and Oriental mythologemes, so ultimately uniform and univocal is the structure of the Gnostic myth. If the Gnostic myth "belongs to the constellations into which the mythic enters in the late horizon of its reception," it can hardly be conceived, as Hans Blumenberg suggests, "from the essential distance"[7] that myth maintains from any kind of theology and metaphysics.

The *Naassene Sermon*, which certainly is considered as a paradigm for a freely literary allegory of ancient and Oriental divine myths, on further investigation proves to be the exegesis of a hymn that stood at the center of a cult ceremony. For an interpretation of the Naassene Sermon, one should take as one's point of departure the metamorphosis undergone by the mystery cults in late antiquity. All of the mystery cults were in fact chthonic cults. The gods of the chthonic cults—Demeter, Attis, and Dionysus—were divinities of vegetation. The mysteries of late antiquity allegorize, that is, translate, the archaic cults and their myths, which were sunk into the terrestrial and subterrestrial worlds, into the celestial. Cults and myths of late antiquity point toward a transworldly if not unworldly fulfillment or perfection for the adepts of the mysteries. It is not much of a step away from the world-fleeing or unworldly perfection of the Gnostic Naassene Sermon. The Naassene Sermon confirms that the philosophical exegesis of the Attis-myth, as it is presented in Sallust (*De diis et mundo*, chap. 4) as well as in Emperor Julian's speech on the divine mother (*Orat.* V), should not be understood as merely an exegetical commentary of Neoplatonic literature, rather than as based on cultic doctrine and praxis. In its center stands a cultic Attis-song that presents the "text" of the sermon (Hippolyte, *Refutatio omnium haeresium* V, chap. 4).[8]

Thus they hastily declare that the things which are said and are done by all men are to be understood in their way, imagining that all things become spiritual. Whence likewise they assert, that even those exhibiting themselves in theatres, not even these say or do anything without premeditation. So for example, he says, when the populace have assembled in the theatres someone makes entrance clad in a notable robe bearing a cithara and singing to it. Thus he speaks chanting the Great Mysteries (but) not knowing what he is saying:

Whether thou are the offspring of Kronos, or of blessed Zeus,
Or of mighty Rhea, Hail Attis, the sad mutilation of Rhea.
The Assyrians call thee the thrice-longed-for Adonis.
Egypt names thee Osiris, heavenly horn of the Moon.
The Greeks Sophia, the Samothracians, the revered Adamna,
The Thessalians, Corybas, and the Phrygians
Sometimes Papas, now the Death, or a God,
Or the Unfruitful One, or Goatheard, Or the Green Ear of Corn Reaped,
Or he to whom the flowering almond-tree gave birth
As a pipe-playing man.

This, he says, is the many-formed Attis to whom they sing praises, saying:

> I will hymn Attis, son of Rhea, not making quiver with a buzzing sound, nor with the cadence of the Idean Curetes' flutes, but I will mingle (with the hymn) the Phoeben music of the lyre. Evohe, Evan for (thou art) Bacchus, (thou art) Pan, (thou art the) shepherd of white stars.
>
> On account of these and such like reasons, these constantly attend the mysteries called those of the Great Mother, supposing especially that they behold the entire mystery by means of the ceremonies performed there. For these heretics have nothing more than the ceremonies that are performed there, except that they are not emasculated: they merely act as if they were emasculated. For with the utmost severity and vigilance they enjoin (on their votaries) to abstain, as if they were emasculated, from intercourse with a woman. The rest, however, of the proceeding (observed in these mysteries), as we have declared at some length, (they follow) just as (if they were) emasculated.

The gods of various peoples are invoked in the hymn itself as metamorphoses of Attis. The Naassene Sermon is a homily on a hymn that is itself already allegorical. It carries the allegorization one step further through a pneumatic interpretation of the hymn, thus performing an allegorization of the allegory. The mystery of Attis discloses itself as a revelation of the god Anthropos.[9] What the example of the syncretistic Naassene Sermon makes particularly clear is how the infinite variation of the mythologemes is used merely for the orchestration of a dogmatic, unequivocal doctrine. This doctrine culminates in the principle that Hippolyte transmits down in his *Refutatio* V, 6, 7: "The beginning of perfection is the knowledge of man. Perfect perfection, however, is the knowledge of God." In itself, this doctrine of the Naassene Sermon is so general that it could serve as instruction for the ascent of any mystic stepladder. Yet, the point of the doctrine is revealed, if one considers that the highest entity bears the name Anthropos. It is only this name that reveals the essence of the divinity. The anthropological funneling that late ancient Gnosticism carries out in its mythologemes, is demonstrated by this Naassene principle. Man becomes, to a degree unknown in all archaic myth, the center of mythology. The emphasis is put on soul or spirit, on the pneuma of man. The knowledge of the fall or the ensnarement of the pneuma is the presupposition for the knowledge of the ascent, or for the redemption of the pneuma. The knowledge of the origin or of the where-from determines the knowledge of the end or the where-to of the pneuma. It is this knowledge that is redemptive. Clemens Alexandria transmits a "programmatic formula [*Programmformel*]"[10] of the Gnostic doctrine in his *Excerpta ex Theodoto* 8, 2: liberating or redeeming is the knowledge of: "Who were we? What have we become? Where have we been thrown into? Where do we hasten to? What are we liberated from? What is birth? What is rebirth?" This touches the essence of Gnostic doctrine. For following the guideline of these questions, the passion of the pneuma and the path toward its redemption are exposed from within the perplexing multiplicty of Gnostic mythologemes. The stations of the ascent and descent of the pneuma are singled out, and the origin and end are always sought after in light of the "we": Who were we? What have we become? The stories of worlds and eons merely orchestrate the destiny of this "we."

II

In the first course of our considerations, I have attempted to show that in Gnostic myth, mythic, and dogmatic modes of representation interpenetrate each other. In the second course it will be imperative to determine more precisely the historical context that allows a formation of the kind such as the Gnostic myth to congeal. The constellation, in which the dogmatic myth of Gnosticism appears, cannot be understood if one tries to grasp the Gnostic myth unhistorically, be it archetypically, or existential-ontologically, as an ultimate Ur-form of thought, or an ultimate attitude toward existence [*Daseinshaltung*] that could not be scrutinized any further. The literary-critical finding, which results in a peculiar fusion of mythical forms of representation and doctrinal teachings, can be understood historically only as the collision of mythic tradition with demythologized modes of consciousness. Indeed, this is because in late ancient Gnosticism, the archaic myth—transformed, but nonetheless with newly gathered strength and not without success—rose against the demythologization or de-figuralization of myth inaugurated by the religion of revelation.

These considerations presuppose that the process of rationalization—couched in the popular formula "from myth to logos"—took place neither exclusively nor even primarily in Greece. It is not the emergence of Greek philosophy and the natural sciences alone that deprives ancient and Oriental myth of its power. It was not only the philosophical concept but rather the religious revelation of the law and of the prophets that destroyed the mythical perspective. Hermann Cohen, in his late philosophical work, and Gershom Scholem, in his studies of the history of Jewish mysticism, have considered this generally neglected aspect of the process of rationalization, and their analyses should be acknowledged here.

Mythic consciousness does not recognize borders between divine, worldly, and human realms. In mythic narrative, the transition between gods, things, and humans remain fluid. Since these borders are not yet definitively established, one form can easily change into another. Then, the dreamlike stage of this mythic unity of gods, things, and humans is exploded by the experience of transcendence proper to monotheistic religions of revelation. Through the doctrine of creation, a sharp distinction is drawn between the divine, the mundane, and the human realms. When God is recognized as the "creator" of world and man, a barrier is erected: on one side, God as creator, and on the other, world and man, both creatures in their respective ways. The de-godding [*Entgötterung*][11] of the world is thus not only the work of Greek philosophy, but primarily the work of monotheistic revelation.

For sharper than the lines of demarcation that pagan philosophy draws between the realm of the divine and the realm of the worldly, between ur-image and matter, is the border that monotheistic revelation sets up between God the creator and his creature. A polemic against the nature myths of ancient Near Eastern religions dominates the law and the prophets. The account of creation in the book of Genesis and the ban on images in the Decalogue liquidate all mythical talk of God: the creation story, in that it excludes any mythical narrative of the birth of the gods and abolishes any opposition of preexisting matter against the creator-God. The classic formulation of medieval philosophy of religion conceptualizes precisely the intention of the biblical doctrine of creation. The formula *creatio ex nihilo* finally bans that remainder of mythical content that had perseveres in the demythologized Greek philosophical speculation about the eternal matter. The Decalogue's ban on images condemns those images in which mythic religions represent the connection between gods, things, and humans, even if only "symbolically" sublimated. Any attempt to grasp the "true" God in an image is put to a stop. From the perspective of the law and the prophets, revelation is to be understood as encounters with the "true" God, not as his humanization in an image. Encounters between God and creature only occur in the medium of the word. Only the revealed word of God, guiding and ruling in the form of law, reaches across the abyss that opened between God the creator and his creature. Man answers the word of God through prayer and by studying the law. In rabbinical Judaism, "study" turns into religious discipline.

Insofar as the mythical discourse on the gods preserves itself as residues and remainders in the accounts of monotheistic religions of revelation, it retains the weight of a poetic metaphor only. Its power or legitimacy as a religious expression, however, has wasted away.[12]

Nature is the theatrical stage of myth where gods, humans, and things perform. The monotheistic religion of revelation has emptied this stage. It strives to distance itself from nature and lets the encounter of man with the "true" God occur on the stage of history.[13] The stage of Gnosticism is neither nature nor history, but essentially man's interiority: soul, spirit, pneuma. The Gnostic myth describes the path of the soul through the multiplicity and the bewilderment of the worlds and eons, the custom checkpoints of the archons through which the soul has to pass in order to reach the transworldly, or more precisely the antiworldly god, that unity which precedes all division and fragmentation in worlds and eons. In the Gnostic myth there is no history of kingdoms and nations as in the Israelite prophecy and Jewish apocalyptic literature. Rather, all external history only mirrors the destiny of a transmundane pneuma.

Gnostic myth takes up again the theme of archaic mythologemes. It signifies the repetition of mythic experiences on a new plane: on the plane of a consciousness that presupposes the rupture of gods and worlds, of god and world. The unity of mythic consciousness, which, however one might understand it, presupposes, in varying metamorphoses, the presence of the divine and his commerce with the world and with man, is destroyed. It can only be regained at a specific prize, achieved by an ascent of the pneuma that out-runs, out-plays, and out-tricks the infinite distance of worlds and eons.

Where the monotheistic religion of revelation, particularly the religion of early Judaism, tore open the abyss between God as creator and lawmaker and between all creatures, the romantic yearning to close this abyss first began to clamor. Gershom Scholem placed his reflection on the context of Jewish mysticism within this historical-philosophical frame. He recognizes this abyss and takes this experience as his point of departure. Jewish mysticism aims to reestablish that unity "which the religion of revelation had destroyed, but on a new plane, where the world of mythology and that of revelation meet in the soul of man."[14] In orthodox Jewish mysticism, the harmonizing impulse toward holding contrary forms of experience in balance is clear. In the heterodox Gnosticism of late antiquity, the encounter between the world of myth and revelation results in a collision. The distance between God and man is equally presupposed in the Gnostic myth, but it is outstripped by cunning and irony. In late ancient Gnosticism, the responsibility for this distance is attributed to the creator-God of biblical revelation as well.

Rebellious Gnosticism ironically had wanted to gloss over the boundary between the creator-God and his creature with its polemic against the creator-God of the Old Testament. An ironic-polemic trait adheres to all Gnostic mythologemes. The creator-God of the Old Testament is acknowledged and exposed as the creator of "this" world in all its evil and darkness. As creator-God, he is degraded to demiurge, to the God of "this" world.

As Gnosticism discovers the "comic" element in the monotheistic doctrine of creation—God as blind tyrant, the creator and lord of this world, *who gloats about what is happening at his feet* (Irenaeus, *Adversus haereses* I, 30, 6)—it exposes the passion of the pneuma as the tragedy of a distant, foreign, and wholly other God, who transcends even the creator-God.

Gnosis, the Greek term for knowledge, achieves in late ancient Gnosticism a specific coloration: secret, revealed, knowledge necessary for redemption, a knowledge that is not naturally acquired, a knowledge that transforms the knower. This knowledge is one of absolute beginning and the conditions that allow this beginning to become ensnarled: it is always already the story of the fall from heavenly powers, of the emanations of eons and worlds down into creation, of "this" terrestrial world, the prison of the soul, of the pneuma. Antiquity and the Orient know paths to redemptive knowledge in other places, such as China, India, and Egypt. Knowledge as concept, however, is the product of Greek philosophy. It is this emphatic concept of knowledge that is presupposed by Gnostic myth even if not always maintained.[15] In Gnostic myth, therefore, the search for truth appears in a much more urgent form than in archaic myth. Philosophy and revelation have already formed criteria for truth that the Gnostic myth cannot dismiss. In the Gnostic myth the idea of its knowledge is included in the unfolding of the mythical event as one of its moments. The act of knowledge is accomplished in the proclamation of Gnostic myth itself.

Gnostic myth is not naïve; rather, it possesses a particular "character of consciousness."[16] Elements of the archaic mythologemes and philosophemes are introduced in Gnostic myth but only as the building blocks of a doctrine about the meandering pneuma ensnarled in worlds and eons. Mythologemes and philosophemes that, taken by their word, transform into mythic metaphors, appear in the Gnostic myth as the rungs of a ladder that can be thrown away after the Gnostic adept has climbed up. Not only is the external framework of late ancient Gnosticism syncretistic, its inner character is as well. The mythologemes of multiple traditions are broken out of their original context and made disposable. Thus, the variability of Gnostic mythology, which can take its subject to the verge of nonrecognizability, is only superficial because internally the Gnostic myth belongs to the dogmatic tradition, since in all of its variations it deploys only one "true" doctrine.

The mythologemes of Gnosticism are not merely adjusted to the demand of the monotheistic religion of revelation, by some kind of "allegorical dogmatization,"[17] and they are not turned into a canon of new (if at time libertine) duties. Instead, Gnostic myth is often only the result of the pneumatic interpretation of the biblical text, the consequence of a Gnostic allegory that polemically reinterprets the biblical original. Nothing indicates more strikingly the affiliation of the Gnostic myth with the dogmatic tradition than the fact that with the emergence of dogmatic myth, the path from allegory to myth can be literary-critically observed. Gnostic allegory, in contrast to Stoic and the Epicurean allegory, becomes the starting point of a new myth that takes off at the end of the stepladder of pneumatic interpretation and is established on itself.

Hippolyte reports on the Perates, a sect of the Ophitean circle (*Refutatio omnium haeresium* V, chap. 11):[18]

None then, he says, can save and set free those brought forth from the land of Egypt, that is, from the body and from this world, save only the perfect serpent, the full of the full. He who hopes on this, he says, is not destroyed by the serpents of the desert, that is, by the gods of generation. It is written, he says, in the book of Moses. This serpent, he says, is the Power which followed Moses, the rod which was turned into a serpent. And the serpents of the magicians who withstood the power of Moses in Egypt were the gods of destruction, but the rod of Moses overthrew them all and caused them to perish.

This universal serpent, he says, is the wise word of Eve. This, he says, is the mystery of Edem, this the river flowing out of Edem, this the mark which was set on Cain so that all that found him should not kill him. This, he says, is (that) Cain whose sacrifice was not accepted by the god of this world, but he accepted the bloody sacrifice of Abel, for the lord of this world delights in blood. He it is, he says, who in the last days appeared in man's shape in the time of Herod.

The Gnostic interpretation of the Old Testament externally proceeds like a kind of rabbinical midrash. The pneumatic interpretation of Gnostic allegorical hermeneutics, however, aims for a deeper meaning that overturns the apparent meaning of the biblical original. The "spiritual" understanding of scripture stands in opposition to the "carnal." Nevertheless, Gnostic allegorical hermeneutics weaves the new myth out of allusions in the biblical narrative.

In the Ophitic excerpts of Irenaeus on the role of Sophia we hear (*Adversus haereses* I, 30, 17):[19]

Their Mother (Sophia), however, tried to seduce Adam and Eve through the serpent to transgress the precept of Jaldabaoth. Eve, thinking she was hearing this from the Son of God, easily believed and persuaded Adam to eat of the tree of which God had commanded them not to eat. But when they had eaten, they received knowledge of that Power which is above all things and forsook those who made them.

The frame of this Sophia-myth is based on an allegory of the story of the fall of man, Genesis 2:3. The Ophites did not acknowledge the creator-God of Genesis, who forbids eating from the tree of knowledge, as the God of the light-world, but rather as the jealous demiurge Jaldabaoth. The allegorical interpretation of the Genesis narrative is no longer part of Gnostic myth. It is presupposed in the narrative and is brought in the context of a new myth about the origin of the world and of man.[20]

In Manichean cosmogony, passed down in the excerpts of Theodor bar Konai,[21] any memory of the Genesis narrative is effaced. The transvaluation of biblical values, once sprung from a pneumatic interpretation of a text of Genesis, has become independent as a new myth:

The Light-Jesus approached unsuspecting Adam and awakened him out of mortal sleep so that he should be delivered from many spirits. And like a just man who finds a human being possessed of a terrible demon and calms him down by his art, so it was with Adam, since the friend discovered him sunk in deep sleep, wakened him, set him in motion, aroused him, drove away the enticing demons from him, and chained up the many Archons far away from him. Then Adam examined himself and recognized who he was. And he (i.e., the Light-Jesus) showed him the Fathers in the heights and his own self (i.e., his soul), cast into (the midst of) all, (exposed to) the teeth of panthers, the teeth of elephants, devoured by the devourers, consumed by the consumers, eaten by the dogs, mingled with and imprisoned in everything that exists, shackled in the stench of darkness. And says: He (the Light-Jesus) raised him (i.e., Adam) up and made him eat the Tree of Life. Then Adam glanced upward and wept, raising his voice powerfully like a lion roaring. He tore his hair, beat (his breast) and said: "Woe, woe unto him, the Sculptor of my Body, woe unto him who has shackled my soul and woe to the rebellious ones who have enslaved me!"

III

At this point the question that can no longer be avoided is this: Why is it that out of "internal" reasons the polemic against the creator-God of the Old Testament dominates the entire thematics of Gnosticism? Why precisely has the transworldly God of the monotheistic religion of revelation been chosen as the preferred object of Gnostic *ressentiment*? Is the Gnostic myth to be dismissed as an example of metaphysical anti-Semitism that accompanies the social anti-Semitism of pagan late antiquity? It is certain that the protest of the late ancient Gnosticism is deeply connected with the rebellion against antimythic Jewish monotheism. But this counterattack comes not only from outside, from the pagan surroundings but also is carried out from within, from the environment of early Judaism. Gnostic myth cannot be understood if the degree to which it is constituted in opposition against the biblical and rabbinic conquering of mythic consciousness is underestimated. The revenge of myth on its conquerors can be acutely grasped in Gnostic mythology. It lives in the revolt against the monotheistic doctrine of the power and creation of the transworldly God. The recognition of the borders, which the religion of revelation erected between creator-God and creature, is also attested to by the protest of late ancient Gnosticism. What has its say in this protest is an experience that strives, once again, to establish consciously that dreamlike unity of mythic consciousness after the boundary separating god, world, and man had been drawn.

As the mythic teachings of pagan antiquity collide with the dogmatic doctrine of early Judaism and early Christianity [*Urchristentum*] in the late ancient gnosis, Gnostic myth as well was forced to create a new form of their conflict: gods, archons, and eons populate the plot in Gnostic myth as dramatis personae but remain anemic and abstract: they are reduced to allegorical figures and marionettes. Gnostic symbolism is shaped by the contradiction between the mythic intentions of late ancient Gnosticism and the boundary making that grounded the myth-liquidating doctrine of revelation.

Late ancient Gnosticism emerges in the immediate environment of early Judaism, and in pagan quarters only, if at all, in those reached by the missionizing propaganda of Hellenistic Judaism, where the doctrine of the creator-God started to take effect against the dominant polytheism. Gnostic myth marks a crisis in monotheistic religion of revelation itself. The mythic reaction to the doctrine of the monotheistic religion of revelation comes from the borderlands of early Judaism, from Samaria, Syria, Transjordania, and Alexandria. This circumstance, essential for a historical interpretation of Gnosticism, is not considered in the foundational work of Hans Jonas, which has dominated the entire field of the study of Gnosticism for decades. Even if his phenomenological analysis remains valid for Gnostic topoi, such as the alien, this world, and the world beyond, worlds and eons, light and darkness, anxiety, erring, homesickness, the noise of the world, the call from beyond, the alien man, and so on, they acquire a different matrix if the problem of Gnosticism is considered from the perspective of the history of Jewish religion—precisely in that reaction against the boundary making of the monotheistic revelation and its interpretation in rabbinical exegesis.

The predominant interpretation of late ancient Gnosticism by the Bultmann school takes the Gnostic alienation from history at face value, or hermeneutically akin to its subject (and dependent on Husserl's unhistorical, absolute phenomenology and Heidegger's existential analysis of Dasein [*Daseinsanalyse*]) had interpreted the ahistorical index of Gnostic doctrine itself unhistorically, that is, phenomenologically. But even the Gnostic negation of history arose in a particular historical constellation. The stronger the loss of reality, the more intensive does the negative consciousness of world and world-creator become, and thus the more enshrouded does the mystery of redemption become. It seems to me to be important, for an interpretation of the history of Gnosticism, to recall the connection between Gnosticsm and apocalypticism. This connection lets us understand how and why the knowledge of the apocalyptic end and redemption is transformed, how under particular historical conditions the formation of a Gnosticism alien to history could emerge, a Gnosticism that sublates the conditions of its emergence. The negation of history in Gnosticism itself has to be conceptualized historically.[22] Gnosticism reveals itself as one of the ways in which Jewish and Christian groups react to the deferral of *parousia*: the accent shifts from the cosmic and historical *parousia* to the entry of the divine into the individual soul. With the decoding of subjectivity, the scene is prepared for Gnostic mythology.

It is our task to grasp more precisely this shift of accent in the move from early Jewish and early Christian [*urchristlich*] apocalypticism to Gnosticism: apocalypticism is still grounded in a salvation history universally accepted in Judaism, under which the history of Israel could be subsumed. The apocalypticist conceives the entire course of history from beginning to end—he describes the history of election from its end retrospectively. His vision has the character of a preemptive eschatological disclosure. The Gnostic describes the voyage of the soul to redemption in a medium in which the stigma of time is extinguished. Gnosticism, so it appears, reformulates the apocalyptic antitheses between both eons, the eon of this world and the one to come, between the dominion of darkness and that of light, without futuristic accent. The historical schema of apocalypticism implodes with the disillusion about any predictions of the end of times and retreats inward. Gnosticism is at least partly an apocalypticism in the crisis of its futuristic element—a crisis that in Christianity leads either to an allegorizing spiritualization of eschatology in orthodox, or heretical Gnosticism, or to sacramentality of the institution of the church that warrants the End in that it anticipates it.[23] The withdrawal from history reduces the drama of salvation to a drama taking place in the human interior, in soul, spirit, pneuma.

Against the dominant interpretation of Gnosticism, I have attempted to present the thesis that late ancient Gnosticism signifies a crisis in the monotheistic religion of revelation itself: in this crisis, the doctrine of the transworldly creator-God becomes questionable. The problem that ignites the protest of Gnosticism and that the monotheistic doctrine of God's creation and omnipotence left unresolved was the question of the origin of evil in the world. The question of *unde malum* is obviously not a sufficient indication to determine what is specific about Gnostic myth. What is however common to all Gnostic mythologemes is the address of the *malum*: the God of the Jews. Initially, Iao, Sabaoth, Adonais, and Eloaios come into play as names of the archons. Early on, however, from among the archons, Jaldabaoth singles himself out as the God of the Jews (Epiphanius, *Panarion haeresium* 37, 3, 6). He is considered the creator of the world, who says of himself: *ego pater et deus et super me nemo*. But immediately, the demiurgic world-ruler is taught in Gnostic myth: *noli mentiri Jaldabaoth, est super te pater omnium Anthropus* (Irenaeus, *Adversus haereses* I, 30, 6).

The strategy of Gnostic myth always remains the same: in order to reestablish mythic unity and to bridge the abyss set up between God and man by the creation-doctrine the creator-God of Genesis must be opposed: the ancient polytheistic myth cannot stand up against the experience of transcendence attested to by biblical revelation. The experience of transcendence had to be surpassed. This occurs in the dogmatic myth of Gnosticism. The transworldly god, degraded to demiurge, vacated the scene for the antiworldly God, who achieves his correlate in the pneuma, the *self* of man. Prior to the encounter with the monotheistic religion of revelation, and the experience of transcendence as abyss between creator-God and creature, this strategy of Gnostic myth would not have been possible nor necessary.

Translated with the assistance of William Rauscher

6

The Justification of Ugliness in Early Christian Tradition[1]

I

Nietzsche's intention to uproot Christian values and to do justice once again to those of antiquity allowed him to focus on the moment when the turnover from ancient to Christian values takes place. As his locus classicus he designates the first Epistle to the Corinthians 1:20ff., as "a first-rate document for the psychology of every *chandala*-morality." In this text,[2] "the contrast between a noble morality and a chandala-morality born of ressentiment and vengefulness" is first brought to light. Paul negates the religious and ethical values of antiquity, but it is also "beauty above all that hurts his ears and eyes."[3] The rapid convulsions of his late aphorisms and fragments block the recognition of Nietzsche's historical insight. For more deeply than any Christian apologetic intent to obscure the distinction between Christianity and antiquity, Nietzsche understood Paul's "*sermo humilis*" as a transvaluation of the religious, ethical, and aesthetic values of antiquity, a process launched in early Christianity and slowly but unrelentingly seeping into the pores of our sensory perception.

What Nietzsche hinted at only aphoristically or polemically, Erich Auerbach presented in his fragments toward a history of our sense of "reality" with a canny eye that also illuminated meticulousness. His approach is "the interpretation of textual passages."[4] Only rarely has the art of interpretation been practiced with such tact, with such powers of perception and a universal mastery of the material. In his literary critical studies, however,

The Justification of Ugliness in Early Christian Tradition 77

Auerbach "strove for something more general": the question concerning the relation between antiquity and Christianity. The interpretation of passages was meant to "illustrate some of the effect of Christianity on the literary means of expression," precisely to illuminate one "aspect of the path of European intellectual history since antiquity." Auerbach chose one of Augustine's homilies as an occasion to investigate more closely the subject of the "*sermo humilis*,"[5] the Christian form of the sublime, and to trace it into the early Middle Ages. He stuck to his theme so tenaciously that these fragments formed a kind of Christological history of literature. Perhaps the path of the development from Augustine into the early Middle Ages is as unambiguous as Auerbach outlines it. Still, our recourse to the first "*sermo humilis*" of the Apostle Paul is meant to identify the inner difficulties and external resistances that prevent the "Christian" impulse from breaking out into the open. Why is such a long latency necessary in order to carry through a subject once it has been raised, so that it finds its first "pure" resonance only in the post-Christian era, since Hamann and Hegel?

Nietzsche's lead ought to be followed here. With their exegetical investigations of the First Letter to the Corinthians along the lines of the history of religion, Walter Schmithals and particularly Ulrich Wilckens—whose work we gratefully invoke—paved the way for an in-depth interpretation of this passage. If today we are able to determine the acutely polemical character of the discussion more precisely than Nietzsche could, his historical insight still remains unsurpassed by the New Testament exegetes. Even though Nietzsche, within a nineteenth-century horizon of understanding, interprets this passage of the First Letter to the Corinthians all too vaguely as a general polemic against Greek wisdom and philosophy (and in this Heidegger follows him in his foreword to the fifth edition of his Inaugural Lecture) he understood the salient point of Paul's teaching of the cross as foolishness, as only Celsus and Porphyry before him had done, a teaching that equals a slap in the face of the noble ethos of antiquity. "Once more I recall the inestimable words of Paul: 'The *weak* things of the world, the *foolish* things of the world, the *base* and *despised* things of the world hath God chosen' (I Cor. 1:27–28): *this* was the formula; *in hoc signo* décadence triumphed.—*God on the cross*—are the horrible secret thoughts behind this symbol not understood yet?—All that suffers, all that is nailed to the cross, is divine. . . . All of us are nailed to the cross, consequently we are divine. . . . We alone are divine. . . ."[6] In this chapter can be found the most radical, but also the broadest formulation of our subject, which reads:

(I:18) For the word of the cross is foolishness to those who are perishing; but to us who are being saved it is the power of God. (19) For it is written, "I will destroy the wisdom of the wise, and the discernment of the discerning I will thwart" (Isaiah 29:14). (20) Where is the one who is wise? Where is the scribe? Where is the debater of this age? Has not God made foolish the wisdom of the world? (21) For since, in the wisdom of God, the world did not know God through wisdom, God decided, through the foolishness of our proclamation, to save those who believe. (22) For Jews demand signs and Greeks desire wisdom, (23) but we proclaim Christ crucified, a stumbling block to Jews and foolishness to Gentiles, (24) but to those who are called, both Jews and Greeks, Christ the power of God, and the wisdom of God. (25) For God's foolishness is wiser than human wisdom, and God's weakness is stronger than human strength.

(26) Consider your own call, brothers: not many of you were wise according to the flesh, not many were powerful, not many were of noble birth. (27) But God chose what is foolish in the world to shame the wise; God chose what is weak in the world to shame the strong; (28) God chose what is low and despised in the world, things that are not, to reduce to nothing things that are, (29) so that no flesh might boast in the presence of God. (30) He is the source for your life in Christ Jesus, who became for us wisdom from God, and righteousness and sanctification and redemption, (31) in order that, as it is written, "Let the one who boasts, boast in the Lord."

(II,1), When I came to you, brothers, I did not come proclaiming the testimony of God to you in lofty words or wisdom. (2) For I decided to know nothing among you except Jesus Christ, and him crucified. (3) And I came to you in weakness and in fear and in much trembling. (4) My speech and my proclamation were not with plausible words of wisdom, but with a demonstration of the Spirit and of power, (5) so that your faith might rest not on human wisdom but on the power of God.[7]

The passage from 1:18 to 2:5 is introduced by the statement in 1:17: "For Christ did not send me to baptize, but to proclaim the Gospel, not with eloquent wisdom [more precisely: 'in wisdom of the Word'], so that the cross of Christ might not be emptied of its power." With an abrupt turn this sentence concludes Paul's allusions to conflicts within the Corinthian community ignited by the understanding of baptism and introduces the discourse of the "Word of the cross."

Initially, the "Word of the cross" is introduced on principle, but with a polemical front against the Jews and Greeks (1:19 to 1:25), and then it is explicated in two approaches. In the first approach with regard to the position of the community (1:26 to 1:31), and in the second in view of the person of the apostle himself (2:1 to 2:5). The construction of this passage is considered an example of a particularly well-structured and nicely executed larger discourse: it is rhetorical to the point of theatricality. If one reads the text aloud and attempts to imagine it spoken, one would note exact word correspondences, rhyming consonance, symmetrically measured sentences often with homonymic endings, and a series of questions, anaphora, and antitheses. The style of the Pauline sermon has been trained on the example of the cynical-stoic diatribe, that moral-philosophical, scholastic declamation that introduces the opinion of others by means of fictional speech with subsequent fabricated retort. It is understandable that the deeply learned, if somewhat old-fashioned Friedrich Blass believes that any Greek orator would have "highly admired the eloquence of this passage." Yet the point of this passage is lost if it is highlighted exclusively as a "piece of the finest writing or eloquence" and considered only with regard to its dependence on the ancient rhetorical tradition.[8] Because in this passage, possibly for the first time in history, the prevalent rhetorical means of expression are put into the service of a cause that revolutionizes ancient perception and experience. For what could seem more foreign to the ancient imagination, be it Jewish or Greek, than the doctrine of the cross? Even in the Corinthian community this doctrine encountered resistance.

In 1:17 Paul summarizes the intention of his Corinthian opponents in the formula *en sophia logou*, in the "wisdom of the Word," from which in 1:18 he authentically distances his own teaching as *logos tou starou*, as "Word of the cross." Through *logos* and *sophia* the cross is depleted, robbed of its meaning. In 1:18 Paul emphasizes the doctrine of the cross as a thesis: for those who are damned, it is foolishness, but for those who are saved, it is God's power. The respective members of this thesis are set antithetically to one another. Damned versus saved equals foolishness versus God's power. Both parts of the sentence are held together by the same subject, which Paul places with emphasis at the beginning: the Word of the cross.[9]

But what does *ho logos tou starou*, the Word of the cross, mean? What it means is, as 1:23 and 2:2 demonstrate, the proclamation of Jesus Christ, namely, he who is crucified: he in no other than this form. With equal emphasis Paul stresses the Crucifixion in 2:1, while polemically clarifying here the address toward which and *against* which his proclamation orients itself. The Word of the cross is considered by the enthusiasts as foolishness. Why would that be? It is a consequence of their rejection of a Christ *kata sarka*. This answer is surprising at first glance but gains plausibility if we presuppose for the Corinthian community a "Gnostic" understanding of redemption and redeemer.[10] For the enthusiasts in Corinth, Christ is *sophia*, the wisdom of God. The exalted Christ is resurrected in their own knowledge (*gnosis*) or wisdom (*sophia*). It is the exalted, heavenly Christ as "wisdom of God" that a Christian belongs to, not the earthly Jesus. If the distinction of a pneumatic Christ from an earthly Jesus, familiar to us from Gnosticism in the second century, is presumed for the Corinthian community of Paul, only then does the conflict between Paul and his opponents gain contour. From this presupposition light is cast on one of the most enigmatic passages of the letter (12:1–3), which perhaps provides the key for more precisely understanding the position of the Corinthians against whom Paul polemicizes. In the community a curse against Jesus, *anathema Jesous*, has been blurted out. Perhaps this curse has been pronounced during some pneumatic speech. The community is unaware whether such a curse could possibly have been spoken *en pneumati theou*, in the spirit of God. First of all, it is astounding that such a question can even arise within a Christian community. The case, however, is not without parallel. Origen attests (*Contra Celsum*, VI, 28), that the Ophites would accept no one into their community who would not first curse Jesus, and the testimony of Origen is beyond doubt. Origen reports on the praxis of the Ophites in an argument against Celsus, who pillories the Ophitean teaching as Christian, and wants to prove that the Ophites cannot be considered Christians. The apologetic tendency of Origen is evident and easily bracketed. Origen attests, if against his own intention, that the curse against Jesus is part of the initiation into the Christian community among the Ophites.[11]

Even in Gnostic circles, however, the renunciation of a Christ *kata sarka* is not necessarily always carried to its furthest consequence in the form of ritual cursing. The Gnostic literature knows an array of mediating efforts that allocate the earthly Jesus an admittedly inferior role in the drama of salvation. Valentinus assigns Jesus to the "psychic" plane. The fleshly Jesus has salvific significance only for the Simplices, and the Psychicists, to whom the "pneumatic" meaning of the Mysterium has not yet (or more exactly, has never) been revealed. If indeed the *anathema Jesous* of the Corinthian community (confirmed by Origen's testimony) attains its meaning only through the distinction of the earthly Jesus from the heavenly Christ, then the question becomes urgent as to what it might be that separates Paul from the Corinthian Pneumaticists, since Paul himself also knows the distinction between a Christ *kata sarka* and a Christ *kata pneuma*. With this distinction Paul, together with the enthusiasts in Corinth, stands in opposition to the original community [*Urgemeinde*] in Jerusalem. It is known how rarely Paul transmits words of Jesus and how little he is interested in Jesus' works. Paul is also a pneumaticist who attaches no salvific significance to the earthly "life of Jesus." But he shies away from the radical consequences inherent in such a distinction, and he dismisses them with the reference to the "Word of the cross." Even if in general his Christology blends into the Gnostic schema of the redeemed Redeemer, Paul still draws the line at the event of the Crucifixion against the radically spiritualizing tendency of Gnosticism. In the doctrine of the Corinthians he can no longer recognize his own distinction of the earthly Jesus from the heavenly Christ. His opponents in Corinth proclaim, so it seems to him, "another Jesus" and "a different Spirit" (II Cor. 11:4).[12] This is why his polemic on this point is so heated. Perhaps this polemic intention also explains why at the opening of the First Letter to the Corinthians the catenation "Jesus Christ" appears emphasized several times, why in the Second Letter to the Corinthians the proper name of Jesus surfaces so often (II Cor. 4:5f.), and finally why in our passage the form *Christos estauromenos*, Christ the Crucified, is emphatically repeated (1:23; 2:1). Christ *kata pneuma*, the heavenly Christ, is to be envisioned as the crucified: this piece, the *sarx*, this remainder of the earthly is what has salvific importance to Paul. This *servo humilis* distinguishes the Christian mystery of redemption from all other mysteries of redemption. The passion itself is the mystery.[13]

The passage 1:18 speaks of the "foolishness of the cross." First of all, the "foolishness of the cross" is a judgment rendered by the wisdom of the world. It decides what is to be considered wise and what is to be considered foolish. This wisdom, however, is overturned by God himself into foolishness (1:20). Thus two valuations stand opposed to one another: the wisdom of the world, and the wisdom of God. Yet Paul takes a position in the midst of the opposing valuation when at the end of the first approach of his argument he speaks of the foolishness (*to moron tou theou*) and the weakness of God (*to asthenes tou theou*). The substantivized adjective in connection with the following subjective genitive (*tou theou*) indicates that Paul speaks of a divine foolishness and weakness emphatically and not merely ironically.[14] The foolishness and weakness of God are initially measured on the value-scale of the wisdom of the world. But Paul turns the wisdom of the world's ironic judgment into an absolute thesis of God's foolishness and weakness. When he speaks of the cross as divine foolishness and weakness, he refers to Christ, and emphatically to Christ as the crucified. The Crucifixion is, in fact, a sign of God's weakness: Paul says *estaurothe ex astheneias* (crucified in weakness, II Cor. 13:4). This "Word of the cross," his fundamental theologumenon—an inexhaustible paradox that Paul brings forward as something given and undoubtable, and unmistakably in the form of ancient rhetoric—is elucidated in the following passages 1:26–31 and 2:1–5: once from the position of the congregation, and then from his position as apostle in the congregation.

The passage 1:26–31 connects to 1:24.[15] The keyword is *kletoi*, the elect. Paul now describes the manner of this election. To ground the thesis that God's foolishness is nonetheless wiser than men and God's weakness stronger (1:25), Paul points to the position of the congregation in the world: not many wise ones according to the flesh, nor the mighty or the noble, are called. *Sophoi* signifies the learned, *dynatoi* the wealthy and therefore mighty, and *eugeneis* the nobly born, those of good pedigree and social status. The Corinthian community is not constituted by those from the higher echelons of society: to the contrary, gathered in it are the foolish or uneducated, *ta mora*; the weak, disenfranchised, and impotent in society, *ta asthene*; and the nameless and thus unsightly, *ta agene*. Paul aims high in deploying the plural form of the neuter, in order to bring the derisive judgment of the higher and upper classes before the community's own eyes. From the perspective of Corinthian society the members of the congregations are not considered persons, but rather a *quantité négligeable*, or pariahs who remain nameless, or, as Paul (1:28) most fiercely sums up, *ta me onta*, a nothing, a genus of person regarded as nothing.

However, the social standing of the congregation—its pariah-existence—is for Paul a consequence and expression of the same divine weakness and folly whose sign is the cross.[16] Paul wants to illustrate to the congregation his Word of the cross, the paradox of the foolishness and weakness of God, by means of their own worldly position, of the election of the ignoble and despised that transvalues and inverts all worldly values. Toward the end of the passage his proposition intensifies. His reference to the transvaluing and inverting position of the congregation is turned into a "metaphysical" judgment on the world as a whole. The social judgment turns into a metaphysical one. God has chosen that which is not (*ta me onta*) in order to nullify that which is.[17]

The passage 2:1–5 connects to 1:3. The keyword is *keryssomen*, we preach. Paul now proceeds to describe the character of his preaching and thus also his charge. In Corinth Paul was reproached that while his letters were weighty and strong, his bodily presence was weak (*asthenes*) and his speech contemptible (II Cor. 10:10). According to this reputation he was regarded as *tapeinos*, meek or insignificant (II Cor. 10:1). His externally weak appearance, his corporeal weakness, and especially his rhetorically awkward style are part of the judgment of the Corinthians. Still, it is far from obvious that it was his sickness that he was reproached for in Corinth. If the judgment of Paul's Corinthian opponents against his weakness is to be meaningful, it must be understood in the context of their doctrine of the pneumatic Christ as the wisdom and strength of God. It thus becomes also understandable that Paul construes his weakness and physical suffering as *imitatio Christi*.[18] In 1:25 he characterized the cross of Christ as the foolishness and weakness of God. God's weakness on the cross justifies his own weakness (I Cor. 4:9–13):[19]

For I think that God hath set forth us the apostles last, as it were appointed to death: for we are made a spectacle unto the world, and to angels, and to men. We are fools for Christ's sake, but ye are wise in Christ; we are weak, but ye are strong; ye are honorable, but we are despised. Even unto this present hour we both hunger, and thirst, and are naked, and are buffeted, and have no certain dwelling place; and labor, working with our own hands: being reviled, we bless; being persecuted, we suffer it: Being defamed, we intreat: we are made as the filth of the world, and are the off-scouring of all things unto this day.

The opponents of Paul deny him the pneumatic proof of his proclamation and denounce him as pneumatically weak (II Cor. 10:2). Paul returns the reproach and uses it as an objection against the Pneumaticists: it is they who act carnally, which for Paul means sinfully.[20] Paul takes up the same reproach from his opponents in our passage and confirms (2:2) that he did not come to proclaim God's suffering [*Martyrium*—Ch. F.] (or as an equally well-attested reading says, the mystery [*Mysterium*—Ch. F.]) according with an overabundance of *logos* and *sophia*, for he did not want to know anything, except for Jesus Christ, and He as the Crucified. Additionally, in 2:3 Paul adopts arguments of his opponents and confirms that he had proclaimed his sermon of the cross with "fear and trembling," that is, in fear of Judgment, and had been among the Corinthians "in weakness." In the concluding verses 4 and 5 of our passage, Paul repeats the antithesis between proclamation and the teaching of wisdom. He juxtaposes "the convincing words of wisdom" of his opponents over and against the evidence of *pneuma* and *dynamis*. His opponents have co-opted *sophia* and *logos* for themselves. Therefore Paul avoids the word "wisdom" for his proclamation in this passage.[21] The "wisdom" of his opponents is convincing according to human manner. The pneumatic *dynamis* of God is juxtaposed with this. Of this divine *dynamis*, however, Paul says (II Cor. 12:9): *he gar dynamis en astheneia teleitai*, it was "made perfect in weakness." This pointed emphasis is uttered by the *kyrios* himself, which happens only rarely with Paul. It summarizes Paul's intention: the perfection also happens in "fear and trembling"; it cannot and should not repudiate the "weakness."

If an acute conflict with the Corinthian community prescribed the course of his discourse, at the same time Paul establishes his thesis against the Corinthian schismatics in the widest horizon. In their teachings he battles against the "wisdom of the world" or the "wisdom of this Aeon." For Paul, the world is constituted of Jews and Greeks as one whole. The Greeks *sophian zetousin*, seek wisdom; the Jews *semeia aitousin*, clamor for signs. "Wisdom of the world" refers to the law of the Jews and the justice that is characteristic of it, as well as the wisdom of the Greeks and the eros-"philosophy" (I Cor. 2:8, unclear whether it is really Pauline?)[22] that is characteristic of it. The cross must be rejected by both "law" and "philosophy" *a limine*. In the end, a detailed philological analysis does affirm Nietzsche's historical insight that Paul denounces the archaic powers of antiquity as a whole. Paul broadens the terrain of the "Word of the cross," initially a polemical formula against the Corinthian pneumatic teaching of wisdom, and turns it into a polemic against the wisdom of the world, against "law" and "philosophy," against Greeks and Jews.

"The Word of the cross" is Paul's idiosyncratic creation, as he alone in the early Christian community elevated the Crucifixion to theologumenon, most distinctly perhaps in Phil. 2:8. In his study, *Kyrios Jesus*,[23] Ernst Lohmeyer splendidly interpreted the Christ-hymn (Phil. 2:5–11), an interpretation that is now widely recognized. We are dealing here with a strophic poem, carefully measured, a piece of early Christian psalm-poetry. The first part of the hymn is composed of three stanzas: in three stations it describes the way of Christ from the heights of divine form, to the humanness of a servant, to the lowliness of death. Heaven, earth, and hell are the three spheres through which Christ passes. With death as a kind of *descensus ad infernos*, the psalm reaches the rock bottom of "lowliness"—it cannot be intensified anymore. From this insight into the material content of the psalm alone, the passage in 2:8, *thanatou de starou*, is revealed as a gloss by Paul. But even formally speaking, this phrase ruins the structure of the poem, because it overshoots the otherwise maintained line length (if it is read as a line itself) of the three-lined stanzas of the poem. As Paul's gloss, it disturbs the rhythm of the psalm; further, the phrase *thanatou de staurou* introduces a new motif into an established early Christian hymn, which had already praised death itself as Resurrection: *his* Word from the cross.

II

One could easily draw a connection between Paul's preaching of the cross to Augustine's *sermo humilis*. *Christus humilis, vos superbi* (*De civitate Dei*, 10:29) is Augustine's formula against the Platonists, which repeats Paul's polemic against the Pneumaticists of Corinth on a new level. However, the connection to Augustine (a theme for Erich Auerbach and Hans Robert Jauss) cannot be drawn without difficulties because on the path from Paul to Augustine resistances accumulate: they serve to prevent the doctrine of the cross from prevailing in the Christian community and from bringing about that alteration of religious, ethical, and aesthetic values that Nietzsche believed to have been discovered in the advent of Christianity.

The difficulties begin with Paul himself. Accommodation of the opponents, first of the Corinthian enthusiasts, and then in general of Gnostic "wisdom," begins in Paul, in fact in the very next paragraph of the First Letter to the Corinthians. If Nietzsche rightfully refers to I Cor. 1:20ff. as first-rate evidence for the advancing transvaluation of the active values, we might claim I Cor. 2:6ff. as first-rate evidence for the advancing accommodation by Christian values of the Greek world. The *sophia* Paul fought against in the first passage is now introduced in the second, in fact, as truth, *en tois teleiois*, for the perfected.

(II Cor. 6) Yet among them that are perfect we speak wisdom, though not the wisdom of this world, nor of the rulers of this world, who are doomed to perish. (7) But we speak the wisdom of God, secret and hidden, which God ordained before the world for our glory: (8) None of the rulers of this world knew: for if they had, they would not have crucified the Lord of glory. (9) But as it is written, "What no eye has seen, nor ear heard, nor entered the human heart, what God has prepared for those that love him"[24]—(10) These things has God revealed to us through the Spirit: for the Spirit searches everything, even the depth of God.

It appears as if Paul, who until now had pointedly set Christ as the crucified (*estauromenos*) against the *sophia*-doctrine of his opponents in Corinth, now also wants to undermine his Corinthian opponents in their wisdom. Naturally outdoing them while also entirely in accordance with their terms, he recounts the Crucifixion in the form of a myth of God's secret wisdom, which remained concealed even to the archons of this world: with cunning, the self-debasing Christ outdoes the archons, and through his Crucifixion, he sets redemption to work. In this passage Paul conformed both terminologically and also with regard to content to the central motifs of Gnostic doctrine of wisdom, so that only Wilcken's sophisticated art of interpretation can discover even in this passage Paul's anti-Gnostic intent. It is certain that the *sophia* that Paul wishes to teach bears all the characteristics of a Gnostic myth. He commences this passage as well with *lalein* (speak), which is differentiated clearly from *keryssein* (proclaim) in the first passage. But *lalein* is a terminus technicus for charismatic speech. The members of the community are characterized as *teleioi*. *Teleios* is, however, a terminus technicus for the Gnostic mystic, for the initiate to the mystery. And the mystery itself that Paul speaks of, which takes place beyond all wisdom of this world, invisible also to the archons of this aeon, is summed up by the typical Gnostic expression *ta bathe tou theou* (2:10). The divine *pneuma* is revealed in the "depths of God." If, however, the human *pneuma* can fathom the depths of God, the perceiver is identical with the perceived. The Gnostic doctrine of redemption, as the identification of the redeemed as pneumaticist with the *pneuma* of the Redeemer, suggests itself as a final consequence. In this profound Gnostic myth the Crucifixion is transformed into a cosmic process. Thus elevated to an indecisive heavenly event, it becomes also "interesting" for the curiosity and ecstasy of the mystics.

Along the path of compromise, which Paul himself forged, the Christian sermon appears to really be in danger of dissolving in the end into a Gnostic mystery. The Gnostics of the second century in fact capitalize on this Gnosticizing myth of the self-concealing redeemer. Valentinus and even Basilides laid claim to the testimony of the first Corinthian letter for themselves. Not without reason the Valentinians contend that the fundamental concepts of their system can be found in Paul, and they appeal to this paragraph with proclivity. We understand why in ecclesiastic circles Paul's testimony had to represent an embarrassment. I refer to the second letter attributed to Peter (3:15f.), who in his strong polemic against the doctrine of wisdom must have had our chapter in mind when he writes:

And regard the patience of our Lord as salvation; So also our beloved brother Paul wrote to you according to the wisdom given him; (16) speaking of this as he does in all his letters. There are some things in them hard to understand, which the ignorant and unstable twist to their own destruction, as they do the other scriptures.

If the ecclesiastic circles do not renounce the testimony of First Corinthians, this is only because it remains a guarantee of an order, taking root in the congregation at that time which Paul defends and confirms in that same letter. If we desist from the echoes and allusions and limit ourselves to the express testimony of the postapostolic era, we are always referred back to against First Corinthians. That applies to Ignatius, to Polycarp, and especially to I Clement, written some thirty years after Paul's death, which from Rome addresses the Corinthian congregation that has once again met with division. Whatever Clement selects from First Corinthians embodies a barb against the schism-makers.[25] Yet Clement does not address himself to his adversaries in Corinth with the formula of the "Word of the cross," but rather with a long and detailed homily on oneness and unity, on order and discipline in the community. Ever since, the purpose of First Corinthians has been established for the church as well: *primum omnium Corinthiis schismae haereses interdicens* (*Muratori Canon* 42f.).

Against the prevailing judgment, which doggedly asserts itself, we have attempted to demonstrate that Gnostic "wisdom" does not first break into the Christian community in the second century. Gnosticism infiltrates Christianity already at the beginning of its history. For Paul, Corinth was the place of engaging that "wisdom" the "Greeks desire." The Letter to the Corinthians is, of course, an incidental text [*Gelegenheitsschrift*] and cannot yet be assessed as "literature." It becomes literature only after it is included in the New Testament canon, together with other letters by Paul and some pseudo-Pauline texts as the opus of Pauline letters. Literature is thus its posthumous destiny, which certainly was not the author's original intention.

Christian writing turns into literature in a narrower sense only with the apologetic writings. These texts actually address a general public. Because the apologists wanted to render Christianity acceptable to a non-Christian public in the form of general literature familiar to it—the apologetic literature renewed, for example, the form of dialogue—they had to make use of the whole line of philosophical-rhetorical arguments. The Christian preaching of the apologists and church fathers connected the Pauline doctrine of the cross to worldly wisdom in the most varying ways. In the apologetic literature the "symbol" of the cross appears for the first time in the light of Greek philosophy. Plato's *Timaios* becomes the founding text for this. Justin is the first to draw on Plato's attestation.

What Plato said in physiological terms (*physiologoumenon*) about the Son of God in his *Timaios* when he writes: "He impressed him upon the universe in the form of the letter Chi" (*eschiamen auton en to panti*), he borrowed in like manner from Moses. [Here Justin refers to Moses's bronze snake interpreted as the figure of the cross, following Ev. Joh. 3:14.] This Plato read, and since he did not properly understand and thought that it was not the form of the cross (*typos staurou*), but the form of the Chi, he said: that his power closest to the first God (*dynamis*) was spread out in the universe like a Chi.[26]

Wilhelm Bousset pointed to this passage already in 1913 and recognized its fundamental importance for the further import of Christian theology.[27] Justin sees manifestations of the schema of the cross everywhere, be it in the mast of a ship, a farmer's plow, or in the flags of the Roman legion. The infinite series of associations furnished by the apologists for the symbol of the cross remains entirely nonsensical if it is not presumed that in the church aspired to displace the cross as an instrument of torture and to attribute to it "meaning" as a cosmic symbol. The material of ancient Christian literature has been collected in many ways but for the most part has been insufficiently interpreted. I refer to Hugo Rahner's Eranos lectures and the publications of the Joseph Dölger Institute.

In the many martyr acts as well, in which—one would initially assume—the death on the cross should once again become a hard reality, the wooden cross is "inflated" and interpreted cosmically. In the so-called *Martyrium Petri* 8,[28] which belongs to the ancient Acts of Peter, we read:

When he [Peter] had approached and stood by the cross he began to say: "O name of the cross, mystery that is concealed! O grace ineffable that is spoken in the name of the cross! O nature of man that cannot be parted from God! O love unspeakable and inseparable that cannot be disclosed through unclean lips! I seize thee now, being come to the end of my release here. I will declare thee, what thou art; I will not conceal the mystery of the cross that has long been enclosed and hidden from my soul. You who hope in Christ, for you the cross must not be this thing that is visible; for this (passion), like the passion of Christ, is something other than this which is visible. And now above all, since you who can hear, can (hear it) from me, who am at the last closing hour of my life, give ear; withdraw your souls from every outwards sense and from all that appears but is not truly real; [. . . —Ch. F.][29] And when they had hanged him [Peter] up in the way which he had requested, he began to speak again, saying: "Men whose duty it is to hear, pay attention to what I shall tell you at this very moment that I am hanged up. You must know the mystery of all nature, and the beginning of all things, how it came about. For the first man, whose likeness I have in (my) appearance, in falling head-downwards showed a manner of birth that was not so before; for it was dead, having no movement. He therefore, being drawn down—he who also cast his first beginning down to the earth—established the whole of this cosmic system, being hung up as an image of the calling, in which he showed what is on the right hand as on the left, and those on the left as on the right, and changed all the signs of their nature, so as to consider fair those things that were not fair, and take those that were really evil to be good. Concerning this the Lord says in a mystery, "Unless you make what is on the right hand as what is on the left and what is on the left hand as what is on the right and what is above as what is below and what is behind as what is before, you will not recognize the Kingdom." This conception, then, I have declared to you and the form in which you see me hanging is a representation of that man who first came to birth. You then, my beloved, both those who hear (me) now and those that shall hear in time, must leave your former error and turn back again; for you should come up to the cross of Christ, who is the Word stretched out, the one and only, of whom the Spirit says, "For what else is Christ but the Word, the sound of God?" So that the Word is this upright tree on which I am crucified; but the sound is the cross-piece, the nature of man; and the nail that holds the cross-piece to the upright in the middle is the conversion (or turning point) and repentance of man.

The polemic in the Acts of the Martyrs against the wooden cross presumes a distinction between the invisible and the invisible cross. From such a reinterpretation of the cross, the way was open to the "Cross of Light," and only as such was the long-despised torture instrument able to be transformed into the sign of victory for the Constantinian epoch.

III

The transformation of the cross from torture instrument to sign of victory also affects the representation of the external *habitus* of the figure of Christ. I Cor. 2:8, the statement on that divine wisdom, "which none of the rulers of this world understood: for if they had, they would not have crucified the Lord of glory," follows Justin's declaration (Dial. 36:6):

For when the rulers of heaven saw Him of uncomely and dishonored appearance, and inglorious, not recognizing Him, they inquired, "Who is this King of glory?" And the Holy Spirit, either from the person of His Father, or from His own person, answers them, "The Lord of hosts, He is this King of glory."[30]

This context becomes more distinct in the Acts of Thomas, 45.[31] The Enemy-Devil says:

For thou art altogether like him, as if begotten of him. For we thought to bring him also under the yoke, even as the rest, but he turned and held us in subjection. For we knew him not; but he deceived us by his form most unsightly and by his poverty and need.

Here the ugliness of Christ becomes the exclusive theme. In the Acts of Peter (*Actus Vercellenses*, 24), Jesaia 53 is explicitly offered as evidence. In a dispute with Simon Magnus, Peter argues:[32]

A curse on your words against Christ! Did you presume to speak in these terms, while the prophet says of him, "His generation, who shall declare it?" And another prophet says, "And we saw him and he had no grace or beauty."

In the ancient church, Jesaia 53 remained the most important testimony for the "ugly" Christ. The Christian Sybilline Oracle (VIII, 256),[33] an apocalypse from the time of persecution which breathed hate against Rome, established this context: "For not in glory but as a mortal shall he come into the world, pitiable, dishonored, unsightly, to give hope to the pitiable."

The judgment of Clemens Alexandria remains ambiguous. Clemens does indeed accept the tradition of the ancient church that Jesus, according to Jesaia 53:2, "was less beautiful than all children of men" (*Strom.* II, 5, 22) and appeared externally ugly (*Paedagog.* III, 1, 3). Christ, however, had to appear inconspicuous and misshapen so as not to distract us, but rather to guide us toward that which is formless (*aeides*) and disembodied (*asomaton*)! Christ did not want to appear in beautiful form at all, so as not to distract anyone from his preaching, "so that no one, because of praise for his comely appearance and admiration for his beauty would neglect to attend to his words, and allow their attention for the transitory to keep the spiritual at bay" (*Strom.* VI, 17, 51). It is thus not surprising that Clemens, despite the chain of early Christian tradition, can abruptly say of Christ that he "exceeded every human nature, so beautiful, that he merited being loved by all of us, that true beauty that we long for" (*Strom.* II, 5, 21).

In the testimony of Celsus, the pagan resistance against the "ugly" Christ has its say. Celsus argues against the Christian belief in the divinity of Christ with an "aesthetic" argument (*Contra Celsum* VI, 75):

Since a divine Spirit inhabited the body (of Jesus), it must certainly have been different from that of other beings, in respect of grandeur, or beauty, or strength, or voice, or impressiveness, or persuasiveness. For it is impossible that He, to whom was imparted some divine quality beyond other beings, should not differ from others; whereas this person did not differ in any respect from another, but was, as they report, small (*mikron*), misformed (*dyseides*), and ignoble (*agenes*).

While Origen recognized that Jesus was "misformed" (*dyseides*), he believed it possible to dimiss the characteristics of "small" (*mikron*) and "ignoble" (*agenes*). Origen wants to derive from Jesaia 53 only that Jesus did not show himself to the people in an entirely magnificent form (*Contra Celsum* VI, 77):

> But again, how did he [Celsus] who said, "Since a divine Spirit inhabited the body (of Jesus), it must certainly have been different from that of other beings in respect of grandeur, or voice, or strength, or impressiveness, or persuasiveness," not observe the changing relation of His body according to the capacity of the spectators (and therefore its corresponding utility), inasmuch as it appeared to each one of such a nature as it was requisite for him to behold it? Moreover, it is not a subject of wonder that the matter, which is by nature susceptible of being altered and changed, and of being transformed into anything which the Creator chooses, and is capable of receiving all the qualities which the Artificer desires, should at one time possess a quality, agreeably to which it is said, "He had no form nor beauty," and at another, one so glorious, and majestic, and marvelous, that the spectators of such surpassing loveliness—three disciples who had ascended (the mount) with Jesus—should fall upon their faces.

Origen thus appears to assume two modes of appearance for Christ. To the Simplices, Christ appears otherwise than to the Perfecti. Origen considers Christ's figure as servant to be valid only for the "multitude, whom one describes as believers": "For those who are only inducted into the faith, he adopts the form of a servant, so that they say: 'We see him, and he has neither form nor beauty.'" They do not move beyond the figure of the servant and do not recognize the whole of *logos*. The crucified thus counts only for the Simplices.[34]

It is fitting in this context that it is precisely the heresiologists Irenaeus and Tertullian in their struggle against Gnosticism who propagated the tradition of the ugly Christ. Irenaeus names the human Jesus not only *infirmus* or *inglorious* (*Adv. Haer.* IV, 33, 12), but also *indecorus* (III, 19, 2). But Tertullian most keenly underscored the human Christ with an anti-Gnostic barb. To the traditional argument from Jesaia 53, Tertullian appends Psalm 21:7: "I am a worm and not a man" as evidence for the ugly

Christ: *Si inglorious, si ignobilis, si inhonorabilis, meus est Christus* (*Adv. Marcionem* III, 17). *De carne Christi* c. 9–17 furnishes an almost expressionistic text on the theme of the ugly Christ. I cite an example, *De carne Christi*, 9, 4–8:[35]

All these marks of the earthy origin[36] were in Christ, and it is they which obscured Him as the Son of God, for He was looked on as man, for no other reason whatever than because He existed in the corporeal substance of a man. Or else, show us some celestial substance in Him purloined from the Bear, and the Pleiades, and the Hyades. Well, then, *the characteristics* which we have enumerated are so many proofs that His was an earthy flesh, as ours is, but anything new or anything strange I do not discover. Indeed it was from His words and actions only, from His teaching and miracles solely, that men, though amazed, owned Christ to be man. But if there had been in Him any new kind of flesh miraculously obtained (from the stars), it would have been certainly well known. As the case stood, however, it was actually the ordinary condition of His terrene flesh which made all things else about Him wonderful, as when they said, "Whence hath this man this wisdom and these mighty works?" (Matthew 13:54). Thus spake even they who despised His outward form. His body did not reach even to human beauty, to say nothing of heavenly glory.[37] Had the prophets given us no information whatever concerning His ignoble appearance, His very sufferings and the very contumely He endured bespeak it all. The sufferings attested His human flesh, the contumely proved its abject condition. Would any man have dared to touch even with his little finger, the body *of Christ*, if it had been of an unusual nature; or to smear His face with spitting, if it had not invited it (by its abjectness)? Why talk of a heavenly flesh, when you have no grounds to offer us for your celestial theory [lit., "why do you suppose it to be celestial"]? Why deny it to be earthy, when you have the best of reasons for knowing it to be earthy? He hungered under the devil's *temptation*; He thirsted with the woman of Samaria; He wept over Lazarus; He trembles at death (for "the flesh," as He says, "is weak");[38] at last, He pours out His blood. These, I suppose, are celestial marks? But how, I ask, could He have incurred contempt and suffering in the way I have described, if there had beamed forth in that flesh of His aught of celestial excellence? From this, therefore, we have a convincing proof that in it there was nothing of heaven because it must be capable of contempt and suffering.[39]

If, at the end of these considerations, I refer to the problem of an "ars humilis" in Christian late antiquity, then it is only to indicate the resistances which stand in the way of a "modus humilis" in art.[40] Precisely in the transition from word to image the Christian experience leaves its own terrain behind—because at *its* beginning stood the Word—and moves into foreign territory where its law and canon are stipulated from the outside. It is less noted but perhaps also significant from an intellectual-historical perspective that images of Christ appear for the first time in Gnostic circles (Irenaeus, *Adv. Haer.* I, 26, 6). In the ancient church itself, the memory of the Old Testament's struggle against pagan divine images remained for a long time too vivid, in order to break the prejudice against a visual representation of Christ. The issue of images had concerned the ancient church long before the iconoclastic controversy in Byzantium, and it had long resisted the image in Christian space. In the earliest preserved images, Christ appears as the good shepherd, as Orpheus, as helmsman of the church, as teacher of the true logos or bringer of miraculous rescue. If Christian art remained predominantly influenced by its commitment to the word of the scripture and stood in the service of doctrine and liturgy as a kind of "biblia pauperum," it is astounding how late a "modus humilis" takes hold in Christian art. Cross or Crucifixion could have very well been able to supply a guideline for a genuine Christian art. Even though in the preceding paragraphs we have attempted to clarify the difficulties confronting the development of the preaching of the cross in ancient Christian literature, it is nevertheless surprising that not a single representation of a cross from the first three hundred years has been preserved. "When we first study the origins of the crucifix, we are surprised to see the centuries go by without our encountering the image we seek. The first century seems to have passed without leaving any trace, any sign that might evoke Christ on the cross. For the second century, the monuments presented cannot be dated with certainty. It is not until the third century that we find occasional marble or terra-cotta fragments, funerary plaques on which can be seen, next to the name of the dead person, a discreet cross, often hidden among the letters of the epitaph. Although the doctrine of the cross was constantly cited by Saint Paul [. . .] although in the second century, Saint Justin spoke enthusiastically of the cross that is in every heart [sic] in his first *Apology*, it is nowhere to be found: neither in private houses, nor in the meeting halls that served as churches, nor in the catacombs, the last refuge against the persecutions."[41] And it is, of course, a long way from the Sethian cross on the Palatine to the radiant golden cross of triumph bedecked with precious stones. The great turning point for the iconography of the cross is its official recognition by Constantine as one of the imperial symbols. The art history of the cross essentially begins only with the erection of the pageant cross in Jerusalem. With the Constantinian turn, the cross changes into a Christian symbol of triumph whose memory of Christ's suffering and death is effaced. The cross turns into a sign through which Constantine captures his victory. *In hoc signo*, it was not décadence that triumphed, as Nietzsche believed in the aforementioned fragment, but rather the Imperium Romanum over Christianity. The *crux invicta* determined the composition, the scene selection, and also the spirit of the passion sarcophagi. Even in the passion scenes on the sarcophagi of the fourth century any trace of suffering is absent. These scenes emphatically avoid the representation of the Crucifixion. Although art of late antiquity was capable already in the third century of representing human suffering movingly, the Christ of the passion sarcophagi does not present a countenance marked by suffering. "Christ had much more of something like an inviolable sovereign grandeur. He always appears more like a victor than a sufferer. He is the young hero on whom death has nothing."[42] Since 340, the *crux invicta* is the norm for all further developments of sarcophagus art in the second half of the fourth century and in the fifth. Christ as victor of the Theodosian era dominates the iconography of the sarcophagus. The middle image of the passion sarcophagi is developed into great scenes of homage that take up the entire front of the sarcophagus. The cross, once a *servile supplicium*, now becomes a royal insignia in the right hand of Christ.

The relief with a Crucifixion scene at the Porta Santa Sabina in Rome is from the fifth century: "The original order of these panels revealed the parallelism between the scenes from both Testaments, but this order was completely forgotten in the repairs undertaken over the centuries. In this way, the Crucifixion found itself relegated to the upper part of the left panel, so far away as to be barely visible. Or perhaps this was the place desired by the artist attempting (timidly) to present a Crucifixion, for it is remarkable that in this door consisting of at least eight big panels, the artist thought it necessary to devote only a small one to such an important subject."[43]

The first miniature of a crucified Jesus that can be dated clearly is found in the so-called Rabulas-codex, which dates to 586. The cross inscription is Syriac, and I see no reason, despite the assertion of learned art historians like Charles Morey and Aloys Grillmeier, to presume a Greek model. Syria and Palestine, above all, have an outstanding rationale for the genesis and development of the cult of the cross: it seems to me that the origin of the image of the crucified Jesus is to be found there. André Grabar advanced the interesting thesis:

> In undertaking the illustration in images of the episodes of the Passion and the end of Christ's terrestrial life through Pentecost, Christian iconographers, then, always confined themselves to themes from theophany. But if the epiphanies of childhood and the miracles that they interpreted from very early on were already familiar to many religions of the time, this was not the case for the group of theophanies of the Passion-resurrection. The cycles of the childhood and miracles of Jesus could thus rely on memories of the pagan iconography of theophany, while the images of the Passion did not recall similar antecedents, and this, in my opinion, is what explains the delay in the creation of an iconography of the Passion. The examples of ancient epiphanies were not enough to compose the first images. What was needed was a particular impulse, and this impulse, as we will see, came from the cult of saints and Palestinian relics.[44]

If it appears to me to be daring to seek the impulse for the development of the Crucifixion scene in the Palestinian cult of the relics alone, it still remains probable that its origin is to be found in Syrian and not in Hellenist sphere. Even the oldest written evidence supporting the existence of a cross with corpse comes from a Nestorian ascetic Dadisho (died ca. 690), a monk from the region of the Persian gulf. In his *Admonitions*[45] we read:

> Bow your forehead to your knees in frequent and long genuflections and beat your head against the ground before his cross with repeated prostrations. [Or]: Genuflect before the Crucifix and recite the Lord's prayer. Then rise upon your feet and embrace and kiss the Crucifix with a feeling of repentance and love. [. . .] Kiss our Lord on his cross, twice on the nails of his right foot and twice on the nails of his left foot [. . .] make a sign on your mouth with the Crucifix.

The crucifix, originally an object of private monastic piety, turns into an object of public cult only in the Middle Ages. The "sermo humilis" in Christian literature as well as in visual art has its origin at the margin of the Imperium and establishes itself only in the decline and downfall of the Roman Empire. Even Augustine's historical theology and "sermo humilis" are eccentric in late Christian antiquity. For late ancient Christianity, the imperial theology of Eusebius remains dominant. The resistances of antiquity as well as those of Christian late antiquity had to be fundamentally cleared out before the "sermo humilis," be it literary, be it visual, could shape the Latin Middle Ages. How foreign it was to ancient sentiment is something that Nietzsche can instruct as in, as he wanted to evoke antiquity once again at the end of the Christian era. *Indeed, what a dreadful place Christianity had already made of the earth when it everywhere erected the crucifix and thereby designated the earth as the place "where the just man is tortured to death"!*[46]

Translated with the assistance of William Rauscher

7

Notes on Surrealism[1]

The first colloquium was organized around the theme of "Nachahmung und Illusion" [Imitation and Illusion],[2] and it attempted to trace the various metamorphoses of the concept of *imitatio* in the period between 1750 and 1830. This colloquium, as its initiators have already established in the invitation, cannot place the upheaval that took place between 1850 and 1920 under such a unified title. The questions, however, that have been posed for the discussion of this colloquium—*What sort of situation produces the dissociation from the traditional attachment to a present object in poetry and visual art? How can the production of concreteness without representing referent [Gegenständlichkeit ohne abbildenden Bezug], unique in each case, possibly be conceptualized aesthetically?*—assume that turn can be sufficiently conceptualized based solely on aesthetic categories. I contest that the dissociation from the traditional attachment to a present object in poetry and visual art that came about between 1850 and 1920 can be sufficiently conceptualized based solely on aesthetic categories. Poetic praxis and theory itself require first of all a historical-philosophical interpretation that determines the historical index of the poetic production as much as of the theoretical principles.

When considered more closely, the prior understandings that determine the analysis of modern poetry break open the closed aesthetic context. In his analysis of the *Structure of Modern Poetry*,[3] Hugo Friedrich used categories such as *empty ideality, ideality without content, empty transcendence, the artificial ego,* and so forth, to characterize modern poetry, which, if they are not only to orchestrate an elegiac complaint and accusation against modernity, must be defined more precisely. Either adjectives like "empty," "without content" [*inhaltlos*], and "artificial" camouflage a historical-philosophical thesis that establishes the norm in a Platonic-Christian metaphysic and measures the deviation from this norm, or such adjectives point toward experiences that exceed the Platonic-Christian horizon. If there are no means other than "negative" concepts to describe the poetry of this epoch, then that which is independent and creative in this negativity must be made visible. This will be tried on the example of a principle of surrealist theory. Our considerations circle around the prefix *sur* in the title "surrealism": What meaning can this prefix have in the context of a purely profane, immanent, and materialist experience? Aragon answered: "The only signification of the word 'beyond,' you are in poetry" [*Seule signification du mot Au-delà, tu es dans la poésie*].

The valorization of fantasy as a medium of poetry, as is prevalent since romanticism, occurs at the price of the loss of the worldliness of its symbolism, which is indicated by the occasional, often even nonobliging character of romantic allegory. Medieval ontology is "symbolically" structured. Nature and holy scripture are both, in different ways, revelations of the noncreated [*ungeschöpflichen*] and therefore also inexhaustible [*unausschöpflichen*] *verbum divinum*. One could only speak of the threefold, fourfold, and multiple meanings of scripture because things and events are, on different levels, copies of an exemplary original image [*Urbild*]. Interpretation, therefore, remains an infinite task in medieval exegesis because the ground, the *verbum divinum*, remains inexhaustible. The hierarchical *chain of being*[4] allows, even provokes the analogy and comparison between Below and Above.

Since the advance of the modern natural-scientific method, which since Bacon, Descartes, and Spinoza provides the guideline for the interpretation of reality, the medieval symbolic interpretation of nature and holy scripture has been robbed of its foundation. Symbolic correspondences are no longer regarded as indication of an infinite mysterium, but are exposed as mystification. The *sensus literalis* alone is considered true or can claim truth. Spinoza, who in his *Tractatus Theologico-politicus* recognized the historical or literal sense of scripture as the only one, wants to construct even ethics *more geometrico*. Since romanticism, poetry as well wants to proceed *more geometrico*. Novalis describes poetry as *beautiful mathematics*, as *mystic* or *artistic mathematics*. This novel combination of poetry with *construction* and *algebra* attests to the fact that modern poetry, despite its opposition to natural science and technology, stands in the shadows of the prevailing natural-scientific concept of reality. The attempt of a *pneumatic chemistry* or a *magical astronomy*, which for Novalis is to represent the whole of natural science as exempla, indicates the burden that the triumph of modern natural science imposes on poetry. The triumph of the natural-scientific interpretation of reality (and the historical interpretation of the word of revelation that goes along with it) pushed the "symbolic" interpretation of the world into poetry and exposed it as a product of fantasy that remains without worldly correlate; thus, it relegated poetry to the path of allegory. The allegorical outlook of the world since the baroque period has its origin in the confrontation of the poetic imagination with the univocal *mos geometricus*, as modern science states it, as it casts out the multivalent symbolic interpretation of reality. With the progress and establishment of the natural scientific method, modern allegory, from the baroque through romanticism to surrealism, becomes fungible and occasional in increasing measure.

The romantic and postromantic catenations of orders and investigations of correspondences do not build any bridge between subjective fantasy and objective world, rather they remain confined within subjective interiority. Thus, for example, the experience of correspondences in Baudelaire (*les parfums, les couleurs et les sons se répondent*) goes together with an almost Manichean split between world and man. At the cusp of modernity, Baudelaire, despite his recourse to medieval-mystic tradition, can state the idea of correspondence only provocatively as paradox because for Baudelaire, analogy and metaphor are products of the imagination. They do not correspond to any order of creation, rather "it [the imagination] disassembles creation, and with materials gathered and arranged by rules whose origin is only to be found in the very depths of the soul, it creates a new world, it produces the sensation of the new."[5] The act of artistic creation here no longer copies an exemplary creation, the order of the world, rather it disassembles and destroys this order, in order to create out of the depths of the soul a new world from its individual parts and to attest to the *sensation du neuf*.

In surrealism, at least in its theoretical reflections, the conclusion is drawn from the situation that we attempted to demonstrate for Baudelaire. The emphasis is put clearly on the interiority of the subject. The analogy or the *correspondance*, which even in its last offshoot remained determined by the medieval model of a symbolic universe, is discarded and heterogenous elements, tattered and without context, are brought together. The individual object is torn out of its established or original context and is placed in unexpected surroundings or imbued with a new application. Already in Baudelaire, the term *surnaturalism* crops up. It is the legacy of romantic language. In Baudelaire this word still remains embedded in a system of correspondences and founded on an *analogie réciproque*, which is, however, no longer visible in a worldly [*welthaft*] way, but instead possesses validity only in the closed circle of poetry. From Baudelaire, these impulses proceed toward surrealism where—at least in its revolutionary phase—the analogous universe is destroyed: world and ego become disunited already in Baudelaire; in surrealism the world with itself and the ego with itself are disunited, and both equally are smashed to pieces. The surrealist allegory orchestrates the worldlessness [*Weltlosigkeit*] of a nihilistic experience, that initially joins itself to the postulates of a revolutionary communism, but in the course of the routinization of the revolutionary impulse it disengages itself from the program of world revolution and emerges ever more distinctly as such in the surrealist work.

The nihilistic worldlessness of the surrealistic experience "repeats" in modernity the nihilistic worldlessness of Gnosticism in late antiquity. If, however, a comparison between Gnosticism and surrealism is not to get bogged down in external and secondary characteristics, the difference between late ancient Gnosticism and surrealistic experience needs to be sharpened and elaborated in view of what nihilistic worldlessness can possibly signify in varying epochs. I first wish to summarize in a few key words the abundance of mythic speculation and soteriological cult-praxis that are concealed by the umbrella term of "Gnosticism" and in doing so follow the analysis carried out by Hans Jonas in the first volume of his *Gnosis und spätantiker Geist* [*Gnosticism and the Late-Ancient Mind*].[6]

The Gnostic experience of the world ought to be our point of departure. Even in Gnostic language cosmos means: order and law. However, the qualifier adhering to this term in Greek is inverted. Order turns into rigid and hostile order, law into tyrannical and evil law. With this inversion of the qualifier, however, not merely is the positive turned into a negative, and thereby all positive quality withdrawn from the ancient cosmos. Rather, the cosmological scheme of antiquity is fundamentally altered. For the idea of the "border" characteristic of the ancient cosmos is transcended in the Gnostic experience. In the Gnostic experience the border, which in the cosmological scheme of antiquity served as guarantor for the harmonic order, turns into an external barrier that is supposed to be transcended. The concept of beyond acquires thereby a concrete meaning in Gnostic language: it is the region of the transmundane god who is conceived as a counterprinciple to the world. The Gnostic divine predicates: unrecognizable, unnameable, unsayable, boundless, nonbeing, are negative predicates. They are to be understood as a negation of the world and polemically determine the opposition of the transmundane god to the world. The juxtaposition between world and transmundane God repeats itself within the human being. The psyche is the dowry of the world powers and in Gnostic language turns into a *terminus* for the natural life that is to be left behind in redemption. It is juxtaposed by the pneuma as an idea of a transcendental, a-cosmic self in the human being, an a-cosmic ego-core, an ultimate, unrelatable interior, in correspondence to the transmundane god. In late ancient Gnosticism the concept of the pneuma as an inner-human transcendence establishes a new idea of freedom, which in its worldly consequences leads to moral anarchism and libertinism. The pneumatic man is a *homo novus* for whom law and worldly wisdom are not binding. The Gnostic pneumaticist is the dandy of antiquity.

Initially this reference to late ancient Gnosticism provides a possibility to free "preconcepts," such as empty transcendence or artificial ego from the odium of the minus. Applied to the Gnostic experience of a nonworldly ego, be it conceived eschatologically or ecstatically, these preconcepts would be overdetermined by a norm of worldliness that Gnostic experience wants to surmount. Could things be similar with regard to modern poetry? Hugo Friedrich's interpretive categories doubtlessly grasp its structure, but the pejorative undertone that adheres to them precisely misses the Gnostic-pneumatic character of this "negativity." Even what M. H. Abrahams considers as *extraordinarily truncated Christianity* in Baudelaire[7] would then have its basis in a particular principle that would have to be developed in the analysis of modern poetry. Because the categories of an orthodox Christian doctrine (which in the concordance of Old and New Testaments always, if in different ways, posits the unity of creator-God and redeemer-God and thus that of created and redeemed world) are useless for grasping the a-cosmism as it articulates itself in Gnosticism and modern poetry, both in its theological as well as anthropological variants.

Our comparison between the Gnostic a-cosmism and the worldlessness of modern poetry is based on the fact that in the protest and provocation of Gnosticism as much as in the protest and provocation of modern poetry the pregiven interpretation of the world as a whole is bracketed. The Gnostic doctrine of redemption is a protest against a world ruled by *fatum* or by *nomos*. This fatum presents itself in the mythological style of Gnosticism as personified powers: astrological determinism. The world as it is represented by the interpretation of modern science and technology and against which modern poetry turned in varying phases since romanticism, regains a mythical coherence as a unified whole: natural-scientific determinism. The poetic protest turns against the enslavement to nature of science and technology, the consequence of knowledge as power that can be wielded only in the form of domination and coercion of a demystified nature.

Obviously, the circle of the modern universe is a circle with infinite radius, so that the protest of modern poetry, in contrast to the Gnostic protest, can never reach a beyond of the world in a strict cosmological sense, no matter how far it strives to advance beyond the boundaries of the world drawn by its scientific interpretation. From this difference between ancient and modern cosmology, the difference of instruments between Gnosticism and surrealism can be determined. In Gnosticism, the pneumatic Self, which stands in opposition to the world in all its forms, still has to guarantee its unworldliness through an unworldly god, beyond the cosmos. The surrealist revolt proceeds against the infinite world posited by the modern natural sciences and technology that is experienced as a system of domination and coercion. But in its escape from this infinite coercive system of the world, it cannot invoke the guarantee of a god beyond the world.

Surrealism knows itself rooted in a modern uniform universe that does not have a beyond. Atheism and materialism are its touchstones of honesty. Still, the anthropological materialism and atheism of surrealist observance cannot seamlessly be derived from the metaphysical materialism and atheism of the nineteenth century. There is a remainder indicated by the prefix *sur* in "surrealism." What meaning can this prefix have in this materialist context? Aragon's answer, *Seule signification du mot Au-delá, tu es dans la poésie* now becomes clearer. Poetry is the only beyond, not because it bridges "this world" [*Diesseits*] and the one "beyond" [*Jenseits*], Above and Below. It is the beyond itself. The word does not bear testimony, rather it is itself transcendence.

Third Session[8]

Surrealism and Gnosis
 Chair: Dieter Henrich[9]

TAUBES (Summary of the paper)—1. Any attempt to compare Gnosticism and surrealism first of all presumes that they are at all "comparable." As one constellation of spirit is being compared with another, the presumption underlying this attempt is that which is comparable is in a certain perspective the same, but at the same time different.

What is comparable between late ancient Gnosticism and modern surrealism lies in the Gnostic and surrealist revolt and provocation that deploys a nihilistic worldlessness (a-cosmism). Precisely a "structural comparison" between Gnostic and surrealist a-cosmism demonstrates the fundamental change of the transcendental points of orientation in antiquity and modernity, and it submits the varying configurations to a historical-philosophical index. Gnosticism and surrealism, the two great manifestations of a-cosmic revolt, do not so much differentiate themselves by the lines of formative dispositions, but rather by the cosmological alphabet that they find in the formulation of their protest.

It is not a matter of uncovering archetypal forms of Gnosticism in surrealist poetry, as was, for example, suggested by C. G. Jung's psychology. Rather, it is only because in this modern configuration of surrealism the archetypal structure of Gnosticism newly construes and regroups itself, that a comparison between late ancient Gnosticism and modern surrealism can have significance.

The historical index of a mythology does not merely state that it belongs to a certain epoch. Above all, it states, as Walter Benjamin subtly notes, that it is only "possible" or readable in a specific epoch because in every structure, however archetypal it may be, time is interwoven. Even an "archetypal" mythologeme is historical and not timelessly eternal. The a posteriori of the epochal index turns concretely a historical-philosophical a priori.

The current attempt does not aim at a literary-historical analysis of surrealist texts. Rather, it intends to elucidate the conditions of the possibility of surrealist poetry in view of the experience and doctrine of late ancient Gnosticism and thus to furnish a criterium that determines more precisely the specifically "modern" form, if only in preliminary terms.

2. Our considerations circle around the prefix *sur* in the title "surrealism." The prefix *sur* in the term "surrealism" corresponds to the Greek prefix *meta,* which, as Hans Jonas notes, presents the fundamental category of movement in Gnostic language and determines the spectrum of Gnostic experience from the most external magical cult praxis to the innermost form of mystic contemplation.

What meaning can the prefix *sur* have in the context of a purely immanent experience? I am in agreement with Walter Benjamin that in surrealism, *a creative overcoming of religious illumination* takes place in favor of a *profane illumination, a materialistic, anthropological inspiration.* It is only a question of *how* this overcoming of the language of religious illumination is accomplished, and *why.*

3. Already in Baudelaire the word *surnaturalism* crops up, a legacy of romantic language. In Baudelaire this word remains embedded in a system of correspondences and founded on an *analogie réciproque,* which is however no longer visible in a worldly manner, but possesses validity only in the closed circle of poetry. The impulses toward surrealism proceed from Baudelaire, where however the analogous universe is destroyed, at least in its first phase: the world has come apart, the ego is disunited from itself, and the bridge between world and ego is shattered.

4. The valorization of fantasy as organ of poetry, as is prevalent since romanticism, occurs at the price of the loss of the worldliness of its symbols, which is indexed by the occasional, often noncommittal character of romantic allegory.

5. The medieval universe is ontologically "symbolically" structured. Since the expansion of the modern natural-scientific method, which since Bacon, Descartes, and Spinoza offers the guidelines for an interpretation of reality, the medieval symbolic interpretation of nature and holy scripture has been robbed of its foundation. Symbolic correspondences no longer count as indications of an infinite mystery but are debunked as mystification. The *sensus literalis* alone is true or can claim truth. Spinoza, who in his *Tractus Theologico-Politicus* recognized the historical or literal sense of scripture alone as being valid, wants to construe even ethics *more geometrico*.

6. The triumph of the natural-scientific interpretation of reality (and the historical interpretation of the word of revelation that is part of it) pushed the "symbolic" interpretation of the world into poetry, demasked as the product of fantasy that remains without worldly correlate.

The romantic and postromantic catenations of orderings and investigations of correspondences do not build any bridge between subjective fantasy and objective world; rather, they remain banned to subjective interiority. Thus for example the experience of correspondences in Baudelaire (*les parfums, les couleurs et les sons se repondent*) goes together with an almost Manichean split between world and man.

7. Our comparison between Gnostic a-cosmism and the worldlessness of modern poetry establishes that in the protest and provocation of Gnosticism as well as that of modern poetry, the aforementioned interpretation of the world as a whole is bracketed. The Gnostic redemption doctrine is a protest against a world ruled by *fatum* or by *nomos*. This fatum exhibits itself in the mythological style of Gnosticism in personified powers: astrological determinism.

The circle of the modern universe is of course a circle with infinite radius, so that the protest of modern poetry, in contrast to Gnostic protest, no matter how far it wants to propel itself over the borders of the world (as given to it by scientific interpretation), can never achieve a beyond of the world in a strictly topographical sense. From this difference between ancient and modern cosmology, the fundamental change of the transcendental point of orientation between Gnosticism and surrealism can be determined. In Gnosticism, the pneumatic Self, which stands in opposition to the world in all its forms, must guarantee its unworldliness through an unworldly God, beyond the cosmos. *This is in a certain sense nothing other than the great projection of the revolutionary uncovered non-worldly self.*[10] The surrealist revolt takes place against the infinite world established in modern science of nature and technology that is experienced as a system of domination and coercion, but in its breakout from this endless system of worldly coercion, it cannot invoke the guarantee of a God beyond the world.

HESELHAUS[11]—J. Taubes himself suggests that the "Gnostic" element of modernity is present already before surrealism when in his points three to six of his summary he refers to Baudelaire and romanticism. In addition, I would like to refer to the literary elements of Gnosticism in F. von Baader and D. F. Strauss (*apocatastasis*-doctrine). In this context the representation of Nirvana in Schopenhauer (*The World as "Representation"*) and Nietzsche's nihilism certainly merit attention as well. Finally in German modernity we have at least three poets who directly take up Gnostic views and continue to develop Gnostic myths: Th. Däubler, A. Mombert, and O. Loerke. Däubler's *Nordlicht*-poetry even contains a mythic/humanist attempt to depict the tradition of Gnostic views in the Western culture.

All of these Gnostic elements in modern poetry belong to the effort to introduce into the field an interpretation against the "natural-scientific interpretation of reality" (J. Taubes), which invokes the spirit (pneuma) and the spiritualizing of the world (pneumaticizing). Consequently, it appears to me that Taubes's differentiation is insufficient, namely, that ancient Gnosticism takes recourse to a nonworldly God, while surrealism supposedly no longer has this guarantee by an otherworldly God. It is precisely surprising that despite the absence of such a guarantee, correspondences with Gnostic views still surface in modernity.

TAUBES—I don't dispute that Gnostic motives are directly taken up in modern poetry, but I would like to warn against a historical analysis of motives, as is prevalent in literary studies, which establishes a net of relations, be they mythographic or terminological, by the guideline of distinct individual motifs. It may be that precisely where Gnostic and hermetic topoi are handed down, the distinct horizon of a Gnostic understanding of self and world vanishes. In the handing down of such Gnostic and hermetic motifs, we are dealing largely with derivative products found in the rubble heaps of tradition and offering no basis for a unified structural interpretation.

ISER:[12] These derivatives, however, are illuminating. In this context one may think of the relation that exists between Yeats's hermetic writings and his poetry. The perfect order detailed in his tracts equally excludes world and self. Yeats's poetry, therefore, is attuned to the idea of an *antiself* [13] and of a perfection characterized precisely by its independence from nature and its worldlessness (*Byzantium* poems). Thus the perfection evoked in the *images*[14] of the *Byzantium* poems is without content, whereby it is indicated simultaneously that this perfection is seen from the perspective of the natural world. For Yeats, this perfection becomes concrete to the extent that sublation of the natural world, and the ego that is conscious of finitude through its subjectivity, is successful (the theme of the *Byzantium* poems). Thus the perfection attributed to the hermetic *images* achieves a revolutionary aspect. This was evinced in Yeats as well in his political activities within the "Irish Renaissance." In the context of the theses provided by J. Taubes it should therefore be asked:

1. Why do these representations of perfection construed from hermetic and Gnostic roots remain ultimately fictions that at the same time thwart the revolutionary impulse?

2. Could an answer to this help clarify the qualitative difference between the two conflicting structural models? This viewpoint appears to be important because the structural comparison between Gnosticism and surrealism is intended to offer points of departure for the elucidation of modern poetry.

TAUBES: 1. Upfront, W. Iser's methodological objection calls for greater precision in my critique of the prevalent motif-historical mode of research. The final products of Gnostic and hermetic language that are born along by tradition can in a particular constellation become constitutive for a binding horizon of poetic self-understanding.

I believe that the oeuvre of Yeats as well as that of Blake prove this insight. Yeats and Blake, who incidentally belong to the surrealist group's calendar of saints, take the traditional Gnostic or hermetic metaphors at their word and fill them with new content, which bears characteristics of a Gnostic mythology as a whole and in detail.

I position myself methodologically between the Scylla of an individualizing interpretation and the Charybdis of an archetypal one. The Gnostic structure, it must be maintained against Hans Jonas, is not only to be assigned to late antiquity. Indeed, the origin of Gnostic experience may lie in the late ancient constellation. However, without any filiation whatsoever Gnostic mythologemes surface in the sixteenth century, not in the form of individual motifs, but in the form of fundamentally determining the basic character, in Isaac Luria's doctrine of *tsimtsum*, the doctrine of the "withdrawal" of God into his own Being. No motif-historical analysis, however subtle, could attribute to "influences" this parallel between late ancient Gnosticisim and Lurianic kabbalah, which develops the great myth of the exile of God from his omnipotence and the theory of the divine sparks "scattered" in the world.

It would also, however, be misleading to conclude from the return of Gnostic mythology that the Gnostic structure is a matter of a timeless eternal, archetypal idea that repeatedly comes into language without being ignited in a particular historical context. It remains decisive when, how, and where the Gnostic structure that emanates from the particular historical constellation of late antiquity becomes "citable."

An archetypal idea is definable not only in its constant repetition, but also, as Benjamin says, in the exhaustion of its history. Thus the comparison between Gnosticism and surrealism was meant to indicate the fundamental change of the transcendental points of orientation and to be put into a historical-philosophical perspective.

2. W. Iser's factual question touches on the "neuralgic" point of Gnostic and surrealist praxis. The conceptions of a *homo novus* construed from Gnostic roots remain ultimately fictions and impede, as W. Iser rightly observes, the revolutionary impulse implied therein because the revolutionary protest, in Gnosticism as much as in surrealism, results in a *révolte pour la révolte*. The a-cosmic presupposition of Gnosticism can provide an approach to the annihilation of the world, but it cannot provide a program to change it.

The first secession from the surrealist group, led by Pierre Naville, advanced every argument against the nihilistic, anarchistic but also libertine consequences of the surrealist premises and embarked on a path into the Communist Party as a church.[15]

... the moral scandals provoked by surrealism do not necessarily entail an overturning of intellectual and social values; the bourgeoisie does not fear them. It absorbs them easily. Even the violent attacks of the surrealists against patriotism have taken on the appearance of a moral scandal. But in a bourgeois republic, no one loses his head over such scandals.[16]

Breton took Naville's objection seriously in his *Légitime défense* (1926), but he did not disengage himself from the anarchistic form of the surrealist protest.[17]

I say let the revolutionary flame burn where it may and that it is not up to a small number of men, in the expectant period in which we live to decree that it may only burn here or there. . . . [18]

If one pays attention to the titles of surrealist magazines the same issue can be observed by tracing the changes of their names. The first surrealist magazine was called *La Révolution Surréaliste*, published by Pierre Naville and Benjamin Péret (1924–29). The second surrealist magazine was called *Le Surréalisme au Service de la Révolution* (1930–33), published by Breton. The first title points toward a specifically surrealist revolution, the second toward the function of surrealism in the service of the general (communist) revolution.

Politics, however, whose method is called nihilism (Benjamin),[19] although it can destroy the old world, cannot build a new one, other than in the poetic imagination, and therefore must embark on the journey into interiority. Yet late ancient Gnosticism as well as modern surrealism have both set free revolutionary energies within the solidified structures of the ancient empire and of modern bourgeois society that opened new forms of human experience beyond the narrow circles of sects and movements.

JAUSS[20]—An explanation is still required for the political-sociological aspect of the emergence of modern poetry, which J. Taubes wants to understand as an opposition against the world of natural sciences and technology. Following the analyses of M. H. Abrams,[21] Baudelaire's political conservatism is beyond doubt, and after 1848 an ever-sharper antidemocratic tendency begins to become apparent even with Flaubert and others. Yet this opposition of the antiromantic authors appears to have originated less from a political than an aesthetic relation to the historical situation. Disdain of the bourgeois *bêtise* and dandyism are the poles that condition their attitude. Dandyism as an "institution outside the law," which in turn imposes the strictest law on itself and beholden to an existence in opposition to all *utilité*, embodied in the political field the extraworldliness of art so to speak in the self, not however a content-dependent protest.[22] Therefore literary modernity since Baudelaire and Flaubert stands in opposition to the taste and the positivistic world understanding of their public, not however to the engineered world as such, which is precisely made accessible here for the first time with the nascent metropolis-lyric.

TAUBES: In these religious-historical notes on surrealism I cannot provide any philosophy of history concerning the metamorphosis within the structure of the transcendental realms in antiquity and modernity, but this much should have become clear from my theses: the "Copernican turn" is not only to be valued as a scientific-historical or philosophical event. The Copernican turn further alters the way in which poetic reality organizes itself.

In his *Theory of the Novel* the young Lukács furnished a *philosophical-historical examination of the forms of the great epic*, which the prevalent literary scholarship, bourgeois or Marxist, has not yet caught up with. I wish our colloquium had arrived at a historical-philosophical examination of the forms of great lyric. Already the antithesis "ancient-modern" demands such a reflection.

The circle that metaphysically determines antiquity and "whose closed nature was the transcendental essence of its life has for us been broken."[23] It is precisely late ancient Gnosticism, which while despairingly attacking the closed Greek cosmos, remains bound to ancient metaphysical presuppositions in its very protest and negation. Just as the Gnostic transmundane God remains, even in his negation, bound to the ancient *mundus*, so the Gnostic "beyond" can still be determined topographically as beyond the sphere of the fixed stars.

Our Copernican world has become infinite, and *that is why the primaeval images have irrevocably lost their objective self-evidence for us.*[24] This insight needs to be made to yield its fruit for the interpretation of modern poetry. The "Copernican turn" takes place in the course of modern lyrical poetry in such an interior realm that one looks for its "description" in vain.[25]

We must learn to read "between the lines," of course, without succumbing to idiosyncratic arbitrariness. Literary criticism should become an interlinear version of the text. As Walter Benjamin cited, Michel Leiris observes that the noise of Paris is referred to in the overt sense in the various places of its naming, and it also rhythmically acted upon Baudelaire's verse: this would be an example for literary criticism as an interlinear version of the text.

KRACAUER[26]—I would like to here step in with a methodological observation on the double character of such structural comparisons: they are as misleading as they are revelatory. They are misleading because they are achieved at a great distance from the given material—from a distant point where all too little of the historical reality resonates. In the case of the comparison set forth by J. Taubes, the real comparandum restricts itself to the phenomenon shared by Gnosticism and surrealism, namely, "loss of worldliness" ["*Entweltlichung*"]. But as soon as it moves in on the respective contours of both situations of origin—the situation in the early Christian centuries and in the nineteenth century—it may very well be seen that important differences emerge between the two, not visible from afar, differences that reduced that which is shared by both to a secondary phenomenon. On the other side, this same formidable distance from the material, which is responsible for the dubiousness of the structural comparisons debated here, also enables them to play a revelatory role. Taken from a great height, they remind one of aerial photographs; just like these, they allow one to catch a glimpse of normally invisible configurations of the broader landscape they survey. Hans Jonas rightly praises Spengler for the fact that from his bird's-eye view, he made visible the phenomenon "pseudo morphosis" of cultures. For the same reason J. Taubes's far-sighted analogy seems to me to be very productive. As an aside, it would be worth a few additional considerations why it is that so often problematic conceptions become the source of durable insight.

TAUBES—What constitutes method in historiography is to be found among its theoretical tools, which initially damage the phenomenon but also rescue it. No historiography can get around the codification of historical reality:

Either our procedure is additive, in which case history presents itself as an infinite series of equally valid events. While such a chronistic method, which avoids every construction of history, does not run the risk of being theoretically refuted, its epistemological value for insight does not transgress the boundaries of an infinite "and-so-on."

Or we base the historiography on a constructive principle, and then different but also comparable constellations crystallize out of the raw material of events. Any constructive principle tends toward abbreviation, without which no progress of insight would be possible. It remains uncertain whether, from case to case, the abbreviations can once again be decoded in the details of historical events.

The comparison between Gnosticism and surrealism intended to determine a current moment in late ancient Gnosticism. "Loss of worldliness" [*Entweltlichung*] appears to me to be too general to articulate this current moment in Gnosticism; rather, if anything, it is "alienation" [*Entfremdung*] of the self from the world and from it-self. The fundamental experience, however, cannot be denigrated to a "secondary concern," neither in surrealism nor in Gnosticism.

PREISENDANZ[27]—I would like to return once again to the fundamental question of a "Gnostic reading" of modern poetry. There is a parallel case: J. Taubes's model lets me think in several places of E. T. A. Hoffmann and Solger, and indeed in the following relations:

1. The fact that the "poetic mind," the "poet hidden" in the self is fundamentally determined by the opposition to the world in all its forms, that all true poetry derives from the misrelation of the "transcendental self" to positive reality, characterizes the thematics and structure of Hoffmanian's narrative art as well as his implicit or explicit poetics.

2. Irony turns into a necessary habit of poetic existence and into a necessary premise of poetic creation because with it the diremption between higher and lower self as well as that between the "inner poet" and all positive reality becomes manifest; in habitual irony the pneumatic self attests that it is subordinate neither to the liabilities nor any of the criteria of the world of creation (J. Taubes's essay above, p. 98–104).

3. Furthermore one can establish in Hoffman and even more so in Solger that poetic existence is the only beyond, that it is the beyond itself. The opposition against all that is established and exists can invoke nothing more than the poetic drive itself. Only in the form of this drive itself (not through it or in it!), following Solger, does the divine, absolute, eter-

nal, nonworldly, or infinite reveal itself in modernity. The divine has been transformed entirely into "the interiority of this general drive"; it evinces itself only more in the autonomous authority of fantasy. The poetic drive is no longer related to transcendence; rather, it itself has turned into transcendence (which is why with regard to Hoffmann's conductor Kreisler, the "mystification of personal existence" is explicitly referred to).

4. Finally, for Solger as well as for Hoffmann, the problem is relevant that language as the medium of such transcendence remains wholly determined by the structures of the world, and that it is precisely because of this that the poetic drive, by entering into the barrenness of worldly language, must constantly destroy itself in inanity.

I do not wish to provoke a further structural comparison with these hints, even though in Hoffmann and Schubert, his usual warrantor, an appropriation of Gnostic views is possible. I relate J. Taubes's considerations to Hoffmann only because he, as is well known, was highly regarded by Baudelaire as well as by many surrealists, Breton, for example; of the "Princess Brambilla," the cleverest piece of "poetic of the poetic" in Hoffmann's work, Baudelaire wrote (*De l'essence du rire*) point-blank it is *comme un catéchisme de haute esthétique*. Is not poetry's character of opposition, which in Hoffmann is repeatedly thematized, and which the confrontation with Gnosticism does help to clarify, the decisive aspect of such reverence?

TAUBES—W. Preisendanz rightfully introduced the problem of irony into the Gnostic reading of modern poetry. In his dissertation, Kierkegaard furnished the means of situating romantic irony in a historical-philosophical perspective. "With irony the subject constantly retires from the field and proceeds to talk every phenomenon out of its reality in order to save himself, that is, in order to preserve himself in his negative independence of everything."[28] Kierkegaard's analysis of romantic irony occurs "with constant consideration of Socrates" and connects the romantic turn of the Spirit [*Geist*] with the turn in antiquity from the spirit of tragedy to the ironical spirit of philosophy: *Socrates primus ironiam introduxit* [Thesis X of the dissertation].

In his historical-philosophical interpretation of irony Kierkegaard encounters Hegel, who in the chapter on "Unhappy Consciousness" thrusts ancient and modern alienation together like a montage. Nothing else was meant by my theses, and they could be understood as proof of the Hegelian analysis, an analysis that modern philosophical or literary criticism has not caught up with, much less overtaken.

FUHRMANN[29]—The parallel Gnosticism-surrealism has clearly been contested. Scholars of literature require an individualizing observation method, while the scholar of religious studies prefers to consider that which is typical. This method has its justification. What is decisive is what one hopes to elicit.

TAUBES—The differentiation between individualizing and generalizing method is itself inherited from romantic hermeneutics, the limits of which I had intended to transcend. But I admit that in the perspective of the historical school, a comparison between late ancient Gnosticism and modern surrealism must be reckoned as a variant of a generalizing typological method, even though as a result the historical-philosophical index, which for me appears decisive for the comparison, does not come into play.

The religious-historical notes were intended to contribute toward breaking the circle of an immanent aesthetic interpretation of surrealism. Only when the aesthetic canon is transcended can the surrealist intention be taken seriously. If this does not pass before an aesthetic last judgment, then this speaks more against the legitimacy of an aesthetic last judgment than it does against surrealist intention.

BLUMENBERG[30]—The confrontation that J. Taubes performs between Gnosticism and surrealism is static and thus corresponds methodologically to the structural comparison between ancient and Gnostic metaphysics on which the concept of Gnosticism in the work of Hans Jonas (fundamental for J. Taubes) rests. This method, however, of determining systematic factors through the alteration of signification, cannot be repeated between Gnosticism and surrealism. If the cosmos that has now become infinite has made external transcendence meaningless and thereby the otherworldly God of redemption homeless, that does not entail that the systematic remainder of transcendence gone inward (mythic: the pneuma) has not been compellingly provided, or has become a question as would have been the case if there were a historical nexus between

Gnosticism and surrealism. Rather, the inner-systematic consequence is trivial: even if the world appears with negative signification because there is "only world" one has to manage a gamut of possible attitudes from within the world. But, I would like to ask, does this immanence-as-remedy automatically entail a preference for specifically determined compensations for the blocked escape? J. Taubes regards the valorization of fantasy as a specifically adequate answer to a loss of world that is supposedly based on the negativity of the determination of the modern cosmos by laws of nature. Fantasy against legality—that sounds plausible. It would, however, be difficult to verify that the legal valuation of nature, stabilized by modernity against the God of salvation and of arbitrariness in nominalism, would have been consciously experienced as oppressive, constricting, or otherwise negatively. On the contrary, an aesthetic reevaluation of nature, an experience of its ugliness, as it begins in the nineteenth century, is bound up precisely with those organic formations of nature in which the moment of legality could not yet be experienced, but rather if anything the tropic irregularity, the proliferating and wasteful madness of eternal self-reproduction against which the human consciousness could posit the joke of creative productivity—for example in the antithesis between city and nature. What further gave offense was the lack of compassion and the social indifference of nature, which is experienced as struggle for existence, pressure of selection, and atomistic dissipation in the overpowering emptiness, as a contrapposto to a new a-cosmic anthropocentrism, which allows the human being to become closest to himself in the constriction of our planet earth, since Malthus appearing to be hopeless. But is the revolt of surrealism really targeted against nature? Or is it not rather the purpose of the way in which Nature is treated to forge a self-affirmation of the human person from the totally hyletic utilizability of the world as it is presented to him, a self-affirmation that succeeds to the extent that this world is not "Nature" any longer? Between self-consciousness and the decomposition of the pregiven world there exists a connection in which is constructed the subject's sovereignty of control over that which it itself had not originally brought forth, not only as self-affirmation but also as the assurance of the possibility of the ultimate act, starting over at ground zero. At that moment at which man had lost his last doubt that nature was not created for him and to his service, he could only bear it in its role as material.

The materialism that conforms to surrealism is not only the continuation of the eighteenth-century hypostasis of the premises of the new physics, but also the consistent exposure and claim to the character of nonhuman reality as pyre matter and thus the only single possible post-Copernican anthropocentrism. The significance of the prefix *sur* in the title "surrealism" around which J. Taubes's considerations circle does not belong to the vertical schema of the *sur-naturel* of Gnosticism and its repercussions in everything "supernatural," but rather to the horizontal schema of that which is possible beyond the reality of nature, what "survives" its decomposition. The analogy established by J. Taubes between the prefix *sur* and the greek prefix *metá*, as Gnosis's "fundamental category of movement" of Gnosticism, is thus only enlightening as it proves to not be tenable.

The decisive structural difference between Gnosticism and surrealism, ignored by J. Taubes, lies in the fact that Gnosticism did not know protest and revolt as forms of reaction. The call of the bearer of salvation [*Heilbringer*] from out of transcendence is not an appeal to any kind of behavior in relation to the world, let alone to an action against the world; rather, the call exhausts itself in the actualization of anamnesis, in the restitution of the relation to the origin of human interiority. It is, therefore, of essential significance for Gnosticism that the origin and destination of the subject symbolized in the pneuma are identical. This identity excludes the possibility for the human being to add to or obtain from his history anything that is essential; it suffices that he is "remembered," in order to restitute himself, since he can obviously no longer "remember himself." The enormous mythic detour of the pneuma through the world and around the turning point of memory does not create any essentially new possibilities. It should not be forgotten that, in one of its decisive elements, namely, in the demonization of the world-creator, Gnosticism emerges from the avoidance of a contradiction in which late Jewish[31] messianism as well as Christian theology inevitably had to get ensnarled, namely, to allow their Redeemer to act and function as if their creator was in need of a radical correction. In non-Gnostic Christian theology, a moment of excess in time and through action enters, by means of the systematic inconsistency of creation and redemption, by means of the inexplicable and reproachable "excess" of salvation over nature. In contrast, the surpassing of the Gnostic cosmos through transcendence is grounded in the ancient concept of reality as "instantaneous evidence" and is therefore possible only as the transvaluation, degradation, and de-potentialization of the undamaged and stable whole. It is precisely the beauty and brilliance of the natural order that has hidden and ruined transcendence. To realize this through memory does not entail any alteration in the conditions of things, rather only its index, and thus neither revolt nor protest. The Gnostic bearer of salvation enters into the world through the cunning of a disguising incarnation, and pneuma slips away from the world through his very de-corporealization. The modern concept of reality of "immanent consistence" allows for an entirely different set of possibilities to disempower Nature vis-à-vis the subject: the factual context of natural phenomena, which is incessantly self-forming and articulating via processes and never given or presupposed as a totality, can be subjected to the decomposition and thereby turned into a substrate by a heterogeneous will of formation. Here beginnings or points of origins can be posited, and quasi-experiments applied to the unknown potential of hyle, and new and surprising elements can be elicited within one and the same horizon of immanence. Not the memory of origin, but the assurance of expectation is the meaning of the anarchist drive toward destruction, toward the minimalization of the liability of a cosmos, which is not so much to be transvalued in toto, but rather to be questioned as a definitive result of its implicit possibilities. Fantasy demonstrates itself as the medium that can become productive only out of destruction. All that was required in Gnosticism to assure the "other world" was the call to remember, to allow the pneuma to come into its own; the guarantee of a potential "new world" in surrealism requires the carrying out of a deconstruction forever incomplete in its radicality, which is driven by the always watchful suspicion of presupposed and ultimate validities. The laws of nature are thus precisely not the quality of reality that constrains the self in its freedom, as is the eidetic in the ancient cosmos. Rather, they are the medium [*Organon*] allied with freedom under whose influence the phenomenal eidetic of nature proves itself to be the accidental status of a process, or the foreground, studded with secondary qualities, of an inexhaustible and disposable potentiality. Modern law of nature cannot be compared with the Gnostic heimarmene because it was designed against the arbitrariness of the miracle and the abyssal uncertainty of the *creatio continua*. From this origin stems its solid, positive quality of consciousness.

TAUBES—H. Blumenberg's critique is pointed primarily against the comparison between Gnosticism and surrealism. The decisive structural difference, according to H. Blumenberg "ignored" by me, "consists in . . . the fact that Gnosticism did not know protest and revolt as forms of reaction." The difference in the interpretation of late ancient Gnosticism cannot be resolved by reference to the material. H. Blumenberg is familiar with the attestations of the church fathers, who denounced the self-consciousnesss of the Gnostics as the ego-maniacal abitrariness and lawlessness of an I loosed from all bondage, and took offense at their extreme negation of the established values, which overturned into moral anarchism and libertinism. He also knows the challenging and provocative transvaluation of canonical texts in the Gnostic allegorical interpretation, which evidence the Gnostic *ressentiment* and declaration of war against all established principles. But he will insist to evaluate all of these revolutionary traits of Gnosticism as mere secondary characteristics to be discarded from a structural interpretation of Gnosticism because the sheer inversion and alteration of signification [*Vorzeichen*] does not yet constitute a new concept of reality that explodes the limits of the ancient experience of reality.

Indeed, Gnostic language entered into a mimicry of the ancient philosophical tradition and in historical-philosophical perspective could legitimately be treated as a variant of Platonism. However, from a religious-historical perspective the Gnostic revolt and provocation acquire an entirely different significance, despite the adaptation of philosophical topoi from ancient tradition. It demonstrates a revolution in consciousness that exceeds the boundaries of ancient experience, if not *de iure*, at least de facto. Thus, so it appears to me, from a religious-historical perspective the comparison between the Gnostic and the surrealist provocation can lead to a reciprocal illumination of both, because the Gnostic revolt, even if conceptually linked to the chain of ancient ideas of reality, already provides a hint toward the modern conception of reality.

Certainly, "the modern concept of reality of immanent consistence [compared to those available to late ancient Gnosticism—J. T.] allows for an entirely different set of possibilities to disempower Nature vis-à-vis the subject." This claim of H. Blumenberg may provide a key to the interpretation of romanticism, but not however to the interpretation of postromantic modernity, where no identical subject opposed to disempowered

Nature can be maintained, but where rather the disempowerment extends over both: subject and object. H. Blumenberg's comment on the connection "between self-consciousness and the decomposition of the pregiven world . . . in which the sovereignty . . . of the subject is constructed not only as self-affirmation but also as the assurance of the possibility . . . of the ultimate action starting over at ground zero" bypasses the intention of surrealism. For the latter destroys the unity of the I—any unity of the I—no less than that of the "world" or of "Nature."

Surrealism wants, as H. Blumenberg himself once established, "to break through the concept of reality of the 'immanent consistence' of its bond to the reality substance of nature," and (if we want to momentarily adopt H. Blumenberg's concepts) is therefore forced "to the desperate effort, only in the ultimate improbability still to become manifest in a kind of 'momentary evidence.'"[32] Which demonstrates that the strict contrast between a concept of reality as that of momentary evidence (ancient) versus a concept of reality as the realization of a coherent context (modern) can historically not be maintained in ideal-typical [*idealtypischer*] purity. Also the contrast resulting from this systematic distinction, between "memory of origin" (ancient) and "assurance of expectation" (modern) should not be carried too far because for modern surrealism as for late ancient Gnosis both of these collapse into each other. The representation of actualized utopia as the return of paradise endures as a topos well into the modern theological Marxism of Benjamin and Bloch.

Breton's first manifesto demonstrates beyond a doubt how the prefix *sur* in the title "surrealism" is to be interpreted: "Without a doubt we could have entirely legitimately drawn on the term supernaturalism [*Supernaturalisme*], as it is used by Gerard de Nerval in his dedication to the Daughters of Fire."[33] The prefix *sur* belongs, as this remark of Breton corroborates against H. Blumenberg's argument, to the schema of the *surnaturel* of Gnosticism and its after-effect. The question remains how the vertical schema of Gnosticism must fundamentally transform itself if it is to become visible in the circumference of post-Copernican immanence. This turn from a vertical to horizontal scheme was and is essential to interpret. I interpreted the prefix *sur* in the title surrealism based on the vertical schema of the *surnaturel* of Gnosticism, while H. Blumenberg interprets it based on the horizontal schema of the verb *survivre*. Testimonies can be procured to support both conceptions. Decisive, however, is (and this was brought out only in the pro and contra of the discussion) that the ambiguity inherent in such a term should not be suppressed if the turn from vertical to horizontal schema is to be sufficiently interpreted. Does not the discussion concerning the presuppositions of the prefix *sur* repeat the argument about Baudelaire's concept of *correspondance*? Does Baudelaire intend a vertical correspondence between natural and spiritual orders, or does he intend a horizontal reciprocal correspondence between the various meanings and things? With Baudelaire as well an unequivocal choice would conceal the process leading from the deconstruction of a Platonic-Christian remainder to an experience of the *sensation du neuf*.

The most contested of my theses provoked H. Blumenberg to articulate the formula of "fantasy contra legality." I accept this formulation, even though like every formula it delineates the thesis only roughly. It "sounds," as H. Blumenberg admits, "plausible. It would however be difficult to verify that the legal valuation of nature, stabilized by modernity against the God of salvation and of arbitrariness in nominalism, would *ever* [stressed by J. T.] have been consciously experienced as oppressive, constricting, or otherwise negatively." Difficult to verify? Precisely when I take H. Blumenberg's fundamental thesis seriously and concede "that the legal valuation stabilized by modernity" is to be understood as a turn "*against* [stressed by H. B.] the God of salvation and of arbitrariness," I am led to conclusions that contradict his. Because if, in this turn, nothing lesser than the fundamental consideration of religious consciousness is at stake, then the resistance against the establishment of the new consciousness of the legality of nature must have been extremely stiff. Nietzsche recognized the legal valuation of nature stabilized by modernity as a caesura between religious and modern consciousness that *closes the gates of religious life for us once and for all*. Shouldn't religious consciousness have resisted this change and metamorphosis before closing time? Testimonies from Donne, Pascal, Blake, and Dostoyevsky could here be brought into the field.

The program of Enlightenment since the seventeenth century aimed squarely at the demystification of the world. Even though the method of *mos geometricus* remained foreign to him, Bacon understood the trend of the new science well and he gathered up the motifs that the Enlightenment would unfold in the course of three centuries. Its struggle centered around the *imagination* and leads, as Elizabeth Sewell says,[34] to a "dismissal of metaphor," which poetry struggles against in ever-new ways. "Fantasy against legality," in its sharpest antithesis, also determines the surrealist revolt. The liberation of the imagination proclaimed again and again by the surrealists seeks to release it from the constraints of the laws of nature.

The aesthetic transvaluation of nature as it begins in the nineteenth century is a highly complex process with contradictory tendencies that our colloquium should especially consider. H. Blumenberg underlines one tendency—art as antinature—that runs from Baudelaire to Valéry. In conflict with this, however, "the tropical irregularity of nature, the proliferating and profligate madness of eternal self-reproduction" is experienced as congenial with the products of fantasy, and thus thrown as counterweight against the legality of nature onto the scales of poetry by Rimbaud or Lautréamont. Similary the "antithesis of city and nature" in the nineteenth century, which H. Blumenberg appropriates for his argument: it is precisely in the nineteenth century, for example in Nietzsche's *Zarathustra,* that disgust for the city develops, which until the nineteenth century was considered as the place of philosophy (*Phaedrus,* 230), where, to speak with H. Blumenberg, "human self-consciousness could . . . posit the joke of creative productivity." Since the nineteenth century the calls for abandoning the "unreal city" (T. S. Eliot) in poetry, literature, and philosophy have multiplied, until philosophy begins to wander off the beaten track entirely against the classical tradition from Ionia to Jena, toward country roads and forest trails.

H. Blumenberg's thesis that "the legality of nature" is supposed to be the "medium allied with freedom," and that the modern law of nature represents a "solid positive quality of consciousness" that is "not to be compared to the Gnostic Heimarmene" reveals the systematic basis of his critique. His thesis is to be situated in the tradition of eighteenth-century Enlightenment. Epistemologically speaking this thesis might very well be legitimized, but it remains one-sided in terms of reception history. It bypasses the arguments of the counter-Enlightenment, which perceive the legality of nature and freedom as contradictory. Certainly, the protest against the legality of nature had initially been a topos of the counter-

Enlightenment since De Maistre. It should be noted, however, that this protest also contains such moments as enter into the protest and revolt of surrealism in the twentieth century.

H. Blumenberg has certainly keenly observed, as he already mentioned in the aforementioned essay "Concept of Reality and Possibility of the Novel,"[35] that the modern concept of reality, as realization of a coherent context, legitimizes the aesthetic (and as I would add, not only the aesthetic) quality of *novitas,* of surprisingly unfamiliar elements, and clear the new of suspicion.[36] However, and here modern experience turns into its opposite, the legality of nature ultimately makes the new appear as something predetermined, thereby in truth reiterating the old. In this contradiction lies concealed a problem that a one-sided interpretation of the process of enlightenment and demythologization, concerned only with the "Legitimacy of the Modern Age,"[37] cannot entirely grasp.

Translated with the assistance of William Rauscher

8

From the Adverb "Nothing" to the Substantive "Nothing":[1] Deliberations on Heidegger's Question Concerning Nothing

I

The manner in which Heidegger stages the transition from the adverbial "nothing" to the substantive "Nothing," in his Freiburg inaugural lecture "What Is Metaphysics?"[2] has a strange effect. In his essay "The Overcoming of Metaphysics Through Logical Analysis of Language,"[3] Rudolf Carnap debunked the switch from "nothing" to the hypostatized "Nothing" as a magic trick and portrayed the entire inaugural lecture, which posits the question concerning Nothing, as an exemplary case of senseless metaphysical speech. Carnap's verdict did not fail to have an effect. Outside a circle of adepts in which the master's words were repeated in paraphrase but without further interpretation, there remained the impression of an embarrassing blunder. In this way, the case of Heidegger's question was closed.

Only recently, in *Durchblicke* Ernst Tugendhat reopened the philosophical discussion with a linguistic investigation and a critique of Heidegger's inaugural lecture. Tugendhat casts his net wide, but it is also tight enough to capture Heidegger's intentions.[4] An analysis of the fundamental terms of Parmenides and of the opening of Hegel's *Logic* precedes the inquest into Heidegger's concerns. With these conceptual preparatory steps, Tugendhat believes to have circumscribed the meaning of the phrase "Being and Nothing" and thus to be prepared for an analysis of Heidegger's key terms. For an analysis of Heidegger, however, Tugendhat suggests a "contrarian process" because for him the meaning of "Being and Nothing" has been unambiguously forged in the interpretation of Parmenides and Hegel: "Because we know now what it [i.e., the formula] means, we can immediately [?] see that it does not fit with what Heidegger means, and we are able to ask why he employs it nevertheless" (p. 152). Heidegger's question concerning Nothing "does not pertain to Non-being at all, but rather to the universal *condition* of the understanding of Being and Non-being" (p. 158). Tugendhat supposes that Heidegger wants to indicate "a particular Non-being" (p. 158), a Non-being that expresses itself in the universal existential proposition "there is nothing." The substantive "Nothing" turns out to be an "objectifying denotation for that which every universal negative existential proposition indicates" (p. 160).

Tugendhat's keen analysis moves too much constrained by a predetermined rhetorical [*sprachanalytische*] discussion as to allow him to render the key terms of Parmenides, Hegel, or Heidegger understandable in relation to his concerns. According to Tugendhat, the Parmenidean argument turns out to be "plainly wrong" (p. 141), and Hegel operates with an "absurd conception" (p. 156) of Non-being at the beginning of the *Logic*. Heidegger introduces the expression "Nothing" in his questioning concerning Nothing in a way that "remains inconsequential" (p. 157)—which "allows" Tugendhat (and therein his own philosophical intentions become clear) to sideline the expression "Nothing" in Heidegger's case and to "seek the objective meaning of Heidegger's discourse . . . aside from it" (p. 157).

Such a method may be justified in a philosophical discussion. Tugendhat rightfully resists "the straight-forward use of words in philosophy" (p. 151). But no less is it possible to eliminate a text's key terms or to reduce them to an understanding, which is prevalent in the contemporary philosophical discussion. The rescue of a text's objective intention by writing off its key terms is not in any way an appropriate hermeneutic method. Too tightly are words and intentions are bound to each other and woven into one another. Such a method has nothing to do with a "historical tolerance" (p. 134) (even though nowadays this is too lightly discarded as a fashionable mantle from the nineteenth century). In its insistence on fundamental terms, such a procedure wants much more to preserve the strangeness of the text against commonplace understanding. The key term that determines the course of discussion cannot "just as well be omitted without any loss" (p. 155) when interpreting either Heidegger's texts in general, or particularly his inaugural speech, in which the question of Nothing unfolds. The key term must be preserved, even at the price of its philosophical integrity. The conception of the inaugural lecture must be developed based on this term.

II

Heidegger's inaugural lecture "What Is Metaphysics?" outlines a particular metaphysical question, taking a few steps toward the question concerning Nothing that Parmenides heeded as the forbidden path:

... Therefore, as it is necessary, the decision has been taken to leave one way unthinkable and unnamable (for it is not the true way) ...[5]

As an exposition to the question of Nothing, the inaugural lecture is an implicit engagement with Parmenides. The position against Parmenides had already determined Heidegger's main work. The very title *Being and Time* can and should be understood as contra Parmenides. For whichever way the term "Being" is interpreted, and whichever meaning the term "Time" acquires in the course of the analysis (whatever kind of temporality this expression indicates); by whichever way the relationship of "Being" and "Time" (and "Time" and "Being") is explicated, the provocative unification [*Ineins*] of "Being" and "Time" stands against the fundamental Parmenidean thesis on "Being":

How could Being be hereafter? How could it have come into being? If it was, it is not, nor if it is going to be in the future. So, coming into being is extinguished and perishing is unheard of.[6]

The discussion of Parmenides in *Being and Time* is almost only casual; we hear that he passed over the phenomenon of "world" (p. 133).[7] The destruction of the ontological tradition, which Heidegger undertakes here, orients itself principally "against the Parmenidean legacy in traditional ontology."[8]

Therefore, when Heidegger touches on the thematic of negation and negativity in *Being and Time,* he speaks cautiously about the "essence of not" [*Nicht*], "Notness" [*Nichtheit*] and "nullity" [*Nichtigkeit*] (p. 331). It is only in the inaugural lecture, which already *presumes* the destruction of the traditional ontology as it emerged in the wake of Plato and Aristotle and consolidated itself in the history of philosophy, that the expression "Nothing" first surfaces together with Parmenides, and the question of Nothing takes center stage.

The way in which Heidegger, in his inaugural lecture, sets the scene for the question of Nothing is only really understandable when it is read as a palimpsestic (as there is no direct indication) a tract against Parmenides. The question of Nothing is staged along with a discussion of the essence of science—"insofar as science has become our passion" (p. 94). The transition from "nothing" to "Nothing" occurs in the passage "What should be examined are beings only, and besides that—nothing; beings alone, and further—nothing; solely beings, and beyond that—nothing. What about this Nothing? Is it an accident that we talk this way so automatically? Is it only a manner of speaking—and nothing besides?" (p. 95). One does not require the acumen of a logician in order to prove that the paradox of this transition from an adverbial "nothing" to a hypostatized substantive "Nothing" is logically untenable. Tugendhat, who subtly reconstructs the lecture's train of thought, can only assert in his interpretation of the decisive point of the transition from nothing to the explosive Nothing that this introduction of the substantive "Nothing" is "unjustified" and "could hardly have been meant seriously" by Heidegger (p. 153).

Yet perhaps it is so. It is perfectly possible to assume that Heidegger would have known to avoid or at least to conceal the logical blunder that Carnap demonstrates, and also that he was able to perceive the rhetorical [*sprachanalytische*] violence in the transition from "nothing" to "Nothing." The violent nature of transition in this act of thought pops out at one's eyes. It seems to me to be chosen intentionally, namely, in the intention of making the transition from "Nothing" to "nothing" reversible, a transition that Parmenides performed paradigmatically for Western philosophy. Parmenides says:

It is necessary to say and to think Being; for there is Being, but nothing is not. These things I order you to ponder.[9]

Nothing is not, *mēden d'ouk estin*, Parmenides decrees.

The "violent character of the Parmenidean act of thought," of which Hermann Fränkel[10] speaks, is largely overlooked because through Parmenides philosophy is headed toward "the call, that calls into the thinking of the West," as the late Heidegger calls this transition in *What Calls for Thinking?*[11] in which Nothing can only appear as null [*nichtig*], as "nothing." Heidegger's countermaneuver, which describes the transition from "nothing" to the way of the Nothing as it has been known and banned by Parmenides and subseqently forgotten by the philosophical tradition, occurs not less violently.

"Parmenides began Philosophy proper," said Hegel in his *Lectures on the History of Philosophy*. This beginning appeared to Hegel

certainly still dim and indefinite, and we cannot say much of what it involves, but to take up this position certainly is to develop Philosophy proper, which has not hitherto existed. (Vol. 1:254)

Heidegger also situates the beginning of philosophy with Parmenides, of course rejecting as "fundamental error" the "opinion" that

the inception of history is primitive and backward, clumsy and weak. The opposite is true. The inception is what is most uncanny and mightiest. What follows is not a development but flattening down as mere widening out [. . .] it makes the inception innocuous and exaggerates it into a perversion of what is great, into greatness and extension purely in the sense of number and mass.[12]

Science and its organization are for Heidegger the last implementation of this Parmenidean beginning. A recourse to their beginning can, and must, be discussed, if their original concerns are to be taken into account. Therefore it is not surprising that where Heidegger comes to discuss science's original concern, he represents them in Parmenidean terms:

That to which the [*scientific*—J.T.] relation to the world refers are beings themselves [*das Seiende*]—and nothing besides. That from which every [*scientific*—J.T.] attitude takes it guidance are beings themselves—and nothing further. That with which the scientific confrontation in the irruption [into the whole of being—J.T.] occurs are beings themselves—and beyond that nothing. (p. 95)

Only in this referral back to the organization of science to its Parmenidean "rootedness" is it meaningful to say of science that "Nothing is precisely rejected by [it], given up as a nullity" (p. 95). Against any attempt to introduce "Nothing" into the discourse, "science must now reassert its seriousness and soberness of mind, insisting that it is concerned solely with being" (p. 96). For scientific thinking, a reference to a substantive "Nothing" can be nothing other than "an outrage and a phantasm" (p. 96). Only an invocation of Parmenides, who lopped off the way to Nothing, allows the outcome of scientific discourse to be summarized in saying that "science wants to know nothing of the Nothing. Ultimately this is the scientifically rigorous conception of nothing" (p. 96). Only in view of the dual "ambivalent" structure of the Parmenidean didactic poem as the condition for the Western concept of knowledge [*Wissenbegriff*] (and dependent and derivable from it: the conception of science [*Wissenschaftbegriff*]) is it meaningful to say:

Science wants to know nothing of the Nothing. But even so it is certain that when science tries to express its proper essence it calls upon the Nothing for help. It has recourse to what it rejects. (p. 96)

The "ambivalent" essence of the null Nothing reflects its origin in Parmenides's doctrine. Heidegger's statement that "it has recourse to what it rejects" can be understood, in an eminent sense, in reference to Parmenidean doctrine. If Heidegger learns anything from the philological scholarship concerning Parmenides, it is about the connection between the two parts of the didactic poem that Karl Reinhardt highlights in his *Parmenides and the History of Greek Philosophy* (1916).[13]

It is not our intention to follow the elaboration and answering of the question of Nothing, as Heidegger develops it in his lecture. For us it is a matter of putting the weakest link of Heidegger's argument, the transition from "nothing" to "Nothing," which Tugendhat believes "could hardly be meant seriously by Heidegger" (153), into a historical context, which for Heidegger however carries a systematic signature. If one were to view from an abstract language-analytic standpoint the transition from the "nothing" of the previous sentences ("beings and otherwise nothing," and so forth), where the word "nothing" appears in its prevalent syntactic-categorical function, to the substantive "Nothing," then the result is certainly that the rhetorical introduction of "Nothing" would be "unjustified."[14] If one observes, however, that Heidegger appends his reflection on the essence of science to his development of the question of Nothing not only (albeit also) due to the occassion of his inaugural lecture, but because Parmenides's doctrine that Nothing is not or that it has nothing in itself opened the path on which the ontological tradition of Western philosophy unfolds, the ontological tradition of philosophy thus forming the presumption of science as system and organization, or, as Niklas Luhmann says more precisely (cf. his contribution "Negation and Perfection" in *Poetik und Hermeneutik* VI, p. 469), then the transition from the adverb "nothing," used in a syntactic-categorically correct manner, to the expression "Nothing," is justified, even meant seriously. If the scientific discourse, where it "tries to express its proper essence" (p. 97), is thrown back on the theses of Parmenides, back on the doctrine that culminates in the statement that Nothing is not, then a countermove must begin with the thesis that within the common adverbial "nothing," the "Nothing" that Parmenides bans conceals itself. Heidegger's transition here from "nothing" to "Nothing" is a kind of anamnesis of the Parmenidean transition from "Nothing" to "nothing," and it is thus set up contra Parmenides. At this point Heidegger does not want to transcend that which has been posed by Parmenides (this happens in the philosophical tradition, which develops a "logic of negation as ontological means of cognition"—cf. Wolfgang Hübener's study of this tradition [in "Positionen der Negativität," *Poetik und Hermeneutik* VI, 1975], pp. 105ff.), but rather wants to return to the point where Parmenides's doctrine marked the way as the constitution of the philosophical tradition. The change in Heidegger's relation to the theses of Parmenides, which since his lecture on the *Introduction to Metaphysics* (1935) he invoked as evidence for his own (transformed?) teaching of Being, represents a problem that cannot be elaborated on here. For this phase from *Being and Time* (1927) to *What Is Metaphysics?* (1929), however, the anti-Parmenidean unfolding of the question of being is the axis around which Heidegger's investigations turn in general and which in particular governs his question concerning Nothing.

III

The return behind Parmenides's crossroads does not occur abruptly in Heidegger. He initiates the last part of his lecture with a "cursory historical review" (p. 108) that culminates in the "fundamental question of metaphysics" "which compels Nothing itself: Why is there something at all and not rather nothing?" (p. 110). In his interpretation Tugendhat singled out Heidegger's reference to Hegel and ignored his comments on the ontological tradition. Perhaps, however, something can be obtained from the few remarks that Heidegger makes concerning the ontological tradition to understand his concept of Nothing. Heidegger designates the path of tradition through two Latin statements and describes his concerns in a Latin formula coined by himself. In these Latin formulas, summations and results of long-enduring processes are compacted. They can serve as points of orientation in order to determine the context to which Heidegger's question of Nothing belongs.

1. Metaphysics speaks "from time immemorial" about Nothingess: *ex nihilo nihil fit*, a statement that of course remains "clearly susceptible of more than one meaning" (p. 107) in the philosophical tradition. Heidegger connects up with Aristotle's classic formulation: *nihil ex nihilo fit*.[15] He relates this formula not only to Aristotelian metaphysics but also to ancient philosophy as a whole. Ancient philosophy from Plato to Plotinus "grasps Nothing in its meaning as that-which-is-not, that is, as unformed matter" (p. 107). Also the Platonic demiurge in the *Timaeus* does not create out of an empty Nothing. An non-created matter is pregiven, the *hyle*, which the demiurge endows with form and to which accordingly he lends an image. The Nothing of matter in ancient philosophy means a Being that is "not yet" formed; an unformed matter bearing a private signature that is most starkly exposed in Aristotle's theory of *steresis*.

2. Heidegger juxtaposes this with the doctrine of theology as a revealed religion (which for him is restricted to "Christian dogmatics"). The orthodox theology of Judaism, Christianity, and Islam "denies" the fundamental principle of ancient metaphysics, "ex nihilo nihil fit" and "thereby bestows on the Nothing a transformed significance, the sense of the complete absence of beings apart from God" (p. 107). The theological doctrine of creation from nothing is condensed in the formation: *ex nihilo fit ens creatum*. Heidegger refers to the interpretation that Thomas Aquinas adduces to the first sentence in Genesis: "creare est aliquid ex nihilo facere,"[16] a formulation adopted from Beda's glossary, which itself invokes the meaning of the Hebrew verb *bara'* in Jewish tradition. Heidegger is inclined to accept that the phrase of *creatio ex nihilo* was coined

deliberately as a battle cry against the philosophical thesis *ex nihilo nihil fit*. The prehistory of this theological formulation is, of course, more complex, and the meaning of the phrase can in no way be so unequivocally determined. Harry A. Wolfson has shown[17] how strongly the Platonic or Aristotelian interpretations of "nihil" resonate in the articulations of the church fathers and the Islamic and Jewish theologians, obscuring the phrase's oppositional signification. It still holds, however, that the phrase *creatio ex nihilo* is entered into the confrontation between the theology of the revealed religions with the presumptions of ancient philosophy, particularly the Aristotelian doctrine about the eternity of the world. The *ex* in the phrase *ex nihilo* indicates that in some form, the *nihil* could be considered the "cause" of creation. The theologians, however, were anxious to fend off any thought of Nothing as a material cause of creation. In the theology of the Middle Ages, however, the relationship between God as *ens increatum* and *nihil* remains unexplained. It is this point that Heidegger's consideration on the rights and boundaries of the creation doctrine takes up: "Therefore no one is bothered by the difficulty that if God creates out of nothing precisely He must be able to relate Himself to that nothing" (p. 107).

3. Heidegger as a matter of fact encounters here a central difficulty in theological argumentation, which the religious historian Gerschom Sholem recently formulated in a way that can easily be read as a commentary on Heidegger's observations:

The paradox in the concept of creation from nothing is also expressed in the formula which Thomas Aquinas uses when he defines creation as an effect of God from without, *operatio dei ad extra*. In creation, God does not bring something to perfection, which is already within his essence. Rather He produces something that is external to this essence. This is however the critical point. How could we think that outside the divine substance, which in itself represents completed being, *ens purissimum*, another incomplete and "creaturely" being can exist, while at the same time taking seriously the thought of the totality of the divine essence? The discussion about creation out of nothing proves itself to be a paradoxical, radical statement. God has the freedom to produce a being which he himself is not. What could be more paradoxical than that? Because how can there be any kind of being, if there is a God, which is not contained with him? The motto of creation from nothing, however, appears to have put a great deal of importance on excluding from the outset an all-encompassment of Being in God himself, a pantheistic turn in the concept of creation. And that in any case is what the sublime dialectic

From the Adverb "Nothing" to the Substantive "Nothing" 133

of Islamic Kalam and none other than the Jewish Theologian Saadia and Maimonides as well as scholastic theology resolved to achieve: the protection of the biblical message of creation against all pantheistic blurring of boundaries.[18]

Yet Heidegger's assumption says that this difficulty in the relating of God to *nihil* is not at all observed by medieval reflection can hardly be established so unequivocally. At the same time as the phrase *creatio ex nihilo* is commonly received by the orthodox Jewish and Islamic theology as well as in the Christian dogmatics, the process of its reevaluation is set in motion. Taking as its starting point precisely the "difficulty" that Heidegger highlights. Scholem exactly investigated this reevaluation of the formula *creatio ex nihilo* and demonstrated that in the mystical tradition, the wording of the phrase remained preserved while its meaning was inverted into its opposite:

> Creation out of nothing, as it surfaces again and again in the mystic tradition, is the creation out of God himself. It is exactly that which all the orthodox doctrines appear to exclude. The Nothing, which is the condition of creation, is He himself. The freedom out of which He creates relates only to Him and not to something which lies beyond him. The Nothing of the philosophers, the Non-Being becomes . . . a substantial Nothing, a Nothing of the over-Being of God. Sometimes in this way God and his Nothing are established as two aspects of his own essence, and sometimes both are regarded from a deeply heretical perspective that invokes the mythical from the deepest abyss. (p. 68)

The process of this revaluation of the *creatio ex nihilo*, which is determined by the conception that God as Nothing, can be equally traced in Ismaili texts of Islamic Gnosticism, in the Jewish kabbalah, and in the Christian mystical tradition since Scotus Eriugena. Even though Eriugena's teachings were pronounced heretical in the early thirteenth century, his doctrine persists in the writings of Meister Eckhart and his students. From there the line can be followed to Jacob Böhme, who repeats Eriugena's thesis that "God made all things out of Nothing and that same Nothing is He himself."[19] It is present as well in Schelling's *Ages of the World*:

> It is exactly a Nothing, but how the pure Godhead is a Nothing is in the sense in which a spiritual poet inimitably expressed it: the tender Godhead is a Nothing and more than Nothing; Who Nothing sees in all, believe me, he sees God. (VIII, 234)

Heidegger does not sustain the mystic-theological tradition from Johannes Scotus Eriugena to Jakob Böhme and Schelling, but he presumes the revaluation of the orthodox phrase *creatio ex nihilo* that persists in the Christian mystic tradition (sometimes concealed once again in orthodoxy, sometimes held in abeyance as a daring metaphor) when he foists on the ancient doctrine of *ex nihilo nihil fit* a meaning "appropriate to the problem of Being itself" (p. 108), which he sums up in a Latin phrase of his own construction: *ex nihilo omne ens qua ens fit.* Philosophically, this phrase achieves a preservation of the ancient doctrine of Being, as its original meaning is inverted into its opposite. Nothing becomes that which the ancient doctrine of Being, ever since Parmenides, which, "not sullied by any No" (Nietzsche) appeared to exclude, a substantial Nothing from which all being as being emerges. The expression "the Nothing" that Heidegger introduces does not mean the *nihil* of the mystic tradition: it is a "Nothing of Dasein" (p. 110). It doesn't occur in ecstasy or mystic meditation, it "occurs" in anxiety [*Angst*], "which reveals to the nothing its ownmost openness" (p. 100). It remains to be ascertained how the most paradoxical formulations of the mystical insight into God are related to the Nothing that Heidegger emphasizes. Orthodox theology always assumed a turn toward the anthropological in the exposed statements of the mystics, particularly in their symbolism of Nothing, and perhaps rightly so.

What Heidegger presents at the end of his lecture as the "basic question of metaphysics" (p. 110): "Why is there being at all and not rather nothing?" itself assumes the negation of the two mutually exclusive theses—the ancient doctrine of Being as well as biblical creation doctrine—intentionally introduced by Heidegger for historical retrospection. Only on the basis of the destruction of the ancient doctrine of Being as well as on the rejection of the biblical creation doctrine can the question, "Why is there being at all and not rather nothing?" be posed to. The question that Heidegger describes at the lecture's end as *the* fundamental question of metaphysics emerges neither from ancient philosophy nor from medieval theology; in this form it can simply not be asked on the grounds of either ancient ontology or biblical doctrine of creation. This form of question is possible only when the twofold basis, the old-European philosophy and theology, begins to quiver. First with Leibniz, whom Heidegger cites in the introduction to the lecture's fifth edition, in order to differentiate himself from the way in which Leibniz states the question: *pourquoi il y a plutôt chose que rien* [why there is something rather than nothing] (*Opp. Gerhard* VII, 602). Heidegger's recourse to Leibniz is actually not a belated addendum, as Heidegger already in 1929[20] mentions the first of Leibniz's "24 Theses": *Ratio est in Natura, cur aliquid potius existat quam nihil* (*Opp. Gerhard* VIII, 289). Then, at a decisive point in late Schelling (which Heidegger astoundingly overlooks in his 1936 lecture on Schelling, published in 1971), which anticipates Heidegger's thematic in his lectuere all the way to the formulation:

If there is Being, then beings are a necessary thought. In its immediate relation to Being however, beings are the potential Being, and so on [. . .] but the entire result relies on the presupposition as to whether there is Being or being. What illuminates herefrom is that the thought *of* beings, namely, an ultimate Substance of Being which is divested of all difference, is not in itself necessary, which the followers of Parmenides or Spinoza pass it off as, but rather only relatively necessary; because if I want to go to the limit of all thought, then I must recognize that it is possible that there might be nothing at all. The last question is always: Why is there anything at all, why is there not nothing? I cannot answer this question with mere abstractions from real Being. Instead, as it could appear, that the real is grounded through abstract beings, it is much rather that these abstract beings are only grounded through what is real. I must always first concede reality before I can arrive at abstract beings. . . . [21]

Schelling's "positive" philosophy is already philosophy "in transition to nonphilosophy" (Odo Marquard), but the question of Nothing still appears in a philosophical manner—"if I want to go to the limits of all thought." For Heidegger, the question of Nothing is no longer a "speculative" question; rather, "it makes possible in advance the revelation of beings as such" (p. 103).

It exceeds our considerations to carry out a philosophical discussion with Heidegger's lecture with the intention, for example, of obtaining language-analytic criteria for the sake of evaluating its theoretical validity. Such a "rescue" of Heidegger's questioning appears to Tugendhat, his most subtle interpreter, to be possible only for human Dasein by sacrificing the fundamental term that determines the theme of Heidegger's inaugural lecture with complete disregard for the transition in the lecture, the transition from nothing to Nothing. How can such a chess game be won whose opening is not meant seriously and in which the Queen, who dominates the game, must be sacrificed right at the beginning? Our concern was on this questioning of Heidegger's, particularly the lecture's astonishing transition from nothing to Nothing in which the questioning and means of argumentation can be made transparent independently of whether these are allowed or forbidden according to the rules of logic or language-analytic theory.

If Hübener, in his meticulous and dense survey on the *Logic of Negation as an Ontological Means of Recognition*,[22] in which the Platonic and Aristotelian variants of a syntax of negation are traced to the farthest ramification, lays by the wayside as "indemonstrable" Heidegger's revolutionary thesis on negation, which he put forth in his lecture (see his contribution "Negation and Perfection," in *Positionen der Negitivität*, p. 106), then he proves against his intention that the spell of Parmenides in old-European philosophy has not yet been broken.

Luhmann has his eyes on Parmenides's spell when he recommends "proving whether the possibility of deploying negation in the occidental tradition is pre-regulated by the idea that reality is thought as perfection [. . .] the perfecting of perfection turns in on itself, and thus perfection can no longer be negated. In this self-determination it serves as a solid measure for critique and justification at the same time" (see his contribution "Negation und Perfektion," in *Positionen der Negativität*, p. 469). Through Heidegger's questioning, possibilities are opened up for understanding negation in a perforated reality: "Nothing does not arise through negation; rather, negation founds itself on Nothing, which emanates from the Nothing of Nothing" (p. 105).

The contemporary resonance of Heidegger's question about Nothing is, of course, not to be ignored. A generation that stood materially and in spirit literally *vis-à-vis de rien* understood Heidegger's question without further commentary. Günter Grass gave the sound of Heidegger's key term resonate in the colloquial language of the Third Reich in his novel *Dog Years*. This trace should be further pursued—precisely in a view of the central term of the inaugural lecture—in a linguistics of politics, as Jean Pierre Faye began to do in his great work on *Languages totalitaires* from 1972. The contemporary index of the metaphysical question of Nothing gives an indication of the secret complicity that exists between philosophy and politics. It also reminds us that a metaphysical question cannot be dealt with in a vacuum.

Translated with the assistance of William Rauscher

9

The Iron Cage and the Exodus from It, or the Dispute over Marcion, Then and Now[1]

I

The history of scholarship on Gnosticism can be read in two ways. First, and especially, it is devoted to the study of late antique Gnosticism. But it can also be read, in the fashion of a palimpsest, as the indictaor of the present intellectual climate. At its critical junctions, the study of late antique Gnosticism served as just such an indicator. I remind you of Ferdinand Christian Baur's work, *The Christian Gnosis, or the Philosophy of Religion in its Historical Development* (1835),[2] in which the Tübingen theologian and church historian investigated Schelling's natural philosophy, Schleiermacher's Christian doctrine, and Hegel's philosophy of religion for the Gnostic *topoi* in them. A century later, Hans Jonas, in *Gnosticism and the Spirit of Late Antiquity* (1934),[3] interpreted the Gnostic teaching by means of Heidegger's Dasein analysis so that the Gnostic form of Heidegger's philsophy itself was brought to the fore.

II

After the Second World War, the Gnostic formulation was introduced once again in the struggle over the "legitimacy of the modern age." Eric Voegelin, in a frontal attack on its legitimacy, denounced it as "Gnostic," first in the *New Science of Politics* (1952), and then in his Munich inaugural lecture, "Science, Politics, and Gnosis" (1959). Hans Blumenberg's defense can only be understood in opposition to the denouncement of the modern period as Gnostic. In *Legitimacy of the Modern Age* (1963),[4] Hans Blumenberg takes up Voegelin's thesis and inverts it, in that he portrays the modern period as the second and conclusive "overcoming of Gnosticism" (p. 78). Blumenberg assumes that the first overcoming of Gnosticism, at the beginning of the Middle Ages, was not successful, and its shadow accompanies the Christian Middle Ages as a question. The Christian medieval period "made its entrance in the confrontation with late antique and early Christian Gnosticism." One could even uphold the thesis "that the unity of its rational desire for system can be conceived as the surmounting of the Gnostic counterposition" (ibid.). The second, and conclusive, overcoming of Gnosticism at the end of the Middle Ages is the result of the triumphant march of science and technology. This event, from the very beginning, is subject to "the power of doubt that the world could not have been originally created for the benefit of humans" (p. 90). Through the project of science, he claims, the "flight into transcendence" as a "solution" has lost its human relevance in the modern period. The burden of modern humanity, then, is of another kind than the one placed on it by Gnosticism and Christianity: "It is responsibility for the condition of the world as future-oriented demand, not as past original sin" (ibid.). In the *cosmos atheos* of the modern age, there is no point of escape "beyond" the world. Therefore, neither can there be any Gnostic exodus from the world in the modern age.

Eric Voegelin's wholesale attack on the legitimacy of the modern age was painted with brush strokes that were too broad; he defined Gnosticism too generally for it to have explanatory power. So it is not surprising that Blumenberg's theses, in general, were convincing. Odo Maquard followed them, most recently in several essays that are collected under the title *Farewell to Matters of Principle* (1981).[5]

III

I do not want to intervene in the dispute between Blumenberg and Voegelin regarding the interpretation of the modern age. Even assuming that Hans Blumenberg's theses carry weight, and that it can be said that the modern age represents a conclusive overcoming of Gnosticism, it has to be asked whether the Gnostic relapse since the 1920s does not announce an end of the centuries-long structure of meaning that is called the "modern age." For perhaps the topos of the "end of the modern age," first circulated as a commonplace of cultural criticism, in fact represents a symptom of a crisis in the self-understanding of the present since the end of the First World War.

Such a turning point was already announced in Max Weber's early study of the "Spirit of Capitalism" (1905).[6] Rarely has the profound irony that pervades Max Weber been noted, when he genealogically relates the "spirit of capitalism" to the Protestant ethic. Weber traced the origin of the rational lifestyle of the capitalist era from the spirit of Protestant inner-worldly asceticism through its dialectical turnover, that is, up to the denial of this ascetic lifestyle in late capitalistic affluent society: "For when asceticism was carried out of monastic cells into everyday life and began to dominate worldly morality, it did its part in building the tremendous cosmos of the modern economic order which today determines the lives of individuals with irresistible force" (p. 181). Insofar as Christian asceticism[7] becomes "inner-worldly," that is, "practical," in the Protestant ethic, "fate" turned our modern world into a "iron cage." But what is it like to live in this "iron cage"? "Nobody yet knows who will live in this cage in the future, and whether at the end of our tremendous development entirely new prophets or mechanized petrification will arise" (p. 182). Max Weber's prognosis at the end of his study of capitalism has, since the end of the First World War, become reality, as the spiritual march of progress through science and technology has come to a stop. The "iron cage" is intentionally described by Max Weber as "fate" ["*Verhängnis*"]—a Gnostic hieroglyph that can be fully deciphered in the various types of attempted escapes from the iron cage.

IV

The Gnostic hieroglyph of that era after the First World War including the legacy of the era and the debate over it may be clarified through the dispute over Marcion. Scholars part ways over Marcion, but the argument about him clarifies what the intellectual-historical and theo-political significance of the sign of "Gnosis" after the First World War might be.

The first to refer to Marcion in intellectual-historical perspective is Ernst Bloch, in *The Spirit of Utopia* (1918).[8] The passage can also be found in the second revised edition of 1923, in an excursus on "the Jews." The religion of the exodus and of the kingdom—as the young Ernst Bloch interpreted it—is borne by a "latent Gnosticism" in the prophets and Jesus, one which articulates a juxtaposition between what is just and what is good, "a juxtaposition that in no way was conceived only by that Christianity that was received outside of Judaism" (p. 330). Marcion remains an impetus all the way through Ernst Bloch's late work. Already in Ernst Bloch, the interest in Marcion is stamped with the specific index of his "modernity." What is "modern" is, first, the odd opposition of an interior to which no exteriority corresponds, and an exterior to which no interiority corresponds—an opposition that neither the old religions and philosophies recognize, nor even the Gnostic systems. In opposition to conventional Neoplatonic dramaturgy and to the Gnostic systems, he is modern also in that the progression of redemption is not exposed in symmetry to the prehistory of the unredeemed. Therefore, redemption is not construed as a return to the reestablishment of an original condition, but rather, as Adolf von Harnack said in his 1921 monograph *Marcion, the Gospel of the Alien God*,[9] "a glorious foreignness is opened up and turns into home." That "something" of which Ernst Bloch still can say at the end of *The Principle of Hope* (1959),[10] elaborating on Harnack, "this something shines into childhood for everyone, yet no one has ever been there: home."

Harnack published his monograph on Marcion in 1921. We read it not (only) as a historical study, but (also) as the evidence of a new religiosity at the end of the liberal-Protestant era. Harnack "seriously" raises the question, "whether Marcionism, as it today must be understood, after its historical scaffolding has been dismantled," is not, in the end, "the solution that has been sought" to the religious problem today; whether the trajectory of the prophets, Jesus, and Paul does not rightly continue only in Marcion; and whether the philosophy of religion should not feel compelled to recognize the antithesis of grace (new spirit and freedom) versus the world (including morality) as the last word (p. 233). I have highlighted the contemporaneity and the independence of the interpretive endeavors of Ernst Bloch and Adolf von Harnack (1918/21—first edition of *Spirit of Uptoia* and *Marcion*; second edition 1923/24), because Martin Buber, reflecting after the Second World War on the course of history since the end of the First World War, points to Marcion as the key figure and to Harnack's interpretation of him at a decisive point in his own writing, with consequences for the central theme of our colloquium on Gnosis and politics.[11]

V

After the Second World War, when Martin Buber tried, in the years after the great affliction, to reduce the sum of what had occurred to a common denominator, he recalled the "Gnostic Marcion" and Harnack's monograph about Marcion. Thus in the first of the four "Addresses on Judaism," collected under the title *At the Turning* (1952):[12]

At the same time that Hadrian brought down Bar Kochba's rebellion, made Jerusalem into a Roman colony, and established a temple to Jupiter on the location of the Second Temple, Marcion came from Asia Minor to Rome and brought with him his own gospel as an intellectual contribution to the destruction of Israel. (p. 28)

I will put aside the question of chronology, which Martin Buber treats somewhat liberally. I believe that Buber does not seek to establish a causal connection, but rather to juxtapose two experiences that are historically concretized: in Marcion, the redeemed soul stands on the one side and existing society on the other, and there is no point in thinking of how to improve the latter. The church did not follow Marcion. It knew that were creation and redemption "torn apart, the basis of its influence on the orders of the world would be removed" (p. 29). At this point, Buber introduces Harnack's work on Marcion. Harnack, who was not at all "anti-Semitic," but on the contrary, the representative of a broad liberalism, held the view that to preserve the Old Testament, in the nineteenth century, as a "canonical document" of Christianity is "the consequence of a religious and ecclesial paralysis." Buber commented, "Harnack died in 1930; three years later, his thought, the thought of Marcion, was transformed into action, not with the means of the intellect, but with those of violence and terror.

Marcion's gift to Hadrian was handed over to others" (p. 30). The nexus between Gnosticism and politics could not have been set forth more forcefully. For Buber, this connection occurs in the perspective of a "concrete messianism" (p. 31), which frames Ernst Bloch's *Spirit of Utopia* as well. Thus a comparison between Bloch and Buber's pro and contra Marcion as a key figure is instructive. Ernst Bloch also spoke of the problem of Gnostic anti-Semitism, and he coined the appropriate term "metaphysical anti-Semitism," but he interpreted Marcion and apportioned his inheritance of this epoch completely differently than Buber did. Already in the *Spirit of Utopia*, he says about Marcion, "Precisely in the fact that Marcion, a great man, conceptualized this god as history, this contrast, this antithesis between the Demiurge and the highest godhead—hitherto unknown and revealed by Christ—in this, this apparent metaphysical anti-Semitism stands closer to messianic intellectuality than the entire later economy of redemption, which also petrifies the Old Testament. This economy of redemption reduces the sequence of revelations to a merely pedagogical measure and thus keeps the actual theological process distant from heaven itself" (p. 30). The events of the Hitler period changed nothing at all. *The Principle of Hope* (1959) also praises Marcion, who understood himself as the consummation of the antithetical Paul, as teacher of the new god, the absolutely alien one, "from whom up to Christ, no tidings had ever come to humanity" (p. 1499). "By destroying the bridge to the Old Testament, Marcion himself just as surely stands upon it" (ibid.). "Stated otherwise: Marcion comes to us not only from Paul; he comes equally from Moses; the true, or alien, god dawns in the God of Exodus, between Egypt and Canaan" (p. 1500). In Ernst Bloch it becomes clear that "utopian messianism stands in total opposition" to the doctrine of creation. Likewise, in his late work *Atheism in Christianity* (1968), Ernst Bloch still calls attention to Marcion's doctrine as "a bold impetus" that supplies the keyword of the antithesis—anti-"law," anti-"righteousness," anti-"creator and ruler of the world"—in which lurks, as meaning, freedom, grace, and homecoming, that is, "something that has never been heard, never been seen, and is yet profoundly familiar; something that, precisely because it never yet has been, is home" (p. 241). Marcion's antithetical keyword certainly has nothing to do with any sort of worldly tension, any enmity with the Jews (Marcion venerated the Jew Paul as his master), remarks Ernst Bloch in passing (p. 238), as if he were answering Martin Buber's great address. Bracketing the anecdotal matters that unite and divide these two utopian figures: the utopian withdrawal to Zion by the one and the utopian legitimization of the October revolution by the other have both been humbled by the course of history. We only want to explore which function Marcion's figure has attained in its historical philosophical reflection, and we want to tie these deliberations on the theme of "Gnosis and Politics" to it.

VI

However much his opinion is colored by partiality, Martin Buber pointed to the historical moment of the Gnostic-Marcionite experience. Even the exodus from the world and history is historically indicated. Marcion is somehow connected with the crisis of concrete messianism, with Bar Kochba's messianic apocalyptic revolt in the time of Hadrian, and he responds to it—with a Gospel that turns inward and sacrifices history. History has no redemption, and redemption has no history. Already Harnack noticed that Marcion interprets the Pentateuch and the prophets of the Old Testament literally. *Les extrèmes se touchent.* For likewise Aquilas (who, in the spirit of the school of Akiva, produced a Greek translation of the Hebrew Bible that was true to the rabbis, after the Septuagint also served Christian missionaries), came from Sinope, in Asia Minor, and is a contemporary of Marcion. Even if the patristic rumors about Marcion's Jewish origins are not to be trusted, the coincidence of Marcion and Aquila remains astounding. Buber also understood something of the "open or hidden Marcionism" that Harnack announced in 1921. This Marcionism promised to be the spirit of the age, be it in Karl Barth's great commentary on the Epistle to the Romans, whose Marcionite character frightened off contemporary theologians; be it in a philosophical work, which first—almost in an unnoticeable manner, but then speedily—gained success as "new philosophy," as a revolution in philosophy: "The sense of the world must lie outside of it. In the world, everything is as it is, and everything happens as it happens; in it there is no value, and if it did exist, it would have no value. [. . .] Therefore there can also be no statements [propositions] of ethics. Statements can express nothing higher. [. . .] For what is higher, the world as it is is a matter of complete indifference. God does not reveal himself in the world." These sentences do not come from a Manichaean tract, but can be found at the end of Ludwig Wittgenstein's *Tractatus logico-philosophicus* (6.41, 6.432; 1921), at whose beginning is the ambiguous sentence—"The world is all that is the case"—a sentence that sounds and is intended to sound positivistic and theological at the same time. It is worth asking what the Marcionite-Manichaean formulae of the 1920s indicate about the historical epoch, and to what difficulties they are responding.

It would be more worthwhile to trace these connections than to "set the spirit of Israel against the open or hidden Marcionism of the gentiles," in general statements of pathos, as Buber does (p. 33). It would provide Buber's historical insight with a frame of reference in the history of religions and contemporary history. It would also need to be asked whether the Marcionite trope approaches concrete messianism (also called "the spirit of Israel" by Buber) only from the outside, or whether it does not also lurk as a silent question on the inside.

Buber's third address is called "The Silent Question."[13] It is the most profound and forceful of his addresses. It stands eye to eye with Simone Weil, a French Jew of the interwar period and of the Second World War, a disciple of Marcion (if ever there has been religious discipleship). For the sake of the coherence of our discussion, I will turn to Martin Buber's depiction of Simone Weil's teachings. Simone Weil, in whose posthumously published writings "a strong and theologically substantiated, far-reaching negation of life is expressed, a negation that logically leads to the negation both of the ego and of society," rejected Israel and Judaism as such without converting to Christianity, for reasons that she intuited based on her religious views. Among them, it was of considerable importance that the church seemed too Jewish to her. "She accused Israel of idolatry, of the one real idolatry, namely, that of the collectivity which she, using a parable of Plato's, called "the great beast." For her, the social realm is the province of Satan, since the collectivity arrogates to itself the authority to dictate what is good and what is evil; it mediates between God and the soul; indeed it supplants God and establishes itself as a substitute for the divine" (p. 68). In ancient Rome, Simone Weil sees the "great beast" in political form; in Israel, she sees it in religious form. Rome and Jerusalem embody the social principle. But Simone Weil "wanted to escape nature, just as she wanted to escape society: reality for her had become unbearable, and for her, God was the power who abducted her away from this reality." It would be carping to ask whether Martin Buber has done justice to Simone Weil's intentions. That he sets her up as an example for the silent question "that moved a generation"—the question he tries to answer forcefully—this proves that Buber has a sense for the fact that as Simone Weil's notes prove, sensitive intellects, even intellectually important Jews (p. 65), are on paths that lead to the "totally other." But the totally other cannot be articulated from the safe harbor of this world, for as soon as it is articulated, it has already been distorted. Thus does Marcion begin his *Antithesis*: "O wonder of wonders, rapture, power and marvel, that one can neither say nor think anything of the Gospel, nor compare it with anything."

In an exciting debate between Barbara Aland and Hans Jonas over the origins of the Gnostic experience, "the starting for all Gnosis," Barbara Aland remarked:

I see the starting point for Gnosis in a boundless joy at being released. Hans Jonas noted that this is a new experiment in dealing intellectually with the Gnosis phenomenon, which puts first the joy of release and then the sense of past oppression.[14]

I believe Marcion's prologue could support Barbara Aland's thesis. The *absconditum* promulgates not horror, but genuine joy.

It would be necessary to take one more glance back to Marcion's time and to ask whether the doctrine of the two powers is in fact only to be found outside Judaism, that is, whether the lines of demarcation between the spirit of Israel and the spirit of the nations can be drawn as clearly as Martin Buber delineates them. A. F. Segal's study, *Two Powers in Heaven: Early Rabbinic Reports About Christianity and Gnosticism* (1977), allows us to surmise that the crisis of monotheistic belief breaks from the inside out. Even within the rabbinic elite, the silent question became "virulent" in the form of Elisha ben Abuya, who received the Hebrew epithet *Aher* ("the other"). G. Stroumsa gathered the sources and has shown that the nickname *"Aher"* is probably a *terminus technicus* for a Gnostic.[15]

In sum, I call for a new reading of the sources and their interpretation, for the possibility of reading the Gnostic-Marcionite trope as a crisis of that concrete messianism that reached its climax in the Bar Kochba rebellion, to which Martin Buber pointed as the basic condition for Marcionism. R. M. Grant, *Gnosticism and Early Christianity* (1959), had already called attention to the inner connection between apocalypticism and Gnosticism. When apocalypticism is a possible answer to the situation that Leon Festinger formulated as "When Prophecy Fails,"[16] then it is perhaps not too bold to reduce Gnosticism to the formula "when apocalypticism fails." From the perspective of the history of religion, the intellectual situation is more complex than the one Martin Buber sketched out; from the point of view of the history of scholarship, it is no less complex. But he exhibited great sensitivity in reading the historical constellation and its interpretation historically. In that, we are obliged to him, if we are also able to read the dispute over Marcion, then and now, with another perspective.

Translation provided by Mara H. Benjamin

10

The Demystification of Theology: Toward a Portrait of Overbeck[1]

The Dispute over Overbeck

In recent decades, Overbeck's name has attained a hallowed aura, in spite of the learned character of his early studies of church history and the fragmentary nature of his later posthumous publications. The more fragments of his literary estate come to light, the more intensified does the riddle of person and oeuvre become. Overbeck's voice was heard more clearly from the grave than it was by his contemporaries. Liberal theology, which grew increasingly uncertain of itself after the First World War, stood by helpless and confused in the face of the claims of the fragments after it had, in its early days, gotten around both Overbeck's *Polemic*[2] and his "Postscript" (1903),[3] which directed its questions against "the modern theology of contemporary Protestantism"[4] sharply and polemically. Carl Albrecht Bernoulli selected some material from the "slips of paper, alphabetically ordered in a full vat"[5]—half quarry, half foundation stone—ordered them by theme, and, in 1919, published them under the title *Christentum und Kultur* [*Christianity and Culture*].[6] Eberhard Vischer, Overbeck's successor to the theology chair in Basel, had in 1913 already summarized the common guild opinion for the guild itself in an article about Overbeck in the *Realenzyklopädie of the Protestant Church*, vol. 24. He wanted to sweep under the rug the texts that Bernoulli had published as "writings that appeared under the name Overbeck," and he regarded an understanding of Overbeck guided by these cryptic fragments as "the most fatal thing" that could happen to his interpretation.[7] Ernst Troeltsch considered them to be a scandal. "Overbeck's behavior is, in truth, indeed almost incomprehensible. I remember that Erwin Rohde came to speak about this multiple times. He believed that Overbeck's theology must nonetheless lie deeper than he himself admits; otherwise, the behavior of this thoroughly honest man would be incomprehensible. [. . .] I can only say that, for me, this publication cast a deep shadow over the personal and the scholarly portrait of Overbeck's character. Because of it, even those writings published during his lifetime have become considerably more suspicious to me." Explaining and exculpating [him,] Troeltsch calls on "Nietzsche's influence," which "tore him away from theology and left him only with the ambition to use his historical-critical expertise, as the theologian of the Nietzsche circle, to completely eliminate Christianity—a plan that he did not, after all, execute." In spite of all his trivial criticism, Troeltsch was on the right track to Overbeck's secret when he closed his review with the judgment: "In spite of all the critiques and all his brilliance, he himself was more theologian than historian, even if a negative theologian."[8]

Overbeck's fragments bore fruit, by contrast, in the circle of those postwar theologians who later took the helm of what would become "dialectical theology." Karl Barth, its first representative, understood those fragments that intended to bring proof "of the *finis Christianismi* in modern Christianity"[9] as a paradoxical "introduction to the study of theology," in which this introduction "could, under certain conditions, just as soon take the form of an energetic exo-duction for the uninvited" (Barth, p. 5).[10] It may remain an open question whether Overbeck wanted to protect Christianity from the modern world or the world from modern Christianity. Barth, in any case, enlisted Overbeck's fragments for his eschatological approach to Christianity, whose critical implications for the relationship between Christianity and history no one else in the nineteenth century had presented as clearly. In his view, Overbeck has understood the fundamental presuppositions of Christianity—the expectation of the *parousia*—as the problem and, on that basis, posed questions to modern theology that to this day have remained unanswered: the question of whether Christianity would be feasible as a historical entity and whether it would want to be so at all; the question of what had become of it and what it is continually forced to become if it suppresses its primary presupposition; the question of whether a theology that expends itself as a negotiator between Christianity and history is not, in fact, acting to the detriment of both.

In the confrontation "with the excessively strange and extraordinarily pious man," Barth was compelled to abandon his first attempt at an explanation of the *Epistle to the Romans*. If "of the first [version], no stone was left unturned," as Barth confessed in the foreword to the second and final version of his commentary, this is especially to be ascribed to Overbeck's "Warning to all Theologians." It was no surprise that Overbeck's successor to the chair of theology in Basel—one of the "putative experts on Overbeck in Basel," as Barth ironically noted—rejected the version of Overbeck that was resurrected in dialectical theology. Vischer called on biographical material for a psychological interpretation of Overbeck that Barth repudiated as a matter of principle because the factual problem posed by Overbeck never could come into view at all in Vischer's biographical-psychological explanation.

In 1941, Eberhard Vischer published and wrote an introduction to the "Confessions" commissioned by the Franz Overbeck Foundation in Basel. Mainly, the publication deals with the pieces that Overbeck had himself presented in the "Introduction" and the "Afterword" to the second edition of his *On the Christianity* in a reworked form. Vischer's introduction and his choice of excerpts are meant to supply the evidence for his thesis, already articulated in 1913, of the one-dimensional development of the professor of theology into an agnostic. Important pieces of the autobiographical fragments that yield information about Overbeck's relationship to modern theology were omitted. At the same time, even these autobiographical sketches themselves, published by Vischer, reveal more (in biographical, psychological respects, more than he could see or admit) about the imbrication of that which is incompatible—an aspect that endows Overbeck's fragments with their abysmal disjointedness. A remainder that cannot be assimilated is left behind, so long as one adheres to making conjectures about Overbeck's belief and unbelief as a psychological problem, or, like Vischer, even chooses unambiguously, but trivially, unbelief. Only from Overbeck's theme, which also dominates his so-called Confessions, can the idiosyncratic moment of this eccentric spirit be determined, this spirit which at the same time possessed the audaciousness of the discoverer.

Overbeck's Theme

Already in his Basel inaugural lecture, "Über Entstehung und Recht einer rein historischen Betrachtung der Neutestamentlichen Schriften in der Theologie" [On the origin and right of a purely historical consideration of the New Testament scriptures in theology] (1871), Overbeck adumbrates the theme of his oeuvre. For Overbeck, to articulate the beginnings of Christianity historically means reading the tradition that had been rigidified in canon and exegesis against the grain. For a historical understanding of the origin, "roughly nineteen hundred of almost two thousand years cannot prove anything," because the tradition spreads a veil of amnesia over its beginnings. As soon as the church erects the canon as armor against the assault of heresy, it no longer comprehends anything of the scriptures it has gathered into the canon and achieves an elasticity for exegesis, which renders the former illusory as a defense. Between us and the ecclesial centuries, to which the period of the Reformation also belongs, "the difference that is certainly significant reigns: that for all of us, those beginnings have become a scientific, historical problem, or—what amounts to the same thing—that for us, the earliest history of Christianity has become past."[11] But the past of origins, however passed, may neither be obtained through a fictionally posited contemporaneity, a form that is characteristic of all traditions, nor may the barriers be taken down between this past and the modern understanding of Christianity through the method of empathy that modern theology employs. Historical understanding is to be had only "at the price of complete separation" from the object, that is, "at the price of the knowledge of how far one stands from it."[12]

What Overbeck realized vis-à-vis the questionable historical method of modern theology intensifies into a general verdict in his untimely meditation *On the Christianity of Our Contemporary Theology*. In the preface to the *Studien zur Geschichte der alten Kirche* [*Studies on the History of the Early Church*], Overbeck seeks, "with all the conciseness and simplicity achievable" for him, to formulate the theses of the polemical text:

> Christianity is too sublime a matter for the individual to be permitted to identify with it so readily in a world to which Christianity is completely alien. Fundamentally, no one does such a thing today, theologians excepted. If the theologians do so, and the public judgment accommodates them, then such judgment is a prej-

udice, and it occurs due to an unwarranted self-deception. But it is precisely the situation in which we find ourselves presently with Christianity, that it is at least somewhat important that the theologians find the appropriate attitude toward the matter and will be able to remain serene for the resolutions to which we are driven, especially in a time in which the strength and simplicity of the faith of earlier times have dwindled, even if they still determine us, and in which a centuries-old and very complicated experience has forced itself between Christianity and all of us. That can, I add today, happen in a great variety of ways, among which will also be found, in any case, the one of scientific enlightenment regarding Christianity. [. . .] But a discipline that calls us, in the religious confusions of the present, to reflection is one with which we can hardly soon dispense, even if a spirit of deception wants to take control of this field presently. . . . (VIIf.)[13]

His attack on the contemporary apologetic and liberal theology is conducted on the very narrow basis of a "critical" theology that both follows and opposes Strauss. Even if this "better" theology conducts itself critically and freely in relation to Christianity, it nonetheless "will be able to protect" Christianity "against theologies that think they represent it when they accommodate it to the world, theologies that, through indifference to Christianity's view of life, either dry it out into a dead orthodoxy that banishes it from the world, or draw it down into worldliness and let it disappear therein. Critical theology will prevent such theologies from dragging through the world an unreal thing they call Christianity, from which has been taken its soul, namely, the denial of the world."[14]

Already during his years in Jena, Overbeck dealt with the problem of the *Anfänge des Mönchthums* [*Beginnings of Monasticism*],[15] a phenomenon for which Catholic theology had long ago lost the purity of understanding of its worthiness, while Protestant theology never had the righteousness to appreciate. In monasticism, Overbeck recognized the institution through which the church could evade the "iron grip" of the pagan state. Since the recognition of the church by the pagan state, martyrdom, its source, dried up. The church produced a replacement for it in the *martyrium quotidianum* of monasticism, and with it "saves nothing less than its own life" for it.[16] In his judgment as to the use and disadvantage of asceticism, Overbeck's analysis departs from Nietzsche's critique of Christianity. For Overbeck regards the ascetic urge in humans as "just as deeply founded" as the opposing libidinal drive, which Nietzsche exposed one-sidedly. For Overbeck, asceticism forms what is fundamental to human culture. Regarding Christianity, however, it may be noted that "its basic character is ascetic; indeed, excessively ascetic."[17] Insofar as Christianity sets "hyperascetic" demands, which contradict human life at its roots, it gets into a hopeless conflict "with humanity or what it itself calls the 'world'" and thus will vanish from among humanity.[18] However, the "most interesting aspect of Christianity" will remain "its powerlessness; the fact that it cannot rule the world."[19] If, however, modern theology (and Nietzsche along with it), in the wake of the Reformation, plays down the ascetic lifestyle as an ephemeral phenomenon in Christianity, then it will push it to the historically "absurd consequence" that Christianity had taken fifteen hundred years to reach its own view of life, one that, up until the Reformation, had remained obscured.[20] In taking recourse to a hypostatized entity called "Gospel" or "ancient Christianity," modern theology seeks to deny the basic ascetic character of Christianity. But in so doing, it reveals its *proton pseudos*. "For there cannot be a belief that is more world-escaping than the one of the first Christians in the imminent return of Christ and the decline of the present form of the world."[21] If early Christianity was not dashed to pieces by the delay of the *parousia*, then it is only because Christian belief, as its expectation of the second coming of Christ was refuted in the course of history, found "a more ideal form" in which it could construct itself in spite of the factual refutation.[22] To Overbeck the ascetic view and conduct of life seemed to be

a metamorphosis of the early Christian [*urchristlich*] expectation of the return of Christ [. . .],[23] for it is based on a continuing expectation of this return. Christian faith continued to think that the world was ripe for its end, and it moved believers to withdraw from it so that they might be prepared for the appearance of Christ that threatened to occur at any hour. The expectation of the return of Christ, having become untenable in its original form, [. . .][24] was transformed into thought about death, changes into the *memento mori* that already according to Irenaeus should accompany the Christian constantly. This greeting of the Carthusians, "remember death!" summarizes the basic wisdom of Christianity far better than the modern formula, "no disturbance should intrude between the person and his original source [God]."[25] That is a stale negation, so long as one forgets that according to the view of Christianity the world itself belongs to what "disturbs."[26]

Overbeck understood the Christian negation of the world in opposition to Strauss, but also in distinction to Nietzsche, with whom he is in broad agreement against Strauss, as an outstanding kind of humaneness.

If Strauss thinks "he has done with Christianity when he critically annihilates a series of fundamental Christian dogmas and especially the church's traditional comprehension of its earliest history," but at the same time "skips over Christianity's ascetic view of life with two or three deprecating and very incidental remarks"[27] and opposes the old belief with a new one, then it must be asked on what standpoint he bases "our life without Christianity."[28] If one compares what Strauss said about the state, war, political penal power, and the working class with parallels in Augustine, then one finds everything in the Christian texts represented "incomparably more profound and at the same time more human and therefore much truer."[29] "Christianity has already come to terms once with a culture like the one modeled by Strauss."[30] A generation that went through the school of antiquity, at whose end Christianity stands, must, in order to maintain its right against Christianity, envision its standpoint as higher, not more lowly, than the common standpoint "of the Philistine of the Roman imperial era,"[31] whom Christianity had already once mastered. It must after all be "of inestimable value" if, over the "whole disastrous dissolution" of our era, "at least the name of Christ hovers as a kind of categorical imperative that condemns it. However, in such a time, hardly could something be more lamentable than the branching off of a kind of religion whose own prophet himself makes hardly a secret of the fact that, for the time being, it can supposedly only be a religion of the middle class."[32]

The bourgeoisie of the end of the nineteenth century, when both the "old" faith of Christianity as well as the "new" faith of the Enlightenment finally decayed into ideology, is historically as well as factually the antipode of Overbeck. Germany of the Second Reich, out of which Overbeck, through the publication of his polemic voluntarily banned himself, made Christianity serviceable as a patriotic vehicle. Upon the conversion of Treitschke, Overbeck's friend since his student days in Leipzig, Overbeck realized what it meant "to convert back to Christianity for the sake of this empire [*Reich*]."[33] When Treitschke, as a Christian, kindled the Berlin Antisemitism Dispute, Overbeck dissociated himself from him for good. Overbeck's letter to Treitschke deserves to be recorded:

What is more embarrassing and—to speak totally frankly since I'm doing so anyhow—more repugnant to me, is another tone—that is, the "Christian" one—that resounds ever more blatantly in your recent publications. First, let there be no misunderstanding here. I don't mean the personal [Christian] feeling that I respect everyone to the highest degree, which it would not occur to me to question with you, as my friend, if it has come upon you. I mean the public usage that you make of this personal feeling in the political debate, and in which I see you losing more and more of your old reluctance, which I always valued, regarding pulling questions of religion into political debate. Only against this loss do I express my reluctance because for this I most certainly do not have respect. And in particular I am of the opinion that a man with your past exposes himself, with his present rhetoric, to the question of what business he has displaying his Christianity in this manner. For in any event it should not be taken so lightly that one day, one might be allowed to do so and at the same time to remain the old Adam in every manner—at least for the public—while one's Christianity cuts a figure as one political expedient among others. Excuse my rudeness, but it concerns a point, one which I take seriously and, if you will, on which I am quite irritable. In my life, I have had cause to keep at arm's length from all mixtures of radical ecclesial tendencies with politics, and so have I done—certainly not because I would prefer so much more a conservative, lemminglike tendency. This is what *I* feel, and what *I* learn from history: that if there is *one* point where one realizes that Christianity has twisted humanity, it is to be found in all the connections that Christianity has entered into with politics, just as I do not doubt at all that here is the point at which it will one day succumb to a general contempt, if this area cannot be kept clean of it. And I cannot think otherwise about the invocation of Christianity in the present racket about the Jews, since it appears to me to be a complete masquerade for which, in modern times, Christianity was not regarded too well, since with battling it, in a dispute of such a nature, can only lead to a further twisting of all simple integrity.[34]

Overbeck's protest against the connection of Christianity with politics springs from his insight into the world-renouncing character of Christianity. Negation of the world is for him the *character indelebilis* of Christianity. "In all seriousness Christianity has never been based on anything in humanity [*unter Menschen*] other than the wretched state of the world."[35] Once, Christianity had thought very differently than today about the "blessings of culture," and since the world (even after Christianity had been in it for almost two thousand years) "has changed astonishingly little, there is no apparent reason why it should not continue to think as it did before."[36]

Christianity and History

The development of modern theology in the decades between the first and the second editions of his polemical work gave Overbeck no cause to waver in his judgment that "a Christianity whose appeasement toward the shaping of the world is hardly a problem" must bring about a "state of things" in which "one will have to esteem Christianity as that religion above all others with which one can do what one wants."[37] In this, the most recent event of the victorious career of modern theology validates him: "Harnack's secular book [*Säkularschrift*], which had more forcefully proved the 'nonessentiality' of Christianity than the 'essence' whose demonstration is announced on its title page."[38] The final sentences of his afterword to *On Christianity* hint at the rich material that Overbeck had subsequently gathered for a critique of modern theology in his last years. This critique was meant to record the last stages of Christian history and to measure the distance to the end point by means of the fate of theology, which hastens ahead of Christianity as its prophet with a wide lead on the way to this very end point. A "Polemic [*Streitschrift*] Against Harnack," designed as an excursus in his *On Christianity*, was meant to make an example of this Christian darling of popular opinion at the turn of the century by relegating both [Harnack and public opinion—Tr.] to inanity. Bernoulli published parts of Overbeck's *Lexicon* regarding the case of Harnack, which amount to an execution.

Adolf Harnack championed a cause that was discredited, both in the circle of current opinion [*Zeitbildung*] itself and in general, in forms which were palatable and acceptable to current opinion [*Zeitbildung*] with purpose and success as a professional modern Christian and theologian. That was once the characteristic task of Abbé, which was naturally, in its generality, bound to neither confession nor nation. Owing to his personal talents and debilities, he lacked nothing to serve this task in the form that was precisely characteristic of Abbé, with the grace and superficiality recognized by the circles of the reigning educated establishment. He is a Protestant Abbé, and, as his success may sufficiently reveal, also because he, as Abbé, gratifies and covers an actual need of the age.[39]

He who has grasped Harnack in his nature as *satisfait* within the contemporary circumstances of the *Reich* will also grasp without further ado what is otherwise ungraspable: that the monument our Kaiser's theological dilettantism had erected in his letters to Admiral Hollmann regarding the Bible and Babel, found its official apologist in him. [. . .] Harnack performed the service of a hairdresser for the theological wig of the Kaiser—just as, formerly, Eusebius of Caesarea did for the Emperor Constantine the Great.[40]

Leaving aside the person of Harnack, Overbeck's charge is aimed at a Christianity *sub specie temporis*: "Nothing may teach how highly esteemed history is at the moment better than the attitude of modern theologians toward it. As the cowardly worshipers of any power and influence that they, as theologians, are, they will be the last to miss an opportunity to pay the required homage to these temporal powers and to betake themselves unto their protection for their own purposes."[41] With the example of modern theology, the following reveals itself to Overbeck as a "basic thesis" (one which he only formulates in the afterword to his *Christianness*, but which he already reads into the polemical work): theology has *always* been modern and therefore has always been the natural traitor of Christianity—but Christianity itself, never. At the beginning, Christianity placed itself outside of all history and, so long as it was important, also as always against it. "According to Christianity's own desire, history and Christianity will never come together."[42] Christianity as history is "something absurd."[43] For Christianity means nothing other than: the divine form of Christ and the faith of the adherents in Christ; it is something transtemporal, which can only be represented *sub specie aeterni*, "that is, from a standpoint that knows nothing of time."[44] Therefore, history is also a chasm into which Christianity had allowed itself to be thrown only with reluctance. If one places Christianity under the concept of the historical, then one concedes that it is "of this world" and, thereby, "inevitably" surrenders it to the law of decay. "The high age of Christianity is, for a serious historical consideration, the deadly argument against its eternality. Christianity has always known this and still today, so long as it lives, continues to know it."[45]

But this insight does not seduce Overbeck into Kierkegaard's rhetorical gesture of "removing the eighteen hundred years of Christian history as though they never were." For whoever thinks in historical categories "cannot let two thousand years be cancelled out as though they are nothing. Christianity, which has lived so long, cannot exist in the world any longer as it once did after all the experiences that it then still had *before it* and now has *behind it*!"[46] Least of all may a theology that is itself permeated by the applicability of the historical approach to Christianity deny this. Rather, with the thought of setting Christianity purely in history, the advent of an age in which Christianity comes to its end and takes its leave announces itself.[47]

Yet in Overbeck's reserved statements, which seem aimlessly to follow the direction of contrary arguments and from time to time change frameworks, his own thesis nonetheless shines through. History is not to be restrained by means of Christianity; rather, history explodes the boundaries of Christianity. "Every attempt to take the Christian periodization of history seriously" must shatter on this fact.[48] The Christian reckoning of time would only be substantiated if Christianity had brought about "a new era." But Overbeck denies precisely this, for "Christianity itself originally spoke of a new time under the prerequisite—one that was not met—that the existing world should perish and make room for a new one. This was, for a brief moment, a serious expectation and, as such an expectation, surfaced continually but fleetingly, never becoming a fact of historical permanence—which alone could have provided the real basis for an incontrovertible account of time, one corresponding to the facts of reality. The world, and not the Christian expectation of it, is what held its own."[49] Overbeck's protest against the Christian account of time and his exodus from Christian history force him into a repetition of the ancient thesis: "What of us is eternal to us has always been in us and is not granted to us only belatedly in a historical moment of our lives. Against this perception of history, not even the experience that we humans have had with Christianity can prevail; rather, it will be affirmed by it."[50]

But an unacknowledged difficulty lies in this reiteration of the antique worldview at the end of Christian history. For Overbeck's historical analysis of the Christian experience as that of a history of blindness and decline, one which is to forge a path back to an antique experience of the world, must also affect his own historical sense. Overbeck's historical reflection must, in the end, dismantle the very construct of historical consciousness itself and reintegrate history—"the eternal essence of history,"[51] as it is called in one illuminating and telling passage—into the perpetually immutable nature of the cosmos and humanity. Overbeck's attempt to repeat the ancient integration of humanity into nature cannot keep itself entirely free of the jargon of a conventional biologism. Therefore his intent does not come to light as a matter of historical reflection but must appear as metaphysical meditation that apparently oversteps the bounds of historical consciousness, in his comparison of the Christian teaching regarding death with the Stoic teaching, in the form of its modern repristination in the early Enlightenment. Overbeck recognizes that Christianity, with its *memento mori*, devoted all its attention to humanity's most sensitive riddle, but he questions whether Christianity did so "in the right way." He preferred Montaigne's and Spinoza's contemplation of death because it pretends much less than the Christian idea to console us about death, while the consolation that it *is* able to bestow does not have the desperate character of the Christian one. To Overbeck, death appears as "the most powerful means" to disperse the shadows that rest upon life; it "can serve as an iron comb to eliminate the lies that disfigure and burden our lives."[52] He was, after all, more Christian than the witnesses of the early Enlightenment to which he refers, reminiscent perhaps of the post-Christian atheism of Jacobsen.

Indeed, we know too much, *too much* in particular of things of which we can know nothing, of last things, of death. How forcefully and beautifully is the latter proved by the description of the three deaths with which J. P. Jacobsen concludes his *Niels Lyhne*: that of the young mother Gerda, who cannot endure atheism; the one immediately following, of the son who is still underage; and finally, a few years later, the death of the householder Niels Lyhne himself, who dies as an atheist, this being the main frame into which other small and insignificant deaths are integrated, the vision of which is altogether exported from the hospital. All of this is done masterfully and in such a way as has only most recently been acquired and could not have been done earlier. For which reason such products of contemporary literature are so much more instructive for the understanding of the past, Niels Lyhne for instance, for that of the Trappists of the church and their composure in the face of death. How piteous do the instruction books of church history appear in contrast to these literary accounts, and those of Christianity in general, which "modern theology" pelts us with, as though it knew itself perfectly well that they are good for nothing other than being thrown at us.[53]

Overbeck put his cards on the table much more in his old age than in his youth, and he no longer clung to theological relics. Rather, from an unconditional surrender of theology, he expected a future for religious heritage that was getting wasted on theology. No longer did he believe himself permitted, as he still had in his polemical text, to set a "critical" or "better" theology against apologetic and liberal ones. His early indication of a "better" theology seemed to him later, when he had judged all theology from the patristic period on to be the "Satan of religion,"[54] as a *lapsus calami*. If he once thought that "many a redeeming idea" of Christianity's ascetic view "could still shine into the misery of the present,"[55] at the turn of the century it became clear to him "that the religious development of humanity up to this point" signifies "an irredeemable aberration and therefore, one to be quietly shut down."[56] "Religious problems" must therefore "be placed on an entirely new foundation, potentially at the cost of that which previously was called religion."[57] But the example of Christian history can still serve as an instructor in spite of its unconditional surrender. The history of Christianity "provides us with the most magnificent example on this path, since the passage from the Old Testament to the New Testament was basically not much different from one suspended in thin air, which thus, even if it was ultimately successful, nonetheless gained acceptance only with corresponding tedium and difficulty."[58] So long as the solution for the religious confusions of the time is sought on the ground of the Bible and that of theological dispute about it, no further progress is possible. For such a solution, Christianity should be disregarded altogether, "which will not happen as long as it is not recognized that we humans will only go forward at all, if from time to time we allow ourselves to be suspended in thin air, and that our life runs its course under conditions which do not allow us to neglect this experiment."[59]

Nietzsche's fate seemed to him to be such an experiment that he, as his friend, experienced close at hand:

Nietzsche's attempt is a serious attempt to grasp the world *completely*, not—or not only—one that grappled with despair on the journey, and which along the way surrendered its vehicle, which Nietzsche had done long before the eruption of his insanity. No one has as of yet reached the destination of the journey that I am speaking of, and in this respect Nietzsche failed no more than others. What failed him was the felicity that other more felicitous people, of whom I knew some, were lucky enough to enjoy. Admittedly he did fail, but only so much, that he would serve as an argument against the journey that he undertook so well and so poorly, as those who were shipwrecked would against the navigation of the sea. Just as he who has reached a harbor will least of all refuse to recognize his shipwrecked predecessor as a comrade in misfortune, so too the luckier seafarers, who on their aimless journey were at least able to preserve themselves with their vessels—with regard to Nietzsche.[60]

In the introduction to the second edition of his polemical text, Overbeck gave an account of his relationship to Nietzsche. He cherished Nietzsche's friendship as the strongest influence that he had encountered on the peregrinations through [his] life, and Nietzsche himself as an "extraordinary man, extraordinary, too, in bearing misfortune."[61] Not that Overbeck had always understood Nietzsche, "who then had already long been on his great journey of self-discovery," not that Overbeck, who was seven years older than Nietzsche "blindly followed him on this journey," which would have "thrown him off his own course."[62] But Overbeck's rejection by his theological colleagues was also dictated at least in part by his "friendship with Nietzsche."[63] Overbeck's polemical text and Nietzsche's first *Untimely Meditation* were, as Nietzsche wrote in his dedication to Overbeck, "a pair of twins from one house."[64]

Even Nietzsche knew that this "anonymous darling of fortune," as Overbeck had referred to himself at some point, was "a lonely seafarer" in his own manner.[65] But Nietzsche was touched by Overbeck's "tranquility and benign steadfastness," which in his contact with him had almost allowed him the last yard of sure footing that could save him from "capsizing."[66] He appreciated Overbeck's labyrinthine statements, which "so politely [. . .] I would almost like to say *cleverly*" devoured his thoughts.[67] His rhetoric is, in fact, entirely cross-grained and, in the syntax, resists any accommodation to normative judgment. His sober prose, in disdain of any pretentiousness, reflects the Medusa's glance of his scholarly eye. "The concept of scholarship with which I have entered my relationship to it is that it is appointed to exercise a kind of last judgment on things, and only thus have I arrived at my concept of theology at all."[68] "As a theologian," Overbeck knows, as he confesses at a decisive point in his *Confessions*, of no other "capability and destiny of theology with respect to Christianity, as to perform a last judgment of it."[69] Admittedly, this judgment does not lie in this "power of scholarship" alone, but rather depends on the "constitution" of the individual who takes this task upon himself. He would have to be "an extraordinary person," one who would also know himself "called upon for extraordinary things."

"Without doubt, I am not such a person."[70] The tension between *this* task of theology and his "awareness" that he "is nothing special"[71] pervades the autobiographical sketches of this "odd" professor of theology,[72] forcing him to abdicate the office of judge. "People are not called to be Last Judges for each other. For as great as their constant aptness is to put on airs of a judge of this manner, they have therefore pushed the whole idea of the Last Judgment to the very margins of their species. Here below, it is in the proper sense of the word *unpractical*."[73] For this reason as well, Overbeck would rather do battle on the side of nonbelief [*Unglaube*]: "For the nonbeliever knows that for humanity, there is no such thing as a Last Judgment, and therefore also nothing that could take its place, even if it merely took on its countenance. *Human* morality in general should make do without any idea of a Last Judgment. One may have serious reservations about that . . . naturally, they can hardly be placated by the admission of such a foolish delusion, as if the judgment that we perform on ourselves, could ever substitute for the Last."[74] The contradiction between an approach toward science and criticism that is continually sharpening as it develops and his prudent, reserved, almost shy manner has allowed him to exert all punches with only the left hand, and ultimately, it thrusts him into the role of an apocalyptic thinker set on remaining silent.

Augustine's *Confessions* describe the path of a late ancient pagan rhetorician into the Christian community, which prepares itself as a church to determine the history of the coming centuries. Overbeck's *Confessions* describes the path of a late Christian professor of theology and church history when Christianity becomes ripe for a critical or for a profane (which is the same thing) historiography, in an interim during which the fronts between belief and unbelief are oddly intertwined. Overbeck's questions for theology have remained unanswered to this day. With Overbeck's question in mind, one may confidently ignore the shifting fashions of theological exegesis and apologetics.

Translation provided by Mara H. Benjamin

PART III

THEOLOGY AFTER THE COPERNICAN TURN

11

Dialectic and Analogy[1]

I

Since Copernicus, Nietzsche once remarked, man is falling from the center of the universe toward an X. Man has not yet found his place in the Copernican cosmos. The Copernican revolution not only antiquated an astronomic theory but also actually destroyed the order of man's universe. Since Copernicus, man's place in the cosmos is an open question, to which modern philosophy repeatedly tries to respond. Kant interpreted his *Critique of Pure Reason* in the light of the Copernican revolution, and rightly so.[2] For what Kant proposes is a philosophy of inwardness, a turn from the universe to human categories. Since the external order of the universe has become meaningless, the only dimension in which man can be at home is his own self. Time as the inner sense corresponds to man's inwardness; therefore, history becomes his home after his place in the natural cosmos has been shaken.

The historical method of the modern era cannot be understood simply as an inquiry into the events of the past. This method became possible only in the frame of a specific interpretation of history that is characteristic for the modern period. It is our thesis that this interpretation of history does not appear in isolation but is related to the basic shift from the medieval to the modern age—the turn from the Ptolemaic to the Copernican cosmology. The dispute around the historical method that was the main issue in the theological controversy of the nineteenth century and that has become the main issue again in the recent controversy on kerygma and mythos[3] involves a consideration of the major principle of modern thought: the principle of history.

It is indeed at first sight paradoxical to subject the principle of history to a historical inquiry. The inquiry into the principle of history is made possible, however, by the very principle itself. Wilhelm Dilthey considered this possibility as the ultimate liberation of the human mind. We cannot share Dilthey's optimism about the ultimate liberation of the human mind through the historical self-consciousness, for a critique of man's historical reasoning which Dilthey envisaged as a systematic basis of his extensive historical research, but never came to develop, would reveal the price such a liberation demands of man's substance. A critique of man's historical self-consciousness would open our eyes to the Medusa that lurks behind the freedom of historicism. Our time has seen many attempts to veil the consequences of historicism. The most recent attempt was made by Martin Heidegger,[4] who wanted to serve the systematic purpose of Dilthey's research and at the same time escape the perilous consequences of the ultimate liberation of the human mind. In order to prepare the terrain for the critique of man's historical reasoning, we must inquire how the principle of history became the guiding pattern of modern thought. The historical criticism that undermined the authority of the scriptures and that became the particular issue in the dispute between religion and philosophy since the beginning of the modern era until today touches only the surface of the problem.

II

Augustine may rightly be called the father of the Catholic Church. In the twenty-two books on the *Civitas Dei* he founded the structure of medieval society and provided the pattern for every Catholic interpretation of history.[5] Augustine's theology of history denies, however, the all-importance of history and removes the fuse from the chiliastic idea that was intrinsic to the eschatology of the early church. The chiliastic prophecy of the Apocalypse of John, which, as a vision of future events, threatened time and again the foundations of the church, was integrated by Augustine into the context of the church. Christ's kingdom on earth should not be expected in the future, and the "thousand years" describe in fact the reign of Christ and the saints in the church. Since Christ the history of the world has become irrelevant. Christian eschatology does not wait for a theatrical spectacle in the arena of history, and its interest shifts to the destiny of the soul at the end of its earthly journey. Man's earthly journey is a transitory pilgrimage "progressing" toward the heavenly city that is not on earth. The *Civitas Dei* and the *Civitas terrena* reflect man's attitude toward reason. Cain is the symbol for man in the *Civitas terrena*, for man in "history." World history is only a succession of Cain-like crimes and a show of man's vanity, pride, and ambition. Cain's victim, Abel, symbolizes the *Civitas Dei*; he foreshadows the destiny of Christ on earth. The history of the *Civitas Dei* is only a pilgrimage on earth, and it would have seemed absurd to Augustine to plot out the history of the world since Christ in any pattern of stages, progressing toward a goal beyond the event of Christ. Since Augustine the eschatology of history was relegated to the outskirts of popular belief, superstition, and—heresy.

The theology of Joachim of Fiore contained the dynamite that was to explode the foundations of medieval religion and society that had been drawn in the light of Augustine's theology of history. In Joachim's theology of history there emerges a principle that will challenge the "chiliastic" reign of the Catholic Church. He envisages a new era in human history that shall supersede the era of the church. The age in which the papal church reigns suddenly shifts into the "middle" between the first period from Abraham to Christ and the new period of the Holy Ghost. I think that it becomes clear how the term "Middle Ages" was coined. The scheme, antiquity—Middle Ages—modern times, is nothing but a secularized version of Joachim's "trinitarian" scheme of history: the period of the Father, from Abraham to Christ; the period of the Son, from Christ until "now" (ca. 1200); and the period of the Holy Ghost. I think that the old "scholarly" controversy of how to fix the date from the beginning of the modern period may be resolved in the light of the fact that in Joachim's theology of history the division between "Middle" Ages and "modern" times becomes relevant in a precise way.

Joachim's theology of history not only challenges Augustine's theology of *history* but marks a change in the theological pattern itself. Joachim's theology denies the "central" position of Jesus Christ, who, according to the orthodox Christian tradition, divides all time into "before" and "after." Christ is submerged in the process of history that is greater than he. The goal of Joachim's theology is not in Christ but in the Holy Ghost, which supersedes Christ, and this marks the pattern for all Spiritualists from the Franciscans and Sebastian Franck and Jacob Boehme through the German idealists, Fichte, Hegel, and Schelling, to the modern Russian "Sophianists," Bulgakov and Berdyaev. The *imago trinitatis* of Christian theology turns into a principle of the historical process, and the different persons of the Trinity mark the different periods of history. Only in the union of the three periods of history does the unity of the Trinity become manifest: the first period is the period of the Father, the second is the period of the Son, and the third the period of the Holy Ghost. The persons of the Trinity—even as the stages of history—are ordered in a progressive succession of divine manifestation. Joachim's "trinitarian" theology of history stands behind Hegel's dialectical method. Hegel, for whom the stage of the spirit is the highest phase of history, insists on the intimate relation between the "principle" of Trinity and his notion of the spirit. The divine, according to Hegel, is recognized as Spirit only if it is recognized as trinitarian. For Joachim the three stages of history are marked as degrees of cognition: from the *scientia* of the first stage through the *sapientia ex parte* of the second stage to the *plenitudo intellectus* of the third. And again we are reminded of Hegel, who interpreted the history of the world according to stages of cognition, until it reaches, in Hegel's philosophy, the *plenitudo intellectus*. For Hegel as well as for Joachim the Middle Ages are identical with the period of the Son. As I have tried to point out in a study on eschatology,[6] these points of similarity in Joachim's and Hegel's theory of history are by no means accidental but rooted in their eschatological notion of the spirit. The principle of history that becomes all-important in modern times and the guide for scientific research stems from the eschatological principle of Joachim and Hegel and necessarily involves a critical approach to the scriptures and the tradition of the church. The critique of the scriptures and traditions of the church that led to the conclusion that the mythology of the scriptures has to be surpassed is not only a consequence of the historical inquiry but is at the very root of the historical approach to tradition.

Joachim's principle of history implies, however, a turn not only in the theological pattern but also in the cosmological orientation of man.[7] Again, Augustine's theology can serve as a point of contrast. Augustine's theology of history, its division between the *Civitas terrena* here on earth and the *Civitas Dei* in heaven, presupposes, as does all Christian theology, the basic Ptolemaic division between below and above. I would suggest that astronomical theories have a relevance beyond the limited realm of astronomy and reflect man's general dwelling in the universe. The Ptolemaic pattern provides man with a clear notion of the vertical axis of the universe: he can divide between below and above in a concrete way. The vertical vocabulary is not yet reduced to mere allegory and metaphor and has its roots in the external order of the cosmos. The Ptolemaic earth has yet a heaven above itself, and whatever happens on earth is only an image of the heavenly idea. The "naïve" hope for a kingdom of heaven that will come "down" on earth is not yet a mythological metaphor but corresponds to the cosmological architecture of reality. The liturgy of the Mass presupposes a charismatic union between heaven and earth, and the hierarchical order of church and society corresponds to the divine hierarchy. The very notion of hierarchy involves a basic division between below and above—in a cosmological as well as in a sociological way. The "body" of the church is an organism where the social and the cosmic coalesce. The principle of analogy may best describe the medieval attitude. "Analogy" is not merely a name for a philosophical concept, diluted and emptied of all concrete meaning, as in modern scholasticism that artificially transplants the principle of analogy into a climate where it cannot develop. For in the Middle Ages the principle of analogy expresses the basic correspondence between below and above, heaven and earth, the natural and the supernatural.

The Copernican revolution, however, not only overthrew an old astronomical theory but also destroyed man's dwelling in the cosmos. The Catholic Church was right in attacking the Copernican theory because the new cosmology indeed threatened the analogy of earthly and heavenly order. It is true that the church later compromised with the new cosmology under the pressure of "scientific" public opinion, which developed in opposition to the church. When the Catholic Church could no longer withstand the public pressure, she did concede the possibility of a cosmology that explicitly denied the correlation of above and below and implicitly destroyed the correspondence of the natural and the supernatural. When the Catholic Church could no longer oppose the Copernican theory, she had to minimize its importance to a "mere" astronomical theory that had no bearing on metaphysics and theology. In truth, however, the Copernican revolution shattered all hierarchical structure, the heavenly as well as the earthly. For a hierarchy is built on the division between what is above and what is below, and these concepts were rendered relative and illusory by the Copernican theory. In the Copernican language, above and below become mere "metaphors" and are not rooted in the external order of the cosmos.

The earth, in the Copernican universe, no longer "reflects" heavenly perfection. The vertical axis crumbles, and above and below can no longer be genuinely distinguished. This situation is at the root of modern theology and metaphysics. The Copernican cosmology may inspire a pantheistic religion and philosophy where no above or below is marked, where the division between the creator and creation is obliterated, where perfection is not sought in heaven but on earth, but a theistic religion and philosophy are forced to retreat into a mere *ordre du coeur*. A cosmology that inspires Bruno's hymns and Spinoza's geometry of ethics outraged Luther and terrified Pascal. For Luther the external world stands under the whip of the law and is rigorously set apart from the light of the Gospel; grace and redemption reign only in heaven, which, Luther emphasizes, has its seat only in the individual heart and conscience. The cosmos and man in the cosmos remain outside the realm of redemption.[1] For Luther and his generation there is no possible analogy between the earthly and the heavenly life, and all attempts at "correlation" between heaven and earth are denounced as the work of Satan. It was the division between above and below that enabled the Catholic Church to "represent" the heavenly hierarchies on earth. Protestant theology attacked the very idea of a representation of heaven on earth through the church and its liturgy as mere idolatry, and it was justified on the basis of the new cosmology that destroyed the basis for all hierarchical order. There was no longer a place for hierarchy and priesthood. The sectarian attack on the church—everybody is a priest; all the congregation is holy—had the "democratic" undertone: nobody is a priest; there is no place for a hierarchical church on earth.

It is a basic, but seldom recognized fact that since the Copernican revolution theistic religion has stood without a cosmology and has been forced to retreat to the domain of man's "inwardness." Tradition and the scriptures that speak in "primitive" and "external" terms of heaven and earth, of the divine kingdom, of creator and creation, must now be interpreted in an internalized and mystical way. It is true that the orthodox tradition is not lacking in hints that heaven may be inside the human heart. But it is a basic difference whether the image is internalized, as in the orthodox tradition, on the *basis* of an established cosmological correspondence, or whether the internalization has not a possible counterbalance in the external order of things and becomes purely metaphorical.[8]

If the cosmological order presupposes the division between heaven and earth, then a bold statement that heaven is in man's heart translates the cosmological order into an *ordre du coeur*. But if the *ordre du coeur* has no correlative in the external order of the cosmos, then its "logic" only proves that heaven is lost. In Copernican cosmology the basic category of medieval theology becomes meaningless—the principle of analogy between below and above, natural and supernatural—and there remains only a dialectic of identity between creator and creation (pantheistic tradition) or a dialectic of their irreparable alienation (Luther, Pascal, Kierkegaard, Barth). In either form the dialectical principle testifies to the fact that the analogy between the natural and the supernatural has become illusory. Karl Barth insists in his Protestant church dogmatics that the only serious difference between Catholic and Protestant theology is the principle of *analogia entis,* and he considers all other reasons for a Christian not to enter the Catholic Church as shortsighted and trivial.[9] Barth denounces, however, the principle of analogy as the "invention of the Antichrist." It is not within the scope of a historical interpretation to take sides in the internal controversy between Karl Barth and Catholic theology, but it seems to me that the principle of analogy was justified in a universe where the natural and the supernatural were distinguished and still related to each other and therefore permitted comparison. It is only in a Copernican universe that the principle of analogy (and all that is connected with it, the liturgy and sacraments that are based on a correspondence of the natural and the supernatural) becomes meaningless. So long as the analogy was cosmologically possible, it was also legitimate in theology, and all the church fathers from Augustine to Thomas Aquinas expressed their theological doctrines naturally in the grammar of analogy. A theology that has lost the cosmological basis for the principle of analogy but nevertheless continues with the method of analogy becomes purely metaphorical. In a Copernican universe a theology that takes its symbols and presuppositions seriously can only proceed by the method of dialectic.

I am not presenting this thesis on the relation of Ptolemaic and Copernican cosmology in order to "prove" the relation of cause and effect in history, as if the cosmological structure would "determine" the ideological superstructure. For the pattern of cause and effect can easily be turned around and would also hold true. Marx developed the series from the economical structure to the ideological superstructure, and Max Weber turned the series around from the spiritual structure to the economic effect. In the present case I would hold that the astronomical theory does not "cause" the change in man's attitude toward the natural and the supernatural but rather "expresses" it. Moreover, the turn from the Ptolemaic to the Copernican cosmology does not come suddenly following an unexpected empirical discovery, but this turn is prepared for by long birth pangs. The beginning of this change in man's orientation toward the natural and spiritual world may be traced back to Joachim's theological speculations on history and German mystical philosophy.

The major difference between Joachim's theory of history and the orthodox Catholic view lies in the historical principle. For Augustine and the medieval theology, history presents man in his transitory state. History is the sign of man's *cor inquietum* that has no stable point until it finds rest in the divine. Joachim's theology, however, transposes the principle of history from the human into the divine realm. Change and process become divine attributes. It is the divine *cor inquietum* that finds no rest until it is fulfilled in man. The myth of the birth of God in man that emerged in German mysticism at the same time as Joachim's speculations (and not entirely independent of them) emphasizes the process in the divinity. The divine process still remains in the Neoplatonic tradition in the realm of transcendence, but in German mysticism the mystical transcendence becomes dependent on man. The Catholic Church was aware that the doctrines of Eckhart and his disciples did not mean the God who created heaven and earth, but a *deus in nobis*.

The philosophy of history of German idealism represents a fusion of Joachimite theology and German mysticism of the divine process. Here the orthodox theistic concepts of a creator standing over and against his creation are seen as "shallow," and pantheistic mystical terms such as *hen kai pan* become the secret symbols of the new theology, already for Lessing. It is Lessing, again, who enthusiastically hailed the "eternal Gospel" of Joachim and the Franciscan spirituals, and in his *Erziehung des Menschengeschlechts*[10] used Joachim's speculations on history as the blueprint for his own theory of divine economy. In the course of the development of German idealism the sense of the "economy of the divine" becomes more and more equivocal as at once a *genetivus subjectivus* and a *genetivus objectivus*. Is the divine economy only an economy of the divine with man without involving the divinity, or is the divine itself in the process? German idealism from Fichte through Schelling to Hegel tends more and more to favor the second version: the living God of the Old and New Testaments is interpreted as a dynamic God, as the divinity in process. Both in its theology and in its epistemology German idealism marks the apotheosis of process over reality, function over substance, energy over matter. In theology such a pattern could lead only to the annihilation of all divine substance and to the deification of the process itself. Change and history become the basic attributes of the divine, and the divine life is subjected to the general *moira* of time. It is true that both Fichte and Hegel point out that the process of divinity they describe is not a process in time but only of a "logical nature." But this cannot obliterate the fact that process cannot become manifest except in time, and here our point is proved by the disciples of German idealism in the nineteenth and twentieth centuries: Christian Hermann Weisse, Johannes Volkelt, and Ernst Troeltsch. The divine is no longer beyond the tragedy of time and change; in fact, it becomes dependent on man's effort and self-realization. Troeltsch in his Protestant *Glaubenslehre* did not hesitate to describe divine life as dependent on the increase of spiritual life in man. Such a liberal *Glaubenslehre* was not far away from the post-Christian theogonies of Hermann Schwarz, Max Scheler, and Leopold Ziegler.

It would be a mistake, however, to imagine that the idea of a dynamic God is limited to the theology of liberal Protestantism or post-Christian theogonies. An activism in the domain of the divine is even so emphasized by the neo-orthodox dialectical theology, which interprets divine revelation solely in terms of action and even while minimizing divine order and stability. Paradoxically, the dialectic of synthesis (Hegel) and the dialectic of antithesis (Kierkegaard) meet in the dialectical theology. *Les extrèmes se touchent* in the dynamistic interpretation of the divine. It is true that, following Kierkegaard's attack on Hegel, dialectical theology was eager to distinguish its negative dialectic from the synthetic Hegelian method of dialectic. But Karl Barth's theology is not identical with Kierkegaard's protest against Hegel, since from Kierkegaard's position no theology would be at all possible. Dialectical theology laid such absolute stress on the antithesis between the human and the divine that, once the contradiction was resolved (and this is the hidden aim of all theology), the new relation between man and God could only be expressed in terms of identity. The extreme alternatives of either contradiction or identity between man and God can only be resolved in the unity of thesis, antithesis, and synthesis. It is true that in dialectical theology the synthetic point of the dialectical pattern is pushed to the infinite. A mathematical simile may best illustrate the formal relation between the antithetical and the synthetical methods of dialectic. A plane passing through a cone parallel to the base always cuts a circle. If, however, the plane is tilted it cuts an ellipse, and, as the plane is increasingly tilted, one focus of the ellipse becomes more and more eccentric until the curve changes from an ellipse to a parabola. The basic dialectic between the human and the divine remains the same in the antithetical and synthetical dialectic; it is only a question of how far the plane is tilted. In the synthetical dialectic the plane is almost parallel to the base (the circle is the mathematical figure of Hegel). In the antithetical dialectic the plane is tilted until it shifts from an ellipse to a parabola (the open parabola is the mathematical figure of Karl Barth).

Our remarks would be ill understood if they were taken as a critique of the dialectical theology, since they only seek to point out that modern theology "must" use a principle of dialectic and not of analogy. There is, indeed, no other possibility to describe the relation between the divine and the human if the cosmological correspondence between the natural and the supernatural is broken but through a dialectic of anithetical terms. But I would hold that the necessity of the dialectical method in theology in *our* cosmological frame does not invalidate the medieval theology of analogy in *its* frame. The dialectical method and the stress on inwardness that mark all the varieties of modern theology only testify to the fact that the creator of heaven and earth is veiled and that the realm of physical reality is lost for religious experience. The principle of dialectic has the advantage over the principle of analogy in formulating our situation. But, I think, it is important to stress that the dialectical principle is our truth, conditioned by the fact that a possible correlation between the human and the divine broke down in our cosmological frame. The principle of dialectic is historically conditioned and cannot be applied universally. Modern theology is in no way entitled to look down on medieval theology that could still presuppose the correlation of the natural and supernatural.

The difference between the medieval and the modern principle may also be traced in contemporary Catholic theology. Surely modern Catholic theology must also formulate its doctrines in accordance with the dogma of the church. The dogma that was last formulated in the *constitutio de fide catholica* of the Vatican (1870) teaches that the principle of analogy should be the rule of all theological method. It is known that Thomas Aquinas was elevated in the last century to the classical doctor of the church. But recent Catholic theology does not insist, as Thomas Aquinas did, on the divine order and hierarchy, on the correlation and similitude of the natural and the supernatural, but rather stresses within the limits of the principle of analogy the paradoxality of the mystery and points to the dissimilitude of the natural and the supernatural. The classical principle of analogy goes through a metamorphosis in the theologies of Henri de Lubac and Erich Przywara and takes the form of a synthetical and antithetical dialectic. It should be obvious that this metamorphosis in Catholic theology is equally determined by the breakdown of medieval cosmology that enabled still a basic and "naïve" analogy between the natural and the supernatural.

Our thesis has been, simply, that the cosmology of a period is relevant for its theology and cannot be dismissed as an external element. This "simple" thesis, however, would remain quite arbitrary despite the fact that it seems natural to assume a connection between the various doctrines of an age and could not command any consequences unless we were able to assume and to investigate a common root of theology and cosmology. I did not refer to the *cosmos* or to the *theos* but to cosmo*logy* and to theo*logy*, and the difference should be obvious. It is man's image of the divine and man's image of the cosmos that are at stake. The *logos* in both cosmology and theology is the human spirit, and all that could and can be stated is that the human image of the divine and the human image of the cosmos depend on each other and "correct" each other. I cannot consider the event of the Copernican cosmology as an event that happens to man *ex machina*. It is man who speaks in his cosmology about his relation to the cosmos. If my argument is granted, then, I think, we can understand why the relation between the cosmology and theology is of such importance that it may serve even as a criterion for separating the wheat from the chaff in our present-day religious thinking. It remains illusionary, for instance, to try to return from Bergson to Thomas Aquinas or from Husserl or Kant to Thomas Aquinas, for the basic presuppositions of Thomas that guided his principle of analogy cannot be renewed at the asking. This thesis does not imply that the presuppositions of Thomas are false; it simply states that they cannot be renewed. The Ptolemaic cosmology is not false over and against the Copernican cosmology that is all true. In both cosmologies man not only describes external structures, but in these images *sua res agitur*.

The principle of history that rules our modern historical research proved to be not only a method of philological investigation of ancient texts but also a fundamental principle that transformed man's reality in the modern era. The dynamism intrinsic in this principle of history transformed man's image of the divine and man's image of the universe, as well as his image of himself. The principle of history destroyed all substance and reduced everything and everybody to a mere function of a general process. This principle must finally turn against itself and transform itself into a mere function of history. This last transformation Dilthey, and not only Dilthey, hailed as the ultimate liberation of the human mind. The other side of the coin, however, is that the liberated human mind may turn against itself and transform its own substance into a function. Hegel saw in this end man's highest achievement—we, however, see also his crisis.

12

Theodicy and Theology: A Philosophical Analysis of Karl Barth's Dialectical Theology[1]

I

Since the emancipation of philosophy from the tutelage of ecclesiastical theology, no theological work has commanded so much attention outside the walls of the church as has the "dialectical theology" of our century. It seems that the general bias against theology that runs through the modern period breaks down before Karl Barth's theology. His work has added a new chapter in the history of the dialectical method. Since the method and program of Barth's dialectics constitutes perhaps the most significant contribution to the general consciousness of our age, it will be necessary to consider his work from the side of philosophy.

Philosophy is an inquiry of human reason unassisted by divine revelation. Theology presents itself as an exegesis of the word of divine revelation. Philosophy can never accept the self-interpretation of theology, but it can try to understand the *meaning* of the theological exegesis. For even in the "alienated" form of divine revelation, by looking at man's nature as it is "in heaven" and judging man's life as it is "on earth," theology can serve as a concrete negation of a status quo that the dictatorship of common sense accepts as man's permanent situation. Could not the theological negation of the mundane realm be catalytic for philosophy in developing categories of dialectics by which it can unmask the conventional element in what poses as man's perennial nature and point beyond the status quo to the ideal standard by which man may be judged?

Theological language is born out of the dualism between the ideal standard and the status quo of man's situation. So long as this cleavage is not healed, there remains a legitimate task for theology. But the language of theology itself reflects the cleavage between the ideal and the ruling norms of man and society. In the moment that the ideal standards that theology has put as a judgment upon man and society are realized in the course of human history, the task of theology has been fulfilled. It is in theology and not in the segmented natural and moral sciences, like physics, biology, or psychology, that man's actual history is reflected. The development of theological language is, therefore, relevant for a philosophy that studies the stages of man's self-realization.

The method of our inquiry is philosophical analysis; its subject, the dialectical method as it is developed in the work of Karl Barth. The aim of this analysis is to point to some general patterns that come to the fore in this theological opus and that seem significant for a philosophical analysis of the *condition humaine*. Such an analysis is guided by the premise that theological discourse is human discourse.

But is there any possibility of inquiring into the meaning of theological doctrines from a universal matrix? If the unity of human discourse is taken as a matrix, then even "theological" statements (that claim validity in a "theological circle" only) *must* be subject to the methods of philosophical inquiry; for all theology, however authoritatively it may present itself as a legitimate exegesis of a divine revelation, is, first of all, human discourse. Even the "word of God" is as a "word" subject to the scheme of the word and thereby to human inquiry. This simple but fundamental premise gives us an opportunity to start a philosophic inquiry of theological discourse.

Symbols developed in the language of theology as a commentary to a canon of sacred scriptures (the form of commentary seems to me essentially connected with a program of a theology that presents itself as an exegesis of a divine revelation) are fundamental for an interpretation of the "naked" human situation. Who would hold it against Columbus that he believed all his life that he had reached India by way of the west, when actually he had discovered a new continent? In a philosophical analysis of theology, doctrines are not sounded out for their concordance with sacred scriptures and established tradition of the churches, but rather are treated as human categories. Theological symbols are man's epigraphy. In these symbols man is writing his own history; they are constitutive of his own genesis.

What is dialectic? The term comes up time and again in various constellations of the history of philosophy, theology, or sociology. But all various forms of dialectic presuppose that the "dialectical method" is based on the dialogue. The dialogue presupposes that no single person is self-sufficient for the establishment of the *logos*. The logos can be realized only in a form of discourse. Since the logos can be interpreted, however, as onto*logical* or anthropo*logical*, the method of dialectic can operate in a twofold way. The logos of Heraclitus is ontological and anthropological: "The logos, though men associate with it most closely, yet they are separated from it, and those things which they encounter daily seem to them strange." The Sophists took the principle over from Heraclitus and developed it into a method of discourse. Dialectics can serve in the process of discourse as a method of questioning absolute dogmatic statements. It may uphold a critical stand against the perennial dogmatism of common sense. The dialectic of Socrates rested on the same critical principle. His discourse was "ironic" intending to shake the naïve confidence of the accepted conventional patterns. But the Sophistic dialectic might also become "eristic" and thus serve as a technique of apology, irrespective of the actual situation (and thereby strengthen the interest of the established canon). This ambiguous use of the method brought it into disrepute and led Kant to condemn the paralogism of metaphysical reasoning as "dialectic." Will the theological negation of the mundane conventional order be able (as a permanent element of critique) to prevent an ambiguous use of the dialectical *sic et non*? Or will the theological base of dialectical theology eclipse the critical element and introduce the apology of the world by the door of a theology?

Theology, according to Karl Barth, is possible only "in the form of a dialogue, in the discourse of question and answer." Only in this movement between question and answer does the thetic-antithetic character of theology realize itself. Theology is "dialectical thought" (*KD* I, 1, 454; *KD* = *Die Kirchliche Dogmatik* [8 vols., 1932–52]). If the dialectical character of theology is to be taken seriously, such a theology must remain an open discourse and cannot close itself in a self-sufficient system. God's "own word," his "theology," would be, as Karl Barth once remarked, "undialectical theology." Man, however, is mortal and cannot claim the "last word" for himself (*KD* I, 1, 460). Can theology resist the temptation to be the "last word" by disguising the mortal word of man as a dogmatic "word of God"?

II

The constellation at the birth of dialectical theology is marked by the union of Hegel's philosophy and Kierkegaard's opposition to Hegel's method of mediation. Hegel developed his philosophy as an exegesis to the prologue of the Johannine Gospel: in the beginning was the logos, and the logos was with God, and the logos was God. The Johannine equations prefigure Hegel's set of identities: God is the logos, the logos is the logic, the logic is the truth, the truth is spirit, the spirit is life. In the frame of such a "circular logic," Hegel develops his scheme of thesis, antithesis, and synthesis on the basis of the Johannine equations. Kierkegaard's opposition aims at Hegel's "mediation" of contradictions, for contradictions cannot be mediated in a "higher" synthesis, but must, according to Kierkegaard, be decided in "either" one way "or" the other. Therefore, Kierkegaard calls his major work: *Either-Or*, in which the "qualitative difference" between the human and the divine is stressed. It was Kierkegaard's "negative dialectic" that inspired Barth's insistence on the hiatus between God and man, on the difference between creator and creature.

But Kierkegaard's opposition to Hegel's synthesis can never be forged into a theology, for it spends itself in a negative rhetoric of protest. If the difference between the divine and the human, the creator and the creature, is introduced into the grammar of a dialectical theology, then the hiatus is stressed only in order to bring the reconciliation between the divine and the human in the act of redemption into better relief. If Barth's theology stresses the negative element in the relation between God and man, then this antithesis has systematically a quite different function from Kierkegaard's repetitious insistence on the hiatus. The theological pattern ultimately emphasizes all the more strongly the synthesis of reconciliation in the state of redemption. Thus the pendulum swings in a wider radius from the negative to the positive pole than either in Hegel's philosophy of reconciliation or in Kierkegaard's negative protest. It is the nemesis of Barth's dialectical theology that it must describe the reconciliation between God and man in a way that outdoes Hegel's dialectic of reconciliation. The specter of Hegel haunts the development of Karl Barth's theology from the beginning to the end. It will be our task to bring this specter into the open.

III

The universality of Hegel's philosophy is contested by the universality of Barth's theology. Hegel's panphilosophical matrix that tried to integrate the realm of theology is challenged by Barth's pantheological premise that serves as a yardstick for all other realms of human theory and practice. It is not accidental that Karl Barth found it necessary to discuss at length the philosophies of Descartes, Leibniz, Rousseau, Kant, Hegel, Feuerbach, Overbeck, Nietzsche, Heidegger, and Sartre. In these discussions he offered a history of modern philosophy that is more penetrating than most current "histories" of philosophy.

The comparison between Hegel's dialectic philosophy and Barth's dialectic theology suggests itself, if one considers the structural scheme that rules their doctrines. The dialectic of Hegel and of Barth is in exegesis of trinitarian Christology. The incarnation is the alpha and omega of man's destiny and provides the schematism for apprehending nature and man. Christology, neither for Hegel's dialectic philosophy nor for Barth's dialectic theology, is simply a theory of the religious consciousness (in a subjective way), but rather the seal by which nature and man are stamped. The *exegesis* of the nature of Christ provides for both the pattern by which the entire range of the natural and human realm is illuminated. Hegel is the last philosopher of the Occident who has made the Christian doctrine of the Trinity and the mystery of the incarnation the cornerstone of his philosophy. Since Augustine's great work *De trinitate*, the doctrine of the Trinity has served as a scheme for theological and philosophical speculations. With Joachim of Fiore the scheme of the Trinity became also the basis for an interpretation of history. Hegel's dialectical philosophy tried to combine Augustine's speculative interpretation of the Trinity with Joachim's historical interpretation of the trinitarian dogma.

It is the same scheme of dialectic that gives structure to Barth's theology. Recent critics of Barth's theology have tried to limit the impact of the dialectical method to only a small segment of his work. But the interpretation of Hans Urs von Balthasar is dictated by the desire to synthesize Barth's theology with the general Roman Catholic theology and philosophy that is ruled by the principle of *analogia entis*.[2] Such an attempt must fail (despite the extraordinary circumspection of an interpreter like Hans Urs von Balthasar). It is not a "misunderstanding" on the side of Karl Barth when he considers the principle of *analogia entis* as "the invention of the Antichrist," which stands as a stumbling block between him and Roman Catholic philosophy and theology (*KD* I, 1, viii). The difference between the principle of *analogia entis* and the method of dialectics is neither in the realm of doctrine nor in the domain of method. It reaches much deeper into the foundation of schematism.

Medieval philosophy and theology are anchored in a cosmological principle. The *analogia entis* presupposes the hierarchical cosmos that is divided into different realms and regions. The principle of *analogia entis* is responsible for the characteristic conjunction "and" that is omnipresent in Catholic theology and philosophy. Nature *and* grace, works *and* faith, reason *and* revelation, scripture *and* tradition, are the bricks of the *duplex ordo*, which provides the skeleton of Catholic philosophy and theology. The principle of dialectics is anthropological, and Karl Barth's theology is significant and meaningful only in the general turn from the medieval cosmological pattern to the modern anthropological scheme. Therefore, he opposes (even in his later orthodox period) the principle of *analogia entis* as a great imposture on the philosophical and on the theological inquiry (*KD* II, 1, 658). For him, the *duplex ordo* of natural and supernatural smacks of "double bookkeeping" (*KD* III, 1, 576).

As a theology of actualism, dialectical theology contradicts the Thomistic philosophy and theology on the basic notion of being. The symbols of creation, sin, and redemption are not interpreted in the pattern of natural-supernatural, but in a temporal (transhistorical) scheme. Its categories are not unfolding the nature of things but unfolding a sequence of events. Only such an ontological philosophy would be adequate to express the basic schematism of dialectical theology that could develop the temporal structure of its categories. Most probably, Bergson's or Heidegger's anti-Aristotelian philosophy would provide the epistemological and ontological foundation of Barth's historical categories—as a kind of "logic of events."

The corpus of Barth's writing can be roughly divided into three periods: (1) the period of a "liberal" synthetic dialectic (up until *Roemerbrief* [1919][3]); (2) the period of negative antithetic dialectic (from *Roemerbrief* [1923] to the *Christliche Dogmatik* [1928]); and (3) the period of an "orthodox" synthetic dialetic from the beginning of his *Kirchliche Dogmatik* (1932). Such a division does violence to the very complexity of Barth's theology and serves only as a guide for orientation in the labyrinth of his immense work. Yet our threefold division may point out the prevalent tendencies and isolate its leitmotifs. I consider it methodologically wrong to play the early period against the later. Neither should one interpret the second edition of the *Roemerbrief* as "classical" and dismiss the late period of the *Kirchliche Dogmatik* as mere petrifaction in orthodox patterns, nor should one dismiss the earlier works as "chaotic" and "expressionistic," as Hans Urs von Balthasar does, and accept with Karl Barth the latest reading of his work as the authentic one. An interpretation has the freedom (and also the task) to bring out the unity of motifs where the author believes he has left not one brick intact of his earliest construction.

IV

The first edition of the *Roemerbrief* (1919), which was not noticed by the general public (and is therefore a rarity even in theological libraries), contains, as Hans Urs von Balthasar first pointed out, the basic leitmotifs of Barth's entire opus. The structure of his first commentary on Paul's Epistle to the Romans is "dynamic eschatology." The drama described starts (like Paul's economy of salvation) from the eon of death, which is the realm of the natural cosmos, and points toward the eon of life, in which the "original harmony" between the divine and the human is reestablished. The movement from this eon to the next is possible, since man has preserved a "memory" of the original identity between the divine and the human. The Platonic anamnesis serves as a catalyst in the "economy of salvation." Paul's theology of history is interpreted in the light of Origen and Hegel as a "fall" of the "Spirit" into the plurality of the world. The anamnesis of the original unity of the divine and the human serves as catalyst but cannot bring about redemption. It can only keep man's "longing" alive and point to man's permanent crisis in world-time.

The unity of the original state is interpreted as a sheer immediacy in the relation between God and man. There is no room for a divine "mystery" in the original state, for the category of mystery expresses a negation that would imply darkness in the divine realm. Man in the state of redemption is a "particle" of the divine *dynamis*, and the redeemer becomes the basis of every single person.

Only when man is divided from his original identity with the divine spirit does he become "flesh." The realm of "flesh" constitutes the hiatus between the "ideal" and the "life." The Kantian or Platonic division between transcendence and immanence, the noumenal and the phenomenal, lurks behind man's state of alienation. In the state of reconciliation, however, Hegel's "pantheistic" category of unity seems to be more adequate. The scheme of pantheism that rules the structure of the first *Roemerbrief* is dialectical, as in the German idealism that had tried to historicize Spinoza's pantheism. In such a perspective the idea of creation must be eclipsed. In the beginning God does not "create" man, but lives in unity with the human. History is not the history of creation, but tells the story of the "Fall" and records the "split" in the divine-human unity. Man's integral restitution is described in terms of Origen's *apokatastasis*.

But whereas Origen's concept of *apokatastasis* remains metaphysical, the first edition of the *Roemerbrief* historicizes the Origenistic scheme. The dynamism of eschatology is historical and is described as a "process of life"—a connotation that recalls Hegel's history of the Divine Spirit. Origen's theology, as I have tried to show in my *Occidental Eschatology*, has strongly determined the philosophy of German idealism since the time of Lessing. Hegel's criticism of a religion of the pure heart is repeated in Barth's critique of pietism and goes to the extreme of equating the "objective spirit" with the "holy spirit" (*Roemerbrief* [1919] = *R* 252).

The doctrine of man in the first *Roemerbrief* is heavily spiritualistic. Paul's doctrine of the spiritual man and Nietzsche's idea of the free spirit fuse in Barth's description of the "aristocracy of the spirit" (*R* 47). Only the masses need "piety," "religion," and "churches." The "free spirits" have left behind all realms of "religion, church, school, Judaism, Christianity, morals, and all idealisms" (*R* 181), and let the realm of the absolute spirit (*R* 80) in a kind of superior patience "grow" organically. The relation of the "aristocracy of the spirit" to the "multitudes" is tainted by the Gnostic division between *pneumatikoi* and *psychikoi*.

V

Whereas in the first edition of the *Roemerbrief* the tendency of the dialectical "movement" is toward the pole of redemption (and the present eon is only used as a dark silhouette that stimulates the spirit of critique), the element of critique comes into the center of the second edition. The antithesis in the ternary dialectic that served in the first edition as a transitional element is emphasized in the second edition to such a degree that dialectical theology becomes a "theology of crisis." The spirit of critique is radicalized to a spirit of crisis. The antithesis takes on the aspect of a perennial contradiction. The negative characteristics are exegetically unfolded in all lengths and at all depths. The smell of death reaches to the highest and most sublime realms of human activity. Man's "longing" for God, which in the first edition served as a catalyst, loses its function in the drama of redemption. For even the "plerophory" of a thirst for God could yet disguise man's pharisaic justice, and his *cor inquietum* might yet serve as subterfuge to escape from before the presence of God.

If the dialectic of the first edition of the *Roemerbrief* can be interpreted in the light of a religious Hegelianism, then the second edition reveals the influence of Kierkegaard's negative dialectic on every page. Man in his totality takes on demonic features and functions only as an antithesis in the divine drama of redemption. His ideals are his wall against the divine breakthrough. Therefore, none of man's attitudes is more ambiguous than his religious life. Paul's dialectic of the law gives to the commentator ample opportunity to develop the realm of religion in the light of the ambivalences that fill Paul's concept of the law. Man as *homo religiosus* is the Pharisee under the law: the higher he climbs, the deeper he falls into the abyss of self-righteousness. Man can never escape the demonic ambiguity: he is simultaneously enthusiast *and* obscurantist, prophet *and* Pharisee, priest *and* cleric. With all the power of rhetoric Karl Barth hammers into our consciousness the equation: man = the antithesis of the divine. In the world of the status quo, man is always the "old Adam."

By admitting man's total identity with "old Adam," however, Barth gestures to a point beyond this total identification of man with the smell of death. All the negativity in the equation man equals death can be revealed only in the light of the totally other, in the light of a life in redemption. Man's natural way of the flesh has its own cycle only in the shadow of the totally other possibility. For only because man is already spirit can he experience himself crucified in his flesh. Thus the spirit functions as the Archimedean point that gives man the opportunity to liberate himself from the conditions of his life. The spirit liberates him from taking the realm of the mundane with ultimate seriousness.

The anthropology that breaks through in the period of the second edition of the *Roemerbrief* is a pertinent commentary on Luther's *simul peccator et iustus*. The epistemological *sic et non* of the philosophical dialectic becomes anthropologically rooted. There is a *sic et non* in epistemological dialectic because the *sic et non* runs through man himself: I am as the new man not only he who I am not, but I am also he who I am not (*R* 204). The simultaneity of the old and the new Adam in man is the ontological root of the epistemological *sic et non*.

Some of the critics, such as Albrecht Oepke, Erich Przywara, and Hans Urs von Balthasar, observed early that behind the dualism between creator and creature lurks the original identity between the divine and the human. It is true that the major theme of Barth's second *Roemerbrief* is the qualitative difference between God and man. The identity of the divine and the human is eclipsed, and the divine as the "totally other" to all mundane and human realms rules the negative dialectic. But even if the motif of anamnesis (*R* 188, 212) has a less important function, the lost immediacy between God and man is not forgotten in the process of man's individuation, which is concretely the process of his separation from God. With the appearance of individuation, the state "where God as God and man as man are not two but one" (*R* 233) is over. Individuation, it seems, is identical with man as a "creature" separated from God. In the state of redemption the unity between the divine and the human is established. Only through redemption does man know that he lives in separation and in death (*R* 186, 216, 264).

The dualism between the old Adam and the new, between "Adam" and "Christ" in man, exists only transitionally. The dualism exists only in transition and surpasses itself (*R* 155). At this crucial point the dialectic theology of our century comes structurally nearest to Hegel's dialectic. The antithesis between the divine and the mundane, which is the basic theme of the second edition of the *Roemerbrief*, comes into relief only on the premise of a presupposed identity.

VI

It seems that the most contradictory criticisms that have been made against the second edition of the *Roemerbrief* are really directed against one and the same point: the dialectical method. If some critics, like H. W. Schmidt and W. Koepp, "accuse" Barth's theology of the *Roemerbrief* of coming dangerously near to a Manichaean dualism and other critics detect in the same theology a principle of pantheism (A. Oepke) at work or theopanism (as E. Przywara and H. U. v. Balthasar like to "classify" it), they really attack the dialectical method from different angles. It is characteristic of the dialectical method that one element can be isolated which is seemingly contradicted by another element. Manichaean dualism and monistic pantheism are only opposites in the catalogue of a library, but they can serve as complementary elements of a dialectical method. Theological critics have pointed to an "unorthodox" radicalism in the second edition of the *Roemerbrief* and tend to forget that Karl Barth's work is a commentary on Paul's Epistle to the Romans. Already the dialectic of grace and law in Paul's Epistle to the Romans comes "dangerously" near Gnostic Manichaeism, on the one hand, and "theopanism," on the other. Paul's Epistle to the Romans has served as the Magna Carta of all great Christian "heretics": Marcion, Luther, and Karl Barth. The only orthodox theologian decisively determined by Paul's Epistle to the Romans was Augustine. But Augustine first joined a Manichaean community and could never obliterate the traces of his Gnostic past. Is it accidental that the orthodox classical *dux studiorum* of Roman Catholic philosophy and theology is Thomas and not Augustine?

Even if the schematism of Hegel's dialectical philosophy and Barth's dialectical theology coincide, is it not necessary to point to a basic difference in the very nature of the reconciliation? In Barth's theology the reconciliation of the contradictions is never developed "out" of the contradictions themselves, but rather is interpreted as the absolute sovereignty of divine freedom. Barth's dynamic actualism not only is "dynamic" but also presupposes as "actualism" a free act that remains forever a divine prerogative. Barth, indeed, describes the movement from man as antithesis to God to man in reconciliation with God in a language that originates in Hegel's dialectical dynamism. But the movement from alienation to redemption is divine freedom and not necessity. The divine act is not law but free love and, therefore, beyond the reach of philosophy.

Barth would have no quarrel with a "philosophy" that would only take care of "neutral" epistemological problems, but he opposes violently any philosophy that theologizes secretly. Is not his violent attack on philosophy dictated by the spirit of civil war? For whereas Hegel's philosophy secretly theologizes, Barth's dialectical pantheology secretly philosophizes. The point of difference that is usually stressed between Hegel's dialectic of "necessity" and Barth's principle of absolute freedom of the divine synthesis might be unimportant for the methodological procedure, but it loses relevance for the actual structure of their doctrines because in the realm of synthesis a state is reached where the concept of freedom and the concept of necessity turn out to be amphibolic and ambiguous.

It is true that (as Barth once remarked) all philosophy has its origin in theology. It is, however, possible to turn around the relation between theology and philosophy. Dialectical theology can point to the development of history from theology to philosophy: theology is the origin. But an equally legitimate interpretation of this sequence might be given from the other side: philosophy is the end. If I emphasize the origin, then the later development takes the form of gradual alienation and eclipse of the origin. If I emphasize the end, the process of development takes the form of gradual fulfilment. The scheme is the same in both interpretations. At no point does the premise of Barth's pantheology contradict the *scheme* of Hegel's dialectic, even if he attacks Hegel's philosophy as "gnosis."

VII

Whereas the second phase of Barth's theology stands overwhelmingly under the impact of Kierkegaard's negative dialectic, the emphasis shifts in the third phase from a "theology of crisis" to a "theology of reconciliation." God's divine judgment is not the theme; rather, the theme is the divine incarnation in the human flesh. The dialectic of Paul (which also served Kierkegaard as a pattern) is consumed in the Johannine theology of incarnation. It is in the period of the *Kirchliche Dogmatik* that seemingly is furthest away from all "philosophical schematism" that Hegel's spirit (and specter!) are nearest.

In the light of the mystery of incarnation Barth writes his great theodicy of the world and calls time and again to witness Mozart's music. It is important to note that, for Kierkegaard, Mozart's music (as well as Hegel's philosophy) lives in the demonic limbo between the aesthetic and the religious realms. Mozart's music is interpreted by Kierkegaard as a music of seduction that is personified in Don Juan. I do not know any statement in Barth's second period that would have pointed to an apotheosis of Mozart. But in the third period the name of Mozart comes up time and again. It is in a spirit opposite to Kierkegaard's that Barth interprets Mozart's music.

In his discussion of David Friedrich Strauss in his history of *Die Protestantische Theologie im 19. Jahrhundert* (Zurich, 1947), Barth closes the chapter with an apology for Strauss against Nietzsche's criticism. Nietzsche ridiculed Strauss as a typical representative of a shallow bourgeois optimism. As an apology, Barth mentions that in the midst of his "fatal" hymn on culture Strauss confessed a preference for Mozart, who ranked for him "as the universal genius" of his period. Anyone who has understood this highest rank of Mozart, Barth remarks cryptically, is to be forgiven for a great deal of "infantile theological criticism" and sentimental optimism. If one considers that, at the time of his violent attack on Strauss, Nietzsche was hopelessly lost in the fetters of the "awful Wagner," then one must admit that Strauss made the better choice (*R* 514).

This remark on Mozart is not a remark on the side concerning musical taste, but is of the highest relevance to the structure of dialectical theology in the period of the *Kirchliche Dogmatik*. It is a new tone that is unheard in Barth's second period. The spirit of Mozart is evoked in the *Kirchliche Dogmatik* at the introduction of the crucial chapter on chaos and the negative. Why does Mozart's music belong in the realm of theology, although Mozart was neither a "church father," nor even a very devout Christian?

Because Mozart's music is, according to Barth, a great theodicy. He knew about the goodness of the creation in its totality in a way in which neither the church fathers nor the reformers, neither the orthodox nor the liberals, nor those who believe in natural theology or those who are armed with the "word of God"—and surely not the existentialists—have known it. Mozart found peace with God in the dark problem of theodicy, a peace that is higher than all praising, vituperating, criticizing, or speculating of human reason. Mozart lets us "hear" in his music what we will see at the end of our days: the fugue of coordination, the world in joint.

He has heard the harmony of creation, to which also belong the somber shadows in which, however, there is no darkness, also the lack that, however, is not an imperfection, also the sadness that does not, however, end in despair, also the grimness that does not degenerate into the tragic, the infinite nostalgia that, however, does not work itself into an absolute melancholy—but therefore also the cheerfulness, but also its limits, the light which radiates only so fully, because it emerges from the shadow, the sweetness that is also bitter and therefore does not cloy, the life that does not fear death, but knows it well.

Mozart listened to the creation without resentment and not in a partisan spirit. Therefore, he produced not his own music, but the music of creation (*KD* III, 3, 327f.).

The apology for the world in its "totality" is the pattern of Hegel's philosophy of reconciliation. Hegel characterized his philosophy as a "theodicy," and he valued the objective spirit more than all praising or criticizing subjective attitudes. Does Hegel's philosophy not attempt to give a sketch of reality in the light of redemption? The fugue of coordination runs through his ternary dialectic. The world never seems out of joint. When Barth describes the place of the negative in the harmony of creation, does he not, in the guise of Mozart's music, give an accurate rendering of Hegel's dialectic? If Hegel ultimately escapes the arrows of Kierkegaard's critique, it is because he contemplates nature and man without resentment and not in a partisan spirit. But it is for this reason that he could fall prey to the illusion that he did not produce his own music, but rather the music of the spheres.

In Barth's late period the symbol of the incarnation does eclipse the catastrophic quality of history. For the incarnation is not a judgment, a death sentence of the world, but rather its foundation. All alienation of sin cannot obliterate the coherence of the world from the beginning to the end. No sin can let man fall into an abysmal separation from the divine. The community of men is not "established" in Jesus the Christ at the end of history, but is already presupposed in the drama of redemption. The Christlike nature of man is a premise in the drama of redemption.

But there are in Barth's "orthodox" period of *Kirchliche Dogmatik* some reservations at work that can be ascribed to his orthodox limitations. Some consequences that are inherent in the premise of a Christological pantheology had to be avoided if a dogmatic of the church were to be developed. It is significant that Barth withdrew the prolegomena volume that started a "Christian" dogmatic and replaced it with a dogmatic of the church. He is aware of the dilemma and faces it squarely: that a dogmatic of the church must at some point become "inconsistent." For "consistency" may be a virtue of reason but surely not of a divine mystery. Our philosophical interpretation, however, which is not bound by the standards that rule in a dogmatic circle, may give at least a hint of some of the "heretical" consequences that would often follow from the premise of a pantheological Christology, even if, in saying this, we run into the danger of being "repudiated" by orthodox theologians as one of those *qui himis crasse delirant*.

VIII

The Christology of the church contains the archetype of the image of man (if the ontological definition of man is, as dialectical theology assumes, based on the act of redemption). The restitution of man in the act of redemption does at least reveal man's inherent possibility. True, the act of redemption is "grace," the prerogative of a divine will. But if the reconciliation between the divine and the human that is fulfilled in the act of redemption starts with the beginning of creation (*KD* III, 1, 150), then creation is in the scheme of redemption. While in the second edition of the *Roemerbrief* Barth emphasizes the judgment in eschatological terms, he centers his *Kirchliche Dogmatik* around an exegesis of the Johannine concept of absolute love. Hegel's earlier writings also reveal that the method of dialectic was first developed as an exegesis of the Johannine *agape*.

The orthodox limit of Barth's theology becomes evident in the crucial issue of man's imitation of Christ. If Christology is the archetype for man's nature, then man's *imitatio Christi* is a meaningful pattern. But Karl Barth insists that man's redemption is consummated in Jesus the Christ. Man does not need to repeat and to imitate Christ's *decensus ad inferos*. The eternal death has been taken from man's shoulders by the sacrifice of Jesus the Christ.

Also Luther's *simul iustus et peccator* (which expresses the anthropology of the second period) is taken over with important qualifications that destroy the paradox of the *simul*. Luther's *simul iustus et peccator* should not, according to Barth, be understood to mean that in the totality, in which we are, righteousness and sin are equally valid descriptions. Such an interpretation would present man as justified and under sin—so that we are permitted to sin as well as being justified. The *simul* only means the continuity of the past into the future. Man's sin "has been," is past; his righteousness "will be," is future! The *simul* does not mean a balance, but rather the suspension of the balance (*KD* II, 1, 706). In the simultaneity of righteousness and sin, however, the anthropological consequence of Christology is expressed. Barth's qualifications of man's dialectic in the *simul iustus et peccator* come from the same source that forced on him the intention to limit man's *imitatio Christi* and accept the life and death of Christ as a sacrifice *for* man and not as an image for his own sacrifice.

Whereas Paul's interpretation of the divine economy of salvation ends in the Calvinistic double predestination of judgment, Barth's theology in his *Kirchliche Dogmatik* culminates in a predestination of love. Predestination is divine grace. Divine grace is ultimately not judgment but love. No negation through sin and death can obliterate the divine will of love. There is grace also in divine judgment. All the darkness of Pauline-Calvinistic interpretation of predestination cannot obliterate for Barth the axiom that in the light of the divine incarnation no damnation of man is possible. Whereas in the second edition of *Roemerbrief* the motif of judgment overshadows the motif of love, the *Kirchliche Dogmatik*, which perceives the world "in joint" in the light of the divine incarnation, goes beyond a "theology of crisis." If the apology for the world in its totality that the *Kirchliche Dogmatik* offers is taken without reference to the negative criticism of the second edition of the *Roemerbrief*, then such a theodicy must end in an apology for the violence and injustice of the world. Would not the arrows Kierkegaard, Dostoevsky, and Nietzsche aimed at Hegel's philosophical theodicy also strike Barth's theological theodicy? Barth's dialectical theology cannot avoid putting the contradiction into divine life itself. God is guilty of contradicting himself in the act of incarnation (*KD* II, 2, 179). In the act of love God makes himself the object of his own wrath. The dialectic reaches into divine life and springs from there into human life. If, however, divine life does not transcend the contradiction, how much does it go beyond the contradiction of human life?

The limits of Barth's dialectical theology are, strangely enough, the same as the limits of Hegel's dialectical philosophy. In both, the spirit is posed as an absolute divine spirit, whereas dialectic presupposes the *dialegesthai* of limited and finite spirits. The absolute spirit does not need a dialogue; we, however, are finite and mortal. We are in need of one another; therefore, human truth, human logos, can be realized only in the dialogue of finite spirits. This dialogue is the foundation of the dialectical method. When Barth's second edition of the *Roemerbrief* was published, it seemed for a moment as if the breakdown of theodicy also could be interpreted in terms of theology. The destruction of the classical cosmos (and therefore also of the classical ontology) was transparent in its pages that gave witness to the decay of conventional society and the natural order. In the destruction of classical ontology the problem of theodicy also was destroyed. Barth's commentary on Paul's Epistle to the Romans was not "theology" but religious literature. Critics like Erich Pryzwara and Hans Urs von Balthasar called Barth's commentary "expressionistic." I doubt if this adjective must be taken as pejorative. True, the language of his *Roemerbrief* is "chaotic" and "expressionistic." True also, the language of his *Kirchliche Dogmatik* is lucid and clear. But may not the chaotic language of the *Roemerbrief* be a sign of a creative situation, and may not the lucidity and clarity of the dogmatics ultimately rest on a yielding to the conventional patterns? What is more lucid than what pleases the dogmatic common sense?

Barth's theology has written a new chapter in the history of dialectics. In the period of the *Roemerbrief* it was an attempt at theology without a theodicy, thus opening the possibility of a religious language in an age of the eclipse of the divine. This language of dialectical theology seemed able even to absorb the atheism of Nietzsche and Overbeck as stages in the purification of man's image of God and could accept the realm of necessity as a veil of the divine. Karl Barth opened the gate to a trans-theistic stage of consciousness, but he opened the gate to this stage as a theologian. Barth's commentary on Paul's Epistle to the Romans was "expressionistic" because it was an attempt to express a new, even unheard-of, situation in theological language: to interpret theologically the eclipse of God that became manifest post Hegel. He knew that with Hegel's philosophy the "capital" of Western Christian tradition was exhausted; he knew that in Harnack's *Wesen des Christentums* or in the *Glaubenslehre* of Troeltsch, liberalism had declared the bankruptcy of Christianity. Nietzsche's elegy on the "death of God" had a concrete and cogent meaning in the frame of Western Christianity. Karl Barth was aware that it was time to start anew.

But with the rise of a restoration period toward the end of the 1920s and the beginning of the 1930s, Karl Barth, who had moved in the language of the *Roemerbrief* beyond ecclesiastical theology, started to publish a *Kirchliche Dogmatik,* which has reached the dimensions of a medieval *Summa*. The dogmatic necessarily presupposes the realm of the visible church as an established institution and must fall back again into the ontological pattern of a theodicy. The dialectics of Barth's magnum opus, however, repeats Hegel's attempt at a total theodicy in nature and history. Will such a theology escape the destiny of all theodicies?

13

On the Nature of the Theological
Method: Some Reflections on
the Methodological Principles of
Tillich's Theology[1]

I

The term "theology" occurs for the first time in Plato's critique of Homeric religion, and ever since Plato's critique theology signals a crisis in religion. The hour of theology is come when a mythical configuration breaks down and its symbols that are congealed in a canon come into conflict with a new stage of human consciousness. When the symbols coined to express man's encounter with the divine at a unique moment of history no longer coincide with his experience, theology tries to interpret the original symbols in order to integrate them within the context of the new situation: what was present in the myth is then only "re-presented" in the theological interpretation.

Theological reflection transforms both the original symbols of the canon and man's consciousness by establishing an equilibrium between them. No human situation is given in absolute nakedness. Only through the symbols of language, through the logos, can man orient himself in his surroundings. The symbols demarcate his horizon and govern, so long as they are meaningful, his thought and action. Theology thus recasts man's horizon by interpreting his situation in terms of the canonic symbols and acts at once as a conserving and as a catalytic force. As apologetics it tries to preserve the original symbols, but, by transferring the symbols of the canon to a changed situation, theology functions catalytically in the birth of a new symbolism. Therefore the task of theology may be described as a dialectic of "perseverance in changing." The equilibrium between symbol and situation is rarely achieved and never more than temporarily. The symbols have their life cycle in the course of theological interpretation and die when theology can no longer translate them into the temporal situation.

Almost from the very beginning of its history the Christian community sought the services of theology, so that the Christian canonic scriptures not only present a body of original symbols but already represent different stages of theological interpretation. Therefore some could assume that the Christian religion had a specific affinity to theological interpretation and that theology is the legitimate successor of revelation. I do not think that such an interpretation does justice to the beginnings of theology in the Christian religion. Christianity had to make use of theological interpretation already in its earliest stages because its symbols of faith expressing the expectations of the first generation conflicted very early with the actual situation of the community. For the Christian community was thrown into history against her expectations and against her will, and the hiatus between the eschatological symbols of faith and man's continuing existence in history is as old as the history of the Christian church.

The function of theology in the Christian church remained the same throughout its history. Theology continually transformed the eschatological symbols to an ever-changing historical situation and carried through this transformation with the help of the Platonic and, later, of the Aristotelian philosophy, turning the eschatological symbols into ontological symbols. Without this perpetual act of transformation, the Christian community would have degenerated into a "narrow and superstitious" sect, and the general culture would have bypassed this community without taking notice of it. But no religion can have the luxury of theology without paying a price for it. Secularization is the price the Christian community had to pay for its development from an adventistic sect to a universal church, and the history of theology is the spiritual account of this price. It would be iconoclastic to deny to a community any right of development, to outlaw all transformation, to declare all commentary as fake, and to argue that only the text is valid. It would be idolatrous, however, to overlook the perennial conflict between text and commentary and to fail to emphasize that the canonic text is "broken" through the prism of interpretation. The history of the development of Christian theology is a tragic history because there is no "solution" to the conflict between eschatological symbols and the brute fact of a continuing history. One may admire the achievement of theology but at the same time be aware of the price involved in such an achievement.

But a situation can arise that makes it impossible for theology to fulfill its task of interpretation. Christian theology, like all theology bound to a canonic text, uses the method of allegorical interpretation and does so by necessity. The entire history of theological interpretation is a running commentary to the original text. But what if the very method of allegorical interpretation becomes suspect? Is a theological exegesis of a Holy Writ possible together with a historical analysis of the text? Does not historical interpretation qua method imply a criticism of all theological exegesis? Whereas theological exegesis must "transfer"—this is the original meaning of translation—the original symbols by the method of allegorical interpretation into a given situation, the historical analysis interprets the text, the canonic symbols, in their original historical context.

In the nineteenth century the historical criticism of religion reached its height. The nineteenth century was a period of Old and New Testament criticism; it was the century of *Leben-Jesu-Forschung*;[2] it was the century of the history of dogma. It remained obscure, however, to most historians, why they were driven into this tempest of historical inquiry. Ferdinand Christian Baur wrote his classical history of dogma under the Hegelian assumption that this development had come to an end.[3] Even if Harnack did not subscribe to the speculative assumptions of the Tübingen school, he nevertheless arrived at the same conclusion when he, the historian of Christian theology, pressed the "essence" of Christianity into a "religion of Jesus," discarding all Christological doctrines as dead weight.[4] It was Nietzsche who discovered (what Hegel and his pupils may have known but did not admit) the driving force behind the passion of historical research: the death of the Christian God. Historical research, Nietzsche observed, works only as a post mortem, dissecting the body for the sake of anatomical study and writing an obituary.

After the First World War, however, a new generation of Christian theologians arose that experienced the catastrophe of war in terms of eschatological symbols. The apocalyptic symbols of the New Testament, symbols that had been the stumbling block for theology throughout the entire history of the Christian church, suddenly spoke with an immediacy and self-evidence that needed no further interpretation. No allegorical translation seemed necessary, for only apocalyptic symbols could express the actual situation. With the First World War a "world" broke into pieces. Man experienced himself as estranged in his social and cosmic setting and did not feel at home in a world he had so painstakingly cultivated to make his own. When the façades of culture and civilization crumbled under the impact of the First World War man was confronted with the realities of life: hunger, destitution, and death. I do not minimize the significance of dialectical theology when I suggest that the situation of the 1920s was catalytic for its development, for a theology is significant only when it responds to a concrete situation.

Karl Barth's commentary on Paul's Epistle to the Romans marks the birth of dialectical theology after the verdict of death had been announced by Nietzsche in the nineteenth century. His commentary is a powerful and penetrating analysis of man's situation and gave voice to man's self-estrangement long before philosophy had taken notice of it. The divine and the human were put in antithesis and any attempt to approach the divine was unmasked—as human *hubris* and illusion. Karl Barth's critique of religion did not fall short of the criticism by Feuerbach, Marx, and Nietzsche. In fact his theological criticism of religion aimed to outdo all secular criticism—in order to bring all human thought and action under divine judgment and to open it to the paradox of redemption. God was experienced in his strange otherness to the world and the last trace of the divine was erased from the human realm so that for all practical purposes the earth was left under the rule of the secular. This analysis of man and his cosmos strangely coincided in its diagnosis with the atheistic interpretation of man's actual situation.

As an analysis of man's situation, Barth's commentary is highly significant, but as a commentary on Paul's Epistle to the Romans, it remains a dubious enterprise, combining revolutionary insight into the meaning of the original symbols with an anachronistic exegesis. The program of a pneumatic exegesis only veiled the confusion concerning the historical method. By stressing the antithesis between the divine and the human to the point of paradox, dialectical theology spelled out concretely man's self-estrangement, but under the cloak of paradox it smuggled in some very unparadoxical stereotypes of Protestant orthodoxy. The later development of dialectical theology into a theological positivism only confirmed the fears of a critic like Harnack that this revival in theology would but contribute a Quixote episode to the history of theology because neither the presuppositions of a pneumatic exegesis nor the conditions for an orthodox supernaturalism could be revived at will. When the first revolutionary impetus of dialectical theology came to a halt and the conservative restoration of dogmatics began (a shift more significant as a general sign of our time than dialectical theology would like to admit), the attempt to develop theology out of man's actual situation had proven itself abortive.

II

It is in such a period of orthodox restoration that Paul Tillich has published the first volume of his *Systematic Theology*.[5] This work presents a challenge to the verdict that the creative development of theology has come to an end. Tillich seriously considers the charge that the history of theology represents a progressive amnesia, suppressing the eschatological meaning of the canonic symbols. He tries to escape the verdict of historical criticism by a solution that is as bold as it is simple: by interpreting ontology in terms of eschatology he charges ontology with eschatological dynamics. Thus he thinks it is possible to interpret eschatological symbols in ontological terms without sacrificing their original meaning. In short, he eschatologizes ontology and ontologizes eschatology in the light of man's present situation.

The starting point of his theology is the experience of despair that marks so much of contemporary art and literature, that comes to voice in existential philosophy and is analyzed in the psychology of the unconscious. Man is seen in an extreme situation that cannot be treated in the traditional stereotypes: neither the ontological speculations of the early Greek church nor the concern of the Reformation with a merciful God and the forgiveness of sin nor the modernistic problem of personal religious life or of the Christian community in the general civilization is at stake. His entire system rotates around the one eschatological problem: man's self-estrangement in his being and his reconciliation in the "new being." When after the First World War the social antagonism between the bourgeois society and the proletarian class seemed to determine man's situation, Tillich tried in a theology of *kairos* to meet the challenge of Marxism in terms of a Christian socialism. Tillich's theological criticism of the bourgeois society wanted to integrate the Marxist-like critique of capitalism. The Second World War has brought a clear shift in his emphasis from social concerns to psychological problems: the class struggle does not determine man's self-estrangement; man's despair transcends the social division of classes. Tillich tries to meet the challenge of existential philosophy and psychiatry, and his theological analysis of man's despair aims to reveal the unuttered theological a priori of their inquiry. Tillich's theology is apologetic, based on a method of correlation. This method determines the scaffolding of the system, which in the first volume is built around the main problems of "I. Reason and Revelation (1. Reason and the Quest for Revelation; 2. The Reality of Revelation)" and "II. Being and God (1. Being and the Question of God; 2. The Reality of God)."

The technique of correlation is not entirely new in the field of apologetic theology and was employed by the Lutheran theologian Karl Heim in a masterly way.[6] In his analysis of the categories of the natural sciences and the concepts of epistemology and ontology Karl Heim unearthed the inner contradictions in their basic axioms and used this crisis in the foundations of science and philosophy to drive man's search for knowledge from intellectual skepticism into an existential despair. Having brought human knowledge to the impasse of despair, Karl Heim turned about to reveal the answer of theology in which all contradictions were resolved and all antagonisms reconciled. Even if the student could not help but admire the author's skill, this technique left him more skeptical toward theology in the end than in the beginning because it gave him the feeling that the method of correlation works like a trick where the theologian, not unlike a magician, pulls the theological answer out of the dark. The analysis of man's situation in no way affected the terms of the theological answer. The crisis of man's knowledge left no scars on theology, and the theological answer did not pass through the mills of the dialectic but appeared superimposed on the analysis.

Tillich's method of correlation is dialectical. His interest in sociology, psychology, and philosophy is not peripheral, but he participates in the cleavages and contradictions, and his analysis of the human situation shapes the theological answer decisively. The theological element of the correlation is forged in his dialectic as much as the anthropological pole. Our interest is not the apologetic technique of correlation but the dialectical principle it involves.

In order to unravel the dialectic of Tillich's method of correlation we would have to discuss his work chapter by chapter. Such a procedure would go beyond the limits of an essay and would, moreover, remain fragmentary since the second volume of his *Systematic Theology* has not yet been published. Therefore I have chosen to treat two methodological points. First, I will consider the necessary presuppositions of a theological system written from an apologetic point of view; this problem centers around the question of theology and authority. Next I will consider the method of correlation; this problem centers around the relation between theology and philosophy.

III

The first sentence of Tillich's introduction contains in a nutshell the problem of theology and authority. For theology is defined "as a function of the Christian church" that must serve the needs of the church. Since the dogmatic part constitutes the most significant element in a system of theology, dogmatics is another name for systematic theology, and the term "dogmatics" is justified because theology "exercises a function of the church within the church and for the church" (p. 32).[7] The church rests on a foundation whose formulation is given in the creeds, and the function of the creeds "as a protection against destructive heresies" makes their acceptance necessary for the church. With the complete union of church and state after Constantine, the doctrinal decisions of the church became also the civil laws of the state, so that the heretic was considered a criminal who endangered the foundations of Christian society. The destructive consequences of the union of church and state have discredited the terms "dogma" and "dogmatics" and brought the subject of dogmatics into disrepute. But this disrepute is, according to the author, only a historical calamity and does not reduce the significance of formulated *dogmata* for a systematic theology because the function of systematic theology is a necessary consequence of the nature of the church.

What are the presuppositions of such a claim? The basis of theology as a function of the church rests, according to Tillich, on the doctrine of the logos that became flesh, of the principle of divine self-revelation that has become manifest in Jesus as the Christ, who is the "head" of the "body" of the church. But the idea of a theology as a function of the church is meaningful only if this doctrine is exposed in a direct way. For there must be a nonsymbolic point of reference beyond all dialectics, the rock on which theology as a function of the church may rest. The dialectical method, however, must always turn the logos that became flesh into a symbol. Surely Tillich is right to insist that a symbol is much more than merely a technical sign. But a symbol remains a "*chiffre*." However, can a *chiffre* carry the burden of a theology as a function of the church?

The tension between the theology of logos and the doctrine of the church not only marks Tillich's theology but also comes to the fore at the most critical juncture of the history of the church. Since the Alexandrian school of theology has turned the logos of the particular event into a symbol of the "pneumatic logos," the idea of theology as a function of the church has become problematic. A theology of the logos must face three major turning points in the history of the church: the theology of Origen, the prophecy of Joachim of Fiore, and the philosophy of Hegel. The church could not but anathematize Origen after long controversies because his theology of the logos tends, even against his will, to overcome the unique event of the logos in the flesh. It is true that neither Origen nor Joachim of Fiore nor even Hegel state that the creeds of the church are fulfilled and superseded. Nevertheless, this statement is implicit in the dialectical principle. The dialectical method is not a coach that can be stopped at will. The arguments around Origen and his pupils in the old church, around Joachim of Fiore and the Franciscan spirituals in the medieval church, and around Hegel and his pupils in the modern church give abundant testimony to this contention.

A theology that has a function in the church cannot function without the authority of the church, and this authority is derived from the credo that Christ as the logos has a continuous life in the community, the church representing the mystical body of Christ. Theology as a function of the church is meaningful only as a continuation of the incarnation, as the logos that became flesh in the *dogmata*.

If the theological task is understood in this rigorous way (and this is one possible interpretation of Tillich's first sentence), then, it seems to me, theology cannot be treated in a systematic way. Not because it is too difficult to prepare a systematic account of the *dogmata* of the church (every catechism does that) but because the incarnation of Christ cannot be treated as a systematic axiom. I do not wish to say that one cannot for pedagogical purposes present the doctrines of the church in a systematic treatise, but one would fail to understand Tillich's basic assumption if one would suppose that he presents theology in the form of a system for pedagogical reasons. The form of his system is connected with the very nature of his theology, and he states explicitly that it has always been impossible for him to think theologically in any other way than a systematic one. *Systematic Theology* as a title implies that theology is a system. Perhaps theology as a totality of consistent assertions about the *dogmata* can be systematic, but a theology that is the function of the church is not so much a totality of consistent assertion as an exegesis of the logos that became flesh. Such a theology is possible only as an interpretation of the divine word of revelation. To know does not mean to construct a system but to understand the word of the scriptures in the light of the authorities of the church. Ecclesiastical theology is based on an *argumentum ex verbo* and not on an *argumentum ex re*.

But Tillich's theology is not an *argumentum ex verbo*. It cannot be accidental that with Tillich "the elaboration of the line of thought has consumed all effort and all space" (p. vii), preventing him from making extensive reference to the scriptures and the classical theologians. In an ecclesiastical theology reference to the scriptures and classical authorities is not an embellishing ornament to prove the author's knowledge, but rather belongs to the very core of the argument.

Tillich's theology, however, necessarily takes the form of a system, since the method of commentary by pneumatic exegesis, as it appears in Barth's dogmatics, is rendered anachronistic through the impact of historical criticism. But at the same time Tillich would like to preserve the role of theology as function of the church under conditions that render the very premise of such a role questionable.

If the proposed interpretation of theology seems too rigorous, one would have to consider its possible alternative and to understand theology and the *dogmata* of the church as the product of creative human imagination. For the historical interpretation of Holy Writ and of the development of dogma in no way permits any conclusion about a continuous act of revelation. The historical interpretation of canonic writings ranges from a conservative reconstruction of minute details in the life of Jesus to a radical denial of any historical existence. Both extremes and the interval between them have to be taken into account by a systematic theology that accepts the results of historical criticism. In fact, the historical interpretation tries to unmask all history as human and only human. A comparison of a historical commentary with any pneumatic exegesis reveals the "unbridged gap" (p. 36) between the two methods. A theology that accepts historical criticism not only "suffers" because of this situation but actually is paralyzed so long as it wants to steer a middle course between historical interpretation and pneumatic exegesis.

It is precisely the "philosophical" element (p. 18) in historical criticism that opposes the assumptions of a pneumatic exegesis. In fact, the philological method was developed in opposition to the allegorical interpretation in order to break the "prejudice" of theology. In charging theology with prejudice, historical criticism aims to emancipate itself from the theological presupposition that truth is *given* to man only by the divine word of revelation. A theology of the church that understands itself in the light of a divine word of revelation would have to unmask the assumption of historical criticism to work without the presuppositions of the given word of revelation as an illusion of the autonomous mind. In order to legitimize pneumatic exegesis, theology would have to carry through a "critique of historical reasoning" and to show that the driving principle of historicism, the "historical consciousness," actually epitomizes human *hubris* and illusion. Leo Strauss, in his study of Spinoza's critique of religion, has developed the genesis of this problem and shown the philosophical implications of historical criticism in such a pertinent way that I do not need to repeat his argument in detail.[8] But not even theological positivism dared to go so far and left the problem of historical criticism in a confused limbo. Erwin Reisner, who pointed out that historical criticism was not only a question of philological accuracy but also had philosophical implications that shake the foundations of Christian revelation, remained a voice in the desert.[9] The church could tolerate the historical interpretation of the canon and the dogma only at the peril of its existence, since such an interpretation reduces the church to one sociological group among others immersed in the conflicts of the world.

Perhaps the time has come when theology must learn to live without the support of canon and classical authorities and stand in the world without authority. Without authority, however, theology can only teach by an indirect method. Theology is indeed in a strange position because it has to prove its purity by immersing itself in all the layers of human existence and cannot claim for itself a special realm. In losing itself in the forms of the world, theology would not betray its destiny. Richard Rothe, the teacher of Ernst Troeltsch, knew something about this destiny of theology.[10] Theology must remain incognito in the realm of the secular and work incognito for the sanctification of the world. Theology should not strive for the vainglory to present a sacred science "separated" from the sciences by special doctrines or dogmas, but rather it should serve in "lowliness of mind" the secular knowledge and life. Would theology miss its point if instead of insisting on a separating circle, it would make itself of no special reputation and take upon itself the form of incognito? In such a fashion, theology would become more likely to present the relation between the divine and the human in our time.

IV

Tillich's systematic theology is not only a theology of the church but also a philosophical theology; therefore, he develops his theology in a continuous correlation with philosophy. His purpose is to define within the limits of a philosophic theology the special topos of theology and to establish a criterion for distinguishing it from philosophy. While philosophy inquires into the structure of being, theology deals with the meaning of being for us. The subject matter of theology is what concerns us ultimately. Only those propositions are theological which deal with their object insofar as it can become a matter of ultimate concern for us.

But here we must ask, "Is there any criterion for determining what should be of man's ultimate concern? Could not everybody put his ultimate concern as theology?" Only those statements, answers Tillich, are theological which deal with their object insofar as it can become a matter of being or not-being for us. The question, to be or not to be, implies a specific theological point. But even the second criterion remains formal. Man's ultimate concern is fundamentally rooted in the ontological question. Ontology is not a theoretical doctrine but an act of questioning in which man asks about the ground of his being. Only in the chapter following the exposition of the two formal criteria of theology does Tillich discuss a material criterion of theology by defining theology as a methodical interpretation of the contents of the Christian faith. This statement remains obscure, however, in its relation to the two formal criteria and makes sense only if we remember that theology is by definition a function in the church. It is the ecclesiastical element in the texture of Tillich's theology that leads him to limit the theological circle and to demarcate the line between theology and philosophy. But this theological circle has a very wide radius. For the only criterion whereby the circumference of the circle can be drawn is again man's ultimate concern with the Christian message. His ultimate concern can express itself through opposition no less than through submission. Are Feuerbach and Nietzsche, then, within the theological circle?

Tillich's division between philosophy and theology poses a crucial problem for philosophy. If philosophy should deal, as Tillich assumes, only with the structure of being in itself, whereas theology deals with the meaning of being for us, then philosophy *qua* philosophy would have to remain in a detached objectivity and forget about man's concrete condition. But is it at all possible to inquire into the structure of being without first considering its meaning for us? For all ontological inquiry into the structure of being, though it develops the most elaborate system of categories, remains fundamentally empty until it has clarified the meaning of being for us. I do not see any possible split between theology and philosophy in the ontological question. For an inquiry into the structure of being, its categories and concepts, which does not beforehand establish the meaning of being for us is doomed to failure. An ontology that stops short at describing objective structures without recourse to the subjective source of this act remains ungrounded.

The division between the universal logos and the concrete logos cannot be interpreted in terms of Tillich's theological circle. The universal logos must at all times be bound to the concrete, otherwise it becomes a mere phantom of generalities. The union between the universal and the concrete cannot be ontologically "dependent" on an event in the course of history. If ontology is eschatologized and eschatology ontologized, then the drama between "being" and the "new being" must be a perennial act. The act of reconciliation must either be an eternal event or it must put an end to man's being in history. The original eschatological symbols of the antagonism and reconciliation between the *protos adam* and the *eschatos adam* had an inner coherence lacking in a theology that has both to reckon with the fact of a Christian history and to turn the eschatological symbols into ontological concepts, making the eschaton break into history at an arbitrary moment.

Such or similar considerations have probably prevented Martin Heidegger from accepting the ontological interpretation of theology that would seem to be the most natural correlatum to his philosophy of being. In sentences that could be taken as a direct comment on Tillich's theology, Heidegger remarked, "If I were to write a theology, which I am sometimes tempted to do, [then] the term 'being' would not be allowed to appear in it. Faith does not need the thought of being, and if it needs it, it is no longer faith. This Luther understood. Even in his own church one seems to forget it" (Zurich, November, 1951).[11] Heidegger remains cryptic as to how he would develop the categories of his theology, but this much is clear: he separates ontology from theology like Kierkegaard and Barth. I cannot but take Tillich's side in this argument, although I doubt whether the ontological interpretation of theology can be confined within the limits of the theological circle.

Is Tillich's *systematic* theology, however, confined ultimately to the theological circle? It is the paradoxical destiny of logos-theology to end in a theology of immanence. This consequence is implicit in the very principle of dialectic. It cannot be denied that Tillich's theology describes the disruptive cleavages of reason and man's alienation in general. But is the reconciliation described theologically, as a "supernatural" breakthrough, as a miraculous healing of the conflict in man? If the supernatural pole is dialectically drawn into the orbit of the world and the divine interpreted in the light of the mystery of incarnation, then the divine becomes immersed in the world, becomes an immanent principle. The divine no longer stands over and against man but is in the depth of his own being. The law of God (theonomy) is no longer a divine decree to man but only "autonomous reason united with its own depth" (p. 85). In such a situation it "is as atheistic to affirm the existence of God as it is to deny it" (p. 237), for God is not a being standing over and against man, calling him, commanding him, arguing with him, but "being itself."

It is important, I think, to inquire into the "topology" of the symbols that are basic to the ontological interpretation of theology. According to Tillich, they are all located in a "depth." The "depth" of reason expresses something that is not reason but that precedes reason and is manifest through it. That which transcends reason is not located "beyond" reason, but the arrow of transcendence points "downward" into the depth. The depth of reason is interpreted as "substance" that appears in the rational structure of reality. Substance also marks the "depth," the "below," and points to that which is "underlying" reality (sub-stantia). The ontological metaphors are even more pointed. The depth is called the "ground" that is creative in every rational act, or the "abyss" that "cannot be exhausted" by any act of creation, or the "infinite potentiality of being and meaningful" that "pours" into the rational structures of mind and reality. The depth is the center of power, and out of the depth all rational structures receive their form (p. 79). All these symbols are metaphorical variations of the unsymbolic term "being itself." The religious symbol for what is called the "ground of being" is God (p. 156).

The point of reference for all these ontological symbols lies in the depth. Since Tillich interprets theology in ontological terms, his basic theological and religious symbols must retain the quality of depth characteristic of Dionysiac theology. Dionysiac theology is an "ecstatic naturalism" that interpets all supernaturalistic symbols in immanent terms. The ecstasy does not lead to a "beyond," in a supernaturalistic sense, but rather signifies an "intensity" of the immanent. In the last analysis, it is the idea of a Dionysiac theology that secretly impels all philosophical theology, and in the convergence and union of the bacchantic dance and the mystery of the cross, I see the mythical original of the dialectical method. Nietzsche's last utterances point in the same direction. At the end of his *Ecce homo*, Dionysos stands symbolically against the crucified. However, in the letters and fragments, written in a last clarity of mind before he entered into the night of madness, the veil is lifted from Nietzsche's ultimate concern: Dionysos and the crucified merge into one symbol. It is the same union of Christ and Dionysos that Hoelderlin celebrates in his last hymns. The theoretical blueprint for the mythical union of Christ and Dionysos is given in the philosophy of Hegel and the late Schelling. The method of dialectic is rooted in Böhme's Gnostic theogony of the eternal yea and the eternal nay. Hence, Tillich's ontological interpretation of theology, which is his most original contribution, adds a chapter to the history of Dionysiac theology in the Christian frame of reference.

It is unavoidable that in the context of a Dionysiac theology some of the biblical attributes and metaphors for the divine, which belong to a paternalistic frame of reference, become "confusing" symbols. It needs all the power of Tillich's interpretation to hold the paternalistic symbols in line with the Dionysiac symbols of his philosophical theology. In the last pages of the volume, for example, Tillich is concerned with the criticism of the personalistic symbols for man's relation to God. The two "central" symbols of biblical faith, Lord and Father, have become a stumbling block for many people. Christian theology has been "unwilling to listen to the often shocking insights into the psychological consequences of the traditional use of these symbols" (p. 288). No doubt this remark touches upon a crucial point, but I would question whether the "traditional use" can be eliminated; that is, I would question whether the symbols can be removed from their original context. No interpretation of a symbol can ultimately uproot the symbol from its natural soil. A symbol explains itself through itself and breaks through all the veils of interpretation. It is important for theology to take the criticism of psychology and sociology seriously, but perhaps it is worth while to consider, even if only for a moment, whether the fact that the paternalistic symbols have become a stumbling block is not in fact a verdict on our spiritual situation. These symbols were in no way disturbing to many generations that shaped their traditional use, and the symbols would never have become so central to the Jewish and the Christian language of faith if their traditional use had conflicted with their meaning. May not the criticism of paternalistic symbols by psychology be the result of a tacit assumption of a theology of immanence?

Tillich's Dionysiac theo-*logy* challenges the ecstatic Dionysiacs like

Ludwig Klages,[12] Keyserling,[13] and other disciples of the pagan cult, who descend into the night and worship earth, race, blood, flesh as sacred powers, abhorring reason as the enemy of the soul. The spirit pulses through the Dionysiac elements in Tillich's theology, which tries to reconcile the powers of the deep that are sacred and the powers of light that are divine. The spirit does not live in enmity with life, but even the abyss of being is illuminated by a logos.

V

Hegel also understood the dialectical method as an explication of the mystery of the incarnation and centered his ontology around Christian symbols. No one can understand the dialectical method unless he refers to Hegel's analysis of "life" and "love" in his earlier theological writings. This analysis is deeply interwoven with an interpretation of the prologue of the Gospel of John. But in the *Phenomenology of the* (human or divine?) *Spirit*, Hegel reveals the secret inherent in the dialectical method of logos-theology. Logos-theology contains, according to Hegel, the method, the way in the deepest sense, leading from the contradictions of alienation to man's self-recognition. The logos that became explicit in theology is the spirit that recognizes itself; it is reason united with its own depth. Hegel also describes the logos as distinct but no longer outside of man and draws the supernatural pole into the circle of dialectic. The dynamics of the dialectical method break through the limits of a theological circle because the principle of dialectic cannot fulfill itself without sacrificing theology as an objective doctrine. Only in the situation of estrangement can man speak about his ultimate concern in an estranged way, in the way of theology; as a doctrine, theology perpetuates the estrangement of man that it set out to overcome. The structure of Hegel's *Phenomenology* testifies to this dynamism of the dialectical method. The *Phenomenology* does not end with a description of the logos-theology, but rather proceeds to a Gnostic theory of knowledge, a doctrine that is neither theology nor philosophy in the strict sense but both at the same time. This doctrine has its source in the Alexandrian theology and in the speculations of Joachim of Fiore. Hegel's doctrine is not a philosophy in the sense of a theory that abstracts from man; it is not a theology in the supernaturalistic sense, for it does not locate the spirit outside of man. In Hegel's logos-theology the supernatural symbols are finally translated into immanent categories.

It is true that Hegel's synthesis crumbled, since he reconciled the contradictions and oppositions of life only in the realm of the idea and relegated nature, matter, and man's material condition to a secondary position. The social and scientific revolution of the nineteenth century burst through the dikes of Hegel's idealistic synthesis. Schelling, in his lectures on the *Philosophy of Mythology and Revelation*,[14] was the first to stress the primacy of being over the "negative" realm of the pure idea—and Tillich started his work forty years ago with an analysis of Schelling's "positive" philosophy. Schelling, who turned the wheel from idealism to a general revolt against Hegel's synthesis, still interpreted being in objective terms, whereas some of Hegel's pupils (Feuerbach and Kierkegaard) shifted the emphasis from the objective pole of being to the principle of subjectivity.

When Tillich defines the object of theology in terms of man's ultimate concern, he tries, if I understand the structure of his ontological theology, to mediate Schelling's primacy of being with Feuerbach's principle of subjectivity. Feuerbach also argued against Hegel that the pure logos needs to be "incarnated" and "realized" in man's concrete existence, and he also understood the principle of subjectivity in reference to Protestant theology. "In contrast to Catholicism, Protestantism has ceased to be concerned with God per se and is interested only in what he means for man. . . . Protestantism is no longer theology but essentially Christology, i.e. religious anthropology."[15, 16] Like Tillich, Feuerbach quotes Luther's famous saying, "As you believe him, so you have him," as his key word. Feuerbach would, like Tillich, insist that theistic religion "has made God a heavenly, completely perfect person who resides above the world and mankind. The protest of atheism against such a highest person is correct. There is no evidence for his existence, nor is he a matter of ultimate concern. God is not God without universal participation" (p. 245). Feuerbach, again like Tillich, no longer envisages matter as an antispiritual principle, but rather interprets spirit as immanent in matter as the ecstasy of nature and the intensity of man's existence. Feuerbach's reference to Protestant theology, however, lost its meaning when in the course of years his naturalism became a positive, undialectical principle. Religion then turned out to be only an illusion and the spirit an ideological instrument. Perhaps all materialism had to end in atheistic revolt in the nineteenth century and sink into a positive materialism because Protestant theology (against which the revolt was directed) equated the divine with the spiritual, excluding nature and matter from redemption.

Tillich's dialectic tries to break this deadlock. His dialectic does not drive toward a reconciliation in the realm of the idea. It is a dialectic that does not relegate nature and man's material condition to a secondary position; it takes the individual, the ephemeral, as seriously as the idea. But in its methodological structure Tillich's dialectic is, like Hegel's, a dialectic of mediation that drives toward a coincidence of opposites. Tillich's theology, like all philosophical theology from Origen to Hegel, considers its interpretation of the canonic symbols as an advance over "naïve" belief. Tillich interprets theological reflection as progress in understanding. Perhaps this is the destiny and the limitation of all theology. For theology must interpret the transition from the myth to the logos as an advance and reflection as an achievement and therefore fails to see that theological reflection presupposes that the original power of the symbol is gone. Theological reflection starts with the resignation that the symbols do not speak through themselves. The ascent to reflection involves a descent from the original relation into an imaginary reconstruction.

Surely, theological interpretation is an achievement, and perhaps it is only by way of dialectic that we can translate the original symbols for the present situation. But perhaps it is the "temporal situation" that forces theology to use the dialectical method. That the theologian has to resort to interpretation is only the reverse side of the fact that the symbols have grown mute. It may very well be that only dialectical terms that border on atheism are appropriate to the present situation. But I would not conclude from this that the dialectical interpretation of the symbols is on a "higher level" than their primitive meaning. For the first generation of Christian believers the coming of the Messiah was a reality and not an ontological problem. Many generations did not stumble over the concreteness of central symbols like Father, Lord, or King of Heaven. I would not hold it against these generations that they could use these symbols naïvely and did not need to develop an allegorical or dialectical interpretation. Anyone who, after two thousand years of Christian history, thinks that he can ignore the hiatus of time is the victim of an illusion, and Tillich rightly reproves all fundamentalist and orthodox theology. But why make a virtue out of a necessity? The progress in theological interpretation throughout history runs parallel with a gradual withdrawal of divine presence. Theological "re-presentation" and theological interpretation are driven deeper and deeper into the web of dialectics because the divine presence is more and more veiled.

It may seem contradictory to push the dialectical principle beyond the limits that Tillich has set and at the same time to interpret his method of dialectics in the light of the absence of the divine. But perhaps the dialectical method implies precisely such a union of contraries, for it is at once a method of opposition (*dia*-lectic) and a method of reconciliation (dia-*lectic*). The dialectic of mediation (Hegel, Tillich) considers the development of theology only as a path of gradual elucidation and illumination. The dialectic of opposition (Kierkegaard, Barth) tries to bypass history and to leap the gap between the original symbols and the present situation. Both uses of the term "dialectic" are legitimate, and strangely enough, in the last analysis, their results coincide. "Dialectical theology" opposes the divine to the human to the degree that the divine became the totally "other" to the world. The theology of mediation involves the divine in the human dialectic to the point that the divine pole of the correlation loses all supernatural points of reference. The two methods seem to contradict each other, but in fact they equally testify to the eclipse of the divine in our present situation.

14

Notes on an Ontological Interpretation of Theology[1]

What seemed impossible in the nineteenth century has happened: theology as a science still exists. Within the realm of scientific studies as taught in the universities, there is apparently still room for theology. What is more, theology as a "positive" science has markedly developed: its literature has reached mountainous, not to say monstrous, proportions. In fact, it is one of the boasts of the age to have made possible the resurrection of theology.

From all this activity, it would seem that we know what the term "theology" means. It is, after all, the label of an academic discipline operating within a well-circumscribed field of cognition. Yet if we look more closely, we are ever more embarrassed to define exactly the subject matter of theology. The self-evidence that theology attributes to the definition of its subject matter is a dubious advantage. For it is exactly the seemingly self-evident that has to be subjected to the *questio iuris*.

The question of the foundation (*Grundlegung*) of theology has fallen into oblivion. And more: in the province of positive theology a dogma has arisen to the effect that this question, which is the ontological question for theology, is superfluous and inadmissible. Positive theology considers it a virtue to have eliminated the ontological question: it enrolls itself in the ranks of those sciences that deny the need for an inquiry into their axioms and start from the *factum brutum* of the subject, if not from the mere fact of an existing academic discipline. It tries to ape such sciences as philosophy, physics, and biology in their "positivistic" demeanor. But a "positive" theology will also share the fate of all the positive sciences. Under the cold eye of the *questio iuris*, the élan and headlong advance in positive exposition will reveal itself as a rottenness in the foundations. What is the use of such a grandiose theological enterprise, if it be discovered afterward that it has been built on crumbling supports? For theology especially, its "resurrection" as a positive science may be only the last gasp before extinction.

All theology, no matter how elaborate and baroque its blueprint, remains unworkable and defeats its own intentions if the *esse* of the θέος (theos) is not beforehand sufficiently elucidated, and if this elucidation is not understood as the basic task. The unease that gave birth to the quest for the θέος (theos) is in danger of being replaced by a facile manipulation of self-evident categories.

An interpretation is ontological when it does not forget this task of elucidation. The term "ontological" refers to no special philosophical discipline, but signifies a method: the way to the ἀρχή (arche). The ontological method of interpretation asserts that only by going down to the ground of all phenomena are the demands of interpretation fulfilled. The way down to the ἀρχή (arche) and the way up to the τελος (telos) are one.

An ontological interpretation of theology has, therefore, to descend to the ἀρχή (arche) of the θέος (theos) and so to ascend to the τελος (telos) of the θέος (theos). The interpretation of the *nihil* as a possible horizon of the revelation of a θέος (theos) is the goal of this inquiry.

This interpretation of theology is ontological and thereby in direct contrast to the discipline of "philosophical theology." Philosophical theology ends in a man's vision of God, and this not only in the welter of homiletical essays but also in the more serious efforts that demand at least logical rigor. But is it even possible to put the question of the θέος (theos) in the dimension of man? Positive theology that is not ontologically founded tends to deteriorate into homiletics, and philosophical theology that is not ontologically founded tends to confuse the *deus in nobis* with the θέος (theos). Philosophy has no right to consider itself a priori as a "natural" foundation of theology, for it then confuses dimensions in the twilight of a *theologia naturalis*.

Nor is it a question here of employing philosophical modes for the ends of religion, integrating them into a theological system (Karl Heim), or of applying the general structures of the *esse* to the theological *existentia* (Rudolf Bultmann). In both of these, theology is reduced to one of the many possible modes of interpretation of the human canon, which all stem from philosophy and which lean on it as a science of formal norms. The *factum brutum* of theology is put on one level with the *bruta facta* of the rest of the sciences. Theology is reduced to a mere science of religion, describing a limited complex of human ποίης (poiesis): the science of religion interprets a document and tells the history of a social unity based on this document as a holy scripture.

But theology means something very different from describing a mundane fact. The *factum brutum* articulated in theology is not to be found in the catalog of mundane facts. The sui generis of theology does not signify a relation within the network of intermundane relations, but rather something essentially apart: the absolute.

It is when the place of theology in the realm of cognition needs defining that inquiry comes to the first fork in the road. If the subject matter of theology cannot be defined in the framework of mundane relations, we are confronted with an either-or:

Either theology can elaborate its own method, for describing the *factum* beyond all objective relations, its own way of indicating the *transcendens*;

Or theology accepts itself as a part of an ontology that drives down radically to the ground of all objective relations.

If theology fails to develop its own method and abandons the attempt to explicate ontologically the *esse* of the θέος (theos) by delegating it to a "decision of faith," then it no longer can claim to be taken seriously, for theology would then have to make ontologically intelligible the meaning of this accession of faith. Is there any other intelligible explication available to theology apart from the ontological method? If not, as part of ontology, theology must subject itself to the neutrality characteristic of ontology.

It is now obvious why the ontological analysis may contain theological elements. Thereby ontology does not justify an independent realm for theology. To the contrary, in integrating theology into itself the ontological interpretation of the *esse* asserts itself as the only sufficiently intelligible one. It is one of the greatest events in the history of the relation between theology and philosophy that ontology has learned to treat the questions of theology in an exact and neutral way without recourse to myth. For it is the first condition of ontology to abandon myth.

It follows that the ontological interpretation of theology is not made from alien territory. Rather does the ontological interpretation arise on a fundament confining and defining the realm of theology. Theology can understand itself only ontologically.

But theology as an essential part of the ontological analysis leads to a paradox that has to be made explicit: How can theology be an element of an ontological analysis whose character is of necessity neutral, and whose neutrality is of necessity atheistic? For when the ontological analysis is not afraid to describe its method as the way to the ἀρχή (arche), does not this signify willful disobedience to a creator? When the relation between the object of the search and the seeker is the relation between the creator and the creature, the search is ultimately not for reflection but for obedience. The creature can only acknowledge the creator and submit to a law given by its creator according to his inscrutable will. If the ontological method demands the radical descent to the ἀρχή (arche), then this implies that the absolute relation between creator and creature is overthrown. It is only the creator who has the right to question the creature so radically that the question reaches the core of its being. The search of the creature can end in nothing but the admission of its failure to fulfill the given law of its creator; it can never end in a reflection in which the core of existence becomes intelligible (Gerhardt Kuhlmann).[2]

At this point, theology is confronted with a second either-or:

Either theology renounces reflection and subjects itself in the form of dogmatics to the sovereignty of a church, synagogue, or mosque, grubbing its subsistence in the explication of a given credo;

Or theology considers itself as reflection, in which case its place is within "atheistic" ontology.

But even before entering into the clear sight of ontological reflection, theology reveals itself as grounded atheistically. Theology as anti-thesis to the λόγος θεοῦ (logos theou), as the responsible response to it, is essentially atheistic. If, however, "atheistic" and "theology" are so essentially related, does not the "a" in "atheistic" (as *a-privativum*) empty "theistic" of its content? Does not the adjective "atheistic" consume the noun "theology"? In the obvious contradiction of these two terms, united by necessity, a dialectic of reversal becomes visible.

Theology and atheism are grounded historically in orthodoxy and Enlightenment. Against all dogmatic Enlightenment for which theology is surmounted, theology's point of departure most be defended. For no matter how crudely and savagely orthodoxy used theology, there is still more truth in theology's point of departure than in the equally crude and savage dogmatic Enlightenment. Most of the arguments of the Enlightenment against theology were, after all, only *Schwärmerei*.[3] But just as theology's point of departure must be defended and so the legitimacy of orthodoxy secured, it is likewise necessary to defend the assertion of atheism and so secure the legitimacy of Enlightenment. For there is more truth in the assertion of atheism, no matter how crudely and savagely made, than in crude and savage orthodox theology that tries to evade the Enlightenment with trifling arguments.

The struggle between orthodoxy and Enlightenment is not antiquated. Enlightenment is still alive today and by far more radical than in the seventeenth and eighteenth centuries. Its atheistic consequences, which orthodoxy has always suspected, are now unconcealed and radically proclaimed. Orthodoxy has had to leave all the mediating positions and retreat to the fortress of an inscrutable God for whom nothing is impossible. The reconciliations and mediations of the nineteenth century broke down. The conciliation of orthodoxy and Enlightenment in Hegel, in whom the will to mediation reached its climax, collapses and splits into the radical positions of Feuerbach and Kierkegaard.

It is sufficient to point to the origin of dialectical theology in the atheism of Feuerbach and to the origin of atheistic ontology in the theology of Kierkegaard to appreciate the reversal that has taken place; Heidegger expounds the whole problem of existence with reference to Kierkegaard. The analysis of the phenomenon of *Angst*, which is central to the existential analytics of Heidegger, is made with an eye on Augustine, Luther, and especially Kierkegaard. The theology of Karl Barth accepts in its entirety the atheistic critique of religion of Feuerbach and makes it the basis and the resting ground of theological viability. (Barth's lecture on Feuerbach gives abundant testimony to this.)[4]

The struggle between Enlightenment and orthodoxy was not decided. The so-called victory of the Enlightenment was ambiguous. All the statements of orthodoxy are based on the irrefutable assumption that God is almighty; once orthodoxy retreats to this fortress, it is even able to hold from there its positions in the field; for if this ultimate assumption is irrefutable, all statements based on it are unshakeable. As the theoretical attack of the Enlightenment failed, it had to try to erect a practical system in which the world and life could be made intelligible without any reference to an inscrutable God. The tool of Enlightenment was natural science. This explains why the methods of mathematics and geometry, and later the method of mathematical physics, could become the criterion for philosophy in modern times. The *mos geometricus* contains the desire for a completely intelligible world and reaches for the ideal of a *mathesis universalis* that may be offered in astronomy or chemistry as a world-formula.

The rational system of the Enlightenment failed at the barrier of irrationality. The dissolution of facticity into necessity did not succeed. It was then that idealism and materialism, these twin modes of interpretation, discovered the radical historicity of man and his world. Since Hegel and Marx, idealism and materialism have been radically historical, and the idea of eternal nature and eternal truth lost. Modern natural science can thus be only one historically conditioned interpretation of the world. It is clear that modern natural science does not ground the Enlightenment but is grounded by it; it is not scientific knowledge that justifies the Enlightenment, but the faith of Enlightenment—atheism—that justifies scientific knowledge.

Atheism, which justifies scientific knowledge, asserts: God is not. This means that in the realm of the "is" assertion, there is no place for God. With an "is" assertion, an object is referred to and described. The sum of "is" assertions constitutes science. What is not an object is not knowable, cannot enter the realm of knowledge, and must be declared by science as null. But "God is not" is also the assertion of theology. For theology has always denied that God is an object and agrees in this with atheism and with science grounded on atheism.

Theology and atheism wish to establish by their statement, "God is not," that God is not an object. Must then theology subject itself to the verdict of the logic of science and abandon God as null, as a nothing, as the nothing? Yes. Theology *must* accept the verdict of the logic of science and plead its case on this nothing.

May the nothing be meaningfully articulated? The nothing can never be an object but is ever and everywhere prior to all as subject. If language is confined to the limits of the logic of objects, then the nothing cannot be articulated. But language must be freed from enslavement to the logic of objects. In the network of the logic of objects there is no distinctive subject, and the grammatical division into subject and object is misleading and deceptive. For in what way does the logical subject of a sentence differ ontologically from the logical object: they are both objects. It is not language that fails; it is the logic of objects that is incapable of expressing an ontological subject. Were language liberated from the logic of objects, even silence could be articulated in it.

In the circle of the logic of objects, God is—if he is not abandoned as null—subdued to the sovereignty of the idea; he is prized as a value among values. Whoever prizes God as the highest value, or proclaims him as the highest idea, commits the highest blasphemy. The superlatives of the mundane realm do not honor God, they desecrate him. The higher in the scale of values God is appraised, the more he is profaned. Theology, therefore, can never be "natural"; for in the mundane relations of the world it does not have its point of departure, but rather its antithesis.

The nothing as the ontological subject is self-evident and without ground. Only a something can be the object of a question; the nothing is the subject prior to all. In every something, the nothing is contained as the ground; in every something as ontological object, the nothing is implied as the subject. All inquiry is directed to the something that has to justify itself; the something has to prove itself as against the demand: Why is there something at all and not nothing?

Theology and atheism reveal God as the nothing. In the past, when attempts were made to determine the relationship of God and world, the notion of *creatio ex nihilo* came to the fore. In this formula, the relation of the *ex nihilo* to the intended, but not explicitly mentioned, *a deo*, remains undetermined. If God creates out of nothing, then he must be related to this nothing. But how can he be "related" to the nothing if God is God? Only if the "relation" between God and the nothing is one of identity, if *deus* and *nihil* are identical. Then *creatio ex nihilo* means *creatio ex deo*.

But if *creatio ex nihilo a deo* means *creatio ex nihilo a nihilo*, then what can be the sense of *creatio*? Is not *ex nihilo fit ens creatum* contradictory to *ex nihilo nihil fit*? This contradiction is resolved in the coincidence of *deus* and *nihil*. If *deus* and *nihil* are identical, then *creatio ex nihilo* and *ex nihilo nihil fit* coincide. *Creatio* means, then, the shattering of the nothing into the many of the something. In the shattering of the nothing, the multitude of somethings is born. In the multitude of somethings, there is the audible longing for the one of the through-shattering-born creation. In the nothing there resounds the birth pangs of the something. Birth as the shattering of the nothing into the multitude of somethings, death as the fusion of the many into the one of the nothing, return eternally upon themselves.

Theological atheism—with its theoretical expression, atheistic theology—is the latest, most incontestable, and most radical consequence of contradictory positions; of theology and atheism, of Enlightenment and orthodoxy. As the most radical consequence, it is also the most primordial beginning. For to be radical means to go to the root, to go to the ground. Theological atheism—with its prolegomenon, atheistic theology—belongs, insofar as recognized labels are appropriate, to the field of ontological analytics in which the most extreme modes of thinking and existence, disbelief and faith, coincide.

15

Theology and Political Theory[1]

In the beginning theology emerged as a problem of political theory. The term itself, "theology," occurs for the first time in a dialogue between Adeimantus and Socrates discussing the place of poetry and literature in the state. Plato assumed that the founders of the state ought to know the general forms in which poets cast their tales and the limits that must be observed by them. It is in this connection that the term theology first occurs, in a question by Adeimantus: But what are these forms of theology, *typoi peri theologias*, that you mean? God is always to be represented as he truly is, Socrates replies, whatever be the sort of poetry—epic, lyric, or tragic—in which the representation is given.

The state's destiny depends on the standard norms of its citizens; therefore, it seemed to Plato important that false symbols and outworn clichés distorting the nature of the divine, as he found them in the epic and the tragic poetry of the Greeks, should be barred from the education of the young. The literature that Plato attacked was the standard literature of Greek education, the symbols he denounced were the basic symbols of Greek mythology and piety. His critique of Greek mythology amounted to no less than the twilight of the Olympian gods, which ushered in the end of Greek society. In such a crisis the term theology was coined; this term itself is a sign of the shaking of the foundations, for it implies that even the story, even the myth revealing the nature of the divine, must render account to man's reason, must justify itself before the court of reason.

For Plato the issue of theology was intrinsically related to political theory. This relation is not astonishing at all, since interest in the theoretical disciplines, such as theology and metaphysics, epistemology, and logic was originally guided by the philosopher's political concern for the community. Is it accidental that Plato developed his theory of ideas in a treatise dealing with the structure of the state? Is not Plato's theory of ideas the epistemological basis for the blueprint of his republic? A community that accepts the sophistic epistemological relativism is, according to Plato, doomed to anarchy or tyranny, since no political authority can be established on the basis of relativism.

It is important to keep this original situation of theology in mind in order to see that its relation to political theory is not a derivative affair, but rather touches the very centers of both. There is, in fact, no theology that should not be relevant for the order of society. Even a theology that claims to be apolitical altogether and that conceives the divine as the totally foreign, as the totally other to man and world, may have political implications. Contemporary theologians are hardly aware of the significant connection between Kierkegaard's theological doctrines, which are today in vogue in Protestant, Catholic, and Jewish theology, and his political theory of authority. Or can anyone seriously assume that a theology opposing all "liberal" mediation between the divine and the human, and stressing "authority" and "obedience" as its key notions, would suddenly turn "liberal" in political doctrine?

As there is no theology without political implications, there is no political theory without theological presuppositions. Proudhon once remarked that we always find theology at the bottom of politics. This statement is quoted by Donoso Cortés at the beginning of his *Essay on Catholicism*,[2] and it is perhaps the only premise, but a very important one, on which those two archenemies of 1848 agreed—Donoso, the defender of Catholic royalism, and Proudhon, the advocate of atheistic anarchism, who aimed his arrows against the "myth of providence." Man, according to Proudhon, must grasp the reins of progress, those reins that have hitherto been held by an incomprehensible providence alone. Providence, which has brought us to this hour, is incapable of taking us any further. Man must take God's place in the chariot of destiny.

It is not accidental that the theological implications of political theory came into the open during the nineteenth-century era of revolution and counterrevolution, for in that epoch a universe of discourse broke into pieces; the parties involved no longer spoke the same language and were therefore forced to go back to the principles that governed their arguments. After Locke and Bayle pleaded tolerance even for atheists, and after atheism became "socially" acceptable in the time of the encyclopedists, the attempt was made, in the nineteenth century, to establish society on a religiously neutral or atheistic territory. It was Hegel—in his *Phenomenology of the Spirit*, 1805—who, though cryptically, interpreted the events of the French Revolution and Napoleonic Caesarism as the rise of atheistic, or better trans-theistic, society. At the end of his book he hinted that the voice announcing the death of God—*Le grand Pan est mort*—that was heard at the end of antiquity was now heard again. The secret whispered by Hegel in the *Phenomenology of the Spirit* (in the last chapter, on "absolute knowledge") became common knowledge in the next generation, through his pupils, and the twilight of the gods (dramatized by Wagner) was put on record by Nietzsche's open proclamation of the death of God.

But with the negation of the transcendent God, the idea of hierarchy and the concept of degree lost their validity. The century that found its most symptomatic expression in Hegel's immanent pantheism and, in a later stage, in Comte's atheistic positivism and in the dialectical materialism of Marx also prepared the path for the absolute sovereignty of the people—for "government of the people, by the people, for the people." No state in the Western orbit in the nineteenth century could resist the contagion of the democratic principle. Predemocratic institutions, even when they withstood the democratic revolution, fought only a strategy of retreat. True, institutions have their own rhythm, and they may show unexpected resistance in surviving critical attacks. But if the inner evidence of its form of life is gone, then an institution continues only as a relic and survives only as a matter of pragmatic utility.

Institutions cannot change the inner principle that sustains them. The institution of monarchy rests on the principle of hierarchy, whose presuppositions are no longer "self-evident" in a democratic era. The divine right of kings is a reality in a monarchical era as much as "government by discussion" is in a parliamentary era. As an ornament the institution of monarchy may survive, but its inner life is gone when the divine right of kings ceases to be accepted as sacred and is challenged by a natural right equal to all men—when the degrees of hierarchy lose to a principle of equality. The institution of parliament may survive as a facade, but its inner life is gone, when its fundamental hypothesis of "government by discussion" ceases to be valid—when open discussion is no longer recognized as an *ultima ratio* because the rationale of argument is no longer experienced as a real way of convincing. A rational argument is then interpreted as a rationalization of egotistical interests and irrational motivations.

The principle of hierarchy in all its manifestations presupposes a sovereign who stands "beyond" the order, who remains "transcendent" to the system of law, who as a *prima causa* guarantees the system of order. All these presuppositions are gone in a democratic era, whose principle assumes a basic identity between the sovereign and the order. There is no sovereign beyond the government of the people, by the people, for the people. The ruler acts as mere "executive," executing the will of the people. Therefore any attempt today (and there are many) to restore a hierarchical order in a democratic era is doomed to failure; it remains a romantic nostalgia or becomes a totalitarian nightmare, since the cosmological, epistemological, and theological presuppositions for a hierarchical order are destroyed.

The idea of hierarchy presupposes an ordered universe arranged in a fixed system of aboves and belows, a system of degrees. The heavens themselves, the planets, and the earth "observe degree, priority, and place." The same idea of order and degree that is revealed in the cosmic realm was carried through by the Middle Ages in the political order and in the realms of art and religion.

The idea of hierarchy was so basic in the Middle Ages that even in the Elizabethan era the cosmos seemed out of joint when degree was questioned or abandoned. Listen to Ulysses, in Shakespeare's *Troilus and Cressida* (I, 3):

. . . when degree is shak'd,
Which is the ladder to all high designs,
The enterprise is sick! How could communities,
Degrees in schools, and brotherhoods in cities, . . .
The primogenitive and due of birth,
Prerogative of age, crowns, sceptres, laurels,
But by degree, stand in authentic place?

Ulysses's speech on degree, written at the end of the hierarchical era, provides good insight into the depth of horror experienced when degree is abolished:

Take but degree away, untune that string,
And, hark, what discord follows!

The passage is an excellent example of the experience of hierarchy at once cosmic and social. The sun and the king, the priorities and degrees in the system of planets, are interrelated with the prerogatives of crowns and sceptres. When the planets in disorder wander, the result is plagues and mutiny on earth. The term revolution, as well as the term opposition, comes from the astronomical vocabulary into political language. The order of the universe and the order of society that become manifest in Ulysses's speech are linked in the chain of hierarchical being. All the parts of the universe partake in the great chain of being that links the hierarchy of degrees into a unity. All degrees are interconnected in a subtle net of correspondences that run through the cosmic as well as through the social and political realms.

The hierarchical principle presupposes an absolute notion of above and below, for only on such a basis can a ladder of degree be established. The division of above and below runs through the cosmology, the psychology, and the theology of the Middle Ages, and it reveals the very horizon into which all things visible and invisible fit. Hierarchy is not only a political concept expressing the "ideology" of a feudalistic society, not only a theological analogy translated into the political order. In the Middle Ages it was so basic to man, cosmos, and God that even the epistemological notion of an "idea" was determined by the image of hierarchy. An "idea," in its Platonic sense, did not "reflect" things visible in the universe; rather, the things of the "lower" changing order partook of and reflected the changeless realm of ideas.

Therefore the breakdown of the medieval hierarchical society cannot be treated in an isolated manner as a political or social event, but must be interpreted in terms of a general breakdown of the hierarchical order in thought, belief, and action, which can be traced through all the layers of human experience. This breakdown can be observed in the turn from the Ptolemaic to the Copernican astronomy, whereby the cosmological basis for a hierarchical order was destroyed (since no division and therefore no analogy between above and below is possible in Copernican thought), as well as in the turn from realism to nominalism in epistemology, whereby the epistemological basis for a hierarchical order was lost (since the objectivity of symbols and concepts was destroyed). It can be observed in the turn from the medieval method of demonstration by analogy to the experimental method of modern science (which, no longer trusting in direct observation, implies that nature is secretive and must be compelled against her will to reveal the truth), as well as in the turn from a theology of an analogy between the realm of nature and the realm of grace to a theology of an antithesis of nature and grace (whereby the theological basis for a hierarchical order is undermined and all representation of the divine in the world becomes illegitimate).

The Protestant theology of inwardness was prepared for by medieval mysticism, which replaced the orthodox concept of analogy (and thus also of separation) between God and man by a theory of identity. The concept of the autonomy of man emerged out of the mystical speculations on the birth of the divine in the human heart, and out of the experience of the identity of the divine spark and man's soul. But the concept of autonomy leads to the atheistic denial of any transcendent law beyond and above man. The fulfillment of man's autonomy is at the expense of the death of God as a creator of heaven and earth and of all visible and invisible order, who gives the law to man. This development from heteronomian theism to the autonomian atheism of the nineteenth and twentieth centuries contains the inner history of theological-political thought in the modern age.

The stages of this development toward autonomy still await to be explored, especially the role of the antinomian ideologies of medieval and modern sectarians—ideologies that decisively prepare for the making of the modern autonomous mind. In the circle of mystical sects the Adamite principle, which is based on the hypothesis that all children of Adam are equal, challenged the aristocratic principle, which is based on privilege and representation. "When Adam delved and Eve span, Who was then the gentleman?" was a popular slogan of those mystical congregations. Cornelius Agrippa, in his pamphlet *De nobilitate*, which was early on translated into English, held that nobility is wicked not only as a result of practice and habit but also by nature. "For among the birds and four-footed animals there is no privileged class of nobility except the one to which those belong that are harmful to other animals and also to men, such as eagles, vultures, hawks,—gryphons and similar monsters. Of the same kind are the lions, tigers, wolves, pards, bears . . . dragons and toads. Among the trees, however, there are none or few that are consecrated to the Gods or held to be noble except such as are quite unfruitful or give no edible fruit to man" (ch. 80).[3]

Most of the writings of the sectarians were destroyed by the church and the inquisition, and we are dependent to a great extent on the indirect testimony of the persecution. In very recent times, however, a new source has been discovered, which, I think, will enlarge our horizon considerably. I mean the iconographic studies. A good deal of iconography of the late Middle Ages—like the works of Dürer, Breughel, Hieronymus Bosch—are oracular pronouncements in a sign language to which we have lost the key. It is a good guess that these works preserve in their images the ideas and rites of sects uncensored by the inquisition. The outlines of such an interpretation have been given in regard to some works of Hieronymus Bosch, especially the famous Garden of Delights, which presents an ideal state that might rule among men if it were not for the forces of hell, the church, and the aristocracy. Hieronymus Bosch, a Dante of the heretics, experienced this world as the plane on which there could be rebirth into the condition of the sinless Adam, into the simplicity and purity of original human nature.

In the shift from medieval to modern philosophy the idea of hierarchical order is replaced by the idea of balance. The idea of balance has not received the attention it deserves as one of the key notions in the grammar of motifs in the modern era, be it in the economical, political, theological, or astronomical realm. In the political realm Harrington and Locke, Montesquieu and Rousseau could serve as signposts to follow up the motif of balance. It should be obvious that the presuppositions of democracy rest on the idea of balance between the legislative and the executive power, and that the idea of a parliament presupposes balance, in the interplay of opposition and mediation of opinions and interests.

At first the idea of the balance of power had a transcendent, a transmundane point of reference, which in deistic theology is interpreted as a function of divine providence. In the deistic vocabulary there is still a "hand" that "holds" the balance. A study of the theological vocabulary of the Declaration of Independence can be revealing in this connection. If we compare the declaration's "rough draft" with the final phrasing, as it reads in the parchment copy, we find a most characteristic example of deistic theology: the divine guarantee is not the presupposition of the declaration, but its afterthought, a suffix.

Thomas Jefferson's first draft, submitted to Franklin, reads: "We hold these truths to be sacred and undeniable . . . " It seems that Franklin substituted "self-evident" for "sacred," and the difference should be noticed. "Sacred" is the divine right of the kings. The divine right presupposes a division of degrees, which is also implicit in the term sacred itself, implying the separated. The sacred is separated from the profane. The sacred and the profane complement each other. The profane means *pro-fanum*: outside of the sacred, before the doors of the sanctuary. You profane the sacred if you act inside the sanctuary as you act outside of it. Natural rights, however, proposing the equality of men, are "self-evident"; they have their justification in themselves and do not appeal to a hierarchical order of degrees.

Jefferson and Franklin agree that from that equal creation "men derive rights inherent and inalienable." But the neutral "from equal creation they derive rights" reads, in the "fair copy," the personal "they are endowed by their Creator with . . . rights." The "creator" of the declaration is the deistic divinity that oscillates between the neutral and the personal and can hardly be distinguished from the general law itself. The very possibility of interchanging the neutral and the personal—the neutral "equal creation" and the personal "creator"—reveals the character of compromise in deism. Deistic theology is in a transition from a theistic credo to a neutralization of the divine. Only in the Lee copy do we find, at the end of the declaration, an addition mentioning a firm reliance on the protection of divine providence. This deistic divine providence is, as the development of the text shows, not the fundamental premise of the declaration, but an annex.

It is of interest, I think, to compare the American Declaration of Independence with the Universal Declaration of Human Rights voted by the General Assembly of the United Nations. The first article of the latter document is phrased in line with the American Declaration of Independence and the French *Déclaration des droits de l'homme et du citoyen*: "All human beings are born free and equal in dignity and rights" (French declaration: "Men are born and remain free and equal in their rights"); "They are endowed with reason and conscience and should act towards one another in a spirit of brotherhood" (American declaration: "They are endowed by their Creator . . . "). The term "endowed" is taken from the American declaration, but "by their Creator" is conspicuously left out, leaving "endowed" hanging somewhat in the air. The Universal Declaration mentions neither the Supreme Being of the French document nor the "divine providence" of the American. The "myth of providence," to use Proudhon's language, the construction of an *être suprème*, was shattered by the theological critique of the nineteenth century, and the text of the Universal Declaration of Human Rights reflects the result of that critique.

Whereas the deistic philosophers of the eighteenth century came to the conclusion that if God did not exist he would have to be invented—and he was invented as the *être supreme*—the atheistic philosophy of the nineteenth century came to the conclusion that the first duty of a free man is to drive the idea of God out of his mind and conscience. Man attains knowledge without him, well-being without him, and a community without him. Each of man's progressive steps is a victory in which he crushes the divinity. If God exists then man must be his slave, and therefore Bakunin comes to the opposite conclusion from Voltaire: if God existed, man would have to kill him. The death of God in the critique of religion belongs to the algebra of revolution of the nineteenth century. The idea of progress crushes the myth of providence.

When the last traces of transcendence are removed from the general consciousness and the principle of immanence takes over, then the idea of balance loses its transcendent point of reference: the balance has to result merely from an immanent relation of the forces involved. In this respect the idea of Spirit in the Hegelian dialectic does not differ from the idea of matter in the dialectic of Marx, Proudhon, or Bakunin. The ruling principle remains in the limits of immanence, yet drives the various antagonistic forces—be they classes, parties, or ideas—toward a synthesis through a pure immanent balance of opposition and mediation.

It would seem that with the proclamation of the death of God, with the neutralization of theology in the Universal Declaration of Human Rights, the chapter on the relation between theological and political theory is closed. Man stands in the light of his autonomous reason. But the authority of reason, which gave impetus to the principle of democracy, was contested in the moment that bourgeois society came to rule. Marx contested the reason of "liberal" reasoning as mere "ideology." This attack is more than a weapon in the antagonism between the bourgeois and proletarian classes, for it undermines the very structure on which liberal society is built. The system of parliament, of government by discussion, loses ground when rational argument is seen as mere rationalization, covering, as we say, irrational motivations. The authority of the rational is challenged by the authority of the primordial archetypes that rule in man's subconscious.

The concept of ideology is only a first step in the direction of a new mythical evidence. Marx limited his suspicion of ideology to the liberal bourgeoisie and thought his own reasoning, for whatever reason, untouched by the original sin of ideology. But what if all reasoning is revealed as mere "superstructure," as mere rationalization of irrational and egotistic motivations? Sorel draws such consequences from Marxism. Sorel, whose doctrine served the actions of violence on both the revolutionary and the counterrevolutionary side, serves as a key to all contemporary political theory.

Sorel translated the spiritual situation of his age into the grammar of politics. He acknowledged as his ancestors Marx, Proudhon, and Bakunin, who probed the legacy of the French Revolution and the philosophy of Hegel. In the *Réflexions sur la violence* the influence of Nietzsche, Freud, and Bergson comes to the fore.[4] Only myth offers a criterion for social action, and through myth alone a group, a class, or a nation may act as a motor in the historical process. It should be obvious that the rise of myth as a political force goes with the decline of religion as a civic platform. With the twilight of the Christian religion—the death of God, as Nietzsche proclaimed the result of the nineteenth century's critique—the protective fences of dogma and ritual were broken, and man's mythical energies set free. Without the rule of reason, however, the mythical energies fall prey to configurations like the "general strike" or "Blut and Boden" or "honor of the nation," for while myth is ingenerate in the soul, its force, when blind, is purely destructive.

The mythical energies cannot be ignored without peril to the society, but they have to be formed into a *nomos*. When a principle is shaken an ancien régime sees only chaos. In such a situation relics of an antiquated form of life try for a revival or a renaissance. But I doubt if revivals, if ossified theologies dressed up in modern vocabulary, will meet the challenge. In our polycultural situation a ghettoid formula will fall short. The uncreated consciousness of our era that pulsates through the various mythologies should be forged into a new concept of reason.

This is a task for philosophy, in the sense that Plato and Hegel understood the term. The chaos of antagonistic mythologies today may then lead, if to nothing else then to a recognition of the inseparable unity of theology and political theory. The secret nexus between the two realms is established by the concept of power. Only when the universal principle of power is overruled will the unity of theology and political theory be superseded. A critique of the theological element in political theory rests ultimately on a critique of the principle of power itself.

PART IV

RELIGION AND CULTURE

16

From Cult to Culture[1]

In chapter XXVIII of *Doctor Faustus* Thomas Mann introduces an interlude on the social life of Adrian Leverkühn that in the context of a radical critique of culture shows the hubris that will eventually overtake the composer. Adrian has just finished a short symphony called *Marvels of the Universe*, a mock-pathetic title stressing the latent Luciferean element in the piece. This musical sacrilege is strangely echoed in the salon society of Munich before the outbreak of the First World War by a theory of myth presaging the rise of a conservative nihilism.

It was in such a society that Thomas Mann himself first came in contact with the ideas of a revolutionary conservatism. This ideology, first infecting the intellectual avant-garde that carried it into other circles, had little to do with the traditional conservative prejudices and attitudes of an aristocratic society. There was no longer anything aristocratic in the spirit of an intelligentsia driven by a revolutionary impetus more disruptive than any liberalism and yet possessing, as though in mockery, a strong conservative appeal.

Since the turn of the century a decaying aristocracy living off the rapidly diminishing capital of its old traditions had been seeking to relate itself to the postrevolutionary conservatism of an intelligentsia revolting against the bourgeois-liberal ethos from the other end, from the standpoint of novelty rather than tradition. From this marriage sprang the demons of fascism and Nazism.

It is strange that the intellectual whom Thomas Mann presents as a model of the ideologues of conservative nihilism should be a scholar by the name of Dr. Chaim Breisacher. His intellectual knowingness and nose for the latest views serve in his case a conservative ideology. I doubt, however, that such general characteristics would have induced the author to bring Breisacher, with his fermenting spirit, into the aristocratic salons of Munich had not memory pointed to a Jewish scholar whose archaistic theory of myth was put to the uses of reaction.

Dr. Chaim Breisacher is described as a person of fascinating ugliness and as a polyhistor who could talk about anything and everything. His major concern is "philosophy of culture," but his ideas are decidedly "anticultural," insofar as he views the whole history of civilization as nothing but a process of decline from cult to culture. For culture is to him only a mocking caricature of archaic cults. He concentrates all his attacks on "progress"—a term of deepest contempt on his lips. Thus he declares it to be the peak of modern arrogance for people to shrug their shoulders at the flat painting of ancient times, as if the development toward perspective art were really a step forward instead of a mere means of producing illusion, a technique that suits the mob. It is true that the art of the ancients lacks the dimension of perspective, but that is not because they were incapable of producing such trick effects. The fact is that they would have considered them vulgar. Breisacher employs the same argument in discussing the development of music. Here too he denounces the change from monody to harmony, generally taken as a sure sign of progress, to be an acquisition of barbarism.

His interest seems to be centered on the theory of decline as such. Polyphonic music becomes the object of his conservative protection as soon as he discusses the transition to the harmonic chordal principle and the instrumental music of the last two centuries. This stage was again the decline of the great art of counterpoint, which had had nothing to do with the prostitution of feeling, so common in modern music. In this general curve of decline he also places the music of Bach, who as the inventor of the well-tempered clavichord developed the possibility of understanding notes ambiguously and exchanging them enharmonically.

Breisacher's cultural harangue reaches its climax when the discussion shifts to the field of religion, touching thereupon his own sphere of origin, the Jewish people and its spiritual history. Prophets and psalmists represent for him an already decayed stage of religion in which every contact with the fundamental realities of ritual has been lost. The "theology" of the prophets or psalmists no longer had any idea of the genuine actuality of Yahweh, the Elohim of Israel. In the magic rites, which at the time of cultic potency forced the Elohim of the people into physical presence, prophets and psalmists could only see "riddles of primeval times."

He is particularly cutting about King Solomon, "the wise," whom he denounces as "an aesthete unnerved by erotic excesses and in a religious sense a progressivist blockhead"[2] typical of the regression of the cult from an effectively present national god into the preaching of an abstract and generally human deity in heaven. He refers to Solomon's prayer in the temple, where the king asks, "But will God indeed dwell on the earth?"[3] as a "scandalous speech." As though Israel's unique task had not consisted in building for its god a dwelling, a tent, and in providing all means for his constant presence. King Solomon's "sermon" was just twaddle and ushered in the poets of the Psalms who exiled the Elohim entirely into the blue sky, singing constantly of a deity in heaven whereas the Pentateuch does not even know the heavens as a seat of god. The Elohim of the Pentateuch (which Chaim Breisacher strangely enough takes to be a homogeneous archaic document) leads his people in a pillar of fire; the God of Israel dwells among the people. While later psalmists piously ask in the name of God, "Do I then eat the flesh of bulls and drink the blood of goats?"[4] the Pentateuch expressly describes the sacrifices as the actual nourishment of Yahweh. These pious litanies of the psalmists were actually a slap of impertinent enlightenment in the face of the reality of the cultic communion.

Breisacher's archaistic interpretation of the Pentateuch, which Thomas Mann describes at length and not without amusement, does not stop at details of the exegesis. He cannot say enough to show the genuine cultic communion with the Elohim of Israel as a magic technique, a manipulation of dynamic forces in which mishaps might easily occur, catastrophic short circuits due to mistakes and failures. Religion as ethics he considers a pale substitute for the sacral acts of the cult. Ethical codes of morality are a typical intellectual misunderstanding of laws rooted in archaic rituals. Prayer is for him only "the vulgarized and rationalistically watered-down late form" of very active and real magic invocation, the coercion of the gods.

I

The negative critique of Chaim Breisacher's propositions that runs through the pages of chapter XXVIII does not, I believe, give a full account of the author's fascination with Oskar Goldberg, whose life and work were his model for the portrait of Dr. Chaim Breisacher.[5] Not only does Mann's Joseph tetralogy draw heavily on the work of Goldberg, but his theoretical statements on mythology are also influenced by that strange historian and philosopher of religion, who after Johann Jacob Bachofen was the most radical interpreter of mythology. He took the language of myth so seriously that from a historian of mythology he evolved into a philosopher of mythology.

It is, I think, significant that Thomas Mann chose Goldberg's theory of mythology for his crucial chapter on myth and humanism. "One has to take away mythology from intellectual fascism and switch it over into humanism," Thomas Mann writes in 1941,[6] thus giving a clue to his great critique of Oskar Goldberg in the portrait of Chaim Breisacher. This "switch-over" of mythology into humanism—the major theme of his exchange of letters with Karl Kerenyi, the Hungarian historian of religion—is preformed by psychology.

It is well known that Thomas Mann's novels on mythical themes are indebted to Freud's psychoanalysis. Yet psychology and sociology (and Freud's psychoanalysis is constructed on sociological rather than on biological premises) are, as Philip Rahv has noted,[7] inherently antimythic. If the union of myth and humanism to which Thomas Mann aspires is to be realized in the coming age, neither a psychology nor a sociology of myth (which can give only an historical account) can satisfy his intention. Therefore Mann is driven time and again to the opposite pole, to the work of Oskar Goldberg, who neither psychologized nor sociologized myth, but rather insisted on the reality of man's mythical experience: the gods.

Goldberg's philosophy of myth is the extreme opposite of the psychoanalytic theory of myth, whose purely formal interpretation is symptomatic of an unmythical age, which can in no way do justice to the constitution of myth in its pristine form. Goldberg's mythological philosophy presented Thomas Mann with the possibility of arresting the total dissolution of myth. Therefore his work remained for Mann fascinating and repulsive at the same time; fascinating because Goldberg's philosophy could be set over against Freud's ideologization of myth; repulsive, because Mann became aware of its regressive nihilistic implications. Mann tried (with poetic license) to steer a course between these alternatives in his interpretation of mythology. Still, in 1937, when Thomas Mann together with Konrad Falke started to publish a journal *Mass and Wert* (dedicated to "free German culture") he invited Oskar Goldberg to contribute.[8]

Goldberg's major work, *Die Wirklichkeit der Hebräer* (Berlin 1925), which presents itself as "an introduction to the system of the Pentateuch," puts the problem of the "mythical reality" into an entirely new perspective. Only one volume of this work was published, and it is doubtful if now after the author's death[9] a second volume will ever appear. The book, though published in 1925, is derived from lectures given in private circles between 1903 and 1908. These dates are not without significance, for they provide us with a clue to the author's cultural "location." Bergson's philosophy, which influenced Sorel's political theory of myth, is also traceable in the conceptual apparatus of Goldberg's theory of mythology.

Yet Goldberg's philosophy of mythology should not be confused with the fabricated mythology so much in vogue in political groups and literary circles since Nietzsche and Sorel. Goldberg understood that Socrates represented a caesura dividing the history of mankind into an *ante* and *post* that cannot be eradicated at will. In fact, for him Socrates was much more to the point than Nietzsche, since the Greek rationalist understood that a society cannot artificially prolong the life of a myth. When, according to Goldberg, does mythology degenerate into a mere literary product? When the pantheon of gods no longer stands behind the myth. Nietzsche, in protesting against Socrates and attempting to return to the ecstasy of tragic greatness, necessarily paved the way for Sorel's literary and political apotheosis of mythology and for the ominous "myth of the twentieth century" culminating in a manipulated mass-hysteria of nations and classes.

The way to a new mythical age must follow the road of Socrates, the road of philosophy. The coming mythical age will be discovered by reason.[10] Goldberg's philosophy of myth presents a classical case for the dialectic of reason that destroys itself "reasonably" and calls for the magical ritual of the mythical age to counteract the tyrannical rule of technology in our civilization. Yet no modern philosopher has been so deeply influenced by the spirit of technology as Oskar Goldberg. For his interpretation of myth and ritual is given in a totally unsentimental and unliterary language, which could be taken from a textbook on electromagnetism. Against his will he testifies to the morphological congruity between magical ritualism and technical "know-how." Unintentionally he explains to us a dark side of our age: the nexus between the magical ritualism and the spiritual conformity of the masses in a technological society.

It speaks for the deep insight of Thomas Mann that he describes the process of reason's self-annihilation by analyzing Goldberg's philosophy of myth. It is, I think, of secondary importance that by 1947 he found Goldberg's highly conservative exegesis amusing and repulsive. It remains that he saved Goldberg's work from total oblivion by incorporating long passages from *Die Wirklichkeit der Hebräer* into chapter XXVIII of *Doctor Faustus*. Out of context some of the passages might strike the reader as comical, but in the context, Goldberg's interpretation of the Pentateuch presents a serious challenge to the accepted theological interpretation of it, be it orthodox, conservative, or liberal. But, as usual, theology met the challenge—with silence.

II

There are basically only two possible interpretations of myth: either you explain the language of myth as a specific symbolic form, or you take the record of mythology as reality. If the realm of myth is to be taken seriously, then, Goldberg argues, it is not enough to refer to "psychic realities," for such a solution evades the fundamental choice between fantasy and reality. If myths tell us about real events, then they testify to patterns that are contrary to the law of nature in which we live. The universe is ruled by a uniform system of natural laws that are valid everywhere and at every time. Only if this uniform system of natural laws is broken can a mythical event occur.

The problem of the reality of the mythical event rests on an ontological premise stressing the tension between spirit and matter. Only under the most difficult conditions can spirit be made to unite with matter. The spirit is not "at home" in the realm of matter. Against all vitalistic theories Goldberg insists on the sovereignty of life in the natural universe. The principle of life connects spirit and the realm of matter. Therefore the element of life is dominant in the texture of nature. Biology is, rightly understood, a transempirical science. Biology is metaphysics. Even if life manifests itself in the empirical realm, the laws of biology have their origin beyond the physical realm. These origins, constituting the "well springs" of life, are the gods of the mythical age.

The gods are the "biological centers" of the various races of mankind. Goldberg is the first after Hegel and Schelling to try a philosophic interpretation of polytheism: the god of one people is distinguished from the god of another people by the difference in biological centers. Every people that is a genuine kin-community has one (or several interconnected) biological centers. The idea of a god is for Goldberg not related to the abstract idea of "humanity," but rather is essentially connected with the idea of a people. The god has for the unity of the people a "biological" meaning. Mythology is, therefore, not a collection of ethnological phantasmagoria, but teaches us something about the actual relation of a people to its "biological" center.

The relation between the god and the people is a covenant. It is, therefore, not unilateral. Also, the people have an important biological role for the gods. Clan members are a potential field for the divine power, and the people as an entity serve as an instrument through which the divine power manifests itself.

The primordial equation (peoples = gods) pertinent for the interpretation of myth limits the power of the gods to ancient times. For only antiquity has known peoples that are concretely related to their biological center. The amalgamation of races, the dissolving of nations in the modern period, reflects the growing fixation of human society on the system of natural laws, culminating in a technology that destroys the last remnants of communities potent in rite and myth. In such a situation only philosophy can break the universal domination of natural laws.

In the covenant between the people and their god a specific boundary is constituted, the historical territory in which the god and the people meet. The god is also the power of the land. The land as an historical unit is related to specific divine powers. The earth of the land is not simply a natural space but also a dynamic divinized reality. Every "metaphysical people" presents a specific reality. Therefore the mythologies vary from people to people and from place to place. The various myths relate a particular story; however, the people telling the story do not know that it is a particular tale they tell but consider it to be universally true. Its gods are presented as "the" gods, its heaven and its earth are turned by the people into "the" heaven and "the" earth. The mythical community cannot see beyond itself, generalizing its experience and creating a generalized "ideology." It bridges the hiatus between its concrete circumscribed horizon of life and the rest of mankind by generalizing its myth. It is, therefore, the task of the historian to translate the language of myth back into its original context. The mythical cosmogonies that tell the story of the creation of heaven and earth actually refer to the heaven and the earth of a specific people.

Goldberg's equation (peoples-gods-lands) is exemplified in his interpretation of the cult. A people needs a territory not only to dwell in but also to actualize its cult. Not every territory is equally suitable for the cultic act. Peoples will migrate in search of a suitable territory where the well springs of its life, the gods, may break through. The land where the god and the people come together and find each other is a cultic territory. The cult presents the union of the biological powers of the people with its source of life. The aim of the cult is the covenant with the gods.

When a people first comes into a territory its earth is dark and void and its heavens above are closed until the cult is established. The territory is the foundation of the cult, but before the cult is established the territory remains neutral ground. Only when the cult comes into function does the earth come alive and the heavens spread above as the firmament. Hesiod in the first part of his theogony does not, as he thought, present a general cosmogony, but rather records the constitution of the cult. The various cosmogonies of mythology do not tell the story of the creation of heaven and earth, but rather give a detailed account of the constitution of cult. Gods and mortals must work together in taming the wild and overwhelming powers in both the divine and human realms. Therefore the first sacred act on the part of the gods is a sacrifice of gods, as much as on the part of man it is the sacrifice of men. Once the common bond between gods and men is established the covenant of the cult comes into being. The covenant is an entirely unmetaphorical symbol. The "symbol" is the contract, the union between two partners. The symbol is a sign of the covenant, by which the gods manifest themselves in the community of men.

The reciprocal covenant between gods and peoples aims to rule the forces of matter. The people wants to emancipate itself from the chains of necessity of the laws of nature. The gods, however, need a mechanism to break through the wall of nature's "iron law." Gods and peoples are united against a common enemy: the natural nexus of the universe. The natural *rocher de bronze*[11] cannot be overcome without specific action and effort. What contradicts the laws of nature is the "miracle" that Goldberg takes as a concrete "biological-metaphysical" phenomenon and not simply as a figure of speech. The miracle is a "political action" of transcendent powers manifesting themselves in the community of men. The powers manifested are the gods.

In the cultic communion the union between the pantheon of the gods and the community of men is perpetuated. So long as "the way up and down is one and the same" the mythical era is real. It rests on the idea of reciprocity between gods and mortals. Men ascend to heaven and gods come down to earth. Such an era has no idea of destiny because the relation between gods and men is still personal. As soon as the idea of destiny rises, the twilight of the gods is near. Man is cut off from the cultic communion with the gods and left to himself. The idea of destiny comes to the fore when a mythical age is drawing to its end and the reciprocity of the cultic covenant interrupted. From the experience of destiny the way is open for the idea of causality ruling in the realm of man as in the realm of nature. Greek tragedy presents this very drama of the gradual eclipse of the gods.

The way from cult to culture leads through the period of fixation in which the relation between a people and its god becomes paralyzed. The "powers" interested in perpetuating and stabilizing the universal rule of natural law tend to outlaw all "miracles," all possible breakthroughs into the realm of nature, cutting off the communion between the people and its biological center, the gods. This process of fixation leads, in the end, to the dissolution of the people as a biological unit.

Technique is substituted for man's cultic communion with the gods. The physical tool can, according to Goldberg, fulfill to a certain degree the function of the ritualistic sacral act, since technique deals on the "unorganic" level with the same problem that the cult deals with in the "organic" realm. Technique and ritual have been in opposition since time immemorial. If a man builds an altar, he shall not build it of hewn stone, for, according to the Pentateuch, by lifting the technical tool on the altar he would desecrate the cultic table.

The forces opposing the cultic union through the process of fixation are symbolized in the image of the Leviathan. This symbol has survived as a mythical relic into modern times and found a striking revival in the essay of Hobbes on "the matter, form and power of a commonwealth, ecclesiastical and civic." For it is precisely through the dissolution of the kin-communities that the artificially organized society, the mortal god of the state, is erected. The state functions as a substitute for and heir to the cultic covenant, institutionalizing the impersonal social contract.

The shift from the cultic community to the society of the state is reflected also in the transition from the concrete national religions to the abstract world religions. The god of the people who broke through the barrier of the laws of nature turns into the creator of the natural order. Whereas the national religions rest on the concrete relation of a people to its biological center, the god of the world religions (when "genuine" peoples no longer exist) represents not a reality but an abstract notion. The god of a concrete people cannot do everything, but what he can do he does with power. The god of the world religions, however, is one who can do everything, possesses all power—and therefore is concretely only an empty formula, an ideological façade that can be filled with any content. In the world religions the relation between god and man is merely fictitious. In the process of fixation the actively present god is turned into an abstract "good lord" who becomes everything and presently—nothing.

The stages of the metamorphosis of god from the active, present god of the people to the general god of mankind can be studied in the literature of the Old Testament. The development from the ritual of the Pentateuch to the *ethos* of prophetism, which in the perspective of progress is usually considered as the step from a primitive ritualism to a "pure" monotheism, is evaluated by Oskar Goldberg according to the specific weight of religious substance inherent in the ritual of the cult and which is lacking in the "pure" monotheism of the prophets or in late philosophy. Yahweh, the Elohim of Israel, goes before his people by day as a cloud and by night as a pillar of fire. He walks among the people and has his dwelling among them. Yahweh, the Elohim of Israel, lives in active presence among his people, whereas King Solomon, the builder of the centralized sanctuary and the enlightened philosopher-king, sermonizes on abstract principles. The late psalmists can see in the gods of the peoples[12] only idols, the work of man's hand. Thus the way is opened for the development of the abstract theological monotheism of Judaism and Christianity.

In the Babylonian exile the people of Israel indeed encountered gods that were mere idols, bereft of all numinal powers because Babylon, like later Rome and today the West, was the incarnation of "culture."[13] The story of the tower of Babel symbolically concentrates within this society all the powers that have been taken away from the biological divine forces and that now join in the building of a technical civilization. This civilization is the activity of the progeny of Cain, the first technician and founder of cities.

Only when the biological communities collapse can the organization of the state flourish. The society of the state aims by technical means to halt the progressive disintegration of the biological community. The Babylonian and Roman deities are gods of the state and not the biological center of peoples. They are civic representatives and their pantheon belongs to the category of civic theology. Babylon is (for the Pentateuch and the prophet Isaiah) a "no people" and its gods "no gods." Only such state gods are treated in the Pentateuch as nonentities, whereas the gods of Egypt appear as potent antagonists of Israel's God. The exodus of the people of Israel out of Egypt is for the Pentateuch primarily a war waged between Yahweh, the Elohim of Israel, and the Elohim of Egypt.

Goldberg's "archaic exegesis" has, I think, led to some striking results by bringing the primordial strata of myth and ritual of the Pentateuch into relief. The cultic communion presupposes the actuality of Yahweh and the negative but active reality of the "other gods." But he defeats his purpose in trying to press the Pentateuch into a "system," thereby necessarily overlooking the manifold strata that run through the compilation of the various books. At this point the historian of ritual himself falls victim to ritualism. The subject of inquiry boomeranged on the method of inquiry.

Goldberg's major impetus was, however, not philological "archaeology" but the fundamental problem of a theodicy. His inquiry led him to the somewhat startling discovery that even the Pentateuch had nothing to do with the general "theological concepts" of divine omnipotence and divine omnipresence. If Yahweh, the Elohim of Israel, is waging war on other Elohim, such a statement is only meaningful if the superiority of one of the parties is, at least for a while, in doubt. Neither can the concept of divine omnipresence be upheld in the view of divine revelations. God is not everywhere but only where he "manifests" himself. The presence of god is limited to the place where his name is known. If god is bound to his manifestation, then he is also limited to a corporeality from which he can be freed, outside the Pentateuch, only by a theological tour de force.

Only if the concepts of divine omnipotence and omnipresence are set aside, can the question of divine justice be asked in a meaningful way. Goldberg's answer implies that the just god is at this time not present, and that his reality and power are eclipsed. Therefore the question of divine justice does not arise at all. Justice is possible in an ultimate sense only when the war waged between the gods comes to an end and the premundane god becomes manifest in the world. Only at the end of history do the *milhamot Yahweh*, the wars of Yahweh, end. Only in eschatological terms can the prophet Isaiah speak about the *yeshu'at Yahweh*, the victory of Yahweh, in the war with the "other gods," when the primordial "one god" will manifest himself as the Elohim of Israel. Since the primordial god is not present in the world, it is the task of the peoples to bring the primordial god into power, thus enacting his liberation from the bondage of being a mere potentiality.

This eschatological theogony reminds the historian of religion strongly of the ideology of Jewish Gnostics in the late eighteenth century, when the radical wing of Sabbatian messianists developed a strikingly similar theology distinguishing the premundane "one god" from the "many gods" in history. Together with the Gnostics, Oskar Goldberg rejects in his philosophy of religion the sterile orthodox division between mono- and polytheism and puts the emphasis on a dialectic between the present and absent god.

The absence of god is a general theme of Gnostic philosophy and literature of the last twenty years. For Goldberg the eclipse of god takes the form of the absence of divine justice in the human realm. The sacral act of the people is a transcendental political action. Whereas other Gnostics apotheosize and universalize the experience of absence, Goldberg tries to coerce god into presence by the magical potency of a sacral act. The sacral act affects as a political action the eschatological revolution.

At a time when the boundaries between cultic mythology and poetic fantasies have been so utterly confused that sheer enthusiasm for mythology can avail itself of the last remnants of prestige vested in religion without committing itself to any definite or rigorous standard of belief or action, and when poetic license manipulates mythic motives frivolously while putting on a mask of seriousness, Goldberg's radical philosophy of mythology has the advantage of facing squarely the problem of mythical reality and consciousness. It teaches us that mythology presupposes the actuality of a mythico-religious form of life. The premise is obscured in all theological or literary interpretations of mythology that can see in it only a symbolic mode of expression. Goldberg's theory of myth is a test case for all myth-enthusiasts who blur the simple but basic distinction between the real and the poetic.

In such a radical theory the partly grotesque and partly nihilistic consequences of a restitution of mythology come into the open—consequences that less responsible and more oracular (and therefore also more successful) hierophants like Martin Heidegger in philosophy or Ezra Pound in poetry fail to come to terms with. In order to establish the union between gods and men or to recover the potency of the sacral act man must first abandon or destroy the entire history of culture. I see Goldberg's originality not so much in his interpretation of myth, later confirmed in rough outline by empirical anthropology and ethnology, as in the terrifying literalness with which he set out to translate myth into reality and in his uncompromising will to take the records of archaic cults and rituals seriously and not merely as a way of flirting with current fashions.

The archaism explicit in Goldberg's philosophy of myth, and latent in the so nebulous conservative nostalgia for it, weakens the foundations of culture and threatens to usher in that tabula rasa of civilization for which conservatives today like to blame the "tyranny of progress." Mythology after Socrates remains illusory. Goldberg's philosophy can only assert that we would have to eat again from the tree of knowledge in order to fall back into the state of innocence. Such is the law of the irreversible process of the history of consciousness.

17

Culture and Ideology[1]

I

In April 1856, on the occasion of an anniversary celebration for the Chartist journal *The People's Paper*,[2] Marx attempted to characterize the signature of the nineteenth century. He undertook this task in view of the progressions in the ability to master nature, which determined the regression of society. He proceeded from one of the great certainties characteristic of the nineteenth century: "At the same pace that mankind masters nature, man seems to become enslaved to other men or to his own infamy. [. . .] This antagonism between the productive powers and the social relations of our epoch is a fact, palpable, overwhelming, and indisputable." In this contradiction between technological progress and social regression, which "throws the pathetic prophets of regression into confusion," Marx recognizes the conditions of the coming revolution. He claims that "in order for the new powers of society to become properly effective, new men are required who will be their masters—and those are the workers."[3] When Marx undertook the analysis of capitalist means of production in *Das Kapital* twelve years later, this had so fully developed that its open secret, the antagonism between means of productive forces and social relations, could now be unraveled. Moreover, these means of production stood first at the beginning of a technological development that would intensify and obscure the antagonism of bourgeois society in new ways. Today, therefore, a new interpretation of its antagonism is required. Marx himself in 1857 was able to use economic categories to describe the "existential forms and determinations" of "modern bourgeois society."[4] He proceeded from the analysis of commodity because the commodity rules the economic structure of bourgeois society. Movement of goods did, of course, exist on the level of precapitalist means of production, but it was first in capitalism that the commodity itself became a determining form for society. "It would be necessary [. . .] for the commodity structure to penetrate society in all its aspects and to remold it in its own image."[5] The commodity first appears in the means of production of modern capitalism as a "universal category" that determines the whole of bourgeois society. This stems from the way in which the commodity as exchange value takes on a life of its own, becoming a thing particularly both sensual and transcendental. It transforms living work itself into a commodity, so that its creator becomes a creature. The economic product is sensual-transcendental because of the secret intervention of social relations. "The secrecy of the commodity-form" is constituted in that it mirrors back in itself a particular social relation between humans, which 'adopts the phantasmagoric form of a relation between things.'"[6] Marx finds an analogy for this social mechanism in the "foggy region of the religious world." "Here products of human minds appear endowed with their own life, among one another and standing in relation to men in autonomous forms."[7] Marx calls this relationship fetishism. The fetishistic character suits the work production insofar as it is produced as commodity. This mode is thus indivisible from commodity production. The abbreviation of the commodity fetish through which Marx describes the social relationship in the economic process of the capitalist means of production is supposed also to later provide the key to an interpretation of the superstructure. While however this abbreviation yields the key to an interpretation of capitalism in both its sub- and superstructures, the problem of the contradiction between technological progress and social regress, which Marx himself had focused on, retreats into the background.

More than half a century has been needed in order to bring Marx's insight into the alteration in consciousness conditioned by the commodity relation into consideration for all cultural sectors. Lukacs deploys the category of commodity in order to interpret bourgeois society. Using this category as a key, Walter Benjamin attempted to describe the phantasmorgia of capitalistic culture on a whole. This work, which was the "dictatorially dominant object"[8] of his labor in his last years, was not written. Among other achievements is a memorandum composed in 1935: "Paris, Capital of the Nineteenth Century."[9] It suggests in its outline which intensity of reflection is necessary in order to detect within the superstructure the commodity fetish, whose "theological quirks" Marx had analyzed in the substructure of the capitalist society. A commentary by Adorno on this draft also exists, since the Hornberger letter of August 2, 1935, should in fact be read as a critical engagement with it. This text and its commentary do not supplant the nonexistent work, but they do lead right into the center of the problem of culture and ideology, into the dispute of late capitalism or industrial society. Two passages, which should be singled out, mark the high-point and the ruination of the phantasmagoria of the nineteenth century. "The phantasmagoria of capitalist culture attains its most radiant unfolding in the world exhibition of 1867. The Second Empire is at the height of its power. Paris is acknowledged as the capital of luxury and fashion." "World exhibitions are places of pilgrimage to the commodity festish. [. . .] World exhibitions glorify the exchange value of the commodity. They create a framework in which its use value recedes into the background. They open a phantasmagoria which a person enters in order to be distracted. The entertainment industry makes this easier by elevating the person to the level of the commodity. He surrenders to its manipulations while enjoying his alienation from himself and others."[10]

Benjamin's general characterization of the high-point of capitalist culture achieves its force in detail: in the interpretation of Grandville's art, which has as its secret theme the "enthroning of the commodity" and the "glint of dispersion" that surrounds it, and in reference to the commodity-utopia of Saint Simonians. Benjamin's allusion to the Saint Simonians is not without interest for the theme of late capitalism or industrial society. This is because from the beginning, industrial society is the signature under which sociology operates. The Saint Simonians revealed this secret signature of sociology and also anticipated its orientation today because they understood its integrated arrangement of industrial rulers, functional hierarchies, systematic organizations in surprising correspondence to feudal hierarchies, ordering of interests and the gradation of dominance. Benjamin says of them, "The Saint-Simonians, who envision the industrialization of the earth, take up the idea of world exhibitions. [. . .] The Saint-Simonians anticipated the development of the global economy, but not the class struggle. Next to their active participation in industrial and commercial enterprises around the middle of the century stands their helplessness on all questions concerning the proletariat."[11]

In the program of the Saint Simonians the "commodity world as Utopia" comes into view, but its back side does not reveal itself: the commodity world as Hell.[12] In an interpretation of Offenbach, whose operetta represented for Benjamin "the ironic Utopia of a lasting domination of capital," "this double sense" could, Adorno claims, "turn out to be extremely appropriate for an interpretation of Offenbach—that is, the double sense of the Underworld and Arcadia; both of these are explicit categories in Offenbach the ramifications of which could be pursued right down to the instrumental details of orchestration."[13]

In the last paragraph of the text, which deals with "Haussmann or the Barricades," the "monuments of the bourgeoisie" are recognized as "ruins" even before they have fallen. For Benjamin, Haussmann becomes the key figure of the epoch. This is because the Medusa-like countenance of capitalist culture, beauty, and violence are manifest in his creations. "Hausmann's urbanistic ideal was one of views in perspective down long street-vistas. It corresponded to the tendency which was noticeable again and again during the nineteenth century, to ennoble technical exigencies with artistic aims." Benjamin saw the true goal of Hausmannian labors as the protection of the city against civil war: Hausmann wanted to make the erection of barricades in Paris impossible for all time. "The breadth of the streets was to make the erection of barricades impossible, and new streets were to provide the shortest route between the barracks and the working-class areas. Contemporaries christened the undertaking 'strategic beautification.'"[14] Culture, its values and goods, found in Benjamin a distant observer. This is because his survey in art and science "has a lineage which cannot be contemplated without dread. The products of arts and science owe their existence not merely to the geniuses that created them but also to the unnamed drudgery of their contemporaries. There is no document of culture that is not at the same time a document of barbarism."[15] Cultural history can never calculate its idea according to this Should and Have. Thus the detachedness in which cultural history presents its contents discloses itself to Benjamin as illusory. Cultural history is always founded on a false consciousness. If the concept of culture is a problematic one for Benjamin, then so is also its ruin into values and goods "which become objects of possession for mankind. The work of the past remains uncompleted for historical materialism. It perceives no epoch in which the completed past could even in part drop conveniently, thing-like, into humankind's lap. The concept of culture, as the substantive concept of creations considered independent, if not from the production process in which they originate, then from a production process in which they continue to survive, carries a fetishistic trait. Culture appears in a reified form. Its history would be nothing but the sediment formed by the curiosities that have been stirred up in the consciousness of human beings without any genuine, that is, political, experience."[16]

This critique of Benjamin's comes formally into agreement with an attack on cultural history and sociology from the Right, which is simultaneously carried out by Carl Schmitt and Christoph Steding. The formal identity of their critiques' line of attack can easily seduce one into speaking of a rightist-fascist and leftist-fascist attack on liberal culture, its history and ideology. Benjamin's criticism, however, is separated from Schmitt's and Steding's attack by an abyss: the difference in how they understand the relation between culture and politics is decisive. If Benjamin refers to a "real, that is, political experience," then he refers back to politics as construction, as overcoming of nature and emancipation from the horror of violence that eternally recurs in a circle. When Carl Schmitt and Christoph Steding refer to political experience, however, they refer back to this horror of violence itself, which persists throughout history. Historical-dialectical criticism since Marx debunked the bourgeois apotheosis of culture because culture in its insularity becomes a substitute for the human emancipation that the political emancipation of bourgeois society did not realize. Bourgeois society could not realize human emancipation, however, and its apotheosis of culture becomes a lie because it leaves untouched the economic fundament where inhumanity continues to reign. For Marxist criticism, the bourgeois ideology of freedom and beauty is mere appearance, but the appearance of a truth that cannot be made manifest in a bourgeois manner. The fascist critique exposes the bourgeois apotheosis of culture as a surrogate and as a powerless superstructure that conceals the horror of the political reality. It criticizes the aloofness of bourgeois culture because it has a neutralizing effect on the barbaric potential of politics that the theoreticians of fascism aspire to let loose. The bourgeois ideology of freedom and beauty is also appearance for them, but the appearance of a lie.[17]

Benjamin once said of his Arcades project that it had to actually be wrested from the realm where madness reigns.[18] This is also true for its method, which Adorno considers as not far from the methods of C. G. Jung and Klage, in which "history and magic oscillate."[19] Benjamin, however, settled himself on the "crossroads of magic and positivism"[20] in order to make those insights available from extreme reactive theoreticians "completely useless for the goals of fascism."[21] If Benjamin tries to capture the fetish character of the commodity in a net of correspondences and analogies, he must set "materially" into immediate relation individually manifest traits from the region of the superstructure with corresponding traits of the substructure. Adorno's critique rightfully addresses itself against this because the materialistic determination of cultural character is only mediated through the cumulative process. "The fetish character of the commodity is not a fact of consciousness; it is rather dialectical in character, in the eminent sense that it produces consciousness."[22] The insight into the universality of commodity fetishism in the nineteenth century could now indicate with utmost precision its social as well as its economic character. This change of commodity fetishism into a total form must also become able to be experienced sensually. The specific character of the commodity in the nineteenth century, that is, industrial commodity production, must be worked out more clearly than Benjamin has done. This is because the relationship between commodity and alienation is present since the onset of capitalism, that is, since the age of manufacture. The "unity" of modernity constitutes itself out of this relationship; however, the physiognomy of the nineteenth century does not. The problem of the commodity form in capitalistic culture can be concretized only through the specific historical categories of world trade and imperialism.[23]

The difference that appears between text and commentary concerning the interpretation of the phantasmorgia of capitalist culture does not stem so much from a difference between the appearance and the violence of phantasmorgia itself; rather, it comes from Adorno's univocal relationship to the constellation of the twentieth century, where substructure and superstructure no longer exist apart from one another, where ideology functions no longer as the façade of a veiled gargantuan interest, and where the material production process as such finally reveals itself as that "which it always was, from its origins in the exchange-relationship as the false consciousness which the two contrasting parties have of one another: ideology."[24] It remains questionable in any case whether the constellation of the twentieth century as Adorno describes it can still be placed under the signature of commodity fetishism, or more precisely: whether the problem of industrial society remains conceivable via a concept of exchange. It should be conceded to Adorno that the universal execution of exchange today "is decoupled from the qualitative character of producers and consumers, from the mode of production, even from the requirement that the social mechanism settle for being secondary." It is to be conceded as well that a "humanity classified as customer, the subject of demands [...] is socially preformed past all naïve representations, not only by the technical condition of productive forms, but as well from economic relations."[25] However, does Adorno's key concept for a critical analysis of society, the idea that profit is primary, still hold for industrial society?

Also if one grants Adorno that in the late capitalist epoch the abstraction of exchange value is not socially neutral, that "in the reduction of men to agents and bearers of commodity-exchange, the domination of men over men" is hidden, as well if one realizes that the industrial social formation does not take place "beyond conflicts and antagonisms or despite them," but rather that its medium is "antagonisms themselves" that destroy society at the same time, the question remains as to whether the gears, gnashing and groaning with untold victims, preserve themselves to this day "only by means of profit interest."[26] Should the analysis of industrial society not be situated closer to the space of naked violence's madness and veiled domination than Adorno ventures? Is the law of exchange not overextended as a universal category for conceptualizing the constellation of the era of technology and industry, if profit-motive subjectively regresses and no longer objectively appears in an unmediated, clearly recognizable form as it does in the epoch of classical capitalism? Adorno's recourse to a universal exchange society befits a certain metaphoric character in view of the conditions of production for industrial society. In the capitalistic organization of society, extraeconomic violence only appears on the margin, for example in crisis situations, in order to regulate universal exchange. In industrial society, however, the quantity of the extraeconomic violent intervention is altered. It means that the situation today, from the point of view of classical theory and praxis of capitalism, is this: the crisis has become permanent. From the point of view of a theory of the current epoch it means: the intervention of extraeconomic violence is the signature of everyday life. Does it appear today—in view of the permanent intervention of extraeconomic violence in the industrial society, as a whole—that domination cannot be miscalculated as an independent factor, or simply as a function of profit motivations? Is it impossible, even in view of the current constellation, to unmask profit-seeking itself as a variant of domination? Is it impossible finally to intensify the classic Marxist thesis concerning the overturning of "rational" capitalism in its late phase into irrationality and to say: this irrationality exposes first the entire *ratio* of capitalism: domination?

When Marx attempted in 1857 to describe in a "rough draft" the capitalist society in its entirety, he struck at the limits of its organization. He recognized as the limits of capital production the organization of capitalist society itself. In the capitalist production process, the technical means for labor pass through "various metamorphoses ... the last of which is an automatic system of machinery." Marx claimed that the capitalist means of production work toward their own dissolution through the development of technology and industry. Because, "to the extent to which [...] large industry develops itself, the creation of real wealth becomes dependent less on labor time and the quantum of dedicated work, and more on the power of agents set into motion during labor time."[27] Through the progress of technology, or more precisely, through the application of science and technology to manufacturing, production, which rests on the exchange value, breaks down. Marx thinks that the process of direct production strips the scantiness and contrariness away from itself. He thus construes the technological development of the productive forces as the explosive factor of the capitalist society. This is because for capitalist means of production, industry and technology are only means for producing "from its narrow-minded fundament outwards." In truth, however, technology and industry develop the material conditions, which "blow up in the air"[28] the capitalist means of production. The problem of the organization of society, Marx concedes, can no longer be placed in accordance with the industrial and technological development under the key of exchange society. After the economic veil is torn, however, violence is capable of hiding itself anew in institutional and bureaucratic entities, which can internalize control through new mechanisms. As soon as the institutional relations of domination are interiorized, economic polarizations can be deactivated, and the antagonisms latent in economic gaps can be dismantled without violence being remediated as a signature of the antecedent process. In the 1856 speech and in the "rough draft" of 1857 in which Marx points beyond the boundaries of economic emancipation, he sets up, if only on the margin, the question of human emancipation in view of technological and industrial development. In the face of technological development, human emancipation requires "new men" in order to "rightly come into agency." So that the new powers of industrial society do not ultimately perpetuate domination and slavery, new men are required who would be their masters.

The question of what form of organization will be established on the other side of the tunnel of economic necessity for the antagonisms is also the secret key to all the theories of the industrial society. It is always a theory of new forms of governance. Exactly because domination is no longer economically necessary, if it is preserved at all it must be defended as anonymous authority. It is well worth the effort to investigate why reactionary theoreticians are, on many accounts, superior in the analysis of the industrial epoch to liberal and Marxist theoreticians. I assume that their relationship to authority and violence is much more intimate than that of the theoreticians of the Enlightenment. The exchange principle still assumes a degree of reason, and its overturning into unreason is, seen from the point of the exchange principle, itself a dialectic and thus a process of reason, which in the organization of the administrated world is no longer visible. The truth of this appearance, according to which the living conditions of the present society are organized in their most inhuman form, must be recognized. But it should be done with the intention to penetrate the element of horror in this appearance of truth.

II

To start with, Nietzsche must be named as the one who introduced the "abyssal antagonism of culture and civilization" into German philosophy almost at the same time as Tönnies. Nietzsche's critique of culture is a critique of civilization as decadence, but its main concern is a defense of culture against the rising plebeians, the socialism of the masses. In the trends of Europe's democratic movements, which strive to create an egalitarian society, Nietzsche sees favorable preconditions for "more encompassing figures of mastery,"[29] the likes of which history has not yet seen. "While . . . the democratizing of Europe will lead to the production of a type prepared for slavery in the subtlest sense," it is "at the same time an involuntary arrangement for the breeding of tyrants—in every sense of that word, including the most spiritual."[30] Nietzsche posed a "seductive and terrible question": "And would it not be a kind of goal, redemption, and justification for the democratic movement itself if someone arrived who could make use of it—by finally producing besides it new and sublime development of slavery [. . .] a higher kind of dominating and Caesarian spirits who would stand upon it, maintain themselves by it, and elevate themselves through it?"[31]

When Marx posed the question about the "new men," which could master the "new forces of society," he envisioned men that are bound to revolt against the inhumanities of domination and slavery. The new enlightenment, which is placed under the sign of Nietzsche, believes itself to be enlightened from the emancipation of man and of the Enlightenment. It draws on the "nature" of humans, which always means violence. It fixes humans, whose consciousness already broke from the compulsions of nature, back into place, be it by means of the ancient belief in destiny or by the means of the sacrificial rituals of primitive religion. This regression of consciousness, in which since-mature man is once again incapacitated, should be signaled by two stations of German sociology, even in the roughest terms: Max Weber and Arnold Gehlen. Sociology is the ideal prolongation of the industrial society itself. If instead of the *œuvres incomplètes* of industrial society's real history, we criticize the *œuvres postumes* of its ideological history, "our criticism centers on the very questions of which the present age says: that is the question."[32]

When Marx analyzed the sensual-transcendental character of the commodity, he looked for analogies in the cloudy realm of the religious world. But, his depiction of the commodity as a fetish is determined by the desire to drive out the commodity's "theological quirks": to demolish the fetish through a theoretical enlightenment of consciousness and through a practical revolution in society. Weber, however, under the sign of Nietzsche, mystifies both rationalization and intellectualization, and even the demystification of the world, to the fate that remains inescapable and that establishes new forms of bondage. Weber sees industrial society "together with the inanimate machine it is busy fabricating the shell of bondage which men will perhaps be forced to inhabit some day, as powerless as the farm hands of ancient Egypt. This might happen if a technically superior administration were to be the ultimate and sole value in the ordering of their affairs; and that means: a rational bureaucratic administration. . . . "[33] This issue was already addressed by Nietzsche, but Weber was the first to analyze it sociologically. The external structure of bureaucratic governance affects the internal structure of the psychic and cultural organization. Outside and inside are both doomed. In Weber, organizational rule and the agricultural state of late civilization continue each other uninterruptedly.

Already in the treatise "The Protestant Ethic and the Spirit of Capitalism," where Weber constructs a religious family-tree for capitalism, he points to the dissociation of the triumphant capitalism from the psychic presuppositions of the beginnings of the bourgeois society, because of its mechanical foundation. Weber's treatise does not exhaust itself in establishing a religious genealogy, but rather culminates in his departure from a time of free humanity: the Puritan *wants* to be a career man, to an obedient humanity: we *must* be so. This change from a free to an obedient career man is what Weber's whole analysis aims to account for. For the Puritan, the care for worldly goods was something like a thin cloak on his shoulder, which he could take off anytime, but "fate decreed that the cloak should become an iron cage."[34]

Capitalist means of production created the "fate" of the iron cage, but this cage of industrial society appears to Weber to be independent from the relations of production. This is his eternally recurring objection to the socialism of the *literati*. Because, even a further elimination of private capitalism would not mean a "shattering of the iron cage" of industrial society, but rather that "now also the *top management* of nationalized or socialized enterprises would become bureaucratic. State bureaucracy would rule *alone* if private capitalism were eliminated. The private and public bureaucracies which now work next to, and potentially against, each other and hence check one another to a degree, would be merged into a single hierarchy. This would be similar to the situation in ancient Egypt, but it would occur in a much more rational—and hence unbreakable—form."[35] The organization of the industrial society, however, appears an inescapable fate to Weber, because for him social relations are constituted only through general immaturity. In the domination of bureaucracy, the rule of humans over one another is concealed. Weber excuses this as fate. Because industrial society does not need anyone to order it, that is, no new man who will first come rightly into agency via new productive forces, it is a matter of "setting an" imponderable *something* "against this machinery [. . .] in order to rescue a remainder of humanity from this paralyzing of the soul, from this solo domination of the bureaucratic ideal of life." This remainder of humanity lives on only in retreat from the public sphere, from social reality.[36]

This retreat of the "ultimate and most sublime values . . . from public life either into the transcendental realm of mystic life or into the brotherliness of direct and personal human relations"[37] only indicates that pure interiority and naked domination fit one another like concave and convex. The fate of our culture is to have our eyes "blinded for a thousand years—blinded by the allegedly or presumably exclusive orientation toward the grandiose moral fervor of Christian ethics,"[38] that we turn our seeing eyes to polytheism: to the struggle of the gods of individual orders and values. "Here, too, different gods struggle with one another, now and for all times to come."[39] Two thousand years of Christian history must be crossed out in order to let ancient polytheism return at the apex of modernity. Only after first being trimmed down so regressively can human self-consciousness be sealed within the steel cage of science of technology.

The concept of fate, which is supported by the men of blind rule, reflects the domination that humans apply to each other. This destiny is only inescapable because it determines itself through authority. This makes Weber's sociological analysis clear, while his mythological talk of destiny transfigures the facts. Weber's analysis as well as his prognosis achieve their force from the constellation of the industrial society itself, which has, in the East as well as in the West, driven the potentialities for domination to extremes. So far as Weber describes what is, so far as his analysis preserves a prognosticated world, it would be powerless to polemicize against it. His complicity with the course of history is something quite different: it misleads him into elevating occurrence to destiny. Weber was directly aware of the haunting concepts of collectivity, as a letter found in his literary estate to Robert Liefmann most distinctly attests to. For Weber collectives are "nothing other than the chance that particular kinds of *actions* take place, actions of specific individual men. Otherwise nothing at all. . . ."[40] Whoever knows this should, when the talk turns to destiny, go ahead and name names.

III

The relapse of consciousness to Greek polytheism is, however, only the first step of regress. To render an apology for industrial culture, Gehlen has to return to the primitive Molochian sacrificial ritual itself. Industrial culture has emerged out of "the collaboration of the exact sciences, technology, and industrial evaluation." In the structure of the bond between science and technology, there is no external reason for degeneration. "There is no reason to connect the consistently advancing results of knowledge and discovery with the thought of decline or mere stagnation." The civilization of industrial society achieves "an infinity structured by advancements and threatened only by violent interruption," even an "immortality."[41] In the collaboration between exact science, technology, and industrial evaluation, "humanity has become completely dependent on the processes of machines [. . .] so that [. . .] the apparatuses we once operated begin to belong to our biological life like the snail shell belongs to the snail."[42] The authority of physicist Werner Heisenberg is called upon: technology "then appears 'almost not as the product of conscious human effort towards the propagation of material power, rather as a biological process on a large scale, in which the structure inherent in human organization are transmitted in broader measure to man's environment, thus a biological process deprived of control by humans.'"[43] This arrangement of industrial culture is no longer controllable by humans, however. Therein lies the question that already starts with Nietzsche and makes its way up to Carl Schmitt: What kind of politics is strong enough to make use of the new technology? For Gehlen this would be "a most deeply conservative attempt to convince [. . .] even this chance to control a metahuman process, which has already relinquished control"—thus "against the effort, counter to the flux of time, to protect man's sense of self and consciousness of self-importance."[44] In order to expel the vices of his "self-importance" as individual from the newly matured man—"spawn of the sixteenth century raised by the nineteenth" (Hofmannsthal)[45]—Gehlen has to return to the difference between "originary man" [*Urmensch*] and "late culture" [*Spätkultur*]; a set formula of Gehlen's which in light of our question can also be read as the difference between "originary culture" [*Urkultur*] and "the present" [*Gegenwart*]. Gehlen sees himself before the "novel task" "to draw the self-actualization and autonomy of the individual, which was won over by the institution, from human nature. [. . .] This same faculty, therefore, which emerges in the thoughts and transactions that people share, confirms itself into one power that in turn lays down its own laws to its very core."[46] One thing certainly threatens institutional power: it is endangered by the challenge of a matured humanity. Therefore Gehlen's sharpest critique takes issue with the claim of a subject that has not fully succumbed to the institutions. He establishes a system of domination so absolute that Weber's question, what do we have against this machinery in order to maintain the *remainder* of humanity free from the absolute reign of the bureaucratic ideal, has to be dismissed as romantic sentiment. "Whoever commits himself with 'body and soul' has no other choice but to let himself be consumed by the appropriate institution, for beyond this, he cannot find a point of entrance. This is the dignity which our time so thoroughly lacks, where the 'subjects' are in lasting revolt against institutions."[47] If Marx speaks of the "elimination of alienness" with which humans are supposed to relate to their own productions, if he says that "man's own action becomes an alien power that subjugates him, instead of him controlling it," and if he claims that humans "must take into their power the exchange, production, and means of their mutual relations," so Marx is, for Gehlen, ensnarled in the illusion of a possible annulment of alienation, whose history Gehlen outlines in his highly illuminative but also highly treacherous essay.[48] Alienation deliberately forms the fundament of his theory of society. The fundamental principle of Rousseau, Fichte, and also of Hegel, that man can only come to himself over other men, is hardened by Gehlen into the principle according to which man can only maintain indirectly a lasting relationship to himself and his own kind and must find himself by means of a self-renouncing detour. This detour leads through institutions, but loss and recovery of man through the institution for Ghelen procede by way of a Molochian ritual of sacrifice. In all seriousness Gehlen says that "at least people are incinerated and consumed by their own creations and not by brute nature, like animals. Institutions are the great preserving and consuming orders and fates that outlast us by far and to whivch we surrender knowingly."[49] People are burned up and consumed not only in Auschwitz and Hiroshima, for the sacrificial ritual is permanent. The exception only proves the rule. That man is a historical being means for Gehlen that he must "allow himself to be consumed" by institutions. The abject phantasmagoria of hell, which Benjamin caught sight of in the nineteenth century, finally reaches its apex in Gehlen: Adorno's correction of Benjamin's image applied really only to the phantasmagoria of industrial culture: that it is not that the ring of Saturn should become a cast-iron balcony, but the balcony should become the real ring of Saturn.[50] In this phantasmagoria, "the *fiction* of freedom and self-determination is more easily preserved than any other," because in the "second nature" of industrial society, "adopted opinions and dispositions can be experienced as one's own. It would require no effort for me," says Gehlen, "to imagine a termite society in which every individual thinks itself free."[51] Subject and object for Gehlen become one, in a derisive inversion of the Hegelian principle that substance is essentially subject.

But every critique of Gehlen runs into the objection: Does Gehlen in his theory of institutions not describe a natural-historical process? Thus is he not the heir of Marx, since he conceives of the structure and history of social formations as natural-historical processes? At least mthodologically, Gehlen's analysis of institutions and Marx's economic analysis appear to proceed from one and the same presupposition. The appearance, however, is deceiving. If Marx describes the economic formation of society as a natural-historical process, then this term has for him a fundamentally ironic appropriateness. The law of capitalist accumulation that Marx describes is a law set by man and an order set by those in power. The law of the development of the economic forms of society is a law mystified into law of nature. It appears as nature, that is, as inescapable only in the kaleidoscope held by the hands of the rulers, in which with every turn, everything ordered collapses into a new order. Marx describes the process of the capitalist economy as it presents itself in the ruler's kaleidoscope. "The concepts of the rulers have always been the mirrors by which the image of an "order" was established."[52] The point of his analysis is that the kaleidoscope itself must be smashed. In Gehlen, however, the thesis that social formation is a natural-historical process transforms into a biological law. While Marx puts the accent in "natural-historical" on history, which breaks through the appearance of natural compulsion, Gehlen puts it on nature itself to make the history of emancipation from it illusory. The ironic and exposing nuance of the adjective "natural-historical" in Marx's work has completely vanished with Gehlen, and the darkness of nature rules for good.

IV

Emancipation is the reduction of human conditions to humans themselves. Alienation is indeed inevitably linked with industrial society, if we take the word of its apologist *à la lettre*. What can be learned from this apologist is *where* the struggle for emancipation takes place today: from the economic field penetrated by Marx to the network of domination and profit in the institutions, which should be understood from a Marxist perspective. Therefore it is not for naught that students today speak of the long march through the institutions. The long march from southern China to the Mongolian border undertaken by the greatest practitioner of the revolutionary war of the present is an event of national war.[53] The pact of philosophy with the partisans, however, unleashes the possibility of battle for the emancipation of man from his institutions within the space of industrial culture itself—that is the secret of the twentieth century and the possibility of its revolution.

The question about the relation of technological emancipation to society for us today turns into a question about the relation of technological emancipation to human emancipation. If it is said of technology that it is to be understood "less as a human effort toward the propagation of material power, and more as a biological process on a grand scale," that is, as a metahuman process, which as such eludes human control, then this is fetishization in the most precise sense of the word, even when it is supported by the authority of a physicist. Because technological emancipation could take place while humans were incinerated and consumed by their own creations, because technological emancipation could take place while the institutions of the industrial society devour them according to the laws of a Moloch ritual, to which men surrendered knowingly, then, as a result, technological emancipation is not human emancipation. We are still very far from exiting history to arrive in *post-histoire*. Rather, we still stand deep in prehistory, where the sacrificial ritual of the institutions is celebrated. With this reference to religious history we don't transform the worldly question of industrial society into a theological one; rather, we transform the theological into the worldly.[54] This is the case if, in the mythologemes of the theory of the industrial society, we exhibit an appearance of the theory that reflects back the appearance of the industrial society.

Accurately, Gehlen establishes the origin of culture in ritual. Culture arose, as we know now even more clearly since Gehlen, in the service of ritual, first magical and then religious. Culture has its basis in ritual, "the location of its original use value."[55] This basis may be mediated; basis it is "recognizable as secularized ritual" even in its most profane forms and expressions. The task would be to interfuse the element of sacrificial ritual in culture itself. Because it is precisely the modern industrial culture which—as a construction—emancipates itself, for the first time in world history, from its "parasitic existence in ritual," from mimetic repetition *in illo tempore*. Where culture was "based on ritual," it is today based on another practice—politics,"[56] as Benjamin observes in a decisive moment. It is based, that is, on construction and history. In this constellation, however, conjuring up the origin, citing the nature of humans and humans as nature means mobilizing the entire force of the Acheron "at the end of a long history of culture and spirit,"[57] in which the power of origin had been disempowered in order to annul even this history. History means not only progress in the mastery of nature, pushing back on its boundaries, but also the transformation of man himself. "The formation of the five senses is a labor of the entire history of the world down to the present."[58] When man acts on and transforms nature around him through this historical movement, he alters his own nature as well.

Gehlen evokes anthropology in order to socially cripple the work of history, which he recognizes, knows, and describes as technology, better than most. Nature becomes historical through technology, but the nature of man, who first inaugurated this conversion of nature into history, must remain fixed on the first man, Adam. The trees of technology, Gehlen claims, grow toward heaven, but the "culture revolution" collapses on the "clung-to status quo" of society. Gehlen says that it is "treading water in the river Lethe."[59] The conversion of Nature into history however presupposes the conversion or the possibility of the conversion of the old Adam into a new Adam. "Only when man has recognized and organized his 'forces propres'[60] as something social," and thus—to develop the trajectory of Marx's dictum—no long separates from himself his social power in the form of *technological* power, can we truly speak of human emancipation.

The emancipation of bourgeois society took place in phases; Marx noted as the first the critique of religion. This remains the presupposition of all criticism because it provided the model for a critique of profane existence: society constitutes an inverted consciousness of world because it is an inverted world. From phase to phase, this critique shifts its center of gravity: from the theological to the political, from the political to the economical, from the economical to the technological. Every level propagates its own illusory appearances, develops its own apologies, but also forges its own weapons of critique.

The critique of the theological veil was essentially the work of an era that gave itself the name "Enlightenment." Its work was political emancipation. Marx begins his critique already with the dissolution of the political veil: political emancipation is not human emancipation. His critique of political emancipation drives him to an analysis of political *economy*. The center of gravity of this critique shifted to the economical: commodity as fetish was the key to opening up bourgeois society to its dark secret. Technology and industry appear in the nineteenth century still closely tied with the economic structure of capitalism. The fantastical development of technology and industry has now spread its own veil over social relations, the technological veil. It is this veil that is to be torn today, and that is why a focus on the economic problem alone remains helpless in view of the hegemonic powers of today. If one wants to take as one's starting point the economic status quo that has become entrenched in the Western world, even if in the only appropriate which is to say negative way, the result would still remain an anachronism.[61] If critical theory measures revolutionary potential in the industrial society according to degrees of economic maturation, then it remains caught up in the illusion of an economism. Even the negation of our economic present as universal exchange society finds itself to be a dusty old fact in the historical junkyard of industrial society. Its triumph in the fantastic development of the productive forces is bought at the price of the regression of the social relations and through the concomitant regression of consciousness. In a society where it is already possible to envision a condition in which violence completely disappears, this violence is enthroned by the hegemony of overpowering institutions. If progress, first a critical concept of the Enlightenment in order to break the compulsions of nature and the repetition of the always-the-same, itself overturns into routine and blind automatism, then the critical edge of this concept is blunted, and progress transforms into an organon of repression.

Even the Marxist concept of progress was not able to withstand the pull of technological illusion. It wants, as Benjamin says in his theses on the philosophy of history, to recognize "only the progress in the mastery of nature, not the retrogression of society; already [displaying] the technocratic features later encountered in Fascism."[62] The fronts have switched places. Today the reactionary theoreticians appear as the ideologues of technological progress, while the theoreticians of enlightenment carry out the business of critique in order to rescue the concept of progress from the technological *stretto*. If progress takes place as a matter of routine, as Gehlen notes,[63] then humans will be taken blindly into bondage by technological progress without being able to constitute themselves as subject in the progress of technology and industry. The separation of the producers from the means of production is the price that is exacted for this progress. As Weber points out,[64] this separation is in no way unique to the economic production process; it is also within the factory, the government administration, the army, and the university.

This reified relation between the means of production and the relations of production is, as Weber says, determined in part in a purely technical manner, through the nature of modern operating facilities, but also simply through the greater efficiency of this sort of human collaboration: through the development of "discipline."

If the nature of today's technology is introduced by Weber and Gehlen as an impressive argument, then this argument has the pretense of truth while remaining a mythologeme. The history of productive forces is evoked, but the history of the antagonisms in the relations of production is conjured away. The idea that within the factory, the university, the government, and the army, that is, within the institutions, where the domination of humans over humans is established as "discipline," but that technological emancipation could enable an association of individuals, that is not based on mastery and slavery, and in which the free development of each is the condition for the free development of all, this thought appears to Weber and Gehlen to be beyond discussion. If sociology as science uncritically adopts the way in which industrial society determines itself from the immediately given, then it only reproduces the appearance of society. It is, however, essential to penetrate and understand the appearances of the illusion: why this illusion establishes itself as "necessary."

Marx took the critique of religion to be essentially complete.[65] For him the critique of heaven transformed itself into the critique of the earth. But how is it so, if the earth is most clearly grasped today by the theological concept: hell's phantasmagoria? Religion was the "sigh of the besieged creature,"[66] in which the protest and demand for real happiness illusorily expressed themselves. In industrial culture, however, the sigh of the besieged creature is drowned by the noise of the illusory happiness, so that the demand for real happiness has become mute. Today, the industrial culture and not "Religion is the general theory of this world, its encyclopaedic compendium, its logic in popular form, its spiritual *point d'honneur*, its enthusiasm, its moral sanction, its solemn complement, and its universal basis of consolation and justification." Industrial culture, not religion, is the measure for "the *fantastic realization* of the human essence since the *human essence* has not acquired any true reality."[67]

The fantastic realization of the human essence occurs today not in heaven but on the earth. The self-alienation of man has reached a degree that allows him to experience his own annihilation as a real possibility and face it as a natural-historical process. The mythologemes of Weber and Gehlen that lie unspoken at the basis of all theories of the present era as an industrial society are an index for the fact that to humans, this fundamental condition of their contemporary existence, the consequences of which they cannot possibly fight against, remains veiled.

Translated with the assistance of William Rauscher

Four Ages of Reason[1]

For Max Horkheimer on his sixtieth birthday, 1966

I

Philosophy is possible only on the premise of the universality of reason. But reason cannot be truly universal so long as violence overtly or covertly rules the relation between man and man. The universality of reason cannot be achieved so long as there is no accord established among the interests of all individuals. History, however, unfolds before us the record of a human society that is split into groups with conflicting interests. The contradiction between the claim of philosophy to the universality of reason, the actual split of society into antagonistic groups has brought philosophy or rational discourse into disrepute. And rightly so. For an inquiry into the meaning of reason that does not take note of the incongruity between the claim to a universal frame of reference and the divided social structure is a chirmeric undertaking.

The reflections concerning the historic function of reason are born of the following questions: How did it come about that a society that had staked its future on the progress of reason ended up in barbarism? Is the progress in technological achievement, both theoretical and practical, necessarily bound up with the decrease of individual and collective rationality? The nexus between progress of technological reason and regress of social rationality may perhaps be determined by an inquiry into the very concept of reason that is ruling our scientific procedures.

But do we not invite chaos if we approach a "systematic" problem of philosophy like an inquiry into the concept of reason by analyzing reason in its historical context? Are we not trapped in the opinions of mortals if we consider the social implications of the concept of reason? Such questions carry weight and cannot be dismissed easily. What is the common premise of these objections? These arguments presuppose that the concepts of mortals are "immortal"—that they are valid without relation to man. In these arguments the nexus between philosophy and history is severed. Philosophy comes to analyze the formal constitutive elements of science, while history deals only with contingent configurations of human opinions. A historical analysis of reason, therefore, would endanger the purity of the scientific pursuit.

II

Philosophy long since developed its own method *more arithmetico*. The analytical character of mathematics saves the mathematical procedure from all dangers lurking in human experience. Mathematical theory abstracts from questions concerning the possible reality of its objects and dispenses with the consideration of the meaning of this abstraction. Philosophical analysis in imitating mathematical procedure surely gains the security of pure operations. But it gains this security only by eclipsing the foundations on which all operations are built—man. If philosophical inquiry, however, is a pursuit that studies the meaning of human concepts, then, it seems to me, it cannot abstract from man as the root of all meaning. Thus it would seem that the price for a pure field of operation is ignorance about the genesis of judgment. It may be that in mathematics such a procedure has its advantages. It becomes, however, grotesque in the formal sciences in the moment when such formal structures are established as a realm in itself, as a reality in itself. An operation that is established in a purely self-subsistent realm without recourse to its genesis in human consciousness only testifies to the alienation of man from the products of his own making, from the products of his own reasoning. The separate realms begin to act as fetishes that control their own maker. There is no basic difference between fetishes that are dressed up as formal logical entities.

The "purity" of philosophical inquiry, of the logical and epistemological pursuit, is usually argued in view of the fallacy psychologism. The validity of a local statement or of an epistemological analysis cannot be made dependent on the state of an individual. It must, so the argument runs, be valid in a domain by itself, irrespective of man. But such a conclusion is warranted only because the subject of logical validity is tested on an abstract and isolated individual removed from the concrete sociohistorical context. The reduction of man to an isolated individual and the positing of universal rules of validity into an abstract realm vitiates the dialectic between individual certainty and transindividual validity. No individual starts as a tabula rasa—he is integrated into a social system of language and signs.

The polemic against a genetic interpretation of rationality succeeds so easily, since it limits the idea of genesis to the psychological nexus, which, indeed, is unable to face the question of universal validity. But reason is a social category: it presupposes that men are speaking. The logical rules are incarnated in language. Language, however, mediates between the isolated individual and the community, between man and society.

If philosophical analysis operates with the human consciousness only in terms of an individual monad, then it is driven to hypostasize a realm of validity since indeed the validity of universal rules cannot be limited to an individual monad. By hypostasizing a realm of validity in the no-where, philosophy loses insight into the *source* of all meaning, into man in his historical existence.

Logical operations are, indeed, valid for all possible judgments, but this rule does not yet give a green light to hypostasize a realm of validity in itself. For both, the logical operations and all possible judgments are mediated by man's historic existence. Even the most abstract sentence is still a "verdict," a spoken word. Even formal logic is "functional" and not an a priori ideal realm. It is the radical division between genesis and validity of judgment that drives philosophy to hypostasize a priori realms. We should indeed guard against confounding the justification of a judgment with its genesis. But does it follow from this that in the explication of the meaning of validity we should abstract from all genetic sociohistoric elements? All philosophy that isolates the subjective pole of reference, be it in a logical or in an existential manner, leads into the antimonies of psychologism, but all philosophy that abstracts completely from all subjective elements in the analysis of reason and postulates a separate realm of validity seems no less to be entangled in difficulties.[2]

III

The metamorphosis of the concept of reason since the end of the Middle Ages contains the history of the stages of Western enlightenment. From the very beginning the concept of reason included a negative element, an element of criticism of the powers and principalities that be. Thus gradual stages of enlightenment produced, as Max Weber has pointed out, a progressive disenchantment of the universe. Man employed reason to dispel nebulae, to free himself for fear and anxiety so that he grew gradually out of his state of dependence on natural and social science. The process of enlightenment proceeds by a gradual elimination of the mythical elements that are contained in our concept and ideas. The "crisis of reason" is marked by the premise that in the end "reason" discovers itself as a theological residuum that has to be abandoned in the process of "rationalization." The process of enlightenment and the progress of rationalization seemed yet identical to the generation of the French Revolution. The progress of technological rationalization seems to us far from identical with the process of enlightenment.[3] A totally "rationalized" reason is a neutral instrument that may serve "enlightened" as well as "dark" purposes. The development toward the rationalized reason may roughly be sketched in three stages.

The end of the Middle Ages is marked by the conflict between the theological and juridical concepts of reason. The theological concept of reason interprets man's reason as a reflection of a divine reason revealed in the sacred scriptures of Christianity. Man's reason has a compass in divine reason. The human intellect is "created" like the rest of the natural order. As a created entity (*ens creatum*) man's reason can explore the realm of things that are also "created" by the divine creator. The inner agreement between man's reason and the realm of natural things is established by the divine order of creation. The theological concept of reason presupposes the hierarchical order of medieval society. Each realm symbolizes by way of analogy the next higher realm. Theological reason "reasons" by method of analogy between realms that are integrated in the hierarchical order.

It is in opposition to the theological-hierarchical order of the universe that the concept of juridical reason is born. Since the twelfth century, Western jurisprudence developed in constant struggle with theology, and this struggle culminated in the separation of jurisprudence from the theological faculties. We are not accustomed to see the revolutionary implications that are contained in the work of the legists of the twelfth and thirteenth centuries. During these centuries, Roman law was rediscovered for Italy and Germany. In the form of a gloss to the *Corpus Juris Justiniani*, the lawyers of the twelfth and thirteenth centuries forged a new concept of reason that was not bound to the "archaic" theological premises of the Roman Catholic Church of the early Middle Ages. It is appropriate to call, like Ernst Kantorowicz, the century from 1150 to 1250 AD (that marks the end of the Middle Ages) the "juridical century."[4] The *Corpus Juris* did not serve for the generation of this century merely as a legal code but also as a source of enlightenment that dissolved theological prejudice and aroused an enthusiasm that we can hardly understand. It is not surprising that during the thirteenth century the Institutions of Justinian are even put into verse. The science of jurisprudence is the first "secular" science of the West with a strongly antitheological bias. Only in concession to the new juridical spirit did the medieval church develop its juridical code of canon law. Since the thirteenth century theology and jurisprudence became antagonistic forces in the Roman Catholic Church. A new elite propagates the cult of justice. Its priests are the lawyers and judges. Their profession becomes a sacred *officium* (and not only a feudal *beneficium*) that equals the "office" of the ecclesiastical priesthood. Lawyers and judges are the hierophants of the mystery of justice (*iusticiae mysterium*). The "cult of iustitia" (a term we find in Frederick's *Liber Augustalis*[5] as a chapter heading: *de cultu iustitae*) challenged the sacramental cult of the medieval hierarchical church. With the "juridical revolution" the jurists become an active elite of the medieval hierarchy. Priest and jurist are separated as "cleric" from the vast body of laymen.[6]

In the juridical revolution of the late Middle Ages the concept of "immanent necessity" is established in the West. This concept marks the end of the theological standard based on the concept of a providential creation. The idea of necessity is first developed in the science of jurisprudence and only from this realm of immanent justice does it migrate into the sciences of nature. The concept of order is gradually emancipated from the idea of creation and becomes at the end of the Middle Ages a self-sufficient base for man's orientation in human and nonhuman realms. Not "Divine Providence" but the *necessitas rerum* establishes the order and nexus of things.

The emphasis on an "immanent" *iustitia* ends the charm of the theological procedures of law in which the "ordeal" is the most usual. The new elite of lawyers tries to minimize the realm of miracles that would limit the universal "rule of law." Ultimately the emphasis on the concept of justice as immanent necessity eclipses the function of divine providence. Providence, divine or human, becomes a plan according to reason.

The notion of "immanent necessity" that is the revolutionary promise of the juridical concept of reason started the emancipation of Western rationalism from its theological base. The concept of reason as the immanent order of justice that was developed in the final phase of Western rationalization still shaped the philosophical and scientific inquiry of Spinoza, Leibniz, and Newton. The immanent world order of modern philosophy and science was still a moral order of justice. At the exodus from the medieval church, the jurists still took some of the sacred images with them—they inherited yet some substance of the *potestas spiritualis* of the Christian church of the Middle Ages. The authority of law was secularized authority, but it was not yet an authority based on naked force.[7]

Compared with the economic concept of reason, the juridical concept that is based on the principle of justice looks like an archaism. In the center of the economic concept of reason stands the subjective motive of profit that eclipses the "objective" element of justice. The problem of a "just" price or "just" wages sounds archaic in the vocabulary of economic language. Such a question violates the law of "pure" economics and is treated in the theory of economics as a mythological relic from the Middle Ages. In "pure" economic terms man's work is to be calculated as an element of cost. The motive of profit stresses a subjective element in the concept of reason. The individual ego is what underlies (*subjectum*) all process of thought and action. The individual is the subject. The self-evident way of reasoning starts, according to Descartes, from the individual ego. It is on the *ego cogito* that the entire order of the universe hinges. All meaning and value is measured with the yardstick of the subject.

Economic reasoning can envisage the objective world only as an object for possible use. *The age of economic reasoning is therefore also the era of scientific discovery.* The external world (and everything outside the *res cogitans* of the individual is external) is reduced to an object that can and should be exploited. Water and land, earth and air are turned by economic reason into a great reservoir that serves man. Life is interpreted in terms of an economic enterprise and the methods of "gaining" life are measured in terms of economic success and failure. What is a man worth? This question does not ask about man's soul or man's character; it refers only to his economic "value." Be reasonable comes to mean: look out for your profit.

In order to use the natural resources with highest profit, nature must become "calculable" in terms of economic profit. Economic reasoning is emancipated from all theological (religious) and juridical (moral) residua that would point to a law "beyond" the subjective profit. The realm of religion and the realm of law are used by economic reasoning only to sanctify and to legalize man's free development and enterprise.

IV

The method of modern scientific inquiry is well summarized in Francis Bacon's remark that "knowledge and human progress are synonymous."[8] The concept of reason that rules the procedure of modern science is spelled out in terms of power, knowledge of human progress. Man dominates nature by the instrument of reason. Kant, in his preface to the second edition of his *Critique of Pure Reason* (a work that carries in the second edition a motto from Francis Bacon), has elaborated more fully the premise of the modern scientific procedure:

Reason . . . must approach nature in order to be taught by it, but not in the character of a pupil who agrees to everything the master likes, but as an appointed judge, who compels the witness to answer the questions which he himself proposes. (BXVI)

The technological concept of reason is ruled by man's will to power. The conquest of nature serves as a standard for man to measure the success or the failure of reason.

In modern times the structure of the universe was studied without illusions, without imputing occult powers, even in the form of innocent ontological categories into nature. Whatever did not fit into the quantifying measure, into *more arithmetico*, became suspect to the standards of modern reason. There is a liberating function in the mathematization of the cosmos that started in the seventeenth century, and formal logic has worked as a great catalyst toward coordinating and unifying man's scientific understanding. Ignoring the various qualities man can dominate nature and society.

But man pays a price for this knowledge in the horizon of power. In exercising reason as power over nature and society, man is alienated from the elements he dominates. He knows only insofar as he can manipulate. The elements of a disqualified nature and a disqualified society become substitutable and exchangeable. The tension between knowledge as a principle of comprehension is not a specific "modern" problem, but rather is fundamentally linked with the act of understanding. Knowledge has at once a liberating function and an alienating consequence. Liberation and alienation are interlocked in the historic development of man's reason. Max Weber and Georg Simmel have described this tension in the function of man's reason in terms of a tragic nature of man. Who could deny that this contradiction has shaped man's historic existence? But to describe man in terms of the contradicting principles of knowledge is to perpetrate alienated forms of reason and to cut off the dimension of hope in the horizon of man to overcome this alienation.

It is important to inquire into the "archaic" beginnings of the function of reason as a principle of domination in order to be able to understand the social meaning of our "self-evident" scientific procedures. Already in the mythical stage of human consciousness the basic elements of the logic of substitution are present: the sacrifice of an animal is a substitute for the sacrifice of the first-born son. In the substitution at the act of sacrifice, however, the sacrificial animal still represents the son in a singular and unique way. The animal becomes a sacred being that is not interchangeable. This element of singularity, this representational function of the sacrifice marks the limits of the mythic consciousness. In man's gradual emancipation from the mythic-religious consciousness representation is turned into universal exchange. An atom is not split in representation of another atom, but merely as a specimen, merely as a substitutional element. Nevertheless the substitution in the act of sacrifice of the animal for the first-born son is a step toward the humanization of man. There is a deeply humanistic element in discursive logic. Reason, rational thought, is interpretation according to a scheme we cannot escape once the first step is taken. It is, therefore, illusory to imagine that we can return to more archaic stages of human consciousness in which we would be freed from the yoke of reason, as some romantics or hierophants like C. J. Jung, Martin Heidegger, or Ludwig Klages would suggest.

Any attempt to restore artificially a mythic consciousness is doomed to failure and remains a romantic nostalgia or becomes a totalitarian nightmare, since the natural and social presupposition for mythology is destroyed. Not by return to earlier stages of human consciousness does man break the yoke of the logic of substitution. The archaism latent in the nebulous conservative nostalgia for mythology weakens the foundations of culture and threatens to usher in that tabula rasa of civilization for which conservatives today like to blame the tyranny of progress. Mythology after the original act of reason remains illusory. We would have to eat again from the tree of knowledge in order to fall back into the state of innocence. Such is the law of the irreversible process in the history of human consciousness. An inquiry into the genealogy of reason should not be conducted for a return to primitive stages, but to point to the human element that is at the root of the pursuit of reason and that is forgotten today in the scientific operation.

The operation of substitution, which we have shown to be central for the development of rational thought, contained in itself a tendency toward universality. But if the human element of the universality of reason is eclipsed, then the universality inherent in the pursuit of reason is transformed into a neutrality of universal exchange.

Durkheim has suggested that the logical structure of primitive classification might be explained out of the forms of the social divisions of labor. The basic categories of reasoning thus should reflect the particular form of social organization and its power over the individual. Durkheim assumed that the forms of thought reflect the structure of solidarity in the tribal community. Whether the primitive forms of thought reflect, as Durkheim assumed, the solidarity of the community, or whether in these forms the role of the ruling group is incarnated is still an open question.

Philosophy, however, could reflect, as a pursuit of universal reason, the consensus of a universal community.

On the basis of its premise that states the universality of reason, philosophy could serve as a voice for the suppressed, underprivileged, and persecuted, but the neutrality of modern technological reason, far from signifying an increasing consciousness of universal solidarity among men, expresses the skeptical separation of reason from the human realm. The process of enlightenment was achieved by a progressive elimination of all mythical residua in human life. None of the categories of the old have survived the critical purge of skepticism. But since Hume the skeptical motor has gained momentum until at the end of the process of rationalization the concept of reason is reduced to a mere tool. Skepticism has purged the idea of reason of so much of its content, of the element of freedom, of the element of happiness, of the element of justice, that at the end the very idea of reason appears like a ghost that has emerged from cloudy linguistic usage.

In the technological concept of reason the universality of reason among men is travested into a neutrality toward the human concern with justice or freedom. They are relegated to an irrelevant domain, to an irrelevant realm of "values." It must then be regarded as a matter of subjective preference whether one chooses liberty or slavery—justice or injustice.

In the perspective of the technological concept of reason, man as a person becomes a medieval atavism that has to be more and more obliterated. The ego of the individual subject is a luxury in the realm of technological reasoning, a residuum of a technological period. The "philosophy" of technological reason is occupied in exposing the bankruptcy of all ideas that go beyond the brute and naked realm of facts.

Wilhelm Ostwald yet tried to formulate an "energetic imperative" as a substitute for Kant's "categorical imperative."[9] In his almost grotesque endeavor we can measure best the implications that lurk behind a gradual elimination of the human element in the pursuit of reason. Be reasonable (translated into the language of an "energetic imperative") can mean only: try to avoid any collision with the mechanical apparatus, try to accommodate yourself to the bureaucracy and management of the society.

The question that haunted Max Weber through all his Herculean work—How is it possible to save some remnants of individuality while the tendency to a universal bureaucracy is becoming the inescapable destiny of technological society?—is today even more pressing than in 1917. What was for Max Weber still a question within the limits of Western society has today acquired universal relevance, since Western technological reason is on its way to conquer the globe. Where the imperialism of Western technological reason failed, as in China and Japan, the imperial conquest of Western technological reason seems likely to succeed. The Asiatic and African nations were not converted to Western religion, but they have become convinced by the methods of Western technological reasoning. The "miracles" of Western industrial production are more impressing than the "miracles" of Western religion. The "converted" nations are embracing the new faith in technology with the neophytic fanaticism that tends to propel the consequences to the utmost.

It is only natural that those who live on the residua of the past are shocked by the courage of the neophytes who are not "inhibited" by such memories to draw the last consequences implicit in the Western concept of technological reason. It is also understandable that such a period abounds in efforts of restoration to save the remnants of the *humanum* in a universal technological society. I doubt if timid and tired restoration can counteract such a universal development. For the disease has reached too deeply in our spiritual and social existence. The development from the theological concept of reason to the technological interpretation of reason is not accidental; it reveals the inner structure of the Western concept of reason: in all its forms this basic concept reveals one structure—the primacy of the principle of power. The technological manipulation of reason reveals the secret of its theological origins. Already the *creator coeli et terrae* is interpreted in the Western tradition in technological terms. Such a concept of reason must complete its cycle according to the principle of its origin.

Therefore it is illusory to seek a balance between tradition and revolution by regressing to earlier stages of the same concept of reason. Such a regression, which lurks behind all romantic remedies of our generation, would not break the basic equation between reason and power that rules the Western concept of reason in all its stages, but would rather perpetuate more archaic forms of domination. Technology cannot be brought under control by a magical formula. The technological rationalization that is on the way to becoming the universal ritual of mankind can only be challenged by an *idea of reason* that has overcome the primacy of the *element of domination*.

In the development of technology, man has reached the stage where the barrier of nature is pushed back to such a degree that man stands for the first time only over and against himself. There is no other object to conquer any longer but man himself. Therefore, the supreme question that confronts our generation is not the technological problem, but the place of reason in the relation between man and man.

In the technological frame of reference the universality of reason has become purely formal: one element can be substituted by another element. Even men become interchangeable parts. Individuals are stripped of their individuality not by external compulsion but by the very rationality under which they live and act. The point is that today the apparatus to which individuals are to adjust and to adapt themselves is so "rational" that individual protest and liberation appear not only as hopeless but as utterly irrational.[10]

Against such a formal neutrality of reason, philosophy can protest only by emphasizing the human conditions for the universality of reason. So long as structures of domination shape and pervert the relation between man and man, reason can function primarily as an instrument of power to subjugate man and nature. The claim of philosophy to the universality of reason contains a promise that relations between man and man are possible that are not tainted by violence, that man's relation to nature is not exhausted in the antagonistic structure of subject and object. The claim of philosophy to the universality of reason is not exhausted in the technical substitution of one element by another, but it contains a promise, a program to redeem man from the structures of domination. If this promise is not fulfilled in the philosophic pursuit, then philosophy has forfeited man's hope for a just and reasonable society and must abdicate its claim to an organization for the unification of the technical sciences.

Reason is the organon of every philosophical pursuit. This is the distinct mark of philosophy by which it is separated from all mythology. But in scientific philosophy today this organon is used only to analyze matters of fact. The element of critique, the counterfactual, the utopian vector is eclipsed in the philosophical pursuit.

But the organon of reason goes beyond the realm of being; it is not chained to the past or bound to the present status quo. Through reason man can transcend a given situation and anticipate the new that is to come. The interest of reason is concentrated, according to Kant, in the three following operations:

What can I know?
What should I do?
What may I hope?

These three questions Kant did not consider arbitrarily chosen, but fundamental for the understanding of man.[11]

Philosophy is an exegesis to the three questions, but only the first two questions—What can I know? What should I do?—have received attention in philosophy. The third question—what may I hope?—has not come into the discourse of reason. Its hermeneutic has not been developed.

In an exegesis of man's hope the task of philosophy lies, if the pursuit of reason should go beyond the tailoring operation of the sciences. Kant, as in many instances, has first understood the issue when he divided his analysis of reason into three parts.

1. into a critique of pure reason as an answer to the question: What can I know?
2. into a critique of practical reason as an answer to the question: What should I do?
3. into a critique of judgment as an answer to the question: What may I hope?

Only if all three parts of Kant's analysis of the function of reason are taken in their fundamental unity are we able to understand that Kant's major interest consists in a gradual ascent from the function of reason as conquest of nature to the function of reason as comprehension of nature. Nature that is subdued by reason as a tool of science is liberated by reason as an aesthetic judgment.

Hegel, in his *Phenomenology of the Spirit*, unfolded the genesis of human self-consciousness. The history of the development of human reason is the story of the conquest of nature by human labor. But human labor is based on the social division between men. Power and work break asunder in the developing division of labor. Power is on the one side, obedience on the other. The relation between man and man is constituted according to Hegel in history through a life-and-death struggle. Only in the last stage of human development does it come to a reconciliation between men. The mutual recognition between men also changes man's relation to nature. Life is no longer organized by the principle of domination.

What religion and art have always anticipated, human life liberated from the principle of domination, in Kant and Hegel for the first time enters into the language of reason. Reason turns into a security for a redeemed life on earth, for a free society. So long as this freedom is not yet real, reason functions as contradiction, as opposition in the process of history. In the technological language, however, the critical function of reason is eclipsed and reason becomes an instrument for the optimum adaption of means to ends. Thus the pursuit of reason becomes an energy-conserving operation. This eclipse of hope, the eclipse of the critical function of reason, seems the *trahison des philosophes* in our age.

19

The Intellectuals and the University[1]

1. Intellectuals are in a profound sense part of the inner history of modernity. To the degree that the feudal order of the Christian Middle Ages meets its dissolution, the hierarchical society that finds expression in the spiritual and temporal orders was replaced by bourgeois society with new principles of order and legitimacy. The new form of legitimization of the bourgeois society, which pulls the transcendental ideal of Christian theology down to earth, is the work of the intellectuals.

The most striking vocabulary for this new form of legitimization has perhaps been coined by Joachim of Fiore toward the end of the twelfth century. His trinitarian theology of history forms the guideline for the interpretation of the different intellectual groups in modern society.[2]

One hundred and fifty years before Petrarch, Joachim understood himself to be at the divide between two eras. If one wishes to categorize him an enthusiast, it is still important to consider that he did not envision either a heavenly beyond or a new form of life experienced via illumination, but on the contrary the realization of an ideal state of things in a chronologically datable future. The idea of perfection, which medieval Catholic theology placed in the beyond, was brought down to earth by Joachim in his image of the future *ecclesia spiritualis*. The consummation was to occur not in a realm beyond death, but rather here, during the lives of men.[3]

Although Joachim understood the new era of the holy spirit concretely as still a monastic order, the idea of a community made up of those perfected in the spirit, who live without institutional authority, was so clearly formulated in his speculations that numerous variations of this idea attaining prominence in the course of modern history can all be principally derived from his conceptualization. Whether it is the humanist or encyclopedic periodization of history into antiquity, the Middle Ages, and modernity, or the philosophical chiliasm from Lessing to Hegel and Marx, or Turgot's and Comte's classification of history into theological, metaphysical, and positivistic-scientific phases, all these attempts of periodization of history, which are determined by the self-interpretation of modern society, remain indebted in their approach to Joachim's historical speculations.[4] Here it hardly makes a difference that the new era Joachim predicts is not enacted as a monastic order of an *intelligentia spiritualis*, that is, not as spirituality, but instead becomes manifest as *spiritus scientiae*, as science.

2. The first indications of a new self-interpretation of the nascent bourgeois society can be detected in the beginnings of the universities during the Middle Ages. If one proceeds from the German example only, then the trace of this context is obfuscated because in the course of the inception of the German universities the antifeudal impetus does not come to light. When Charles IV founded the first university in the German empire there were already fifteen universities in Italy, eight in France, six on the Iberian Peninsula, and Oxford and Cambridge in England. The founders of Prague's Charles University expressly mention Paris and Bologna in their founding document. Since then, these foreign models, and Paris above all, were most often evoked when new universities were founded in the German empire.[5]

Of course, the German copies differ from the French original in one respect. They are collectively, whether royal or civic, foundations by the powers to be. What fell to German doctors and scholars *auctoritate regia* as privileges and rights,[6] precisely that element of cooperative autonomy that remains constitutive for Western universities to this day if often only formally, in Paris had been fought for in a long and difficult struggle during which the external and internal constitution of the university took shape.[7] It was precisely in Paris that masters and students came together in defense against ecclesiastic and governmental claims, to form an autonomous community, an *universitas*. The earliest evidence for this concept can be found in 1213 in Paris and unequivocally means the *universitas magistrorum et scholiarum*, precisely that confraternity of lecturers and students who organized themselves to protect their common scholarly interests.[8] This community itself, and not the governmental or ecclesiastic authorities, created the forms of self-government that remain characteristic of the university today.[9]

One usually understands these institutions of cooperative self-government as medieval forms and hardly considers how unusual or actually how modern the institution of the university appears in the high-medieval era of feudal society. In their structure, the universities disrupted the feudal-hierarchical structure of medieval society. Even if we are still able to integrate the universality of the medieval university into the common conception of the Middle Ages, this becomes impossible when we consider the university's social structure. For the university brings together people of all estates[10] into one community. Even though masters and students divided themselves according to regional origin [*Landsmannschaften*], initially it remained immaterial which land or culture they came from.[11] It is astonishing that there was no privilege of birth, not even in the case of selecting rectors and deans, and this at a time when in all other aspects of public life, including the ecclesiastic orders, the nobility unquestionably laid claim to privilege and received it accordingly. In this regard, the new university cooperative, similar to the mendicant orders of the thirteenth century, pointed beyond the feudal and hierarchic structure of the Middle Ages.

The university also transcended the ecclesiastic differentiation between laymen and clerics. With the claim of a new *ordo* extolled by the university, these fundamental concepts of the church mutated as well. Since the founding of the university, *clericus* no longer referred only to a man of the cloth but also to the student and to the scholar, even if he had not received ecclesiastic ordination.[12] As a secular or "laicist" term, *clericus* has been preserved in French and English usage: "le clerc" or "the clerk" refers to the intellectual, who stood in contrast only to the uneducated as the layperson.

The community of masters and scholars represented a new class. As

Friedrich Barbarossa articulated before the Diet of Roncaglia in his first imperial privilege for the protection of scholars, they were *amore scientiae facti exules*, homeless out of love for science.[13] These homeless unite themselves into the *universitas*, a community of masters and scholars. Even in Paris, no university would have been set up if on the Seine's left bank a few intellectuals had not gathered students around themselves on their own initiative, without authority, office, or commission, supported only by their own intellectual effectiveness. In his autobiography, the "historia calamitatum," Abelard vividly recounted his conflict with the ecclesiastic authorities.[14]

That with the university a new social form and authority emerged that demolished the structure of medieval society probably nowhere becomes as clear as in the attempt by Alexander von Roes, the *canonicus* of Cologne, who attempted to supplant the representation of society by the two powers—*sacerdotium* and *regnum*, papacy and kingdom, spiritual and worldly sword—common in the Middle Ages, with a doctrine of three powers or *principatus*. Alongside *sacerdotium* and *regnum* Alexander placed *studium* as a third force, as it was embodied in his view by the university of Paris. The university, which represented the sciences, appeared with Alexander as a new power on par with the state and the church.[15] It is not at all accidental that the beginnings of the universities coincide with the reception of ancient tradition: the beginnings in Bologna coincides with the "rediscovery" of Justinian's code of law around 1100 and with the beginnings in Paris with the natural-scientific and philosophical writings of Aristotle, translated into Latin only from the beginning of the twelfth century onward.

These natural-scientific writings of Aristotle, of which the West had become aware only then, turned into a source of the emerging pantheistic heresies. In 1210, David of Dinand and Almarich of Bena were convicted of heresy by a Parisian synod, which further forbade them from lecturing in Paris, in public or in private, about the "libri naturales" of Aristotle and its Arabic commentaries, on the pain of excommunication. The *viri literati* from Almarich of Bena's circle connect the impulses of the Aristotelian philosophical tradition and his Neoplatonic commentaries with Joachim's doctrine of the Spirit. It cannot be a coincidence that the same Parisian synod that issued the first ban against Aristotle's scientific writings also condemned the doctrine of Joachim. The fact that in Paris we hear little about spiritual *intelligentia* and contemplative perfection, and that more philosophical concepts are introduced in place of theological-historical symbolism, can be easily explained by the milieu that prevailed in the universities: "What was fulfilled and grasped so differently and lead to so many diverse expressions as well was, there as here, the same ideal: a religious position beyond the standardization of the letter, beyond the objectification in the church, dogma, sacraments, the time of the spirit, unmediated divine agency in and through perfected individuals, and sublation of the tension between divine and human action."[16]

The important and richly varying history of the reception of Aristotle cannot be outlined here even in its crudest characteristics. If soon after the midcentury lectures on the previously forbidden writings found their way into the curriculum of the Parisian arts and sciences, even though the ban had not been lifted, this was because in the meantime the teachings of the Stagirite had been tamed by the orthodox interpretation of Albertus Magnus and Thomas Aquinas.

3. With Siger of Brabant, however, Aristotlean philosophy enters into the realm of medieval Christianity as a revolutionary moment.[17] What in pre-Christian antiquity was predominantly merely a cosmological-theological theory about the eternity of the world and an ontological speculation on the spirit, in the Christian era attained an anthropological accent. Siger's theory of intelligence—*intellectus unus in numero in omnibus hominibus*[18]—paves the way for that form of modern spirituality that found its most reflected expression only in Hegel's teaching of the objective spirit, but that secretly propelled all humanist and encyclopedic conceptions of a unified human culture. Siger of Brabant is the first intellectual in the bourgeois sense. The turn from the Middle Ages to modernity cannot be grasped more acutely than in the final statements of his "Quaestiones de anima intellectiva."[19]

Vigiles et studeas atque legas, ut ex hoc dubio tibi remanente, exciteris ad studendum et legendum, cum vivere sine litteris mors sit et vilis hominis sepultura.

[Be alert and study and read, such that you, if a doubt remains with you, will be thus spurred toward studying and reading, because to live without science is death and a woeful grave for humanity.]

Here the emphasis shifts from restrained and dogmatic exegesis of scripture and tradition to autonomous research. The austere discipline of canonical exegesis itself provokes the new ethos of research. Since the defeat of the Latin Averroeists, the universities were more and more integrated into the ruling system of scholasticism that, depleted of all progressive tendencies, remained dominant within the universities up to the eighteenth century. Since then and until the era of Humboldtian reform, the relationship of the intrinsically productive spirit to the university system had always remained precarious. In the seventeenth and eighteenth centuries neither humanist nor scientific research took place within the universities. One can say that in these centuries the universities were more interested in maintaining the status quo, degenerated into professional institutes that served the training of magistrates and jurists, ministers and teachers, and following the church schism, became subservient to their respective denomination.

The essential steps taken by the bourgeois intelligentsia[20] from humanism to the Enlightenment occurred outside the university. We connect the intellectual elite of this epoch with the salon and the coffeehouse more than with the university. For it is the coffeehouse more than the university that was among the breeding grounds of political and spiritual unrest. The coffeehouse became the salon of the homeless and impoverished writers, and the authorities became compelled to take action against the discussions in the coffeehouses, while the disputations at the university evidently caused them much less concern. The salon and the club of the prerevolutionary epoch in France, as Necker notes, "were set up as a court of law before which anyone who drew attention to himself, must appear: it is public opinion (opinion publique)."[21]

4. Hegel said of the French Revolution that in it men stood on their heads, that is, on their thoughts, and that they constructed reality accordingly. The revolution was prepared by the literary agitation of the *philosophes*. In the first half of the eighteenth century, the *philosophes* targeted religion, literature, and art with their critique. Only when they collected their work in the *Encyclopédie Française* did the political intention of their agitation take effect, at least indirectly. Robespierre described the encyclopedia as the "introductory chapter to the revolution." Their intentions were realized in the revolutionary era by the *idéologues*.[22] The

group of *idéologues* that met at the salon of Madame Helvétius in Auteuil considered itself the heir to the tradition of prerevolutionary *philosophes*.[23] The *idéologues*, who imagined the order of the republic as a pedagogical province, reorganized the French school system after the Thermidor. The Ecole Normale, the Ecole Centrale, the Ecole Polytechnique, and above all the Institut National were founded according to their plans. Just how decisive the influence of the pedagogical institutions of the *idéologues* was on revolutionary France can be seen in the fact that it was very important to Napoleon to be accepted as a member of the Institut, and in that he still signed the proclamations of his Egyptian campaign as "général en chef, member de l'Institut." In Napoleon, the *idéologue* appeared on horseback.

Or so it seemed, because the hopes that the *idéologues* placed on Napoleon were dashed.[24] Bonaparte began to place more and more value in a social order anchored in positive orthodoxy, and since the closing of the concordat he got into an ever-deeper dispute with the group whose membership he once so coveted. In 1803 he dissolved the section of the Institut that was devoted to the moral-political sciences, where he must have assumed the kernel of resistance to his politics resided, and rightly so. In doing so he condemned the *idéologues* to ineffectiveness. As a substitute, Napoleon set up a section for French language and literature at the Institut, with the particular mandate to create a dictionary of the French language and to translate Greek, Latin, and Oriental writers into French. It was a noble but infinite and thus insignificant task, with which the Académie Française and the Institut National pass their time up to this day. The Institut was transformed from the bearer of a revolutionary-critical intelligentsia into a Confucian state-loyal *mandarinate*. With its new task of regulating the meaning of words, the Institut had, in fact, taken on the business that Confucius himself had described as the most important one.

Obviously, this change from a critical-revolutionary intelligentsia to a technological-organizational one cannot be explained solely through Bonaparte's intrigue. The time of philosophical and political discussion in France was over when the postrevolutionary bourgeois society consolidated itself, and—skeptical of all the *idéologues*' arguments—began to settle in a new objectivity. If Napoleon defamed his earlier comrades in 1812:[25]

C'est à l'idéologie, à cette ténébreuse métaphysique, qui en cherchant avec subtilité les causes premières veut sur ces bases fonder la législation des peuples, au lieu d'approprier les lois, à la connaissance du cœur humain et aux leçons de l'histoire, qu'il faut attribuer toutes les malheurs de notre belle France.

[It is the doctrine of ideology—this blurry metaphysics that pedantically seeks for the primary causes and based on these, seeks to erect the legislation of peoples instead of adapting the laws to the knowledge of the human heart and the teachings of history—that must be blamed for all the misfortunes of our beautiful France.]

Then in these words he summarizes the spirit of an epoch.

This accusation could have been leveled just as well been by Saint Simon, who appointed himself the Napoleon of the sciences. Saint Simon and his student Comte formulated their theses eye to eye with the program of the encyclopedia of the eighteenth century. The old encyclopedia was driven by a critical or destructive spirit. The new system was supposed to be integrative and constructive.[26] The new science, which Comte would later call sociology, was consciously drafted against the critical, analytic-corrosive, negative doctrine of the *philosophes* and the *idéologues*. The argument that Saint Simon brought in the course of the anti-Enlightenment was new, and it cast a shadow on the future. His thesis was that the industrial revolution evolving behind the back of the bourgeois political revolution produced a new feudal hierarchy and system of domination that lent new weight to the counterrevolutionary rhetoric of de Bonald and de Maistre. The connection between the counterrevolution and the Ecole Polytechnique remains notable. It kept alive the mistrust against the intellectual elite in France during the nineteenth century. It stands behind the theses of George Sorel, the engineer and student of the Ecole Polytechnique, who delivered in his *Le procés du Socrate* (1889) and *La ruine du monde antique* (1894) a critical genealogy of the intellectual elite in the history of the West, only to turn into an apologete of naked violence and of political myth.

5. The *philosophes* and the *idéologues* of the end of the eighteenth and the early nineteenth centuries belong to the prehistory of intellectuals. The term "*l'intellectuel*" first emerges toward the end of the nineteenth century in France, specifically in the fight about Dreyfus. Maurice Barrès took Clemenceau to be responsible for the term, a neologism, which

according to Barrès betrayed a fairly poor sense of the French language.[27] Clemenceau used it in an essay in *L'Aurore* on January 23, 1898. That the term emerged as a catch-phrase during the affair of the Jew, Dreyfus, injects into the term all those mysterious undertones, which in an integrated Christian society append themselves to the word "Jew": without fatherland, rootless, and cynical. In his novel *Les déracinés*, Maurice Barrès caricatured the intellectual type in the form of the Kantian professor Boutellier and thus opened that series of novels, which thematize the fate of intellectuals and which remain characteristic for French literature to this day.

The Dreyfus Affair created *le parti intellectuel*, that band of professors and writers, which in the struggle to repeal the verdict entered as a new class into the politics of France.[28] The "Manifesto of Intellectuals" of 1898, in the middle of the Dreyfus Affair, was essentially a product of the Ecole Normale Supérieure and created the presuppositions for the "Republic of Professors," which represented the Third Republic in the first decades of the twentieth century.

The Dreyfus Affair still could produce unequivocal divisions in France: on one side the forces of the ancien régime, the church and the military; on the other, the bearers of revolutionary tradition, the intellectuals. From elementary school to the university, the republic of professors had built a unified cadre of *clercs* who as secular clergy confronted the clergy of the church. Therefore, the intellectuals in France stand, to this day, more uniformly on the Left than other intellectuals in Europe, gathering themselves around the flag of the revolution and regarding the proletariat as the guarantee of their aspirations.

After the collapse of Vichy and during the first years of the hegemony of Résistance rule, the fronts of the Dreyfus Affair seemed to have reemerged. However, the position of the intellectuals was darkened by the shadows cast on their conscience by the terror of Russian Bonapartism. In the 1952 controversy between Sartre and Camus the unified front of the intellectuals was shattered.

The crisis of the intellectuals provides the theme for the key novel *Les mandarins*, in which Simone de Beauvoir documents the endless discussion of this circle, almost like a protocol. The intellectuals in France, as the title suggests, deteriorated into a class of mandarins; of course, this time not through an external *ukase* as during the time of the *idéologues*, but rather through the aporia immanent to their situation. While during the Dreyfus Affair, the liberal intellectuals knew that they had right on their side and regarded their opponents as representatives of the hegemonic power and the incarnation of prejudice, in 1959 Sartre, who wanted to continue the intellectual tradition at any price, was faced with the choice either to betray the proletariat in order to serve the truth, or to betray the truth in the name of the proletariat.[29]

6. The German reform of the university system is to be counted among the most important trends during the era of the French Revolution. The higher education reform was perhaps the only social reform that could be realized on German soil in the transition from feudal to bourgeois epochs. Pedagogical reform was the surrogate for political emancipation: education alone was supposed to ennoble, and thus to conceal, the lack of political hegemony.

Humboldt and the idealist philosophers constitute a new beginning that remains groundbreaking for the history of the modern university, first on the European continent, then later in America and today also in Asia and Africa. During the brief era of classicism and German idealism, the productive spirit found itself at home in the university. In his 1811 rector address, Fichte, perhaps a bit too enthusiastically, yet in tune with an entire generation, put the university in the place of the church.

The self-understanding of the university, as it is passed down to us in the lectures of Fichte, Schelling, and Hegel, is not entirely free of a chimerical aspect, but in these blueprints the cornerstone for the university as the new church was laid, as well as the principles and rites of this new institution: the freedom to teach and to learn. Thus German professors were able to imagine themselves both as bourgeois magistrates as well as priests of the absolute, without ever realizing the inherent contradiction.

Hegel is the last professor of the idealist epoch, and already the first generation after Hegel, in which the revolutionary implications of the officially conservative philosophies of state and religion were discussed, came into conflict with the state, the church, and the universities. Feuerbach had to give up his lecturing post in Erlangen due to his religious-philosophical positions, Ruge lost his teaching position in Halle due to his political and social agitation, and Bruno Bauer was dismissed from his teaching position in Bonn because of his radical theological views. David Friedrich Strauss was chased out of Zürich, and Marx was not even allowed to finish his habilitation. The quietist fathers, who were still able to reconcile reason and reality, if only in "concept," understood the university as a place of reform: for them, Enlightenment was education. The activist sons, however, held that the realization of the Enlightenment was possible only through changing the conditions of society, which was to include educator and educated. Marx summarized these theses in one sentence, new and subversive for the whole generation of sons:

The philosophers have only interpreted the world; the point, however, is to change it.

Precisely in light of Hegel's "last" philosophy, in which philosophical thought consummates itself and the world becomes reasonable and "intelligent," Marx demands that philosophy now step out of itself and become worldly and revolutionary-practical.

7. Realization and action were also the concern for the Russian intellectual elite in the middle of the last century. Like Marx, they also wanted no longer to interpret the world but to change it.[30] In this circle the concept of "*intelligentsia*" arose, which nowadays is predominantly used for intellectuals in developing countries, where a traditional archaic society, similar to Russia in the middle of the nineteenth century, is sucked into maelstrom of industrial civilization. Russian society was actually divided into only two classes until well into the nineteenth century. The aristocracy monopolized property as well as education, while the masses of farmers dumbly vegetated. Neither the bourgeois class nor the ecclesiastic leadership played a significant role in society as a whole. While the revolts of peasant groups disturbed the autocratic order, de Maistre noted at the start of the nineteenth century that the autocratic system would not be threatened by peasant rebels like Pugachev, but rather that a possible "Pougatchev d' université" could seriously endanger the authority of the state.

The word "intelligentsia" is probably the Latin word "intelligentia," knowledge or understanding, spoken with a Russian accent. The term first appears in 1860, but it concerns those groups that in the 1930s split in the conflict over Hegel into Western-leaners and slavophiles. These figures live on today for us in the novels of Turgenev and Dostoyevsky. In his memoirs Alexander Herzen retained some of the atmosphere of these circles:

> They discussed these subjects incessantly; there was not a single paragraph in the three parts of the Logic, in the two of the Aesthetic, the Encyclopedia, and so on, which had not been the subject of desperate disputes for several nights together. People who loved each other avoided each other for weeks at a time because they disagreed about the definition of "all-embracing spirit," or had taken as a personal insult an opinion on "the absolute personality and its existence in itself." Every insignificant pamphlet published in Berlin or other royal residence or province was ordered and read to tatters and smudges, and the leaves fell out after a few days, if only there was a mention of Hegel in it.[31]

That a small group of students regards itself so profoundly as the incarnation of Reason gives the Russian word "*intelligentsia*" a farther-reaching resonance than the French "*l'intellectuel.*" While the French *intellectuels* could connect to the tradition of *philosophes* and *idéologues* and could take root in French society through the army of teachers and the wide-reaching roots in the school system, the Russian intelligentsia remained hostile to and alienated from the Russian reality. In the universities young noblemen came together with students from different classes, and thus those who belonged to the intelligentsia saw themselves as *rasnotshinzi*, "of different status," or without any particular status. From here the famous division into fathers and sons emerged: the fathers brought the French ideas of humanity, freedom, and fraternity to Russia and attempted, similarly to the philosophers and Humboldt in Germany, to enact these through Enlightenment or education. The sons, however, like Marx or the young Hegelians in Germany, did not expect anything from a pedagogical Enlightenment. For them, the Enlightenment was only to be realized through revolutionary practice. The government stood in hostile opposition to the universities and suspiciously followed every move in the student circles.

In 1917 the "Pougatcheves d' université" came to power, but with it the fate of the group was sealed. For in the new society, which the revolutionary intellectuals set upon to establish, the conditions under which they had first formed themselves were liquidated. The prerevolutionary intelligentsia thrived on a moral and ideological critique of the autocratic regime. After the revolution, the ruling party demanded the construction of a technical-organizational intelligence and claimed the legacy of the ideological critique for itself.

It is part of the self-understanding of communist society, which knows itself on the pinnacle of science, that a particular place is to be reserved for the intelligentsia within the social system. Thus alongside the orthodox binary division of society into workers and farmers, there is another version, in which society is composed of the working class, peasantry, and intellectuals. Science is regarded as the norm of society. As a result, on the one hand, Soviet intelligence can be considered a social stratum "of a new socialistic kind as has never occurred before in the entire history of man," and on the other, it can be claimed, in a manner that perpetuates a chiliastic aspect, that "with the triumph of communism the intelligentsia as a distinct class will disappear, because every person is to become intelligent or intellectual."[32]

8. The mutation of the intelligentsia from a critical-ideological group to a technical-organizational stratum, which we have noted in the development of Russia, can also be observed in Western industrial society as well. The first generation of revolutionary intelligence in the United States was particularly close to the prerevolutionary *philosophes* of France,[33] but with Jackson's victory, the "common man" of the early nineteenth century came to power and installed a distrust of intellectuals.[34] Since then, "the professor" has belonged to the common figures of comic strips. Only when the open border, the frontier, was closed off and the tensions within American society intensified, the self-understanding of the common man was disrupted.

With Woodrow Wilson, an intellectual, a university professor, comes into power again. Roosevelt's New Deal called on intellectuals as experts and planners to overcome the economic crisis that followed the "return to normal" in the 1920s. The president's brain-trust became more important, and the intellectuals altered the traditional configuration of administrative bureaucracy.[35] Of course, the pragmatic nature of Roosevelt's reforms disappointed a great number of intellectuals who were fascinated by the more intransigent and ideologically more coherent experiments in Russia, and who were attracted to the status of the intellectuals during the first phases of the Bolshevik revolution.[36] The rise of National Socialism and the subsequent incipient popular-front politics allowed these intellectuals to initially overlook the terror and bureaucratic impulses in Russia or to regard them as the lesser evil. There were even brief periods in the 1930s and 1940s in which a noticeable sector of American intellectuals went partly Marxist, partly Stalinist, partly Trotskyite. McCarthy's accusations, which wanted to nail the position of the American intellectuals to this past engagement in a wholly different situation in the 1950s, however formulaic, did not strike out at nothing.

> It has not been the less fortunate, or members of minority groups, who have been selling this Nation out, but rather those who have had all the benefits the wealthiest nation on earth has to offer—the finest homes, the finest college educations, and the finest jobs in the Government we can give.[37]

McCarthy's agitation left deep marks on the United States, because his accusations against the intellectuals were dictated by the anxiety that with the development of industrial society, which through production and organization was based on the apparatus of modern science, a stratum of intelligence was coming to power, which could attempt to govern a scientificized society from the standpoint of science. Therefore, the political immaturity and unreliability of the intellectuals, and even their betrayal of America had to be demonstrated. Concerning the question of the political status of the technical-organizational intelligence or the scientific elite, the government itself took the same tack as McCarthy and, as the case of Oppenheimer illustrates, dismissed the claim of the intellectuals to participate in the military and political decisions, which had become possible only through the new scientific prosperities.[38]

The public humiliation of Oppenheimer by the Personnel Security Board and, even more so, the appeal's decision of the Atomic Energy Commission was aimed at a whole social stratum. Oppenheimer was put to trial after the attempt of the intellectuals to secure their rise to power had already failed. Like the trials in Moscow, this public hearing was only the epilogue, after the defeat. In Oppenheimer's case, psychological defamation was the chosen weapon. "Fundamental defects of character" had to be demonstrated for the man, who since Einstein's death had been the primary figure of the scientist in America. When Oppenheimer conducted his defense as a meticulous exploration of conscience, which often took on the form of self-accusation, the victim identified with the aggressor.

Neither in the accusation nor in the defense were the social and political moments that determined the case discussed. Instead, a case history of pathology was opened, which confirmed the dominant prejudice that intellectuals were too complex for political authority. After the verdict in Oppenheimer's case, it was clear that intellectuals were not qualified for political decisions. They neither control them as elite, nor influence them as a "veto group"; instead, they are at best allowed to occupy positions of experts and gofers of civilian and military authorities.

9. These defeats brought a large number of the natural and social-scientific intellectuals back to the American universities. The grandchildren returned to the universities after the breakdown of the utopia, or after the "end of ideology," as it is called in America, and carried out the business of Enlightenment or education like the generation of their idealistic grandfathers once did, but certainly with a bad conscience. If the attempt to bring the world into reason by way of revolutionary praxis failed, the educators are left imprisoned in a splendid isolation, self-reliant, and they were thus seduced into regarding the reflex of social praxis for the thing itself. Yet if they do not pose themselves as the measure of all things human, in a vain and out-of-touch way, then the question cannot be avoided: Who educates the educators?

Thus today, as it once was in the case of the prerevolutionary Russian intelligentsia, the theme of alienation has become the most important topos of the American intellectual community. Certainly, the difference in accent in interpreting what alienation means remains more important than the thematic congruence. For the Russian intelligentsia, alienation from the "cursed Russian reality" was a constant appeal to overcoming the conditions that caused it. By determining alienation as metaphysical or socially universal, the postrevolutionary American intellectual elite created for itself an alibi for the lost chance to change the world or to reform or revolutionize it according to the blueprints of reason. It is precisely the extreme form that alienation as negative utopia has maintained since Huxley's *Brave New World* or Orwell's *1984*, mediated in social-analytical terms through William H. Whyte's *The Organization Man* or David Riesman's *The Lonely Crowd*, which can appease the conscience of the intellectuals and corroborate the status quo, whose beneficiaries they themselves are.[39] If alienation encompasses and holds sway over the whole, the interior as well as the exterior, society as well as the individual, then questions such as those posed by the Russian intelligentsia, "Who is to be blamed? What is to be done?" become groundless or dismissed as superficial.

10. In the Soviet Union, the contradiction between scientific freedom and the claims of industrial society, steered by terror-powered politics, is most clearly palpable. This contradiction, however, holds sway over progressive industrial society as a whole. Industrial society is integrated, even before being governed in a totalitarian manner, because the totalitarian form can be achieved not only through a politically terrorist coordination but also through an economic and technical coordination, which does not inevitably have to be conducted in a terrorist manner. In the industrial society, political violence and economic power convey themselves through a technological form as it has been manufactured by science.

The industrial society is in an extraordinary sense a scientificized society [*verwissenschaftlichte Gesellschaft*]. Its production and organization can only be guaranteed in an administered, extremely rationalized enterprise of science, and the scientific enterprise has its exact correspondence in the mentality that it puts to work. The sciences produce a neutral apparatus that can be steered by any government. The critical substance that first renders scientific progress possible is consumed in the progress of the industrial society, which factually organizes the organization of men according to the guidelines of the scientific system.[40]

11. At this point, the reflection ought to be further developed and the position of the intellectuals in the university more closely determined. The task of scholarship is not only to demystify the exoteric nature in praxis but also to abrogate the esoteric human mystification. But is the university itself not comprised by the law, which governs the administrated world? How should the university be able to secure its critical enterprise when it is dependent more than ever on the ruling powers, the state, and the economy, which alone are capable of furnishing the means for sponsoring research? It would be entirely appropriate in the course of its development if the university, as organization of the sciences, would structure itself by the very principles it provides for the organization of industrial society. It is difficult to resist the force of this argument, yet everything depends on withstanding this temptation because as the institution of the university

adapts itself to the most progressive elements of our society, the drive toward bureaucratic regiment only intensifies. Wherever this takes place, university labor begins to approach a factory-like form of production.

We are thus faced with a paradox: scientific knowledge should be at the pinnacle of its time, but the institution that develops and mediates this knowledge is to retain in an untimely approach the archaic remainder of its internal and external constitution. Of course, if it does so only to preserve the privileges of a status, it has to degenerate into a helpless apology for itself. But who guarantees that while it preserves the remnants of *its* freedom, the university wants to preserve freedom itself?

The freedom of science, the claim to autonomy and self-rule, which has been characteristic of the university since its inception, was in the Humboldtian reforms, borne by the aspirations of a liberal bourgeois society. The ideas of freedom and reason were critical ideas, weapons of critique for the sake of replacing the prebourgeois feudal sovereign order with more rational and more productive forms of social life. In the industrial society, the ideas of freedom and reason can no longer be preserved in the traditional forms without being usurped by an archaic or illusory element, yet what is humane about this institution depends on it. The idea of science, on whose model the university and industrial society have organized themselves, has itself become ambiguous. It reproduces the reification of society, against which it has been used as a weapon since the Enlightenment. Science, which the Enlightenment used as the means to accomplish the exodus of men from their self-imposed immaturity, now conveys their incapacitation. The scientificized society turns the society under tutelage.

The totalitarian impulse of industrial or scientificized [*verwissenschaftlichte*] society confronts us with a form of irrationality that is difficult to penetrate.[41] This is because the rule of science appears as the incarnation of reason itself, and since this rule elevates the standard of living for the masses through technological progress, the circle closes, an event against which any opposition would seem futile. The more that technological progress appears to create the conditions for a free realization of human possibilities, the more it reinforces society's status quo. Thus intellectuals can only act as experts in a Confucian capacity while their reformist or revolutionary impulses cease altogether.

Technological progress obscures the fact that the system of the sciences remains subordinate to a political hegemony, which predetermines what part of reason and freedom can actually be introduced into reality.[42] The same law that governs the administrated world counts for science as well. This now-usable science has, as Max Weber emphasized in his famous speech in front of the students in Munich in 1919, become neutral in the face of the values of the social praxis, which in turn is left without guidance regarding the questions: For what end should science be, and how should it be employed?

Indeed, a critique of science admittedly remains a dangerous business today. The accusation was already raised in 1920 against Weber's normativizing statements that "the old science in its human sense has been shaken" and is to be replaced by "a newly visionary and not merely thinking science" that "must be knowledge in the only ancient magical sense, one which expresses an unequivocal ability to meet its destiny, not an accumulation of information."[43]

When thirteen years later this mystified knowledge did meet its destiny, Martin Heidegger asserted in his rector address on the "Self-Assertion of the German University" in what sense "the will to science" comes to power "as the will to the historical and spiritual mission of the German *Volk* as a *Volk* that recognizes itself in its state."[44] This new science knows of "its impotence in the face of Fate."[45] "Knowledge service" along with "labor service" and "military service" are "equally necessary and of equal rank" for the teachers and students "bound through the *Volk* to the destiny of the state in its spiritual mission."[46] Anxious about an all-too-contemporary science, Heidegger retreated to a knowledge born by the *Volk*. In a dogmatic concept of the *Volk*, however, and in the postulation of an ostensibly shared destiny between humans as condition for science and as agents for action, Heidegger negates in the course of counter-Enlightenment the idea of science as a universal power and the idea of a society emancipated from the compulsions of nature.

Any critique of the sciences has to be examined as to whether it cites the irrational forces, the irrational character of the order of being or existence, in order to bind, out under tutelage, or disempower man with their magic, or whether it carries on the process of demystification and illuminates precisely the entanglement of science with the irrational praxis of industrial society, and thus tears from the intractable-rational veil off its irrationality. The critique of the sciences cannot fall back onto the ever more specious privileges of an educating intelligentsia that positions itself defensively in relation to the development of modern science and the modern industrial society, and that defends a culture patched together by the arts and the humanities as a marketable tradition. Precisely through the separation of a culture-bearing from a technical-organizational intelligentsia a double bookkeeping is fixated, one that stabilizes a reactionary, classical canon of culture, on the one hand, and a science degenerated into technology, on the other. The process of demystification remains univocally our course. What is at stake is in the process of demystification to guide the technological understanding toward reason.

Industrial society first made it possible for humans to dissociate from the histories of mythical origin and to take a few steps toward a world history with which they need to reckon. Today for the first time the postulate of the Enlightenment, to coax people to move out of their self-inflicted immaturity, can become a reality. If, however, the scientificized society itself overturns into tutelage and terror, this is not the result of a blind or transcendental fate. The fate that rules in this inversion is a social nexus of blindness—the penetration of which is the task of Enlightenment. If science does not adopt any sort of reflection on this dazzlement, then it will inevitably morph into the most proficient means of incapacitating mankind.[47]

How can the critical function of the sciences be institutionalized, and who is to bear it? The intellectuals—this free-floating intelligentsia, which divested from any interests, carries out the business of Enlightenment? We have intentionally chosen the example of Martin Heidegger to show that intellectuals and philosophers are not protected from betrayal either, and that while intellectuals can tear away veils, they can also weave them. But that much can be learned from this betrayal, that an intelligence that retreats from the process of production of the industrial society is not in the position to penetrate the dazzlement of the scientificized [*verwissenschaftlichte*] society, but can only abide in absolute negation. This absolute and admittedly only verbal negation morphs into an apology for the respective ruling authorities and falls back into obscurantist mythology.

This also is still worthy of consideration because in the mythologemes of earth and *Volk* a true claim announces itself, if only in horridly distorted form: the memory of the unity of man and nature. "This means, however," as Walter Benjamin suggests at the end of *One-Way Street*,

> that man can be in ecstatic contact with the cosmos only communally. It is the dangerous error of modern men to regard this experience as unimportant and avoidable, and to consign it to the individual as the poetic rapture of starry nights. No, it is not; its hour strikes again and again, and then neither nations nor generations can escape it, as was made terribly clear by the last war, which was an attempt at a new and unprecedented commingling with the cosmic powers. Human multitudes, gases, electrical forces were hurled into the open country, high-frequency currents coursed through the landscape, new constellations rose into the sky, aerial space and ocean depths thundered with propellers, and everywhere sacrificial shafts were dug in Mother Earth. This immense wooing of the cosmos was enacted for the first time on a planetary scale, that is, in the spirit of technology. But because the lust for profit of the ruling class sought satisfaction through it, technology betrayed man and turned the bridal bed into a bloodbath. The mastery of nature, so the imperialists teach, is the purpose of all technology. But who would trust a cane wielder who proclaimed the mastery of children by adults to be the purpose of education? Is not education above all the indispensable ordering of the relationship between generations and therefore mastery, if we are to use this term, of that relationship and not of children? And likewise technology is not the mastery of nature, but of the relation between nature and men.[48]

Translated with the assistance of William Rauscher

On the Current State of Polytheism[1]

I

That one has "Difficulties with the Philosophy of History" is one thing, that these difficulties entice an ingenious mind like Odo Marquard's into a "Praise of Polytheism" is another one altogether. Odo Marquard exhibits sensitivity for historical constellations and is distinguished by a particular gift for arriving at an orientation of the present by way of an academically normativized philosopheme. Marquard first signaled the turn to aesthetics as a medium of knowledge. In the search for a salvaging and powerful form of reason that could rescue us from the aporias of "pure" and "practical" reason, the turn to aesthetics is foretold already in Kant's *Critique of the Power of Judgment*. From Kant's aesthetic turn, the path leads to the "System Fragment" in which Hegel, Hölderlin, and Schelling, first brought together at the Tübingen seminary, outlined at the turn of the nineteenth century the program of a "mythology of reason": "Monotheism of reason and of the heart, polytheism of the imagination and of art, that is what we need!"[2] In this program, which accompanies the history of the German spirit all the way to its demise, "monotheism" and "polytheism" are roughly equal. Since then the scale of "polytheism" has begun to tilt. Not only has the aestheticization of ethics and politics progressed quite far but also, since Nietzsche, has the aestheticization of truth, with the consequence that we are enthroned not only beyond good and evil but also beyond truth and falsehood on the "Olympus of Appearances," as supermen [*Übermenschen*]. But have we not in truth landed in the cave/hell[3] of appearances, in which no measure of the judgment of good/evil, true/false remains calibrated, and all is declared as "will to power," a *bellum omnium contra omnes*,[4] against which Hobbesian terror pales to an idyll? Enlightenment has enlightened itself and reveals itself as mythologeme.

From this perspective it is understandable that aesthetics is academically elevated to an organon[5] of knowledge, and that the question of style takes precedence over the question of truth. It is understandable that, not so much the content, but an analysis of forms determines the course of our considerations, and that the surface, not the substance of philosophical questions, is what keeps our hermeneutic interest in suspense. Odo Marquard, who insightfully and conceptually articulates the larger connections and schemes, handily summarizes what occurs today in many different variations throughout the humanities as the praise of polytheism. What once began innocently in the realms of philosophy of art and literary criticism and is exercised across various corners of the German academic republic has now plunged us into debt spiritually and in the philosophy of religion. What first began as commentary on myth and literature, residing between "terror and play," has now raised the stakes with the gravity of the question about God and the gods. The work on myth in mythology and literature has now put us into a mythogenic intellectual situation.

Our situation turned mythogenic ever since it was recognized that "even when all possible scientific questions have been answered, the problems of life remain completely untouched." This sentence could have come from Max Weber. It appears at the end of Wittgenstein's *Tractatus logico-philosophicus* (sentence 6.52) and attests to the powerlessness of reason at the end of the First World War. Toward the end of the Second World War Horkheimer and Adorno described the *Dialectic of Enlightenment* (written 1944, published 1947) in an even gloomier tone: "The world as a gigantic analytical judgment, the only one left of all the dreams of science, is of the same mold as the cosmic myth that associated the cycle of spring and autumn with the kidnapping of Persephone."[6] Certainly their diagnostic thesis that "Enlightenment reverts to mythology" lights up as the writing on the wall of our consciousness with the experience of fascism's epochally triumphant procession that destroyed the moral and political fundaments of old Europe. During the Biedermeier days of our post*histoire*, however, in which a lot happens but nothing takes place anymore, this writing on the wall has turned into the sober record of the spirit of the epoch. The horror of mythos executed in the first half of the twentieth century has lost its force for the liberal pluralist *juste milieu* of our current age. The old gods, demystified, rise again from their graves. Not, however, in the form of inhuman forces, as one generation ago, forces that had grasped for power over our lives and in the battle for values competed irreconcilably with one another; rather, they are called to fill the "playroom of the imagination" of those contemporaries who, as Claude Lévi-Strauss remarks, "feel torn between science and sensibility."[7]

Even today as a plea for mythos and mythology may be, for the most part, brought forward trivially, Marquard's *In Praise of Polytheism*,[8] which is garbed in a façade of a playfully belletristic rhetoric, allows a glimpse behind it, of a seriousness that asks for decisions. Borne by a common prejudice toward a form of life that generally privileges paganism, his thesis reaches further than the trendy fascination with mythos and polytheism. It reaches into the realms of sketching ethical orientation and epistemological truth. Marquard's programmatic call to arms is not called *Farewell to Matters of Principles* for nothing. He does not practice any sort of romantic reconstruction of mythos, he is not occupied with the "effective potential of mythos"[9] *in aestheticis*, nor is he interested in the "presence of myth"[10] as compensation for the "indifference of the world."[11] Rather, his "praise of polytheism" takes place at eye level with the crisis of history and its philosophy, from the perspective of the self-consummating disintegration of Hegel and Marx in Marxist theory and praxis.

II

In order to present, establish, and question Odo Marquard's thesis, the problem of mythos and Enlightenment must be explored more deeply: first as a question of ethical character and the function of myth; second as a question concerning the relation between polytheism and history. It would be bold and to no avail to merely repeat here the various theoretical explications of myth, even if only cursory. Whether in our understanding of mythos we connect to Walter F. Otto and Karl Kerényi, the previous generation's significant exponents of mythological research, or whether we follow Mircea Eliade and Claude Lévi-Strauss, this generation's most significant and opposing exponents of mythological research, what they all have in common is that they explain mythos mythically. None of them determines an Archimedean mental situation of mythical thinking, and in so doing, produces a "mythos of mythology."

I take the opposite direction. In order to explore the function of myth from an ethical standpoint, I would like to attempt to consider the constellation in which an exodus from the mental situation of mythical thinking takes place. This was the concern of the great introductory piece "The Concept of Enlightenment" by Horkheimer and Adorno, in relation to which the subsequent excurses and supplements are conceived of as corollaries only. It seems to me that, from a perspective of history of religion, the weakness of Horkheimer's and Adorno's monumental outline is that they want to demonstrate the "escape of the individual subject" from the mythic powers with the example of Odysseus. Indeed, Odysseus's ruse is a form of self-assertion in the face of the overwhelming superiority of the mythic forces. But his ruse is a kind of casuistry of mythical consciousness; it circumvents the mythic powers, deals with them, but does not break their spell. Horkheimer and Adorno exposed the "*ur*-history of subjectivity" in Homer's *Odyssey* because it is there that they saw evidence for their double thesis: myth itself is Enlightenment, and Enlightenment reverts into mythology. In doing so they themselves ultimately remained within the frame of the mythical trope, according to which Enlightenment can achieve only episodic but not fundamental force. Odo Marquard ties into this prejudice, characteristic of their general thesis. Why should the double thesis:—myth itself is Enlightenment and Enlightenment reverts into mythology—only be proved in the Medusan gaze of catastrophe? If this double thesis holds in general, an "enlightened polytheism" might mediate the tension and opposition between mythos and Enlightenment. Polymythy as a humanizing process protects us from the terrorism of Enlightenment as the executioner in the trial of history and can spare the world, as it is, from being altered. And Enlightenment can function as a filter that extracts the dark modes of myth, ritualized by a repetition compulsion—thus creating a reconciling, and perhaps even reconciliatory, version of that *Dialectic of Enlightenment* that Horkheimer and Adorno could interpret solely as catastrophe. What should be on today's agenda therefore would be a "dialectic of Enlightenment," in the Biedermeier style of the liberal *juste milieu* evolving as a farewell to matters of principle.

If mythology is not only to designate a literary genre of stories about Gods, heroes, and demons but is also determined by a particular horizon of consciousness,[12] then together with Paula Philipsson one can speak of "genealogy" as "mythical form"[13] in which the series of conceptions and births merges into a nexus of guilt. The interconnectedness between the generations is compelling and plausible for the nexus of guilt and atonement in mythic consciousness. To this perspective, Ezekiel 18 marks a turning point in the history of religion. It is indeed a constitutive chapter in the "ur-history of subjectivity" because in the prophet's speech the power of the mythical nexus of guilt and atonement within the chain of generations is broken and the mythic horizon of consciousness is decisively transcended. Guilt and atonement through the chain of generations: this is the bracket that holds together the logic of what transpires between gods and humans in various tribes and cultures. This is the case also in Israel of old, whose God reveals himself to the community as "merciful, gracious and patient," "abundant in love and truth," where it states in Exodus (34:7): "Keeping mercy for thousands [yet] visiting the iniquity of the fathers upon the children, and upon the children's children, unto the third and to the fourth generation."[14] This nexus of guilt and atonement in generational chain comes alive precisely in times of emergency and crisis. It is not surprising that during the time of the destruction of the First Temple a saying was circulated: "The fathers have eaten sour grapes, and the children's teeth are set on edge." The word is doubly passed-down, once in Jeremiah (31:29) and again in Ezekiel (18:2), both testimonies to the downfall, once within the nation, once in exile. At decisive points of their prophecies both Jeremiah and Ezekiel take a stand against fate, which echoes from this saying, be it resigned or cynical. The prophecy of Jeremiah of a "new covenant" with the "house of Israel" is introduced with a counterdictum: at the same time that saying will no longer be recited, rather "everyone shall die for his own iniquity: every man that eats sour grapes, his teeth shall be set on edge" (Jeremiah 31:29). The very same proverb or cynical statement is taken up by Ezekiel as motivation for a great didactic speech:

Chapter 18. "It is a mistake," Hermann Cohen says, in his late work *Religion of Reason Out of the Sources of Judaism*,[15] where he comments exegetically and philosophically on this chapter of Ezekiel's prophecy—it is a mistake to consider Ezekiel's examination "as long-winded; this fullness of detail is rather a proof of the novelty of the idea"—against the mythical nexus of guilt and atonement in the chain of conceptions and births, in the interconnectedness between the generations: "As I live, says the Lord God, you shall not have occasion any more to use this proverb in Israel. Behold, all souls are mine; as the soul of the father, so also the soul of the son is mine: that soul that sinneth, it shall die" (18:3–4). These verses give testimony of the highest order to the ur-history of subjectivity—in the process of the demythologization of the "spirit" that Horkheimer and Adorno took on as their task decades after Hermann Cohen's late work. When the mythic spell is broken, humans acquire what since Ezekiel we have called a "soul": his ego. "Thus the new man is born: in this way the individual becomes the I."[16] This ego, however, is not a "man without qualities,"[17] who is indifferent in good as in evil, in truth as in falsehood. What for Nietzsche and for today's Nietzsche-lings, mythically blinded as they are, appears merely as a reversal of instinct from outside inward, for Ezekiel is the key to repentance: "Cast away from you all your transgressions, whereby you have transgressed, and make for yourselves a new heart and a new spirit" (Ezekiel 18:31). Hermann Cohen comments, "In the recognition of his own sin, man became an individual. Through the power to create for himself a new heart and a new spirit, however, he becomes the I."[18] The new heart and new spirit broke through the mythical form of consciousness. A recourse to mythology, an evocation of myth "*in illo tempore*" here and today implies a suspension of the ethical, the dissolution of the I, whose ur-history we have sketched in Ezekiel. Odo Marquard will have to allow the question whether his late "praise of polytheism" outlines that philosophical choreography by which that academicized "cosmics" in West Germany and in France can aggrandize themselves. It was certainly *Difficulties with the Philosophy of History*[19] that induced Odo Marquard to intone the "Praise of Polytheism." We must, therefore, finally consider the relation between polytheism and history.

In the eighth lecture of his *Lectures on the Method of Academic Study*, Schelling concerns himself with the "Historic Construction of Christianity." The title of this lecture already points toward Schelling's thesis: its historical character is what differentiates Christianity from polytheism because in Christianity reality is understood as a "moral realm," and "the universe in general considered as *history*" (V, 287). History, however, not only is a new lens for reality that in and of itself remains the same, but also is the index of a reality that is in transformation. Thus the "opposition that the new world thrusts against the old . . . is sufficient in and of itself, to gain an insight into the essence of Christianity and all its unique characteristics" (V, 292). It may seem, as the late Schelling elucidates his early insight, as if the differentiation between polytheism and Christianity is solely a concern of "the theologians. This is not at all the case. Christianity does not merely belong to theologians; it belongs just as well to the genuine historians" (XIV, 20). Historical scholarship is "genuine" only when it relates the change of consciousness of history to the change of being in history. In his last lectures Schelling differentiates a "philosophy of mythology" from a "philosophy of revelation" with great deliberation, a differentiation that roughly corresponds to the common distinction between "prehistory" and "history." However, this differentiation that still holds sway in today's *sciences humaines*, orienting itself along the lines of the distinction between "oral" "written" cultures, remains "external and contingent" (XI, 231). "The prehistorical would be an essentially, internally different time if it had a different *content* than the historical." Prehistorical and historical epochs are, for Schelling, no longer "merely relative variations of one and the same time, they are two essentially different times, discontinuous to one another, mutually exclusive but as well limiting times" (XI, 231ff.). In other words, the project of the later Schelling is not "Being and Time" but "Being and Times." Mythic time and the time of revelation are qualitatively different. Revelation is a predicate of history and requires its own scale. Such a scale, however, has been systematically taken apart by the Enlightenment critique of religion from Spinoza via D. F. Strauss to the school of the history of religion in the twentieth century. In the battle with the Catholic Church in France, with the Anglican and Lutheran orthodoxies in England and in Germany, the first deistic, then atheistic Enlightenment turned deaf to the differentiation of epochs and of the forms of consciousness before and after Christ. The creation account of Genesis in the Old Testament and the Gospels of the

New Testament are today treated as a kind of myth. The turn away from mythology in the biblical horizon of consciousness has been glossed over and sacrificed to a general bias for "natural" revelation and religion. The result of the seventeenth century's critique of religion remains ambiguous. Revelation as a unique phenomenon of the Christian era is abolished, revelation itself declared mythology, and thus the ground is prepared for a general, formalized concept of mythology. What the more recent histories of religion pursues is nothing less than an apology for polytheism, after two thousand years of Christianity have blinded our eyes. With the religio-historical apology for paganism and the philosophical *praise of polytheism*, a mythical horizon of consciousness is not merely indexed but also produced. Recourses to mythos post Christum are in truth only repetitions of Julian's apostasy. Already in the fourth century it was overcome by the Galilean[20] when memories of the reality of the gods still hovered in the air. Two thousand years post Christum all recourses to literature that find their apotheosis in the "Gesamtkunstwerk" remain condemned. Yet this can arouse interest only so long as the aesthetic judgment is deployed as an eminent organon of knowledge, even of the problems of "pure" and "practical" reason.

I have drawn on Schelling's philosophical distinction between mythology and revelation in order very roughly to trace the possibility of a demythologized concept of history. If we are not successful in constructing a historical concept of history, then the project of modernity is not safe from a retreat into a Nature that remains eternally the same, and a lapse back into a mythical horizon of consciousness will be in order. Then it could be that acheronistic powers will flood the "Olympus of appearance"[21] on which an enlightened polytheism wishes to settle. I took recourse to Schelling because Odo Marquard also calls on him as his chief witness in his *Praise of Polytheism*. Certainly no philosopher since Vico—and Vico was not a professor of philosophy—described so strikingly the historical character and function of polytheism in the formation of peoples as late as Schelling. But no one was more clearly aware that post Christum, the gods can no longer be invoked, but can only be conjured.

It was said of Marx that he discovered a new continent of reflection and knowledge: the continent of history. I do not take this theory to be false, even if it favors Marx one-sidedly. What is correct about it is that the continent of history was not discovered by Hegel. Hegel's *Phenomenology* is the Odyssey of consciousness. Hegel describes the way of consciousness through history in the course of which time, however, is obliterated. Thus the doctrine of post*histoire* rightly connects to the Hegelian figure of the "phenomenology of spirit." Marx and Schelling, however, both speak, contra Hegel, of "prehistory" and "history." This is not only a difference in nomenclature but also concerns the situation of consciousness post Hegel mortem. Marx's "abolition of philosophy" and Schelling's caesura: "positive philosophy" of an "absolute empiricism" against the "negative" movement of thought from Ionia to Jena,[22] stand together in secret alliance. Can Marx's revolutionary program be saved only by the reactionary philosophy of Mr. von Schelling? Friedrich Engels at least was attuned to the materialistic overtones in the lectures of the old Schelling, and Lenin would not have been shocked if his consortium for the study of Hegel also took the step from Hegel to late Schelling. Thus my offer to Odo Marquard is as follows: to advance from a philosophy of mythology to a (self-evidently!) "enlightened" philosophy of revelation. In this way some difficulties of history and its philosophy could, if not be abolished, at least be rectified.

"One would do well to advise Mr. Schelling to reconsider his first writings," writes Karl Marx, a statement that Marxists also should consider self-critically with regard to Marx. In his master's thesis Schelling dealt with the biblical story of the fall of man and in his dissertation with the "Myths, Historical Legends, and Philosophemes of the Ancient World" in order to make them objects of historical knowledge of both being and consciousness. If the young Marx allowed the "science of history" to count as the "only" form of scientific reflection, and all sciences of nature as historical, then Schelling and Marx meet in their discovery of the continent of history with the intention to better mark the boundaries for the object of historical knowledge. While for Marx this object is demarcated by circumstances that occurred and were transmitted and that prohibit making history transparent from all sides, for Schelling the boundary is located in the constitution of the autonomous subject itself.

The program of a "critique of historical reason" is the agenda of philosophical reflection since Dilthey's *Introduction to the Human Sciences*.[23] The title of the program is consciously related to the threefold form of the

Kantian critique. This is because Kant was concerned first and foremost with a justification of knowledge. The philosophy of history as a "critique of historical reason" aims toward a concept of knowledge that draws on certain epistemological presuppositions that Kant articulated in his three critiques, the consequences of which he himself recoiled from as a "son of the Enlightenment." If the "Copernican turn," initiated by Kant is interpreted from a historico-philosophical intention, then the result is a change of perspective on the concept of history. As is well known, Kant exposed the categorical network of natural law as a form of appearance of the subject. But a "thing in itself" remains hidden behind the laws of nature, and behind the forms of appearance of time, the inaccessible "event in itself" also remains hidden. Kant recoiled from the consequences implied in his doctrine of the I [*Ich*] as the foundation of the consciousness of time and, as a result, of history. This is where Schelling and Marx pick up and carry forth Kant's intentions.

A central task of a future "critique of historical reason" would be to establish the foundation for the reflection that with the discovery of the phenomenality of categorical laws of history, a concept of knowledge is required that can introduce temporal extensions of past and future into the experience of a particular present of an "I." Past, present, and future are not fixed points on a one-dimensional chronological timeline; rather, past and future are entwined within each respective present of the self and are determined anew in each other's light. Kant's refusal to draw the consequences had been noticed and criticized early on. Theoretically each event bears within itself the measure of its time within itself, as was noted by Herder in his *Metacritique of a Critique of Pure Reason*. Romanticism and historicism took up Herder's objection and referred back to those "multiple, uncountable times within one time." Ranke theologically formulated the historical axiom that every epoch was "immediate to God." As the princeps of German historiography, however, Ranke understood his theologumenon as the legitimation of an "objective representation" of history, without any awareness of the epistemological presuppositions on which such a form of historiography fundamentally depends. Thus Ranke was able to ignore the self of the historian. He virtually institutes the maxim "to quasi dissolve the self," so that to the historian in the "bordello of historicism" events can appear as they "really were."

History, indeed, strives to articulate the past "historically." To do so, however, should mean to determine the unique temporal index for every event. This is not to be determined (if indeed the "Copernican turn" of Kant's critique also affects our concept of history) out of a belief that every epoch is supposed to be "immediate to God." History is not "immediate to God," and neither are any of its epochs. History is the story of the eighth day of creation, that is, the story of Adam's fall, of the world, that understands all of what that fall was and is. If history is the predicate of revelation, so does the content of this predicate reveal itself as the court of martial law.

The story of the fall of man begins immediately after the seven-day labor of creation has been concluded. The account of creation prior to the fall does not describe any event in time. Whatever in it bears the index of time does so from the perspective after the fall. The beginning of history is severed from the narrative of the seven days of creation and introduces the eighth day. God's creation is said to be "good," even "very good." But with the eighth day a new theme is introduced: the history of Adam. His history is, however, the story of his fall or his transgression. It is intended to explain how evil entered into the world. Evil, therefore, is not the result of a mythical divine struggle. The biblical narrative cancels out all "prehistorical" mythos and lets Adam bear the burden of evil alone. All mythical remnants within the biblical narrative are rendered subordinate to the story of Adam.

The story of Adam's fall remains quite purposefully hidden within the books of the Bible. The law and the prophets as well as the Gospels do not take recourse to Adam's fall. Paul's messianic reflection on the "second Adam" first renders the story of Genesis citable. The ur-history, the "archaeology" first becomes significant eschatologically. It is only from the perspective of the "second Adam" that light is thrown on the "first Adam." Archaeology and eschatology constitute an ur-history in the eminent sense that in the course of history itself remains concealed. Revelation in the strict sense occurs only at the beginning and end of history, which are interlocked in secret agreement. The course of history itself is a state of martial law become permanent.

III. General Orientation and Notes on the Literature in Question

The publication of the work results of the research group "Poetics and Hermeneutics" Colloquium IV, 1968, which appeared in 1971 under the title *Terror und Spiel: Probleme einer Mythenrezeption*, edited by M. Fuhrmann (Munich: Wilhelm Fink Verlag), opened a new phase in the scholarship on mythology: the philosophical phase. Hans Blumenberg's essay "Wirklichkeitsbegriff und Wirkungspotential des Mythos" provided the guideline and Odo Marquard's essay "Zur Funktion des Mythologiephilosophie bei Schelling" the historical contextualization. Both essays served as foci around which the ellipsis of the colloquium circled. In Blumenberg's monumental work *Work on Myth* (German edition: Frankfurt, 1978, English edition: *Work on Myth*, Cambridge, 1985) the labor of the research group matured into a complete work. In Odo Marquard's essay "Lob des Polytheismus," first a lecture in Berlin in 1978, than published in one of the volumes of the colloquium, *Philosophie und Mythos*, edited by H. Poser (Berlin and New York, 1979), and again in a collection of essays by O. Marquard, published with the provocative title *Farewell to Matters of Principle* (German edition: Stuttgart, 1981; English edition: New York, 1989), that labor matured into a program. At that point I was provoked to articulate my refusal to Odo Marquard and implicitly to Hans Blumenberg. From Odo Marquard's authorial biography we can easily read the path of the entire "skeptical generation" that is now in charge—intellectually and ideologically. No one of that generation was as witty as O. Marquard, nor as dazzling, and at the same time as enchanting. It is the intent of the somewhat cryptic thoughts of this essay to break this spell—in conversation with Marquard and in memory of Schelling/Marx.

Thoughts are free, but not without consequence. That a "praise of polytheism" is put forth at precisely a point where the question of *comment peut-on être païen?* [how can one be pagan?] is posed, where a "European alternative of faith" is probed, where Alain de Benoist tries out what today it could mean To Be Pagan [German: *Heide Sein* (Tübingen 1982), translated from the French *Comment peut-on être païen?* (Paris, 1981)] caused me to prick up my ears. I attempted to redo our intellectual alphabet and starting from Horkheimer/Adorno's *Dialectics of Enlightenment*, first published in Amsterdam (Querido, 1947), then, after many pirate copies, released by the authors in Frankfurt (1969), I returned to Hermann Cohen's *Religion of Reason Out of the Sources of Judaism* (Frankfurt: J. Kauffmann, 1929; second edition, republished in Wiesbaden, 1978; English edition: New York: Frederick Ungar, 1972).

The fact that in the last part I call on Schelling and Marx as witnesses is intended as targeting the orthodox theses on Schelling and Marx, represented by Hans Jörg Sandkühler's *Freiheit und Wirklichkeit: Zur Dialektik von Politik und Philosophie* (Frankfurt, 1968), which put the student revolt, the first event of German Spirit after the demise, onto the track of orthodoxy. Not just Schelling but Marx as well, whose death will soon approach its hundredth anniversary, are still in the future, lest our history is not to end in total horror, in "post*histoire*."

Philosophy has a secret connection to politics, and even aesthetics do not remain without consequence. The program of demythologization, whether in classical philology, or in (Protestant) theology, is a product of the protest against the rampant "myth of the twentieth century." At the beginning of the 1940s it did attain a political acuity with Walter Nestle on the one side, and Rudolf Bultmann on the other. It is a sign of the times that nowadays a certain uneasiness with thesis is spreading, as well as the fact that it is philologically and philosophically represented as dated.

Next to the established historiographical report on the theme of myth—German edition: Jan de Vries, *Forschungsgeschichte der Mythologie* (Freiburg, 1961); English edition: G.S. Kirk, *Myth: Its Meaning and Function in Ancient and Other Cultures* (Berkeley, 1970; translated into German, Berlin, 1980)—noteworthy from the perspective of philosophy and the humanities is Alfred Bäumler's monumental as well as violent piece on "Bachofen, der Mythologe der Romantik," introducing the volume of selection from Bachofen, *Der Mythos von Orient und Occident*, edited by Manfred Schröter (Munich: Beck, 1926), provided with an appendix "Bachofen and the History of Religion," in 1965, that appeared as a separate volume, *Das mythische Weltalter*. The same material is interpreted in a much more discreet and striking manner by Fritz Kramer, *Verkehrte Welten: Zur imaginären Ethnographie des 19. Jahrhunderts* (Frankfurt, 1977; second edition, 1981).

Translated with the assistance of William Rauscher

21

Psychoanalysis and Philosophy:
Notes on a Philosophical
Interpretation of the
Psychoanalytic Method[1]

I

Freud's *The Interpretation of Dreams* appeared in 1900. Until that point, psychoanalysis had moved only within the confines of a medically oriented psychology and was preoccupied with the resolution of pathological phenomena. In *The Interpretation of Dreams,* however, Freud turned to an area not determined by pathological symptoms. The dream is a phenomenon of normal psychic life and occurs for every healthy individual.

A quarter-century later, Freud attempted in his *Autobiographical Study* to determine in hindsight the function of his epoch-making work:

If dreams turned out to be constructed like symptoms, if their explanation required the same assumptions—the repression of impulses, substitute-formation, compromise-formation, the dividing of the conscious and the unconscious into various psychical systems—then psychoanalysis was no longer a subsidiary science in the field of psychopathology, it was rather the foundation for a new and deeper science of the mind that would be equally indispensable for the understanding of the normal. Its postulates and findings could be carried over to other regions of mental happening; a path lay open to it that led far afield, into spheres of universal interest.[2]

The analysis of dreams gave Freud insight into unconscious psychic processes. He attempted to show that the mechanisms that create pathological symptoms are also active in normal psychic life. In this way Freud transformed "psychoanalysis into depth psychology," and as such dissolved the boundaries of its view toward the humanities.[3] Psychoanalysis now stood eye to eye with philosophy.

How did philosophy respond to the claim of psychoanalysis? I recall first of all how psychoanalysis was initially received by the medical guild. Ten years after the appearance of *The Interpretation of Dreams*, medical authorities could still publicly declare that psychoanalysis was "not an object of discussion for a scientific congress," but rather "a matter for the police."[4] The confrontation with psychoanalysis in medicine has since taken on a quieter form, even if an underground rumble is still audible. Either anonymously or by name, important pieces of psychoanalytic theory have become part of the teaching of academic psychiatry.

In philosophy and the humanities, however, the times of blind polemics are not yet over. Granted, the style of the psychoanalytic method has found its imitation in the analysis of philosophical texts. In his interpretations, Martin Heidegger made use of methods that—at least formally—evoke the style of psychoanalytic exegesis. If an interpretation merely rehearses that "which has expressly been *said*" by an author, then, Heidegger claims, "from the outset it is not an interpretation, insofar as the task of such an interpretation remains to make visible specifically that" which the author "had brought to light in his groundwork over and above the explicit formulation." This, however, the author is "no longer able to express."[5]

In every philosophical insight what is decisive for Heidegger is not

> what is said in uttered propositions. [. . .] Instead, what must be decisive is what it sets before our eyes as still unsaid, in and through what has been said.
>
> Certainly, in order to wring from what the words say, what it is they want to say, every interpretation must necessarily use violence.[6]

This apology for violence is certainly Heidegger's own addition to the art of interpretation, but his differentiation between the explicit formulation and the foundational layer of a text, between expressed statements and the unsaid that permeates that which is said, is impossible to implement without elements taken from the Freudian art of interpretation. But even beyond his art of interpreting philosophical texts Heidegger is indebted to the psychoanalytic method in the course of his analyses.

> All fundamental-ontological constructions that take aim at the unveiling of the inner possibility of the understanding of Being must, in projecting, wrest from forgetfulness that which is apprehended by the projection.[7]

The founding philosophical act, like that of psychoanalysis, is an anamnesis, a re-remembering of the forgotten. Heidegger de-masks and exposes the vulgar or everyday understanding of human existence and wants to bring original, still concealed possibilities into the light of day. Thus we can answer his rhetorical question, "What does this method have to do with psychoanalysis?"[8] by saying: quite a lot. This context becomes evident only if we are ready to abandon Heidegger's lofty philosophical tone and pay attention to the way in which he poses his questions. In any case, the silent suspicion that Heidegger practices against Freud is distinctly out of place.

Karl Jaspers publically took a stand against psychoanalysis. This weighs all the more seriously as Jaspers himself had taken a route from psychopathology to philosophy. I refer to the first of three lectures that Jaspers presented in Heidelberg in 1950, a half-century after *The Interpretation of Dreams*. This lecture bore the promising title "The Challenge by the Scientific Method" and reached a wide circle with its publication in the journal *Der Monat* (vol. 26, Nov. 1950). It thus can serve as representative of his critique of psychoanalysis.

Jaspers provides three arguments for his thesis, of which the first and the third can be scrutinized according to an intellectual-historical and philosophical analysis, while his second argument only deals with generalities that neither offer themselves up to evaluation nor contribute to the point. I start with the second argument in order to leave the field open for the aspects of his critique of psychoanalysis that should be taken seriously. Jaspers claims that the manner of its therapeutic effect remains questionable: any psycho-therapeutic treatments can produce results in the hands of effective personalities, and the procedure of psychoanalysis produces successes and failures just like any other method. While in academic medicine enormous almost incredibly successful cures have been made possible during the past hundred and fifty years, so that the average life of Western man has been extended by twenty years, it appears that the successes of psychotherapy have not increased at all. They can hardly do so owing to the very nature of things.[9]

Appearance may deceive, and without further detailed study and an exhaustive comparison of various methods, this argument remains only a rhetorical gesture. His reference to "the satisfaction which some patients derive from a devoted concern for themselves and for their whole biography"[10] is so vulgar that we can treat it only with silence.

Jaspers's first and third arguments, however, weigh more heavily. The first suggests that psychoanalysis confuses "the understanding of meaning with causal explanation." "The understanding of the meaning of something evolves from the mutuality of communication: causality is foreign to this process of meaning making. . . . "[11] Already prior to Jaspers this view has been expressed often and repeated just as much following him. Freud, so the prevalent opinion goes, fell for the deterministic positivism and materialism of the vaining nineteenth century and remained blind to the question of meaning or purpose in human action. There is no doubt that psychoanalysis adopted some of its terminology from the scientific language of the 1880s and 1890s. But if one does not observe that in psychoanalytical theory these terms attain an entirely new coloration, then this is really only an antiquarian inventorial endeavor.

More still: one remains blind to the revolutionary implications of the psychoanalytic method if it is not realized that it overcomes the causal explanation of psychic events in order to advance an immanently goal-oriented form of understanding, that is, precisely an "understanding of meaning" in psychic phenomena. Many years ago Franz Borkenau called attention to this turn in Freud's research in a brilliant if unusual essay. If one hears Jaspers's arguments repeated so often, then revisiting Borkenau's insights in his essay seems necessary.[12] Freud inherited the extremely mechanistic psychology of the late nineteenth century—every psychic event had to have an external psychological cause. But Freud broke with this mechanistic psychology already prior to his first psychoanalytic works.

In his work on aphasia, which was ahead of its time, he proved that although general lesions on the organ of speech can lead to speech disturbances, it is still impossible to determine a specific coordination between the specific psychic lesion and the respective resulting speech impediment. The latter is determined much more fundamentally by the sequence in which the patient acquired his language ability. In this way [so Borkenau rightly claims], a historical process, i.e., the idea of a purely external determination of a psychic phenomenon, was undone even if the importance of this was not clear to Freud at the time.[13]

As Freud carefully approached the formulation of the psychoanalytic method during the last years of the outgoing nineteenth century, he was driven toward the assumption that psychic disturbances were above all indications of disturbances of the sexual development. This insight could have been easily integrated into the context of a physiochemical theory and therapy. It is surprising therefore that Freud renounced any physiological therapy, dismissed any biochemical influence on sexual development, and developed his therapy exclusively from the uncovering of his patients' repressed psychic experiences. Of what, however, does the purely immanent coherence in psychic events uncovered by Freud consist? The psychoanalytic method attempts to render intelligible to the patient who suffers from symptoms (which he cannot overcome so long as he cannot understand them) the concrete biographical context of the experiences from which the symptoms arose. It attempts to disclose the symptom as a meaningful formation, as an—admittedly inexpedient and needlessly agonizing—balance of antagonistic wishes and prohibitions between the infantile "I want" and the social but equally interiorized "you should." Psychoanalysis thus understands the symptom, as Borkenau felicitously phrases it, "as a goal-driven [*zweckhaft*] (but as such not necessarily functional [*zweckmässig*]) behavior."[14] What is discovered in psychoanalytic theory are thus "not causal contexts, but goals."[15] The decisively new element in the psychoanalytic method consists precisely in the fact that it does not deny external causalities, such as the biologically conditioned drives, but only gets a grip on them by means of the explication of their often encrypted and repressed goals.

We must, therefore, turn Jaspers's statement on its head if we want to reckon with the trajectory of psychoanalytic theory. The psychoanalytic method surmounts causal explanation and develops a method that does not merely promise the understanding of meaning, like the existentialist homily does, but also casts a light deep down onto the bottom of the human structure of drives that is inherently foreign to meaning making, and then proceeds to explicate these within the context of an analysis of meaning. Freud did not write an "explanation" of dreams that would have constructed the dream event out of physiological or biochemical elements, but rather an "interpretation" of dreams that attempts to place even the most nonsensical tatters of dreams and delusions into a coherent framework of meaning. The psychoanalytic method knows no other medium than the word of the patient. And cure here means that the shattered coherence of meaning of his communication is reassembled.

The last argument that Jaspers furnishes in his critique concerns the model of neurosis:

> Only a tiny percentage of human beings suffer from this mechanism, this gift of fate, by which they encounter their own spiritual or intellectual processes, the acts of their own free will transposed into physical phenomena, as something foreign to themselves and beyond their control. Most people repress, forget, leave unsettled, suffer, and endure the worst without transforming it into physical symptoms.[16]

This, however, means to completely bypass the epochal character of Freud's *Interpretation of Dreams*, half a century after its publication. While in its first steps psychoanalysis was only concerned with the resolution of pathological phenomena and was often forced to make assumptions with consequences disproportionate to the importance of the case at hand, in 1900 *The Interpretation of Dreams* transcended the limits of the psychoanalytic perspective.

It is precisely this dissolution of the limits of Freud's method that caused it to surge in different directions after 1900: first as an analysis of historical life in general, then as a theory of the current epoch that provoked Jaspers to make his summary complaint that psychoanalysis abets totalitarianism. He discovers in psychoanalysis "the claim to a total knowledge of man," even a "'total' conception of man, which is structurally analogous to totalitarianism in politics" (24). That is, he pronounces in elegantly and in the terms of a critique of ideology precisely the same thing that was articulated more clearly half a century earlier by a medical authority of the time: psychoanalysis is no object of discussion for science; it is a matter for the police.

However, despite Heidegger's rejection of psychoanalysis and its near-denunciatory caricature by Jaspers, the younger generation has become aware of its philosophical implications. In fact, the most important attestations to the philosophical understanding of psychoanalysis come from the extreme right- and extreme left-wing of the critique of ideology. In an important essay, "On the Birth of Freedom Out of Alienation,"[17] Arnold Gehlen demonstrates that an "invisible thread [runs] from Fichte to Marx to Freud" (350), because in the wake of German idealism, both Marxism and psychoanalysis develop in very different ways the matter of freedom's birth out of alienation. Man realizes his freedom when he recovers control of those products of his own agency that have slipped away from him. The idealistic conception of "lost freedom," of alienation and the illusory, deceptive autonomy and sovereignty of that which is produced by us, lingers on in socioeconomic form in the work of Karl Marx.

Without anyone noticing it, this Fichtean formula has through psychological use become popular worldwide: in Freud. Because what are dreams, tics, the unconquerable compulsions and anyhow the entire neurotic arsenal other than unconscious products of the ego's autonomy which become alienated from it and which confront it with their superiority, and which now analysis dissolves as it "renders them conscious," reconstructing them in their genesis and course of development, thus reinstating the ego's freedom and sovereignty over its own nocturnal births.[18]

Indeed, this genealogy of psychoanalysis to Gehlen represents a heavy debt. Psychoanalysis lives on not as a strict theoretical construction of psychology but as a perspective, a worldview. Its theoretical categories, however, which Freud derived from the psychic life of the individual, "are weirdly deformed and ultimately shattered when they are overburdened with collective-psychic content."[19]

This is precisely what Herbert Marcuse would disagree with. He tries to show that the prevalent interpretation of the Freudian categories construes, too univocally and abstractly, the relation between the individual-psychological center point and the social-psychological periphery. This is because Freud does not simply proceed from individual to social psychology; rather, Freud's theory is sociological "in its very substance."[20] Precisely Freud's seemingly purely biological categories are in essence categories of social history. Marcuse not only provides a philosophical genealogy of fundamental psychoanalytic concepts but also integrates Freudian theory into the great tradition of philosophy and subsumes it under philosophical criteria. The history of philosophy as a whole stands under the signs of logos or reason. The principle of reason, however, reveals itself in the process of the history of philosophy as the reasonableness of the principle of efficiency.

The history of ontology reflects the reality principle that governs the world ever more exclusively: the insights contained in the metaphysical notion of Eros were driven underground. . . . Freud's own theory follows the general trend: in his work, the rationality of the predominant reality principle supersedes the metaphysical speculations on Eros.[21]

The traumatic metamorphosis of the human organism into an instrument of alienated labor appears to Freud to be an irreversible fate. This concept of fate puts him in close proximity to Georg Simmel and Max Weber. Freud's late work *Civilization and Its Discontents* is the psychoanalytic variation of the analysis of an inescapable "tragedy of culture," which Georg Simmel and Max Weber sought to determine sociologically and and to substantiate philosophically. Freud, however, like no one else before him, identified the multiple forms in which the repressed Eros returns in a world alienated from pleasure and subjugated by work. This is the point to which Herbert Marcuse's critique takes on, as he attempts to think with Freud against Freud.

The idea that a culture without repression is impossible is a cornerstone of Freudian theory. Freud—and in this Marcuse agrees with him—"regards the primordial life struggle as 'eternal' and therefore believes that the pleasure and reality principles must 'forever' strive against one another."[22] This accounts for the unhistorical character of his category. Yet, thus according to Marcuse, Freudian theory contains elements that tear the veil of this rationalization. In his extraordinarily exciting book on *Eros and Civilization*, Herbert Marcuse performs this extrapolation from the Freudian theory, by opening up perspectives and deriving from it propositions, which it contains merely in a reified form. Marcuse develops the theoretical construction of a culture beyond the efficiency principle, in which he inverts elements of Freud's theory into their opposites, but by demonstrating them as consequences of their historical substance.

The question about the connection between philosophy and psychoanalysis can be posed only within the terrain circumscribed by Gehlen and Marcuse. This philosophical analysis was deployed in Germany in the last few years in an excellent text by Odo Marquard submitted as his habilitation to the philosophy faculty of the University of Münster under the cryptic title *Über die Depotenzierung der Tranzendentalphilosophie* (1962).[23] In a recent essay Marquard dealt with "Some Connections Between Aesthetics and Therapeutics in the Nineteenth Century."[24] Here he attempted to clarify the romantic turn from aesthetics to therapeutics in a comparison between Schelling and Freud. However, I would like to consider the relationship between the dialectic and psychoanalytic methods.

II

The analysis of man according to the guideline of history, carried out for example by Hegel and Marx, is replaced around the middle of the nineteenth century by an analysis of man according to the guideline of psychology. Nietzsche demands that psychology be elected the queen of science. Since then, psychology has appeared as the path to mankind's fundamental problems. Freud is positioned within this turn, and his psychoanalysis gives it a particular acuity. And still, the problem of history poses itself anew in Freud. Not only did Freud provide fragments of a theory on history in his various "metapsychological" writings, but, and this is my first thesis, psychoanalysis as a method is historical through and through. Psychoanalysis differs from all other variations of psychology as the most radically historical. Its fundamental design is historical. It works with histories of illness and with the biography of the individual as a constitutive part of its therapy. The concepts of the psychoanalytic method are historical because psychoanalysis tries to discover the past, how it is manifested in the patient's present life or how it wreaks havoc. This is possible only because of the existence of both memory and the repression of memory. Man is essentially historical because he remembers. Memory introduces the element of history into human life, beyond the biological processes of growing up, maturing, and dying. A reflection on the process of psychoanalytic therapy necessarily encounters the problem of the historical method in general and, as I claim, particularly the problems of the historical-dialectic method. It is the explicit thesis of these reflections that Freud's psychological writings in general and his metapsychological writings in particular answer questions posed by Hegel's dialectical method and philosophy of history. That is, *sub specie* Freud the fundamental problems of Hegel appear in a new light; *sub specie* Hegel, the fundamental problems of Freud appear in a new light.

Hegel connects the epistemological process of self-consciousness from sensual certainty to reason with the historical process of humankind from enslavement to freedom. For Hegel, the forms of consciousness appear simultaneously as cosmic circumstances. In this constant transition from philosophical to historical analysis, Hegel intends to substantiate the historical character of the fundamental philosophical concepts. This appears most distinctly in his first great work, which bears the title the *Phenomenology of Spirit*. I want to single out two benchmarks in Hegel's work—the beginning and the end of the *Phenomenology*—and to learn to understand them anew, retrospectively, so to speak, *sub specie* Freud. I take for my guideline the Hegelian concept of truth as a progressive disclosure that occurs through the communication of one self-consciousness with another. This communication occurs precisely through reciprocal "recognition," or through language.

In this way Hegel principally differs from the tradition of modern philosophy—from Descartes to Kant—where consciousness in its solitude must turn to God, who guarantees the truth of human knowledge, which in turn can allow consciousness to return to the realm of appearances. For Hegel, this guarantee of truth occurs in the communication between one consciousness and another—precisely in language, where universal self-consciousness develops or forges its path and where truth discloses itself step by step. This problem is posed on all levels of the *Phenomenology of Spirit*, and I will only single out one paragraph from the beginning and from the end respectively. At the beginning Hegel speaks of natural consciousness and says:

Natural consciousness will show itself to be only the Notion of knowledge, or in other words, not to be real knowledge. But since it directly takes itself to be real knowledge, this path has a negative significance for it, and what is in fact the realization of the Notion, counts for it rather as the loss of its own self; for it does lose its truth on this path. The road can therefore be regarded as the pathway of doubt, or more precisely as the way of despair.[25]

Hegel presents us with the natural consciousness, not the naïve one. It is the consciousness of all of us, whether high or low, educated or ignorant.

What is characteristic of this consciousness? *Sub specie* Freud, I would like to say, that the natural consciousness is not conscious of itself, or that it remains "unconscious" to itself. Consciousness is not an exclusively false consciousness: it sees, but does not see itself. What Hegel narrates on the path of the *Phenomenology of Spirit* is precisely the structure and history of this consciousness that is unconscious of itself: how it becomes conscious of itself on this Odyssey—or as we might say in light of Freud—*Oedipey* of the Spirit. This is not to say that it learns something new, some sort of addendum: in the end consciousness can only "acknowledge" what it has always already known, and what is the root of its knowledge: itself.

But I believe that this is also a key, *sub specie* Hegel, to better understand Freud. It is perhaps a better understanding than even Freud himself understood in his first works, better than he *could* understand in the first furtive steps of his new method. The unconscious is not a world in the background, an object that hides behind consciousness; rather, it is fundamentally the unavoidable mode by which natural consciousness is what it is. One will have to speak of an ontological status of the unconsciousness of natural consciousness. The concept of the unconscious is, to be sure, infamous for its paradoxes and also offered cause for the sharpest critique. This is because, logically, we are faced with the following alternatives: either the unconscious can be made transparent, can be made manifest with the psychoanalytic method, and then it is no longer unconscious, or it lacks any processing in consciousness, in which case the unconscious cannot be at all demonstrated in the processes of consciousness, with the consequence of losing any conceptual relevance and thus becoming superfluous as a category. If one remains beholden to the mechanical image of the unconscious as a repository of traces, it cannot be clearly, conceptually represented.

The tradition of philosophy from Descartes to Husserl, which takes as its origin in *ego cogito*, does not even approach the acuity and verve of doubt, of which Hegel speaks in this paragraph. The "science of the *experience* of consciousness" that Hegel develops in his *Phenomenology of Spirit* "can thus be regarded as the pathway of *doubt*, or more precisely as the way of despair." Hegel purposefully underlines the term "doubt." From Hegel onward the problem of false consciousness presents itself and is thematized by Marx, Nietzsche, and Freud, in ways that vary but nevertheless belong together. This is the *novum* of post-Hegelian philosophy, that it fosters suspicion of consciousness and its structures. The problem of doubt is carried into the Cartesian fortress of *ego cogito* itself, or, in other words: for Descartes and philosophy in his tradition, consciousness and meaning belong together. Marx and Freud destroy this philosophical equivalence of meaning and consciousness: false consciousness emerges as a question, socioeconomically in Marx and psycho-economically in Freud.

Hegel's *Phenomenology of Spirit* conceives itself as "science of the *experience* of consciousness." It represents the immanent history of human experience. This is clearly not the experience of common sense, or the experience of natural consciousness; rather, it is the matter of an experience already on the way to real cognition. He who walks along this path of the experience of consciousness must already be at home in the element of philosophy. The "we" that appears so often in the text of the *Phenomenology of Spirit* and so confusingly interrupts the course of the analysis does not refer to the natural consciousness of common sense, but rather to the self-consciousness of the philosopher. This way of the experience of consciousness is not a lonely path. Consciousness does not pull off a Münchhausen-like feat, pulling itself up by its own bootstraps; rather, it stands eye to eye with the "we." Who is this "we," which so often surfaces in the *Phenomenology*? It is us who with Hegel have arrived at the end of the path, from where we can recognize the insurmountable barrier of natural consciousness. It would, however, so Hegel claims, be a short-circuit if the "we" of absolute knowledge wanted to share its "knowledge" with natural consciousness. "What we would claim to be its essence would not be its truth at all, but only our knowledge of it,"[26] just as it would be equally short-circuitous if the analyst read his patient's history from his symptoms and imparted to him his discovery. Such a short-circuit is condemned to failure because the patient would clearly not be able to recognize this truth. It would only have been read into him without he himself being able to read it, or as Hegel says: "The essence or the criterion would lie in us, and that which was to be compared with this standard, and on which a decision was to be passed as a result of this comparison, would not necessarily have to recognize that criterion."[27] Thus, natural consciousness has no other way to truth than the long road of experience that brings consciousness to the point where it can decode its truth in itself.

The function of negation is decisive for the dialectical method, and it is exactly at this point that the dialectical character of the psychoanalytic method most distinctly demonstrates itself. If this method can be reduced to one problem then it is—if I understand correctly—the problem of repression. The entire apparatus of psychoanalysis serves to better grasp this concept. The theory of the unconscious is born by the interpretation of repression.[28] Freud can therefore say that "the whole theory of psycho-analysis is, as you know, in fact built up on the perception of the resistance offered to us by the patient when we attempt to make his unconscious conscious to him."[29] Repression, Freud says, is the key to all of psychoanalytic theory, and negation is the intellectual substitution for repression. Its "no," Freud claims in his extremely important essay "On Negation" (1925),

is an indication of the same[. . . .] With the help of the symbol of negation, thinking frees itself from the restrictions of repression and enriches itself with material that is indispensable for its proper functioning.[30]

Negation first becomes a theme in the constitution of the ego because "there is nothing in the id which can be compared to negation."[31] It becomes clear only in the interpretation of the process of repression why the dream provides the hermeneutic guideline for the psychoanalytic method. The dream is the only place in which immediacy articulates itself without the blemish of negation. Denial does not take hold in the dream, and thus a level is reached in which the process of repression has not yet fully taken its course.

We cannot follow the individual steps on the path of the development from consciousness to self-consciousness; instead, we want to take up our question again from the end of the *Phenomenology of Spirit*. The self of self-consciousness has passed through its own history:

This way of becoming [so Hegel claims] presents a slow procession and succession of spiritual shapes, a gallery of pictures, each of which is endowed with the entire wealth of Spirit, and moves so slowly just for the reason that the self has to permeate and assimilate all this wealth of its substance. Since its accomplishment consists in Spirit knowing what it is, in fully comprehending its substance, this knowledge means its concentrating itself on itself, a state in which Spirit leaves its external existence behind and gives its embodiment over to Recollection.[32]

Memory preserves history and is the deeper and actually superior form of Substance. Spirit, which remembers its history, is freed from the burden of the past. "Absolute knowing, or Spirit that knows itself as Spirit, has as its path recollection."[33] Why *memory* as the way of the spirit that knows itself as such, or of absolute knowledge? Why is the task of science an anamnesis or remembering?

In Freud's *Studies in Hysteria* we can retrace the beginnings of the psychoanalytic method. Here we learn that hysteric patients who have "repressed" various of their feelings and exhibit corporeal symptoms can lose these, when they remember and articulate the traumatizing circumstances while under hypnosis. But we must be more precise: it appeared to Freud that it is not the hypnotic or cathartic method that suspends hysteric symptoms, but rather the remembering of the traumatic event and its communication to the doctor. Hypnosis was the medium for recalling memory and breaking down the resistances, which in a waking conscious state hindered its ascension. It became, however, clear to Freud that with hypnotic catharsis, the hysteric symptoms receded only temporarily and that the patient was not released from his hysteric *condition humaine*. The decisive factor was *communication*. From this Freud arrived at a rational conception, or more precisely, at a historically biographical conception of psychic illness in general.

The path from hypnotic catharsis to analysis was a path from a punctiform ecstasy, that expands and illuminates consciousness in a flash, to a rational, steadily progressive revelation of the past that, precisely because it is not remembered, keeps the individual under its spell. It was no longer a matter of an acting, as in hypnosis, but of an understanding. This insight led Freud to the method of classical psychoanalysis, which from this perspective reveals itself as a rational and historical method. For Freud it was not enough to let the scenes take place for a second time, in which neurotic symptoms remain preserved as residue. Rather he was concerned that where "Id" was, "I" should come to be, that the Ego can interiorize its past as Ego and that it should not prevail in him as something foreign. Freud understood illness as a specific form of failure of re-membering [*Er-innerung*], the failure of the process of interiorization or of Ego-constitution.

Like Hegel's dialectical method, the psychoanalytic method is a "science of the experience of consciousness," which constitutes itself on the way from the experience of unconscious consciousness "in itself"—as Hegel says—to conscious self-consciousness "for itself." Just as Hegel does, Freud describes the actual effective genesis of the self. Freud is also the only one to pose the question of absolute knowledge after the process of disintegration of the Hegelian philosophy. The fact that Hegel's dialectical method and the psychoanalytic method are comparable was recognized by Jaspers, albeit in a way that is wrong in every detail and correct only with the comparison. Therefore it is fruitful to cite the gross misunderstanding of a philosopher like Jaspers, even as it is enunciated in the ire of a blinded polemics. Surely, this can be done only if we are ready to separate his insight into the congruence of the methods from the pathetic rhetoric of his denunciation.

III

If in his psychoanalytic theory Freud participated in the course of the dialectical method, then where does he proceed beyond Hegel and Marx? Hegel and Marx grasped the self-production of man as a process: self-production in the element of work, in the historical process from the master-slave relationship all the way to mutual recognition. Hegel had initially attempted to develop the dialectical relationship in the element of love, but then gave this comparison up because love appeared to him as nondialectic, or nonhistorical and natural-like. Freud was able to introduce the dialectical method into areas that as natural or ecstatic regions appeared to elude the law of history. Sexuality is for Freud a prefiguration of the master-slave relationship and its overcoming in mutual recognition that determines the course of historical development. If the historical plane is the forum for human desire, desire for recognition, if to speak of the origin of self-consciousness means to address necessarily the life-or-death struggle for recognition, then it is indispensable, and this is Freud's decisive insight, to speak of the apparently animalistic, but in truth human desire of sexuality. It is precisely in the natural context of sexuality that the historical situation arises, even has its origins. Freud underlines the Hegelian term "desire" and in his opus explicates the libidinal development of the individual.

Therefore, Freud does not sketch out a phenomenology of the *spirit*, of the self-identical spirit, but rather places the priority in *nature*. When already Marx disrobed Hegel's dialectic of its mystical shell, namely, the priority of spirit, in order to get to the sensual priority of natural existence, in the wake of Feuerbach he opens up the possibility for a dialectical analysis of "sensuality." Marx, however, remains beholden to the limits of Hegel's model. For him, "Nature taken abstractly, for itself, fixated in a division from man, is nothing."[34]

The purely natural material in which *no* human labour is objectified, to the extent that it is merely a material that exists independently of labour, has no value, since only objectified labour is value.[35]

The development of the mastery of reason through the organization of work is a process that for Marx is part of political economy and not of psychology. But certainly we should not understand the economic categories already in Marx in the sense of a scientific discipline stuck in its tracks:

In the succession of the economic categories, as in any other historical, social science, it must not be forgotten that their subject—here, modern bourgeois society—is always what is given, in the head as well as in reality, and that these categories therefore express the forms of being, the characteristics of existence, and often only individual sides of this society [. . .] and that therefore this economy by no means begins only at the point where one can speak of it *as such*; even *scientifically*.[36]

The somatic-psychic preconditions of this development that Freud uncovered make it possible to trace the problem of work and economy back into the shadowy libidinal structures of human existence. The fact that history affects the natural, sensual, and even sexual level of humanity does not yet occur to Marx. Thus it is not at random that in Hegel and Marx the problem of love in the analysis of historical processes is swept under the table or is displaced from the text into the notes.

Freud himself points to the opposition between history and love or sexuality. Sexual love is a relationship between two people for whom a third can only be disruptive, while history deals with relations among a much greater number of people.

In the developmental process of the individual, the program of the pleasure principle, which consists in finding the satisfaction of happiness, is retained as the main aim. [. . .] This is different with the process of culture. Here the main issue is the goal to bring about a unity among human individuals. The aim of happiness still remains, but it is pushed into the background. It almost appears as the creation of a great human community would work best if one did not have to worry about the happiness of the individual.[37]

The question of history arises, for Freud, from the tension between Eros, which is prehistorical and eternally reoccurring, and a forward-moving Labor, which must master the world. The price for the progress of history lies in the forfeit of happiness, which is paid through the elevation of a sense of guilt. The fact that humanity, as species or individuals, is still ruled by archaic forces is to be counted among Freud's deepest insights. In Freud's sense, "archaic" or "original" has at the same time both a structural and a historical significance. The archaic drive-structure was predominant in the prehistory of the species. It was transformed in history proper, but remains effective as underground, preconscious or unconscious, in the history of both the human individual and the species, and certainly most visibly in early childhood. Historical development remains overshadowed by this beginning. The primordial event: patricide, remorse, and the constitution of the fraternal bond as society exists as ur-history beyond the course of history. There is no development that does not remain under the shadow of this event. The primordial event of Ur-history, whether of the individual or of the species, remains isolated and lurks within history's further progress. Sure enough, this Ur-history is itself historical and by no means a metatemporal Platonic idea. Thus, in Freud the beginning of history becomes thematized in a way that does not occur in Hegel or in Marx. The beginning or origin of history, which overshadows and overtakes all further events, is the question of the beginning, of *auctoritas,* or of authority.

Thus, we find in Freud a double scheme: on the one hand, the evolutionist scheme of both historical and libidinal development; on the other hand, the scheme of the eternal return of the same, the discovery of the fundamentally regressive or conservative tendencies in the total effect of the drives. The status quo of natural reality, which always already precedes the course of history, also always overtakes it. These conflicting tendencies in Freud's theory destabilize the edifice of psychoanalysis. Freud falters as to whether to negate the renunciation of the drives as repression and as pathological aberration, or to affirm it as sublimation in support of history. The psychoanalytic method wears the same two-faced visage that Hegel's dialectical method does. It is also the last broadly conceived theorem of a critique of bourgeois society post Hegel. It is precisely because of this that this "self-criticism of bourgeois society has become a means of making bourgeois self-alienation, in its final phase, absolute, and of rendering ineffectual the lingering awareness of the ancient wound, in which lies hope of a better future."[38]

This ambiguity in the theoretical construction is also the reason why the reception of Freud (similar to that of Hegel) has unfolded into right- and left-wings. The conflicting exegeses were provoked by the problem of the transition from nature to history: in his analysis of this problem Arnold Gehlen puts the emphasis on the permanently repressive elements in the construction of human society. The psychoanalytic theory is not, according to him, suitable to provide the motives for our immediate social behavior, which copes with durable relations in need of stabilization, relations between individuals who must live together. As individual psychology, insofar as it describes persons whose social sensor has fallen ill, it may produce results. But as an analysis of the stabilizing function of society, which has to dam up all the chimerical hopes and fantasies of individuals, it works poorly. The social alienation from the individual's aspirations to happiness and freedom remains permanent. Gehlen here can easily call on Freud: "Individual freedom is not a cultural asset."[39] The more the apparatus, which guarantees social progress, is developed, the more oppressive are the sacrifices it demands from individuals in order to sustain the drive structure required for the construction and continuity of society.

This is where Marcuse introduces his critique of Freud.[40] His emphasis is the utopian goal of history as the path to freedom. Do the taboos, on which social progress rests today, have to be guarded so anxiously because the temptation, as it expresses itself in the individual's pleasure principle, grows stronger and stronger, and in view of increasing productivity also more and more objectively reasonable? If, as Freud underscores, "civilization obeys an internal erotic impulse which causes human beings to unite in a closely knit group,"[41] then, so Herbert Marcuse concludes, culture stems from pleasure, and the goal of historical development is subsumed under the pleasure principle. Marcuse can also refer to Freud's pronouncements for his utopian interpretation:

The same thing occurs in the social relations between humans as has become familiar to psycho-analytic research in the developmental course of the individual libido. The libido attaches itself to the satisfaction of the great vital needs, and chooses as its first objects the people who have a share in that process. And in the development of mankind as a whole, just as in individuals, love alone acts as the civilizing factor in the sense that it brings about a change from egoism to altruism.[42]

Thus, moving provocatively beyond Freud, Marcuse claims that even labor, which has a significant share in mediating the transition from nature to history, is originally libidinal. A person begins to work because he achieves pleasure *in* work and not only *after* work. Thus, in contrast to Freud, work appears to him in a utopian perspective as a possibility for developing human abilities, as a form of free play. Schiller's *Letters on the Aesthetic Education of Man* constitutes the backdrop of this new utopia.

Freud however, just like Hegel, remains ambiguous in this conflict, allowing for both a conservative and utopian interpretation of social development. Hegel completed his great opus with the echo of the thundering cannons of the Battle at Jena. He saw his time, the epoch of the French Revolution, as a time of birth and a transition to a new period. The time of transition persists to this day. What with the French Revolution announced itself on the European continent today affects the entire globe in world wars and revolutions. And what Hegel says of his time and his work, the *Phenomenology of Spirit*, is still valid, in a much more literal sense, for our time and for the phenomenology of the soul that Freud opened up before us in his works:

> . . . the spirit of the age, growing slowly and quietly ripe for the new form it is to assume, disintegrates one fragment after another of the structure of its previous world. That it is tottering to fall is indicated only by individual symptoms here and there. Frivolity and again ennui, which are spreading, the undefined foreboding of something unknown—all these betoken that there is something else approaching. This gradual crumbling to pieces, which did not alter the general physiognomy of the whole, is interrupted by the sunrise, which, in a flash and a single stroke, brings to view the form and structure of the new world.[43]

Translated with the assistance of William Rauscher

22

Religion and the Future of Psychoanalysis[1]

Freud insisted time and again that psychoanalysis is not a philosophy but a therapeutic method. Nevertheless, this method that developed out of the study of some cases of hysteria drew into its orbit the arts and the humanities, philosophy and religion. For psychoanalysis as a therapeutic method carried far-reaching implications for the understanding of man.

A revolutionary doctrine such as psychoanalysis could make its way into the general public only against the powerful resistance of current ideologies and established institutions. The resistance to the psychoanalytic method should not surprise the historian. What should astonish us is the rapid success that analytic method has achieved in recent decades. Did the resistances against psychoanalysis break down before the success of a therapeutic method, or did the theory and practice of analysis undergo a change? Did psychoanalysis adapt its theories to the established ideologies? Did the post-Freudian development of psychoanalytic theory obscure its critical implications for the life of society? Does it now serve to reinforce our existing institutions?

Prior to the First World War, religion represented the stronghold of resistance to the claims of psychoanalytic theory. This opposition on the part of religion was not accidental. Freud had committed psychoanalytic theory to the premises of atheism. Beyond a general acceptance of atheistic views current in the late nineteenth century, Freud and his followers studied religion in terms analogous to the study of individual neurosis. Religion became a supreme instance of a primordial neurosis of humankind.

Freud belonged to the avant-garde of "free spirits" anticipated by Nietzsche, those who were sensitive enough to discern that with the decomposition of theism in the West the foundations of our morality had collapsed. Far from being tormented like Nietzsche by the greatness of the event, Freud took the end of religion for granted and dared to prophesy that the abandoning of religion will have to take place with fateful inexorability of growth and that we are just now in the middle of this phase of development. It must make us suspicious that within two decades of Freud's death psychoanalysis and religion now exhibit such marked signs of friendship.

Many reasons mingle to account for this shift. Surely one of them is the challenge and collapse of socialist messianism in the West. Faced with the challenge of secular chiliasm, theologians and clerics have found in psychoanalysis a secular version of the doctrine of original sin that helps undercut the claims of the Marxist chiliasm.

When the hopes that the Western intelligentsia had invested in the transformation of the social structure were bitterly disappointed, Freud's antieschatological view of man and history could be used as an argument against the "illusions" of all chiliastic hopes that expected the transformation of men through the transformation of the societal structure. Even in the new society man remained the old Adam possessed by his drives and instincts, unredeemed from his lusts, and therefore even more apt to stumble into barbarism when the conservative fences around the political order were removed. While Marxism as secular version of chiliasm interpreted the history as a transitory stage of man on his way to the "reign of freedom" in the future, Freud insisted that man can never jump over the shadow of his past. As much as the early years of childhood exert a decisive influence on our adult life in a way that later events oppose in vain, likewise the past of our collective history turns the progress of history into a farce. Man moves in history as in a circle, reproducing many versions of "the same old story."

Once this conservative element in psychoanalysis became obvious the ice of resistance in our society against psychoanalytic theory and practice melted, and Freud's discoveries about man's conduct and motives turned quickly into the most recent syllables of the divine. Religion and psychoanalysis equally stressed the authority of the past and could join in the affirmation of the past as a guide for human conduct on an individual as well as on the societal level.

I

Religion is a Latin term, which originally designated the civic cult of the Roman polity. Biblical literature does not know the term. Still the congregations whose experience is reflected in the books of the Old Testament as well as in the writings of the New Testament are classified as "religions." This is not a small philological detail, of interest only to the linguist or to the exegete. The fate of Christianity is embedded in this shift of language as in a nutshell. What was once a way of salvation, a hope for the redemption of man, has become an established religion in the realm of the world. In the term *religio* Rome was victorious over the hope of redemption. It is impossible at this stage of history to break the ambiguity in the term religion that comprises two contradictory elements: religion as a civic cult, and religion as a way of salvation, redeeming man from the authority of the powers and principalities of the world.

A way of salvation is, as the Latin adjective *salvus* or *salus* indicates, concerned with redeeming man from the powers that break and disrupt his life. Man's life is threatened by forces from without and within man. A message of salvation professes to heal the break in human existence, to redeem it from the burden of guilt under which man is breaking down. The conflict between religion as a way of salvation and psychoanalysis as a therapy focuses on the notion of salvation as a way of healing, as a way of redeeming man from his guilt. While psychoanalysis and religion as a civic cult could easily come to terms in the stress on the authority of the past, the relation between religion as a way of salvation and psychoanalysis as a therapy freeing man from the burden of his guilt is a more complex one.

While in the *Future of an Illusion* Freud makes use of the ideology of progress as developed in the age of Enlightenment to combat religion, his theoretical writings reveal an insight into the indispensable role of religion in the genealogy of guilt. Since the genealogy of guilt presents also the story of the origin of human society, Freud is forced against his ideology to describe the crucial role of religion in the origin and history of society. The edifice of society is built on an original crime and the perennial rites and customs symbolizing atonement. "The totem was, on the one hand, the corporeal ancestor and protecting spirit of the clan, he was to be revered and protected. On the other hand, a festival was instituted on which day the same fate was to be meted out to him as the primeval father had encountered. He was killed by all the brothers together (totem feast, according to William Robertson Smith). This great day was in reality a feast of triumph to celebrate the victory of the united sons over the father."[2]

Even if the original fate of the primeval father certainly became forgotten in the course of thousands of centuries, the original act lives on, according to Freud, in veiled and repressed forms in the unconscious of humanity. Since this original act has occurred, guilt haunts man and "it is not really a decisive matter whether one has killed one's father or abstained from the deed: one must feel guilty in either case."[3] The history of mankind is thus turned into a story of man's "original guilt." Society must foment an ever-increasing sense of guilt. "That which began in relation to the father ends in relation to the community. If civilization is an inevitable course of development from the group of the family to the group of humanity as a whole, then an intensification of the sense of guilt . . . will be inextricably bound up with it until perhaps the sense of guilt may swell to a magnitude that individuals can hardly support."[4]

II

Never since Paul and Augustine has a theologian taught a more radical doctrine of original guilt than Freud. No one since Paul has so clearly perceived and so strongly emphasized the urgent need to atone the act of original guilt as has Freud.

It is not a matter of sheer speculation that Freud conceived his work, his theory, and therapy, in analogy to the message Paul preached to the gentiles. "Paul, a Roman Jew from Tarsus, seized on this feeling of guilt and correctly traced it back to its primeval source. This he called original sin; it was a crime against God that could be expiated only through death. Death had come into the world through original sin. In reality, this crime deserving of death had been the murder of the father who later was deified. The murderous deed itself, however, was not remembered; in its place stood the fantasy of expiation, and that is why this fantasy could be welcomed in the form of a Gospel of salvation (*evangelium*)."[5]

Freud penetrates deeply into the dialectic of guilt and atonement that is the central motif of Paul's theology. He endows Paul with a "gift for religion in the truest sense of the phrase. Dark traces of the past lay in his soul, ready to break through in the regions of consciousness."[6] While the Mosaic religion did not progress beyond the recognition of the great father, Paul, by developing the Mosaic religion became its destroyer. The Mosaic religion had been a father-religion, while Paul became the founder of a son-religion. Paul's success "was certainly mainly due to the fact that through the idea of salvation he laid the ghost of the feeling of guilt."[7]

It cannot be accidental that whenever Freud discusses the message of Paul, he takes the Apostle's side and "justifies" his message of salvation. In the religion of Moses (which represents for Freud the paradigmatic case of religion as authority), there is no room for a direct expression of the murderous father-hate. Therefore, the religion of Moses and the prophets came only to increase the guilt of the community. "Law and Prophets" have burdened man with the sense of guilt. It therefore seemed significant to Freud that the lightening of the burden of guilt proceeded from a Jew. "Although food for the idea had been provided by many suggestive hints from various quarters, it was, nevertheless, in the mind of a Jew, Saul of Tarsus, who as a Roman citizen was called Paul that the perception dawned, 'It is because we killed God the Father that we are so unhappy.'" Surely, Paul first formulated this "historical truth" in the delusional guise of the glad tidings. In Paul's message of salvation "the murder of God was, of course, not mentioned but a crime that had to be expiated by a sacrificial death could only have been murder." Original guilt *and* salvation from the burden of guilt through the sacrificial death of the Son of God became the basis of the new religion founded by Paul. "The strength which this new faith derived from its source in historical truth—enabled it to overcome all obstacles."[8]

What fascinated Freud in the message of Paul was the implicit confession of guilt contained in his good news. The evangel was at the same time a dysangel, the bad news of the original crime of man. The delusional form of the news is the "good" news that this guilt is expiated in the sacrificial death of the Redeemer. For in this form the confession of guilt is still veiled. Freud considers himself the first to break the spell and to dare to delineate the secret guilt that haunts man. What Paul could only acknowledge in the illusion of a "good news" was spelled out by Freud without illusion. Guilt cannot be expiated through the sacrificial death of a Son of God; it can only be acknowledged. By the conscious acknowledgment of guilt man liberates himself from blind bondage. Freud did not conceal to himself in serious moments that his "theories amount to a species of mythology, and a gloomy one at that." In this context Freud's tract on the *Future of an Illusion* may take on some unexpected meaning. It may turn out that this seemingly "progressive" humanist tract really pits the tragic and the eschatological interpretation of man against each other. While the tragic consciousness can only go so far as man's awakening to his original guilt, the eschatological consciousness expresses man's hopes to overcome his guilt. While in the tragic consciousness man can never be absolved but can only bear the burden of his guilt in a heroic gesture, the eschatological man stakes his hope in a future reconciliation and atonement. For the tragic man, the hope in a future is an illusion. The future can only repeat the past, perhaps on a more conscious level, but never can man break the cycle of history.

It is no accident that the mythical *numina* that Freud calls to the fore are named with Greek names: Eros and Thanatos, Logos and Ananke. There is no hope for redemption from the powers of necessity, from the claws of death. History is caught in an eternal cycle of constructing and destroying. It is illusory to hope for man ever to break the cycle.

III

The atheistic premise of Freud's psychoanalytic theory and therapy is not simply a residue of bourgeois optimistic humanism that lingered on among educated classes of the nineteenth century, but belongs within the history of tragic humanism since Nietzsche. The death of the Christian God proclaimed by Nietzsche through the mouth of his prophet Zarathustra inaugurates the rise of new mythologies. Nietzsche was well aware that the question revolved around where to lay "the greatest stress": on the eternal return, or on the eschatological history. In the Dionysiac-tragic horizon "the eternal hourglass of existence is turned over and over, and you with it, a dust grain of dust." On the eschatological horizon, history does not turn around and around, but rather comes to an end.

Nietzsche, who styled himself as "Antichrist" and as "the last disciple of Dionysos," has best put the ultimate difference between the eschatological and tragic view. Both Christ and Dionysos figure as suffering gods. What separates them is the sense given to their suffering, whether eschatological or tragic. "In the first case suffering is the road to a holy mode of existence; in the second case existence itself is regarded as sufficiently holy to justify an enormous amount of suffering."[9]

Freud's psychoanalytic method develops in the horizon the tragic Dionysiac humanism. If there is progress, then it is solely toward opening man's eyes to the tragic structure of reality. Thus the difference between religion as a way of salvation and psychoanalysis as a therapeutic method rests in the hope for reconciliation. Is human life "hopelessly" lost to the process of construction and destruction, or can it nourish the hope to overcome all destruction? The young Nietzsche in a paper written while still at college summed up the issue under the title "Fate and History." Freud's theoretical writings and practical therapy presuppose fate as the ultimate category. Even the patterns of evolutionary history (that are really the residue of nineteenth-century anthropology and sociology) are bracketed into an overreaching cycle of eternal recurrence. Freud, like Nietzsche, was convinced that the end of the Christian religion will lead the way out of two thousand years of falsehood and illusion. Religion was an illusion because the hope for reconciliation, for the atonement of guilt, is ultimately an illusion. Guilt cannot be overcome but only acknowledged.

Surely the psychoanalytic critique of religion can serve as a critical measure to discern all magical elements in the eschatological hope. Insofar as religion acts as a magic operation of atonement in which the person seeking reconciliation is not regenerated and transformed, it falls fully under the severest judgment of Freud. In the struggle between the priestly magical and prophetic-personal element in eschatological religion, psychoanalysis can help to unmask the retrogressive form of magic manipulation that replaces the regenerative and revolutionary act. But is the eschatological hope itself an illusion? If the eschatological hope is illusory, then the future itself turns out to be an illusion. This last difference between faith as hope and faith as illusion emerged already in Paul's confrontation with the Stoic philosophers. "Mankind," says Léon Bloy, "began to suffer *in hope* and this is what we call the Christian era."[10] With Nietzsche and Freud this very hope is put under the suspicion of illusion. The success of Freud's psychoanalysis thus indicates to the historian, if such indications were still necessary, that the West has entered a post-Christian era.

Notes

ACKNOWLEDGMENTS

1. Now Jacob Taubes, *The Political Theology of Paul,* trans. Dana Hollander, comp. Jan Assmann and Aleida Assmann (Stanford: Stanford University Press, 2003); originally published as *Die politische Theologie des Paulus: Vorträge gehalten an der Forschungsstätte der evangelischen Studiengemeinschaft Heidelberg, 23.–27. February 1987* (Munich: Wilhelm Fink Verlag, 1996).

2. Aside from the Paul book and this current volume, the translation of the *Abendländische Eschatologie* is under way, as *Occidental Eschatology.*

PREFACE

1. See Introduction, p. xii.

2. The production of these groups was published by Taubes in three volumes, see p. 345n13 below.

3. Such protocols exist for other essays assembled in this volume as well, but the surrealism essay is the only one in *Vom Kult zur Kultur* for which the protocol was included.

4. See p. xix in the Introduction to the German edition.

5. Mark Lilla, "A New Political Saint Paul?" *New York Review of Books* 55, no. 16 (Oct. 23, 2008).

6. Taubes's intellectual biography is now in preparation by Jerry Z. Muller of Catholic University of America. Further, Taubes's son Ethan is working on a biography of his father. Susan Taubes, Taubes's first wife, wrote a fictionalized autobiography about her life with Taubes, *Divorcing* (1969); it is a brilliant piece that should be republished. An edition of Susan Taubes collected work and papers is currently being prepared under the supervision of Siegrid Weigel at the Zentrum für Literaturforschung in Berlin.

7. Giorgio Agamben, *The Time that Remains: A Commentary on the Letter to the Romans,* trans. Patricia Dailey (Stanford: Stanford University Press, 2005). The French translation was published in 2000.

8. *Saint Paul: The Foundations of Universalism*, trans. Ray Brassier (Stanford: Stanford University Press, 2005); originally published in French in 1997.

9. See the volume edited by Richard Faber, Eveline Goodman-Thau, and Thomas Macho, *Abendländische Eschatologie: Ad Jacob Taubes* (Würzburg: Königshausen & Neumann, 2006). That volume is the result of a conference on the occasion of Taubes's Jahrzeit, the tenth anniversary of his death and the fiftieth anniversary of the publication of the *Eschatologie*. The thirty or so lectures and essays in that volume demonstrate Taubes's presence across the disciplines. The volume includes a bibliography by Josef R. Lawitschka (p. 561) that has been eminently helpful to us in tracking down the original versions of the essays assembled in our volume.

10. See, for instance, Elettra Stimilli, ed., *Il Prezzo del Messianismo*, translated by Astrida Ment into German as *Der Preis des Messianismus: Briefe von Jacob Taubes an Gerschom Scholem und andere Materialien* (Würzburg: Königshausen & Neumann, 2006).

11. It ought to be pointed out that the language is also conditioned by the circumstances of the production of the work. Hence, the essay on "Messianism and Its Price" was occasioned by Taubes's participation in the World Congress of Jewish Studies in 1979.

INTRODUCTION

1. Schönberg's string quartet op.11 in f-sharp minor, which sets to music Stefan George's poem *Rapture*, with its opening line "I feel air from other planets," represents (less than George's lyric itself) a key text in the circle of Jewish emigration that included Adorno, Horkheimer, and Marcuse. Marcuse, a close friend of Taubes's, quotes this line in his book *One-Dimensional Man: Studies in the Ideology of Advanced Industrial Society* (Beacon Press, 1991). See also A. Assmann and J. Assmann, "Air from Other Planets Blowing: The Logic of Authenticity and the Prophet of the Aura," in *Mapping Benjamin: The Work of Art in the Digital Age*, ed. Hans Ulrich Gumbrecht and Michael Marrinan (Stanford: Stanford University Press, 2003), pp. 147–57. On Taube's relationship with Marcuse, see J. Taubes, "Revolution und Transzendenz. Zum Tod des Philosophen Herbert Marcuse," *Der Tagesspiegel* (Jan. 31, 1979).

2. Norbert Bolz, "Erlösung als ob. Über einige gnostische Motive der kritischen Theorie," in *Gnosis und Politik*, ed. J. Taubes (Munich/ Paderborn, 1984), p. 271.

3. "The Price of Messianism," *Journal of Jewish Studies* 33, nos. 1–2 (1982): 595–600; cf. also "Scholem's Theses on Messianism Reconsidered," *Social Science Information* 21 (1982): 665–75. Cf. "Der liebe Gott steckt im Detail. G. Scholem und die messianische Verheissung," *Die Welt* (Oct. 5, 1977).

4. We thank David Stein for an account of this event.

5. "Die Entstehung des jüdischen Paria-Volkes," in *Max Weber*, Gedächtnisschrift der Ludwig-Maximilians-Universität München zur 100. Wiederkehr seines Geburtstages 1964, ed. K. Engisch, B. Pfister and J. Winkelmann (Berlin, 1966), pp. 185–94. This essay, which out of great respect for Max Weber and Gershom Scholem obscures Taubes's own position, has not been included here.

6. "Nachman Krochmal and Modern Historicism," *Judaism* 12, no. 2 (1963): 150–64.

7. While in the case of the essay on Weber, the contradiction between views expressed there and elsewhere depends on concessions to varying contexts and is uninteresting to this extent, we have in this case taken the contradiction to be a productive one and important enough to highlight it by placing the two essays next to one another.

8. On the ahistorical character of rabbinical Judaism, see in particular Y. H. Yerushalmi, *Zakhor: Jewish History and Jewish Memory*, The Samuel and Althea Stroum Lectures in Jewish Studies (Seattle: University of Washington Press, 1981); but also A. Funkenstein, *Perspectives of Jewish History* (Berkeley: University of California Press, 1993).

9. "The Issue Between Judaism and Christianity," *Commentary* 16, no. 6 (1953): 525–33.

10. M. Buber, *Zwei Glaubensweisen* (1950; reprinted, Gerlingen, 1994). Martin Buber and Karl Ludwig Schmidt, "Zwiegespräch im jüdischen Lehrhaus in Stuttgart am 14. Januar 1933," *Theologische Blätter* (Sept. 1933): 257–74; cf. K. L. Schmidt, "Die Judenfrage im Lichte der Kapital 9–11 des Römerbriefs," *Theologische Studien* 3, no. 2 (1946).

11. Hans Blüher and Hans Joachim Schoeps, *Streit um Israel. Ein jüdisch-christliches Gespräch* (Hamburg, 1933). Franz Rosenzweig and Eugen Rosenstrock, "Judentum und Christentum," in *Franz Rosenzweig. Briefe* (Berlin, 1935), pp. 638–720; a new, critical edition in *Franz Rosenzweig. Der Mensch und sein Werk. Gesammelte Schriften* Section: Letters and Diaries, vol. I (Den Haag, 1979), pp. 189ff.

12. On the historicity and relevance of Gnosticism, see J. Couliano, *The Tree of Gnosis: Gnostic Mythology from Early Christianity to Modern Nihilism* (San Francisco: HarperCollins, 1992); as well as the volumes edited by Thomas Macho and P. Sloterdijk, *Weltrevolution der Seele* (Zurich: Artemis and Winkler, 1991).

13. The three volumes that resulted from the group meetings are *Der Fürst dieser Welt. Carl Schmitt und die Folgen* (Munich: Wilhelm Fink, 1983); *Gnosis und Politik* (Munich: Wilhelm Fink, 1984); and *Theokratie* (Munich: Wilhelm Fink, 1985).

14. First in "Terror und Spiel," *Poetik und Hermeneutik* IV (Munich: Wilhelm Fink, 1971), pp. 169–86. See also various discussion contributions by Jacob Taubes in this volume.

15. Harold Bloom also takes up this aspect when he interprets romantic poetry as a repetition of the revolt of Gnosticism against the aniconicism of Judeo-Christian monotheism. (Cf. Harold Bloom, *Ruin the Sacred Truths: Poetry and Belief from the Bible to the Present* (Cambridge, MA: Harvard University Press, 1989).

16. The text's historical level of meaning was pitted against "arbitrary" allegorical interpretation, whereby however the "prophetic" references between events in the Old and New Testaments was still preserved. In his work on the patristic and medieval traditions of figural interpretation, Erich Auerbach took on the Protestant perspective and thereby provided it with far-reaching significance in literary scholarship. Cf. Erich Auerbach, "Figura" [German, 1938], in *Scenes from the Drama of European Literature: Six Essays* (Meridian Books, 1959), pp. 11–76. During the same time, Leonhard Goppelt adopts similar accents within the field of New Testament scholarship. Cf. L. Goppelt, *Typos. Die typologische Deutung des Alten Testaments im Neuen* (1939; reprinted, Darmstadt: Wissenschaftliche Buchgesellschaft, 1981).

17. *The Origin of German Tragic Drama* (London: Verso, 2003), p. 233.

18. M. N. Ebertz, *Das Charisma des Gekreuzigten. Zur Soziologie der Jesusbewegung* (Tübingen, 1987). G. Theissen, *Soziologie der Jesusbewegung* (Munich, 1991); and *Der Schatten des Galiläers* (Munich, 1993).

19. First in "Die nicht mehr schönen Künste," *Poetik und Hermeneutik* III (Munich, 1968), pp. 169–86.

20. First in "Positionen der Negativität," *Poetik und Hermeneutik* VI (Munich, 1975), pp. 141–53.

21. See also Scholem, "Der Nihilismus als religiöses Phänomen," *Eranos Jahrbuch* 43 (1974; Leiden, 1977): 1–50.

22. "Gnosis und Politik," *Religionstheorie und Politische Theorie* 2 (Munich and Paderborn, 1984): 9–15.

23. Cf. K. Löwith, "Die philosophische Kritik der christlichen Religion," in *Sämtliche Schriften* Bd. 3 *Wissen, Glaube, Skepsis* (Stuttgart, 1985), pp. 96–162.

24. Cf. for example B. K. Berger and R. MacLachlan Wilson, "Gnosis," in *Theologische Realenzyklopädie* 13 (Berlin, 1984), pp. 519–50; K.-W. Tröger, ed., *Altes Testament, Frühjudentum, Gnosis* (Gütersloh, 1980); Ewin A. Yamauchi, *Pre-Christian Gnosticism: A Survey of Proposed Evidences* (1973).

25. Thomas J. J. Althizer, ed., *Toward a New Christianity: Readings in the Death of God Theology* (New York, Chicago, San Francisco, and Atlanta, 1967), p. 219.

26. In addition to those mentioned here, essays belonging to this group include "Theology and the Philosophic Critique of Religion," *Cross Currents* 5, no. 4 (1954): 323–30; also in *Zeitschrift für Religions- und Geistesgeschichte* 8 (1956): 129–38 (widely comparable with "On the Nature of the Theological Method") as well as "The Copernican Turn on Theology," in *Religious Experience and Truth*, ed. S. Hook (Edinburgh and London, 1962), pp. 70–75.

27. "Dialectic and Analogy," *The Journal of Religion* 34 (1954): 111–20.

28. "Theodicy and Theology: A Philosophical Analysis of Karl Barth's Dialectical Theology," *The Journal of Religion* 34 (1954): 231–43.

29. "On the Nature of the Theological Method: Some Reflections on the Methodological Principles of Tillich's Theology," *The Journal of Religion* 34 (1954): 12–25.

30. Cf. the autobiographical details in *The Political Theology of Paul* (Stanford: Stanford University Press, 2003).

31. *Review of Metaphysics* 2, no. 8 (1949): 97–104.

32. G. Scholem, *The Messianic Idea in Judaism and Other Essays on Jewish Spirituality* (New York: Schocken: 1995), pp. 282–304.

33. Susan A. Taubes, "The Absent God," first printed in *The Journal of Religion* (1955). Susan Taubes, née Feldman, daughter of a well-known psychoanalyst who emigrated from Budapest, studied religion at Harvard with Arthur D. Nock and later, like Taubes, taught at Columbia University. She took her own life in 1969. Eds.: A critical edition of her work is being prepared by the Zentrum für Literaturforschung in Potsdam under Sigrid Weigelt.

34. "From Cult to Culture," *Partisan Review* 21 (1954): 387–400.

35. Manfred Voigts, "Jacob Taubes und Oskar Goldberg," *Zeitschrift für Religions- und Geistesgeschichte* 43 (1991): 76–83; as well as Oskar Goldberg, *Der mythische Experimentalwissenschaftler. Ein verdrängtes Kapital jüdischer Geschichte* (Berlin: Agora, 1992).

36. Eds.: It should be pointed out that this summary of biblical criticism is hardly adequate. It may represent Wellhausen's approach correctly. But Wellhausen's anti-Jewish tendencies, particularly with regard to Jewish law and therefore Judaism as he knew it, have long since been exposed. See, for example, Charlotte Klein, *Anti-Judaism in Christian Theology* (London: SPCK, 1981); and Jon D. Levenson, *The Hebrew Bible, the Old Testament, and Historical Criticism* (West Minster, Eng.: John Know Press, 1993). Further, the biblical scholarship of the past two decades at least has been strongly inclined to question the chronological priority of the prophetic literature.

37. See p. XXX. There the quote is concerned with Walter Benjamin's concept of politics.

38. In. Theodor W. Adorno, ed., *Spätkapitalismus oder Industriegesellschaft? Verhandlungen des 16. Deutschen Soziologentages* vom 8.-11. April (Frankfurt and Stuttgart: Enke, 1969), pp. 117–38.

39. On Taubes's critique of Gehlen's theory of institutions, see also J. Taubes, "Das Unbehagen an der Institution. Zur Kritik der soziologischen Institutionslehre," *Interdisziplinäre Studien*, Bd. 1: *Zur Theorie der Institution*, ed. H. Schelsky (Düsseldorf, 1970), pp. 68–76.

Notes

40. J. Taubes, "Four Ages of Reason," *Archiv für Rechts- und Sozialphilosophie* 42 (1956): 1–14.

41. In *Universitätstage 1963, Universität und Universalität* (Berlin: Walter de Gruyter & Co., 1963), pp. 36–55.

42. "Zur Konjunktur des Polytheismus," in *Mythos und Moderne*, ed. K. H. Bohrer (Frankfurt: Suhrkamp, 1983), pp. 457–70.

43. "Religion and the Future of Psychoanalysis," in *Psychoanalysis and the Future*, A Centenary Commemoration of the Birth of Sigmund Freud (Psychoanalysis 4, nos. 4–5), ed. B. Nelson (New York, 1957), pp. 136–42; the German edition printed in E. Nase and J. Scharfenberg, eds., *Psychoanalyse und Religion* (Darmstadt: Wissenschaftliche Buchgesellschaft, 1977).

CHAPTER 1

1. Eds.: This essay was published originally in English in three versions, each with only small additions, all in the same year. Originally, the essay was presented as a talk at the World Congress of Jewish Studies in Jerusalem 1981, published as "The Price of Messianism," in *Proceedings of the Eighth World Congress of Jewish Studies*, Jerusalem, Aug. 16–21, 1981, Division C (Jerusalem, 1982), pp. 99–104. It further appeared under the same title in the *Journal of Jewish Studies* 33, nos. 1–2 (1982): 595–600. The version presented here is based on the one published in the *Journal of Jewish Studies* (JJS). The translation in *Vom Kult zur Kultur* (VKK) is based on this version; see VKK, p. 13n3. However, if this is so, then the editors decided not to include in their version the footnote that Taubes himself put at the beginning of his essay in JJS, which I left as a footnote here; see below n. 3. Josef R. Lawitschka's bibliography, "Eine neu-alte Bibliographie der Texte von JACOB TAUBES, zecher le-veracha (dem seligen Angedenken)," in Faber, Goodman-Thau, and Macho, mistakenly has the VKK translation based on the Proceedings version, see p. 567, n71. Be that as it may, the only difference between the two texts is the footnote in question. That note is of interest insofar as Taubes was determined to expose the politics of the academic World Congress in the republication of his essay in JJS. Finally, the text was published a third time under what Taubes claims was the original title of the talk, namely, as "Scholem's Theses on Messianism Reconsidered," *Social Science Information* 21, nos. 4–5 (1982): 665–75. In this version, Taubes adds an introductory section with Scholem's brief biography and the English text of Scholem's "Theses on Messianism," copied (and corrected) from David Biale's *Gershom Scholem, Kabbalah and Counter-History* (Cambridge, MA: Harvard University Press, 1979). The essay exists also in a different German translation in Elettra Stimilli's edition of *Jacob Taubes—Der Preis des Messianismus: Briefe von Jacob Taubes an Gerschom Scholem und andere Materialien* (Würzburg: Königshausen & Neumann, 2006). The translator, Astrida Ment, notes that she bases the translation on the version in the *Proceedings*.

2. Eds.: In the version of the essay in *Social Science Information* ("Scholem's Theses . . . ") this section is entitled "When Prophecy Fails" (see p. 668), which is a reference to Leon Festinger's classic 1956 book *When Prophecy Fails: A Social and Psychological Study of a Modern Group that Predicted the Destruction of the World*, that he wrote with Henry Riecken and Stanley Schachter (originally University of Minnesota Press, reissued by Pinter & Martin, 2008).

3. JT: The original title of this communication, read at the World Congress of Jewish Studies in Jerusalem in 1981, was "Gershom Scholem's Theses on Messianism Reconsidered." The Steering Committee of the Congress asked me to "neutralize" the problem; hence, "The Price of Messianism."

4. Eds.: In "Scholem's Theses . . . " Taubes claims in a note there: "I have myself given a more detailed analysis of the inner dynamics of the messianic idea in 'The Price of Messianism,' *Journal of Jewish Studies* 33, nos. 1–2 (1982)," p. 675 n8. However, the text of JJS presented here contains mostly cosmetic changes and could not be categorized as "more detailed analysis."

5. Eds.: In "Scholem's Theses . . . " the JBL reference is moved into the notes as exact reference: "From Schweitzer to Scholem: Reflection on Sabbatai Svi," *Journal of Biblical Literature* 95, no. 4 (1976): 529–58.

6. Eds.: In "Scholem's Theses . . . " Taubes entitles this section "Early Christianity and Sabbatian Messianism."

7. Eds.: (Stimilli p. 47 n17) Cf. K. Marx, "Der 18. Brumaire des Louis Napoleon" (1852), in *Marx-Engels Werke*, vol. 8 (Berlin, 1978), pp. 115ff., n59, p. 618; and G. W. F. Hegel, *Werke*, vol. 12 (Frankfurt, 1970), pp. 339ff.

8. Eds.: Taubes has this term (Enlightenment) in German in the original English version of the essay.

9. Eds.: In "Scholem's Theses . . . " Taubes adds the reference: "Cf. G. Scholem, *Du Frankisme au Jacobinisme* [Paris: Seuil, 1981]. Marc Bloch Lectures." Published also in Hebrew in G. Scholem, "Caryera shel Frankist" [Career of a Frankist], *Zion* 35 (1970): 127–81.

10. Eds.: In "Scholem's Theses . . . " Taubes gives this last section the title of his talk in Jerusalem, enforced by the Steering Congress of the World Congress.

11. Eds.: The page number refers to the publication of the essay in the collection of Scholem's essays on messianic themes in *The Messianic Idea in Judaism,* as do all the other page numbers Taubes cites in the essay. This particular essay was published also as Gershom Scholem, "The Neutralization of the Messianic Element in the Early Hasidim" (Joseph Weiss Memorial Lecture), *Journal of Jewish Studies* 20 (1969): 25–55.

12. Eds.: VKK mistranslates this famous Talmudic phrase (see Babylonian Talmud Berakhot 8a) as "vier Höfe der Halacha." The "four yards" here refer to measurement, not space. The Talmudic phrase is, "Since the day that the Temple was destroyed, the Holy One Blessed Be He has nothing in the world but the four cubits of halakhah alone."

13. Eds.: The Talmudic phrase has played a crucial role in religious Zionist discourse from Rav Avraham Yitzhak Kook onward. See Aviezer Ravitzky, *Messianism, Zionism and Jewish Religious Radicalism* (Chicago: University of Chicago Press, 1996).

CHAPTER 2

1. Eds.: This essay was published in English in Paul Arthur Schilpp and Maurice Feldman's anthology, *The Philosophy of Martin Buber* (La Salle, IL, 1967), with Taubes's essay as chapter 20, "Buber and Philosophy of History," pp. 451–68. It is signed by Jacob Taubes, as located in the Department of Religion at Columbia University. The version of the essay presented here is based on that publication. Paradoxically, the German translation (or version) of the essay appeared earlier in the German "translation" of the same book, as "Martin Buber und die Geschichtsphilosophie," in Paul Arthur Schilpp and Maurice Friedman, *Martin Buber* (Stuttgart: Kohlhammer, 1963), pp. 398–413. Although the German book was published four years before the English version, it appears that the latter was the original, as the German version of the volume is introduced: "The only authorized translation of the volume, *The Philosophy of Martin Buber*, to be published in 1963 [*Einzig autoritisierte Übertragung des 1963 erscheinenden Bandes* The Philosophy of Martin Buber]." The English volume apparently ended up taking four years (until 1967) to be published. The German edition lists Curt Meyer-Clason as translator of all those essays in the book that did not have a German original manuscript, with Taubes's essay among these, which would suggest that the editors had a manuscript in English from Taubes himself. *Vom Kult zur Kultur* does not cite the source of its text, but its version is entirely identical to the German version published in 1963. It remains somewhat unclear whether Taubes wrote the essay in English or German. The German version contains quite a few variances, although none of them substantive. I note the variances in my endnotes. As to the German version in the volume by Schilpp, the editors claim that "in part the translated manuscripts have been reviewed by the authors [*die Übersetzungsmanuskripte wurden zum Teil von den Autoren selbst überprüft*]," so presumably Taubes would have agreed to the German translation. Altogether it seems to me that the English version in the Schilpp volume reads somewhat less elegantly and less poetic than the German and that it tones down some of Taubes's explicit (although far from dramatic) criticism. See, for example, n44. I am choosing the 1967 English version as my text for this edition only because Taubes presumably either wrote it himself in English—judged on the evidence in the published volume—or authorized the translation, if after all the German was the original. The reader should note that the counting of sections followed here differs from the one presented in VKK, since we are following the 1967 English version.

2. This quote from Paul, "the first great Christian interpreter of history" in the following sentence, is left without parentheses and quotes in the English text of 1967. The German version (1963 = 1996) has the citation inserted into the text.

3. The last two sentences of this paragraph present a somewhat shorter, less elegant version than the German one in VKK. The German version reads instead (my translation): "But Buber intends to strike at the root of Hegel's monological concept of history. In order to strike at the root of the Hegelian philosophy, Buber reaches back to the Christian theology of history, since the tree that bears Hegel's philosophy is rooted in Paul's theology of history. In his critique of the Hegelian philosophy of history Buber first comes face to face with Paul's 'Heilsgeschichte'" (VKK, p. 51).

4. Not in German version.

5. German version: "the crucified and risen Messiah."

6. German version omits "as the 'good news.'"

7. This subclause makes no sense—as if the "princes of this world" had one leader—and it is phrased differently in the German version: "For had they known this mystery, then the leaders and princes of this world, whom Paul calls on occasion the 'god of this aeon,' would not have fallen into the trap" (p. 51).

8. German version: "earthly powers and heavenly principalities."

9. Again, this subclause is not clear. German version reads, "Paul's concept of salvation history," with no further subclause.

10. None of these terms are in parentheses in the German version. For the phrase "form of slave," cf. Paul's epistle to the Philippians 2:5–8: "Let the same mind be in you that was in Christ Jesus, who, though he was in the form of God, did not regard equality with God as something to be exploited, but emptied himself, taking *the form of a slave*, being born in human likeness." The latter phrase, "nailing it to the cross," is from Colossians 2:14; see next note.

11. Instead of this last sentence, the German version inserts a long quote from Colossians 2:13–15, one of the pseudo-Pauline epistles in the New Testament: "And when you were dead in trespasses and the uncircumcision of your flesh, God made you alive together with him, when he forgave us all our trespasses, erasing the record that stood against us with its legal demands. He set this aside, nailing it to the cross. He disarmed the rulers and authorities and made a public example of them, triumphing over them in it."

12. JT: [Buber,] *Two Types of Faith* (1951), p. 88.

13. JT: Ibid., p. 86.

14. JT: Martin Buber, "Prophecy, Apocalyptic, and the Historical Hour," *Pointing the Way* (1957), pp. 192ff. [Ch. F.: p. 194].

15. This introductory paragraph again is unclear, and even imprecise. It differs quite pronouncedly from the German version. That version reads: "However, in which kind of ground can the Hegelian philosophy of history take root? From

which ground do the roots, that is Paul's *Heilsgeschichte*, draw their nourishment, and (to stay with this image) through them the entire tree? The theology of history of Paul grows out of the ground of the apocalyptic faith, as we know it from 'the apocalyptic writings of Jewish and Jewish-Christian coinage in the age of late Hellenism and its decline.' The apocalyptic experience of history is often connected with the teaching of Israelite prophecy. Therefore, Buber feels compelled . . . "

16. JT: Ibid.

17. German version inserts reference: Numbers 23:23.

18. JT: Ibid. [p. 197].

19. German version here reads "Heilsgeschichte," rather than "message of the crucified Messiah." The paragraph presents in part at least a paraphrase of Buber. Thus Buber uses the phrase "dogmatic encystment."

20. JT: Ibid. [p. 198].

21. German version: "Buber juxtaposes the apocalyptic message with. . . . "

22. JT: Ibid. [p. 201].

23. JT: Ibid. [p. 202].

24. This summary presents a montage of sentence fragments from Buber's essay. Buber writes, "The mature apocalyptic, moreover, no longer knows an historical future in the real sense. The end of all history is near. 'Creation has grown old,' it notes as a point unalterably established; this is stated still more penetratingly in the Baruch apocalypse: 'The procession of the ages is already almost past.' The present aeon, that of the world and of world history, 'hurries powerfully to the end.' . . . The proper and paradoxical subject of the late apocalyptic is a future that is no longer in time, and he anticipates this consummation so that for him all that may yet come in history no longer has an historical character" (p. 203).

25. JT: Ibid. [p. 203].

26. German version: "*spätjüdische Apokalyptik*," that is, the postbiblical, but prerabbinic Jewish apocalyptic literature. However, that choice seems problematic, and I find it hard to believe that Taubes would have used it for the following reason. It was German Protestant scholarship, represented prominently by Julius Wellhausen, that has often referred to this literature (or this time period) as "*Spätjudentum*," for supersessionist reasons, with the assumption that Judaism comes to a conclusion with the arrival of Jesus. See also the next chapter where Buber himself refers to the abuse of the term "*Spätjudentum*" in Protestant scholarship (chap. 4, p. 7).

27. German version does not have this didactic sentence.

28. German: "*Geschichtsphilosophie wandelt sich in Geschichtsprophetie.*"

29. JT: [Buber,] "Herzl und die Historie" (1904), *Die jüdische Bewegung* (1916), pp. 156ff.

30. German: "*jüdisch-völkischer Humanismus.*"

31. German has "in our century after World War I."

32. German has "messianisms" instead of "movements."
33. JT: [Buber,] *Pointing the Way,* [pp. 203–4].
34. JT: Martin Buber, "The Validity and Limitation of the Political Principle," *Pointing the Way* (1957), p. 25.
35. German has "German philosophy of history from Hegel to Heidegger."
36. German has "Jewish messianism against Christian eschatology."
37. JT: Martin Buber, *Drei Reden über das Judentum* (1920–23), p. 91.
38. Taubes uses "mythic-immanent" in the previous sentence, and clearly both sentences should have the same term. The correct term is probably "mystic-immanent."
39. This paragraph is arranged slightly differently in the German version.
40. JT: [Buber,] *Pointing the Way,* [p. 194].
41. JT: Buber, *Prophetic Faith* (1949), p. 209.
42. JT: [Buber,] *Pointing the Way,* [pp. 198–99].
43. JT: Ibid. [p. 199].
44. Here the English version of 1967—adapted in the present volume as well—skips two sentences that sharpen the critique of Buber's and Taubes's own understanding of the concept of the apocalyptic: "If we adapt the scale by which Buber measures the difference between prophecy and apocalyptic literature, it seems to us that Buber remains blind to the fact that in Deutero-Isaiah and in the entire later apocalyptic literature a completely new form of alternative emerges. Because Buber recognizes the concept of alternative only in the prophetic literature—with a concept of alternative that affects the course of history only magically superficially—he closes himself off to the new internalized form of alternative, which is indeed one of the fundamental themes in apocalyptic literature (and in the history of the West!)" VKK, p. 59, even highlights this sentence, while the version in Schilpp's 1963 German *Martin Buber* does not.
45. This sentence again presents a free rendering of the German, if the German were original, or otherwise a different version: "The new form of alternative, which considers the course of history to be fixed and determined in advance, and which subdivide humanities into those, who recognize the necessary advance of the 'New,' and those who do not recognize or sense the new, even if can already like a change of pressure in the atmosphere, produces an unprecedented activism in the apocalyptic communities and group" (VKK, p. 60; Schilpp 1963, p. 407).
46. VKK, p. 60, highlights the last sentence, but the version in Schilpp's *Martin Buber*, p. 407, does not.
47. JT: Buber, *Two Types of Faith* (1951), pp. 109ff.
48. JT: *Prophetic Faith*, pp. 234f.
49. This sentence is marked as a quotation (without citation) in the German version.

50. JT: Martin Buber, *For the Sake of Heaven*, 13 (1953, 2d ed.), foreword to the second edition.
51. JT: Ibid., pp. 108ff.
52. JT: Ibid., pp. 114ff.
53. JT: Ibid., p. 280.
54. JT: Ibid.
55. JT: Ibid., p. 284.
56. JT: *Two Types of Faith*, p. 78.
57. JT: G. F. W. Hegel, *The Phenomenology of Mind* (1910), pp. 667f.
58. This sentence is highlighted in VKK, again without parallel in Schilpp.
59. Again, this last part is highlighted in VKK.
60. Again, this sentence is highlighted in VKK.
61. JT: Augustine, *Sermones*, ed. Denis, 24, 11 transl. Karl Löwith, *Meaning in History* (Chicago, 1949). [This quote serves as the epigraph to Löwith's book.]

CHAPTER 3

1. Eds.: This essay was originally published in English under this title in *Judaism* 12, no. 2 (spring 1963): 150–65. The German translation in *Vom Kult zur Kultur* is based on this publication. The version presented here follows closely the 1963 version, leaving Taubes's footnotes in place, with only slight editorial corrections marked as such, and some orthographic adjustments. Further editorial remarks are noted in these endnotes. The author's bio at the beginning of the article reads: "JACOB TAUBES holds jointly a chair in history of religion at Columbia University and the Free University of Berlin. He is presently teaching at the latter institution."
2. JT: Friedrich Meinecke, *Die Entstehung des Historismus* (Munich and Berlin, 1936). [Ch. F.: Translated subsequently as J. E. Anderson and Friedrich Meinecke, *Historism: The Rise of a New Historical Outlook* (London: Routledge and Paul, 1972).]
3. Tübingen, 1922.
4. JT: *Phenomenology of Mind*, 2d edition (London, 1931), p. 80.
5. JT: Ibid., pp. 85ff.
6. JT: See Nahum N. Glatzer, *Die Geschichtslehre der Tannaiten* (Berlin, 1933). [Ch. F.: The terms are left in German in the published English version of the essay. The correct citation would have been: *Untersuchungen zur Geschichtslehre der Tannaiten: Eine Religionsgeschichte* (Berlin: Schocken Verlag, 1933).]
7. JT: It surely would be falsifying the record if we accept an easy and neat division and would equate apocalyptic with Christian, and rabbinic with legal. There is an intensive stream of apocalyptic literature in the Jewish tradition, also after the secession of the Christian sect. But the relation between halacha and the historic form is not devoid of deep tension.

8. Surely, Taubes refers to Scholem's work, and in particular the *Major Trends in Jewish Mysticism* (New York: Schocken Books, 1954). In the footnote on the same page Taubes mentions Scholem's name. It is not clear why Taubes does not spell out the reference here.

9. JT: I cannot see (as does Rotenstreich, following Scholem) the Sabbatian theology of history as a kind of prologue to the historic consciousness developed in the period of the Enlightenment. The Sabbatian messianism was surely a violent breakthrough of subterranean forces in the Jewish mind, but (a) it remained an episode in Jewish history, and (b) its failure was a cause for an even more radical suppression of the historic sense.

10. Julius Guttman's *Die Philosophie des Judentums* (Munich: E. Reinhardt) appeared originally in German in 1933. It was translated into English by David W. Silverman originally for Schocken as *Philosophies of Judaism: A History of Jewish Philosophy from Biblical Times to Franz Rosenzweig* (New York: Schocken, 1964), and republished more recently as *The Philosophy of Judaism* (Northvale, NJ: J. Aronson, 1988). The English translation in turn is based on the Hebrew translation, to which Taubes refers in his text here: *Ha-Filosofyah shel ha-Yahadut* (Jerusalem: Mossad Bialik, 1951; reprinted, 1983), which is a revised and enlarged edition of the German original. Julius Guttmann died in 1950.

11. As so often, Taubes does not provide precise citations, rather than relying on Schwarzschild's dissertation cited in his endnote above. Rotenstreich's *Jewish Philosophy in Modern Times: From Mendelssohn to Rosenzweig* (New York: Holt, Reinhart and Winston, 1968) appeared after Taubes's article, but provides access to Rotenstreich's approach in one volume. Rotenstreich (1914–93) was professor of philosophy at Hebrew University and therefore one of Gershom Scholem's colleagues.

12. JT: See Steven S. Schwarzschild, *Two Modern Jewish Philosophies of History, Nachman Krochmal and Hermann Cohen* (an unpublished dissertation, Hebrew Union College, Cincinnati, 1951).

13. JT: See *Kitbe Rabbi Nachman Krochmal*, ed. S. Rawidowicz, 2d ed. (London, 1961). [Ch. F.: *The Writings of Nachman Krochmal* has not been translated into English.]

14. JT: Ibid., p. 31.

15. JT: Ibid., pp. 220–40.

16. *Vom Kult zur Kultur* here translates "*in den späteren Jahren seines Lebens.*"

17. Victor Cousin (1792–1867), ed. *Proclus* (6 vols.) (1820–1927).

18. Eds.: Krochmal does not provide a citation here. The midrashic tradition cited in the Babylonian Talmud (B. Megillah 29a) reads: "We have been taught that R. Simeon ben Yohai said: Pause and consider how beloved are Israel in the sight of God. Wherever they were exiled, the *Shekhinah* [divine Presence] was with them. When they were exiled to Egypt, the Presence was with them, for Eli was

told, 'Did I not reveal Myself to your ancestor [Aaron's] house when they were in Egypt?' (I Samuel 2:27). When they were exiled to Babylon, the *Shekhinah* was with them, as it is said, 'For your sake I had Myself sent to Babylon' (Isaiah 43:14). When they were exiled to Elam, the *Shekhinah* was with them, as it is said, 'I will set My throne in Elam' (Jeremiah 49:38). When they were exiled to Edom, the *Shekhinah* was with them, as it is said, 'Who is this that comes from Edom, with crimsoned garments from Bosrah?' (Isaiah 63:1). And when they are redeemed, the *Shekhinah* will be with them, as it is said 'The Lord your God will return with your captivity' (Deuteronomy 30:3). Scripture does not say, '[He will] cause to return your captivity,' rather it says '[He will] return [*with* your captivity],' proving that the Holy One will return with them out of the several exiles. Thus also it is said, 'Come with Me from Lebanon, My bride, with Me from Lebanon; look from the top of Amana, from the top of Senir and Hermon, from the lions' dens, from the mountains of the leopards' (Song of Songs 4:8)."

19. Ibid., pp. 40–41.

20. The "personalistic" language of the midrashic tradition here would be the *Shekhinah*, the quasi-hypostacized "Presence" of God, his representative in this sphere.

21. JT: *'ad 'omek acharit ha-yamim.*

22. JT: *ha-ma'amin ha-maskil.*

23. The Hebrew phrase is biblical in origin and used widely in that context, especially in the prophetic literature, and especially by the author of the book of Jeremiah, here with eschatological overtones. See, for instance, Jeremiah 23:20, 30:24, 48:47, 49:39. Cp. Isaiah 2:2, Ezekiel 38:16, Hosea 3:5, Micha 4:1, and especially Daniel 10:14.

24. JT: *Jüdische Rundschau* (Berlin, 1907), p. 54.

CHAPTER 4

1. Eds.: This article was first published in English in *Commentary* 16, no. 6 (Dec. 1953): 525–33. The editors of the journal introduced the article with the following note: "The argument between Judaism and Christianity, Jacob Taubes here points out, is generally distorted by the historical success of Christianity. But success and truth belong to quite different realms; here, at a time when there are attempts on both sides to obscure the fundamental theological difference between the two faiths, the ancient disputation is once again canvassed, without regard for the fact that Christianity spread throughout the world while Judaism remained the religion of a small people, and from this discussion some clarifying—though old—facts emerge. Mr. Taubes was born in Vienna in 1924 and received his doctorate in philosophy and theology from the University of Zurich. He has been a fellow at the Jewish Theological Seminary of New York and the Hebrew Universi-

ty in Jerusalem, and he is now a Rockefeller Fellow at Harvard University. He has written one book, *Occidental Eschatology,* and many articles for journals of philosophy, and he is now at work on a study of 'political theology,' which will deal with various neglected relations between theology and political theory," p. 525. The text presented here is based on the text as it can be found in *Commentary.*

2. *Vom Kult zur Kultur* here chooses *ethnisch* as the translation for "racial," which updates the linguistic convention.

3. The German translator(s) in *Vom Kult zur Kultur* add the reference: Romans 11:28.

4. John 14:6. The *Vom Kult zur Kultur* edition mistakenly refers to John 14:16.

5. It deserves emphasizing that Taubes is one of the few and one of the earliest, if not the earliest, Jewish intellectual to recognize and pronounce this fundamental problem in Rosenzweig's text.

6. For the citations of some of the literature referred to here, please see the discussion of this essay in the Introduction, p. xxviii–xxx, where the editors of VKK provide some references. Max Weber apparently did not require referencing, since he deploys the term *Spätjudentum* throughout. Emil Schürer's *A History of the Jewish People in the Time of Jesus Christ* (originally published 1886–90 and since then reedited various times) has suffered from similar problems of supersessionism. The reference for Herberg is Will Herberg's essay "Judaism and Christianity: Their Unity and Difference. The Double Covenant in the Divine Economy of Salvation," *Journal of Bible and Religion* 21, no. 2 (April 1953): 67–78. He writes—and here I am quoting because of the enormity of the statement—"as Rosenzweig puts it: man is either a pagan or a Jew or a Christian. (Islam presents a problem; Rosenzweig does not regard it as a distinct way, nor do I; I think rather it is a kind of Jewish-Christian heresy)," p. 75.

7. Herberg writes in the aforementioned essay: "'Israel,' says Franz Rosenzweig, 'can bring the world to God only through Christianity.' Despite all hostility through the ages, Jewish tradition has always 'freely acknowledged the divine mission of Christianity' as 'Israel's apostle' to the nations. This, if one may venture to put it that way, is Christianity's service to Judaism," ibid., p. 75.

8. JT: The meaning of the Latin *perfidus*—"faithless" or "infidel"—is not quite the same as the English "perfidious," which necessarily includes the meaning "treacherous."

9. See Gerschom Scholem, *Sabbatai Sevi: The Mystical Messiah* (Princeton, NJ: Princeton University Press, 1973); "Sabbatianism and Mystical Heresy," in *Major Trends in Jewish Mysticism* (New York: Schocken Books, 1964), pp. 287–324, and Sholem's essay on "Redemption through Sin," originally in Hebrew, but translated by Hillel Halkin in *The Messianic Idea in Judaism* (New York: Schocken, 1971).

10. Scholem, *Major Trends in Jewish Mysticism,* p. 307.

CHAPTER 5

1. Eds.: This essay, as all the other ones in this section, was published originally in German and has been translated for this edition. See Manfred Fuhrmann, ed., *Terror und Spiel: Probleme der Mythenrezeption* (Munich: Wilhelm Fink Verlag, 1971), pp. 145–57. For a discussion of the original venue and context of this particular essay, see the detailed explanation in the introduction to the volume, pp. xxxi–xxxii, which we will not repeat here. Again, we are leaving Taubes's footnotes in place, but where relevant we replaced the German publications with their English translations. One general remark on the translation of the essay: we have opted for "Gnosticism" instead of "gnosis" for rendering the German term "die Gnosis" into English. In German it is sufficient to add the definite article to *Gnosis*, in order to differentiate between "gnosis" as knowledge or cognition in general and "gnosis" as the term for the late antique religious phenomenon that has come to be known as Gnosticism.

2. We translated the phrase "*in seinen Späthorizonten*" into the somewhat awkward "in its late horizon," since this is a phrase coined by Hans Blumenberg in his contribution to the volume, in which Taubes's essay appeared, and Taubes adopts it from there. See Hans Blumenberg, "Wirklichkeitsbegriff und Wirkungspotential des Mythos," in *Terror und Spiel: Probleme der Mythenrezeption*, ed. Manfred Fuhrmann (Munich: Wilhelm Fink Verlag, 1971), p. 28.

3. JT: See Walter Benjamin, *The Origin of German Tragic Drama* (London: Verso, 1985).

4. JT: S.H. Blumenberg, "Wirklichkeitsbegriff und Wirkungspotential des Mythos," in "Terror und Spiel: Probleme der Mythenrezeption" (*Poetik und Hermeneutik* IV) (Munich: Wilhelm Fink Verlag, 1971), p. 42.

5. The German is *Allegorese*, which is mostly synonymous with *Allegorie*, although it refers more precisely to the practice of allegorical exegesis or interpretation. Where stylistically possible, we render Allegorese as "allegorical hermeneutic," otherwise as allegory.

6. JT: Ibid., p. 20.

7. JT: Ibid., p. 42.

8. JT: Cited according to the English translation of the text, *Philosophomena or The Refutation of All Heresies*, trans. F. Legge (New York: Macmillan & Company, 1921), pp. 141–42 [Ch. F.: with minor corrections based on the Greek.]

9. JT: P. Pokorny, *Der Epheserbrief und die Gnosis* (Berlin: 1965), pp. 90f.

10. JT: H. Jonas, *Gnosis and spätantiker Geist*, Bd. I (Göttingen, 1964), p. 201.

11. One of the Heideggerian terms that are extremely difficult to translate into English.

12. JT: See Gerschom Scholem, *On the Kabbalah and Its Symbolism* (New York: Schocken Books, 1965), p. 117.

13. JT: Scholem, *Major Trends in Jewish Mysticism* (New York: Schocken Books, 1971), p. 8.

14. JT: Ibid.

15. JT: H. H. Schaeder, "Urform and Fortbildung des manichäischen Systems," *Vorträge der Bibliothek Warburg* 4 (1924/1925): 100. Jonas's sharp criticism of Schaeder's entry, ibid., p. 57, does not apply to Schaeder's fundamental considerations.

16. JT: Jonas, ibid., Bd. II/1 (Göttingen, 1954), p. 14.

17. JT: Essay by H. Blumenberg, p. 27.

18. JT: *Refutation*, p. 155.

19. JT: *St. Irenaeus of Lyons Against the Heresies*, trans. Dominic J. Unger (New York: Paulist Press, 1992), p. 98.

20. JT: H.-M. Schenke, *Der Gott "Mensch" in der Gnosis* (Göttingen, 1962), p. 72.

21. JT: Cited according to the translation by J. F. Hendry in R. Haardt, *Gnosis, Character and Testimony* (Leiden: Brill, 1971), p. 295.

22. JT: C. Colpe, "Mythische und religiöse Aussage ausserhalb und innerhalb des Christentums," *Beiträge zur Theorie des neuzeitlichen Christentums*, ed. H. J. Birker und D. Rössler (Berlin, 1968), p. 30.

23. JT: R. M. Grant, *Gnosticism and Early Christianity* (New York: Columbia University Press, 1959), p. 27.

CHAPTER 6

1. Eds.: This essay was published originally in German, as "Die Rechtfertigung des Hässlichen in urchristlicher Tradition," in *Die nicht mehr schönen Künste: Grenzphänomene des Ästhetischen*, ed. Hans Robert Jauss (Munich: W. Fink, 1968), pp. 169–87. We should also point to the poignant discussion of Taubes's essay recorded in that volume, under the question: "Is There a 'Christian Aesthetic'?" see *Die nicht mehr schönen Künste*, pp. 583–609. It included people like S. Kracauer, H. Blumenberg, and H. Jauss, to name but a few. Taubes's essay was translated for the current volume. The context of this volume explains the third part of this essay and its extensive quotations from literature on early Christian art, which obviously is not Taubes's field of expertise. By the same token this section demonstrates Taubes's interdisciplinarity and willingness to read widely. The essay contains longer quotes in Latin (from the early Christian author Tertullian) and French (from French art historians) for which Taubes did not provide translations. We are replacing those quotes with their translations and put the original Latin and French texts in these endnotes. Thanks to Emily-Jane Cohen who provided the translations of the French quotes.

2. Taubes applies Nietzsche's quote to the passage from I Corinthians, whereas Nietzsche himself refers to his own *Genealogy of Morals*, in which the contrast is brought to light.

360   Notes

3. JT: *The Anti-Christ*, chaps. 45 and 51, cited after W. Kaufmann's translation.

4. JT: E. Auerbach, *Literatursprache und Publikum in der lateinischen Spätantike und im Mittelalter* (Bern: Francke Verlag, 1958), pp. 20ff. [Translation from the German by Ralph Manheim, *Literary Language and Its Public in Late Latin Antiquity and in the Middle Ages* (Princeton, NJ: Princeton University Press, 1993), pp. 19–20ff.]

5. JT: Ibid., p. 25.

6. JT: Nietzsche—see note 1. §51.

7. Taubes cites Luther's translation and introduces it as such. Our text is based on the *The New Oxford Annotated Bible: New Revised Standard Version* translation (NRSV).

8. JT: J. Weiss, *Beiträge zur Paulinischen Rhetorik* (Göttingen: Vandenhoeck & Ruprecht, 1897).

9. JT: Cf. U. Wilckens, *Weisheit und Torheit* (Tübingen: J. C. B. Mohr, 1959).

10. JT: Regarding Basilides's doctrine of salvation, Irenaeus relates that (Adv. Haer. I, 24, 4): "Et liberatos igitur eos, qui haec sciant, a mundi fabricatoribus principibus; et non oportere confiteri eum, qui sit crucifixus, sed eum qui in hominis forma venerit et putatus sit crucifixus et vocatus sit Jesus et missus a Patre, uti per dispositionem hanc opera mundi fabricatorum dissolveret. Si quis igitur, ait, confitetur crucifixum, adhuc hic servus est et sub potestate eorum qui corpora fecerunt; qui autem negaverit, liberatus est quidem ab iis, cognoscit autem dispositionem innati Patris." [Ch. F.: Those, then, who know these things have been freed from the principalities who formed the world, so that it is not incumbent on us to confess him who was crucified, but him who came in the form of a man, and was thought to be crucified, and was called Jesus, and was sent by the Father, that by this dispensation he might destroy the works of the makers of the world. If anyone, therefore, he declares, confesses the crucified, that man is still a slave, and under the power of those who formed our bodies, but he who denies him has been freed from these beings and is acquainted with the dispensation of the unborn father.]

11. JT: W. Schmithals, *Die Gnosis in Korinth* (Göttingen: Vandenhoeck & Ruprecht, 1965), p. 45.

12. JT: Ibid., pp. 52f.

13. The German is phrased: "*Das Martyrium selbst ist das Mysterium.*"

14. JT: Wilckens, pp. 36ff.

15. JT: Ibid., p. 41.

16. JT: J. Bohatec, "Inhalt und Reihenfolge der 'Schlagworte der Erlösungsreligion,'" in I Cor. 1:26, *Theological Zeitschrift* IV (1948): 252.

17. JT: Wilckens, p. 43.

18. JT: Schmithals, p. 148.

19. JT: Ibid.
20. JT: Schmithals, p. 142.
21. JT: Wilckens, p. 51.
22. JT: H. Schlier, "Kerygma und Sophia," *Die Zeit der Kirche* (Freiburg: Herder, 1956), p. 207.
23. JT: E. Lohmeyer, *Kyrios Jesus* (Heidelberg: C. Winter, 1928).
24. Cp. Isaiah 64:4.
25. JT: I Cor. 1:11–13 = I Clem. 47:1; I Cor. 12:12 sq = I Clem. 37:5, 38:1; I Cor. 13:4–7 = I Clem. 49:5. W. Bauer, *Rechtgläubigkeit und Ketzerei im ältesten Christentum* (1934), p. 252. [*Orthodoxy and Heresy in Earliest Christianity*, ed. Robert Kraft and Gerhard Krodel (Philadelphia, PA: Fortress Press, 1971).]
26. Justin, *First Apology*, chap. 60 ("Plato's Doctrine of the Cross"). The translation of this passage in the *Ante-Nicene Fathers* reads: "And the physiological discussion concerning the Son of God in the Timaeus of Plato, where he says: 'He placed him crosswise in the universe,' he borrowed in like manner from Moses, for in the writings of Moses it is related how at that time, when the Israelites went out of Egypt, and were in the wilderness, they fell in with poisonous beasts, both vipers and asps, and every kind of serpent, which slew the people; and that Moses, by the inspiration and influence of God, took brass, and made it into the figure of a cross, and set it into the holy tabernacle and said to the people, 'If ye look to this figure, and believe, ye shall be saved thereby' (Numbers 21:8). And when this was done, it is recorded that the serpents died, and it is handed down that the people thus escaped death. Which things Plato reading, and not accurately understanding, and not apprehending that it was the figure of the cross, but taking it to be a placing crosswise, he said that the power next to the first god was placed crosswise in the universe" (*Ante-Nicene Fathers*, vol. 1: *The Apostolic Fathers, Justin, Irenaeus*, ed. A. Roberts and J. Donaldson, p. 183). Taubes summarizes Justin's paraphrase of the biblical narrative. The remark in the square brackets is his. In the translation offered in the main text above I chose to preserve the references to the letter Chi (rather than replacing that with crosswise), since that is what Taubes does in the German, and the editors of the *Ante-Nicene Fathers* do in the notes.
27. JT: W. Bousset, "Platons Weltseele und das Kreuz Christi," *Zeitschrift für die neutestamentliche Wissenschaft* XIV (1913): 273ff.
28. JT: Edgar Hennecke, ed. Wilhelm Schneemelcher, trans. A. J. B. Higgins a.o., *New Testament Apocrypha*, vol. 2 (Philadelphia, PA: Westminster Press, 1963–66), p. 469.
29. Taubes here skips a few sentences without marking the lacunae: "close these eyes of yours, close your ears, withdraw from actions that are outwardly seen, and you shall know the facts about Christ and the whole secret of your salvation. Let so much be said to you who hear as though it were unspoken. But it is time for you, Peter, to surrender your body to those who are taking it. Take it,

then, you whose duty this is. I request you therefore, executioners, to crucify me head-downward—in this way and no other. And the reason, I will tell to those who hear."

30. The English translation is based on *The Ante-Nicene Fathers*, vol. 1: *The Apostolic Fathers, Justin Martyr, Irenaeus*, ed. Alexander Roberts and James Donaldson. The quotations within this passage are taken from Psalm 24.

31. JT: Ibid., p. 307.

32. JT: Ibid., p. 733.

33. JT: Ibid., p. 745.

34. JT: Origen, in *Mt.* 12, 30 GCS X, 1, 133f. (ed. E. Klostermann).

35. JT: Tertullian, "On the Flesh of Christ," in *Ante-Nicene Fathers*, vol. 3: *Latin Christianity: Its Founder, Tertullian*, Philipp Schaff (Edinburgh: T. & T. Clark, WM.B. Eerdmans Publ. Co.), p. 530. [Ch. F.: Taubes quotes and cites the Latin source here, without providing a translation. For the Latin text, see endnotes.]

36. Taubes begins his Latin quote with the second paragraph of this chapter of Tertullian's amazing text. The referent of the demonstrative pronoun is the first paragraph we provide here, since it demonstrates what Taubes means by "expressionist" nature of the text: "We have thus far gone on the principle, that nothing which is derived from some other thing, however different it may be from that from which it is derived, is so different as not to suggest the source from which it comes. No material substance is without the witness of its own original, however great a change into new properties it may have undergone. There is this very body of ours, the formation of which out of the dust of the ground is a truth which has found its way into Gentile fables; it certainly testifies its own origin from the two elements of earth and water—from the former by its flesh, from the latter by its blood. Now, although there is a difference in the appearance of qualities (in other words, that which proceeds from something else is in development), yet, after all, what is blood but red fluid? what is flesh but earth in an especial form? Consider the respective qualities—of the muscles as clods; of the bones as stones; the mammillary glands as a kind of pebble. Look upon the close junctions of the nerves as propagations of roots, and the branching courses of the veins as winding rivulets, and the down (which covers us) as moss, and the hair as grass, and the very treasures of marrow within our bones as ores (Lat.: *metalla*)."

37. The translator notes: Cp. Isaiah 53:2, and Tertullian's *Anti-Marcion* in the same volume, p. 153.

38. The translator notes: Matthew 26:41.

39. Taubes quotes this entire text in Latin, from *Corpus Christianorum* S.K. 1954, Tertullian, II, 892f. (ed. A. Gerlo), without providing the German translation. The Latin quote in his text is the following, with the antiquated u- changed to the conventional v- here: "Carnis haec omnia terrenae originis signo et in Christo fuerunt, et haec sunt, quae illum dei filium celauerunt, non alias tantummodo

existimatum quam ex humana tantum substantia corporis [. . .] sed nihil novum, nihil peregrinum deprehendo. Denique verbis et factis tantum, doctrina et virtute sola Christum hominess obstupescebant. Notaretur autem etiam carnis in illo novitas miraculo habita. Sed carnis terrenae non mira condicio ipsa erat, quae cetera eius miranda faciebat, cum dicerent: Unde huic doctrina et signa ista? Etiam despicientium formam eius haec erat vox adeo nec humanae honestatis corpus fuit, nedum caelestis claritatis. Tacentibus apud vox quoque prophetis de ignobili aspectu eius, ipsae passiones ipsaeque contumeliae loquuntur, passiones quidem humanam carnem, contumeliae vero inhonestam. An ausus esset aliqui unque summo praestringere corpus novum, sputaminibus contaminare faciem nisi merentem? Quid dicis caelestem carnem, quam unde caelestem intellegas non habes? Quid terrenam negas, quam unde terrenam agnoscas habes? Esurit sub diabolo, sitit sub Samaritide, lacrimatur super Lazarum, trepidat ad mortem—caro enim, inquit, infirma—sanguinem postremo fundit. Haec sunt, opinor, signa caelestia? 'Sed quomodo,' inquitis, 'contemni et pati passet, sicut et dixit, si quid ex illa carne de caelesti generositate radiasset?' Et ex hoc ergo convincimus nihil in illa de caelis fuisse, propterea, ut contemni et pati passet."

40. JT: Because M. Imdahl elsewhere address the question of the "ars humilis" and thus ties in with Sedlmayr's research, I limit myself to a few indications that place the emphasis slightly differently than Sedlmayr and Imdahl.

41. Taubes quotes this entire passage in French, leaving it untranslated. For our edition, Emily-Jane Cohen has kindly provided the translations of all three French quotations in this essay. Taubes's French text is the following (with corrections from the VKK edition): "Quand on étudie pour la première fois les origines du Crucifix, on est surpris de voir les siècles s'écouler sans rencontrer l'image recherchée: le premier siècle semble passer sans laisser aucun vestige, aucun signe qui puisse évoquer le Christ en croix; pour le IIe siècle, les monuments présentés ne peuvent être datés de façon certaine; il faut arriver au IIIe siècle pour trouver des rares débris de marbre ou de terre cuite, plaques funéraires sur lesquelles on voit, à coté du nom du mort, une croix discrète, souvent dissimulée au milieu des lettres de l'épitaphe. Bien que la doctrine de la Croix soit sans cesse rappelée par saint Paul [. . .] bien qu'au IIe siècle saint Justin dans sa permière Apologie, parle de la Croix en termes enthousiastes, la Croix, qui est dans tous les coeurs [JT: *sic*], ne s'extériorise pas; nulle part elle ne se dresse, ni dans les maisons particulières, ni dans les salles de réunions qui servaient d'Eglises, ni dans les catacombes, dernier refuge contre les persecutions." Citation provided by Taubes: P. Thoby, *Le Crucifix, des Origines au Concile de Trente* (Nantes: A. Bellanger, 1959), p. 11.

42. JT: F. Gerke, *Christus in der spätantiken Plastik* (Berlin: Florian Kupferberg, 1941), p. 32.

43. P. Thoby, *Le Crucifix*, p. 23. Again, Taubes quotes the entire text in French, without providing the translation. The editors did not provide the citation, and

there a number of mistakes in the French text in VKK. His French text (with corrections from Thoby) is the following: "L'ordonnance primitive de ces panneaux montrait le parallélisme des scènes des deux Testaments, mai celui-ci a été complètement oublié dans les réparations subies au cours des siècles; c'est ainsi que la Crucifixion se trouve réleguée en haut du battant de gauche, si loin des regards qu'elle est à peine visible; peut-être d'ailleurs cette place fut-elle voulue par l'artiste présentant—timidement—un essai de Crucifixion, car il est remarquable que, dans cette porte qui comprenait au moins huit grand panneaux, l'artiste ait cru devoir n'en consacrer qu'un petit à un sujet aussi important."

44. Again, Taubes quotes this entire text in French without providing a translation. His French text is the following, with corrections vis-à-vis the text provided in VKK: "En entreprenant l'illustration par l'image des épisodes de la Passion et de la fin de la vie terrestre du Christ jusqu'à la Pentecôte, les inconographes chrétiens restaient donc toujours dans le cadre des thèmes de théophanie. Mais, tandis que les épiphanies de l'Enfance et des Miracles qu'ils interprétaient dès une époque très ancienne étaient familières à bien des religions de ce temps, il n'en était pas de même pour le groupe des théophanies de la Passion-Résurrection. Les cycles de l'Enfance et des Miracles de Jésus avaient donc pu s'appuyer sur des souvenirs de l'iconographie païenne des théophanies, tandis que les images de la Passion n'évoquaient point d'antécédents semblables, et c'est ce qui explique, selon moi, le retard apporté à la création d'une iconographie de la Passion. Pour composer ses premières images les exemples des épiphanies antiques ne suffisaient plus. Il a fallu une impulsion particulière, et cette impulsion, nous le verrons, est venu du culte des saints et des reliques palestiniennes." Citation provided in Taubes's text: André Grabar, *Martyrium: Recherches sur le culte des reliques et l'art Chrétien antique*, vol. 2 (Paris: Collège de France, 1946), p. 255.

45. JT: E. Peterson, "Das Kreuz und das Gebet nach Osten," *Frühkirche, Judentum und Gnosis* (Freiburg/Br.: Herder, 1959), p. 15.

46. JT: Nietzsche, *Daybreak*, trans. R. J. Hollingdale (Cambridge and New York: Cambridge University Press, 1997), pp. 46–47.

CHAPTER 7

1. Eds.: Taubes contributed this essay, just like the preceding two, to an interdisciplinary colloquium in 1964 that was part of the research group on *Poetics and Hermeneutics* (Poetik und Hermeneutik). The contributions plus the notes of the discussions based on the individual contributions were edited and published by Wolfgang Iser as *Immanente Ästhetik, Ästhetische Reflexion: Lyrik als Pradigma der Moderne* (Munich: Wilhelm Fink Verlag, 1966). This colloquium was preceded by another one on the topic of "Imitation and Illusion," referred to in the opening paragraph. For a more detailed discussion of the colloquium see the Introduction.

Taubes's contribution itself, included here, is relatively short (pp. 139–43 in *Immanente Ästhetik*), while the resulting discussion ("Dritte Sitzung," or third session, also included here, as in VKK) takes up significantly more space, pp. 429–42. VKK adopts the discussion session without further comments from *Immanente Ästhetik*. It is not entirely clear why the editors of VKK include this discussion session, while they neglect to do the same for "The Dogmatic Myth of Gnosticism" (here, Chapter 5), where the discussion session published in *Terror und Spiel* (see Chapter 5, n1) provides interesting and important disagreements between Blumenberg and Taubes. The same would be true for *Die Rechtfertigung des Hässlichen*, see Chapter 6, n1.

2. JT: Cf. *Nachahmung und Illusion*, ed. H. R. Jauss (Munich: Eidos, 1964).

3. Taube cites the German title, *Struktur der modernen Lyrik: Von Baudelaire bis zur Gegenwart* (Hamburg: Rowohlt, 1960). In the meantime, this book has been translated by Joachim Neugroschel as *The Structure of Modern Poetry: From the Mid-Nineteenth to the Mid-Twentieth Century* (Evanston, IL: Northwestern University Press, 1974).

4. English in the German original.

5. Taubes quotes the text in French only, without citation. His French text, with his introjections, is the following: "elle (the imagination) décompose (disjoints, dissolves) toute la création, et avec les matériaux amassés et disposés suivant des régles dont on ne peut trouver l'origine que dans le plus profonde de l'âme, elle crée un monde nouveau, elle produit la sensation du neuf." The text is from Charles Baudelaire, *Salon de 1859: Lettres à M. le Directeur de 'La revue française,' III: 'La reine des facultés'* (1859), in *Œuvres complètes* (Pléiade ed., 1961) (S. H., trans.), p. 1038. The entire passage in English, including the preceding phrase quoted by Taubes is this: "It is imagination that has taught man the moral sense of color, of contour, of sound and of scent. It created, in the beginning of the world, analogy and metaphor. It disassembles creation, and with materials gathered and arranged by rules whose origin is only to be found in the very depths of the soul, it creates a new world, it produces the sensation of the new. As it has created the world (this can be said, I believe, even in the religious sense), it is just that it should govern it."

6. Hans Jonas, *Gnosis und spätantiker Geist* (Göttingen: Vandenhoeck & Ruprecht, 1934–35). The latest (fourth) edition of the original publication of 1934 was published in 1988. This important work has remained untranslated.

7. Taubes cites the phrase in the original English of M. H. Abrams's contribution on "Coleridge, Baudelaire, and Modernist Poetics" to the colloquium (cf., *Immanente Ästhetik*, pp. 113–43, and especially p. 122).

8. See n1. The discussion is introduced by Taubes's summary of his paper, hence the repetitions.

9. At the time professor of philosophy at the University in Heidelberg.

10. JT: H. Jonas, *Gnosis und spätantiker Geist* (Göttingen: Vandenhoeck & Ruprecht, 1964), p. 249.

11. Clemens Heselhaus, at the time professor of German language and literature in Giessen.

12. At the time professor of English in Cologne.

13. English in the German original.

14. English in the German original.

15. The German text in VKK and *Immanente Ästhetik* cites the following passage in French without translation: "... les scandales moraux suscités par le surréalisme ne supposent pas forcément un bouleversement des valeurs intellectuelles er sociales; la bourgeoisie ne les craint pas. Elle les absorbe facilement. Même les violentes attaques des surréalistes contre le patriotisme ont pris l'allure d'un scandale morale. Ces sortes de scandals n'empêchent pas de converser la tête de la hiérarchie intellectuelle dans une république bourgeoise ... " Naville's text has not been translated into English, so I thank Emily-Jane Cohen for providing a translation of this passage.

16. JT: P. Naville, *La Révolution et les Intellectuels (Que peuvent faire les surréalistes?)* (Paris, 1926).

17. As previously, the German text cites the passage in French without translation: "Je dis que la flame révolutionnaire brûle où elle veut e qu'il n'appartient pas à un petit nombre d'hommes, dans la période d'attente que nous vivons, de décréter que c'est ici où là seulement qu'elle peut brûler." Breton's text has not been translated into English, and I thank Emily-Jane for providing a translation of the French.

18. JT: A. Breton, *Légitime Défense* (1926).

19. From Benjamin's *Theological-Political Fragment*.

20. Hans Robert Jauss, at the time professor of romance languages at the University of Konstanz.

21. M. H. Abrams, at the time professor of English at Cornell University, in his lecture on Baudelaire at the colloquium, on "Coleridge, Baudelaire, and Modernist Poetics," in *Immanente Ästhetik*, pp. 113–38. See above, n7.

22. JT: Such laws of dandyism are, for example, "The dandy has to aspire to being sublime without interruption. He has to live and sleep in front of a mirror" (Baudelaire, *Complete Works* [French] [Paris: de la Pléïade, 1951, p. 1200]). Or, "these beings do not have any other purpose than cultivating the idea of beauty in their person" (here also the concept of "institution beyond the laws"). The dandy, whom M. H. Abrams describes as a secularized saint, could be related back to the stoicism that Baudelaire himself invoked (ibid., p. 899, here also the rule: "[The passion of the dandy] is the pleasure to astonish, and in the proud satisfaction never to be astonished oneself." On the opposition of the dandy to nature, see also pp. 1191, 1199 ("The Woman and the Contrast to the Dandy"). [Ch. F.: The quotes

are in French. We translated them here, but with reference to the French edition, *Immanente Ästhetik,* Taube worked with. The references refer to Baudelaire's reflections on "The Dandy."]

23. JT: Georg Lukács, *The Theory of the Novel,* trans. Anna Bostock (Cambridge, MA: MIT Press, 1971), p. 33.

24. JT: Ibid.

25. JT: See also John Donne, *The First Anniversary: New Philosophy Calls All into Doubt . . . , the Poems of John Donne,* ed. H. Grierson (Oxford: Oxford University Press, 1939).

26. Siegfried Kracauer, that is, listed at a private New York address in the volume.

27. Wolfgang Preisendanz, at the time professor of German literature at the University of Konstanz.

28. JT: *The Concept of Irony,* trans. Lee M. Capel (New York: Harper & Row 1966), p. 274.

29. Manfred Fuhrmann, at the time professor of classics at the University of Kiel.

30. Blumenberg, listed as holding a position in philosophy at the University of Bochum.

31. Blumenberg here uses the term "*spätjüdisch*" (late Jewish), that derives from traditional Protestant Christian historiography, according to which Judaism is superseded by Christianity. "Late Jewish" therefore refers to what nowadays is referred to as early Judaism.

32. JT: "Wirklichkeitsbegriff und Möglichkeit des Romans," in *Nachahmung und Illusion,* ed. H. R. Jauss (Munich: Wilhelm Fink Verlag), p. 26.

33. [Ch. F.: Again, the German text leaves the French untranslated, without a precise citation: "A plus juste titre encore, sans doute aurions-nous pu nous emparer du mot Supernaturalisme, employé par Gérard de Nerval dans la dédicace des Filles de Feu." I thank my mother Barbara Fonrobert for helping me with the translation of this passage.]

34. The reference is left without citation. But see Elizabeth Sewell, *The Human Metaphor* (Notre Dame, IN: University of Notre Dame Press, 1964).

35. Thus the approximate translation of Blumenberg's essay "Wirklichkeitsbegriff und Möglichkeit der Romans," in *Nachahmung und Illusion,* ed. H. R. Jauss (München: Wilhelm Fink Verlag, 1964), pp. 9–27. The essay had a significant reception in German scholarship, but it has not been translated into English.

36. JT: Ibid., p. 13.

37. Robert M. Wallace translated Blumenberg's *Legitimität der Neuzeit* (1973, 2d edition) as *The Legitimacy of the Modern* Age (Cambridge, MA: MIT Press, 1983).

CHAPTER 8

1. Eds.: This essay was originally published in German, in "Positionen der Negativität," *Poetik und Hermeneutik* VI (Munich, 1975), pp. 141–53. See the Introduction for more explanation on the provenance of the essay. We are translating the essay for this edition. It should be pointed out that in German every noun is capitalized. Therefore, the original German title—"Vom Adverb 'nichts' zum Substantiv 'das Nichts'"—provides another subtle yet important means by which to differentiate the adverb "nothing" from the substantive nothing. In order to make this material difference more apparent in the English we have chosen to retain the capitalized "Nothing" to differentiate the substantive from the adverbial form.

2. The German original, *Was ist Metaphysik?* was translated into English by David Farrell and appears in the collected essays volume, Martin Heidegger, *Basic Writings* (New York: Taylor & Francis, 1978). All the following references to this work, which are here maintained in Taubes's style, refer to this edition.

3. JT: R. Carnap, "Überwindung der Metaphysik durch logische Analyse der Sprache," *Erkenntnis* II (1931): 219–41.

4. JT: E. Tugendhat, "Das Sein und das Nichts," *Durchblicke*, Festschrift für Martin Heidegger zum 80. Geburtstag, ed. Vittorio Klostermann (Frankfurt, 1970), pp. 132–61.

5. JT: Fragment VIII, trans. by Leonardo Taran, in *Parmenides: A Text with Translation, Commentary, and Critical Essays* (Princeton, NJ: Princeton University Press, 1965), p. 85.

6. JT: Ibid.

7. All the references to Martin Heidegger's *Being in Time*, which in the original German publication of this essay appear in the text in brackets, refer here to the English translation by John Maquarrie and Edward Robinson. See Martin Heidegger, *Being and Time*, trans. John Maquarrie and Edward Robinson (New York: Harper & Row 1962).

8. JT: E. Tugendhat, p. 153.

9. JT: Fragment VI, op. cit.

10. JT: H. Fränkel, *Dichtung und Philosophie des frühen Griechentums* (Munich: C. H. Beck, 1962), p. 420.

11. See chap. 9, in Heidegger, *Basic Writings*.

12. JT: Heidegger, *Introduction to Metaphysics*, trans. Gregory Fried and Richard Polt (New Haven, CT: Yale University Press, 2000), p. 165.

13. JT: Heidegger, *Being and Time*, p. 265.

14. JT: E. Tugendhat, op. cit., p. 153.

15. JT: Aristotles, *Metaphysics,* IV, 5, 1009, a31.

16. JT: Thomas Aquinas, *Summa Theologie* I, qu. 45, a1.

17. JT: H. A. Wolfson, *The Meaning of Ex Nihilo in the Church Fathers, Arabic and Hebrew Philosophy and St. Thomas, Mediaeval Studies in Honor of Jeremiah Danis Ford* (Cambridge, MA: Harvard University Press, 1948), pp. 355–70.

18. JT: G. Scholem, "Schöpfung aus Nichts and Selbstverschränkung Gottes," in *Über einige Grundbegriffe des Judentums* (Frankfurt: Suhrkamp Verlag, 1970), p. 59.

19. JT: Böhme, *De Signatura Rerum* VI, 8.

20. JT: Heidegger, *Vom Wesen des Grundes* (Halle: Max Niemeyer, 1929), p. 48.

21. JT: Schelling, *Philosophie der Offenbarung* WW XIII, p. 242.

22. See "Die Logik der Negation als ontologisches Erkenntnismittel," in "Positionen der Negativität," *Poetik und Hermeneutik* VI, ed. Harald Weinrich (Munich: Wilhelm Fink Verlag, 1975).

CHAPTER 9

1. This essay was first published in German as "Das stählernde Gehäuse und der Exodus daraus, oder Ein Streit um Marcion, einst und jetzt" and served as the introduction to the second volume of the series *Religionstheorie und Politische Theologie*, edited by Taubes under the title *Gnosis und Politik* (Munich and Paderborn: Ferdinand Schöningh, 1984), pp. 9–15. See also the Introduction to this volume. The interdisciplinary Arbeitsgruppe (research group) on "Theory of Religion and Political Theology," of which Taubes was a member, produced three volumes, edited by Taubes, with the first volume on Carl Schmitt, under the title *Der Fürst dieser Welt: Carl Schmitt und die Folgen* (Paderborn: Ferdinand Schöningh, 1985) and the third one under the title *Theokratie* (Paderborn: Ferdinand Schöningh, 1987). The second one on Gnosticism is the product of an interdisciplinary colloquium in 1982. For the purposes of this essay, we are leaving in place Taubes's page references to the German editions.

2. Baur's *Die Christliche Gnosis, oder Die Religionsphilosophie in ihrer geschichtlichen Entwicklung* (1835) has remained untranslated.

3. Jonas's *Gnosis und spätantiker Geist* has remained untranslated as well, although the German edition underwent three editions. More recently, Jonas's reception in the Anglophone world is undergoing a renaissance. See Hava Tirosh-Samuelson and Christian Wiese, eds., *The Legacy of Hans Jonas: Judaism and the Phenomenon of Life* (Leiden: Brill, 2008).

4. Taubes refers to the German date of publication. Blumenberg's *Die Legitimität der Neuzeit* was translated into English by Robert M. Wallace as *The Legitimacy of the Modern Age* (Cambridge, MA: MIT Press, 1983), based on the second edition of 1976. Taubes's page citations in this section refer to the German edition of 1963.

5. Taubes, of course, refers to the German version of 1981, *Abschied vom Prinzipiellen*. This has been translated as *Farewell to Matters of Prinicple* (New York: Oxford University Press, 1989).

6. Translated as *The Protestant Ethic and the Spirit of Capitalism, and Other Essays* (2002). Taubes's references are not precise here. Our translation cites the Penguin Classics English translation of 2002 by Peter Baehr and Gordon C. Wells, thus smoothing over Taubes's inaccuracies in the German essay.

7. VKK wrongly has *"Auslese"* instead of *"Askese."*

8. Again, Taubes obviously refers to the German edition, *Der Geist der Utopie*, which was published in 1918. Bloch's book has most recently been translated by Anthony Nassar as *The Spirit of Utopia* (Stanford: Stanford University Press, 2000).

9. Harnack's book on Marcion (*Marcion: das Evangelium vom fremden Gott, eine Monographie zur Geschichte der Grundlegung der katholischen Kirche*) remains untranslated. It was republished in German by the Wissenschaftliche Buchgesellschaft in 1960.

10. Cp. Neville Plaice, Stephen Plaice, and Paul Knight's translation of *Das Prinzip Hoffnung*, as *The Principle of Hope* (Oxford: Blackwell, 1986).

11. On the colloquium, see n1.

12. The translator notes the complicated reference situation: Buber's "Addresses" exist in an English edition: *At the Turning: Three Addresses on Judaism* (New York: Farrar, Straus and Young, 1952). Taubes refers to four "speeches" in his essay. But obviously, this English edition has only three addresses. The German *An der Wende. Reden über das Judentum* (Köln and Olten: Hegner, 1952).

13. "Die heimliche Frage." In the English edition of *At the Turning*, this is actually the second lecture.

14. This quote is left in English in the German text. See Barbara Aland, ed., *Gnosis: Festschrift für Hans Jonas* (Göttingen: Vandenhoeck & Ruprecht, 1978).

15. Taubes must be referring to G. Stroumsa, "Aher: A Gnostic," in *The Rediscovery of Gnosticism: Proceedings of the International Conference at Yale, New Haven, March 28–31, 1978*, vol. II, ed. Bentley Layton (Leiden: Brill, 1980–81), pp. 808–18. See, however, also Alon Goshen-Gottstein, *The Sinner and the Amnesiac: The Rabbinic Invention of Elisha ben Abuya and Eleazar ben Arach* (Stanford: Stanford University Press, 2000).

16. *When Prophecy Fails*, ed. Leon Festinger, Henry W. Riecken, and Stanley Schachter (Minneapolis: University of Minnesota Press, 1956).

CHAPTER 10

1. Taubes published this text originally in German, as his introduction to the edition of *Franz Overbeck. Selbstbekenntnisse: Mit einer Einleitung von Jacob Taubes* (Frankfurt: Insel Verlag, 1966), pp. 7–27.

2. JT: Franz Overbeck, *Über die Christlichkeit unserer heutigen Theologie, Streit- und Friedensschrift* (Leipzig, 1873; reprinted, 1903), trans. John Ebert Wilson as *On the Christianity of Theology* (San Jose, CA: Pickwick Publications, 2002). From here on referred to as *On the Christianity*. References are made to the English edition.

3. Postscript here refers to the Afterword to the second edition of *On the Christianity of Theology*, published thirty years after the original publication. One word on the translation here: Wilson (see first endnote of the current essay) translated the text as *On the Christianity of Theology*. Our translator, Mara H. Benjamin, had originally suggested *On the Christianness of Theology*, since Christianity is the term for *Christentum,* the cultural phenomenon and religion itself, while *Christlichkeit* refers more to the nature and character of that cultural phenomenon. "Christianness" would therefore have been more accurate. However, as we refer to Wilson's translation, we keep "Christianity" in the references. We mostly follow Wilson in rendering Taubes's references to that text by Overbeck, at times with some minor adaptations. Furthermore, Wilson left the subtitle ("Streit- und Friedensschrift") untranslated. Taubes, however, often refers to this text as "*Streitschrift,*" which we render as "Polemic."

4. JT: Ibid., pp. 200ff.

5. JT: Franz Overbeck*, Christentum und Kultur. Gedanken und Aufzeichnungen zur modernen Theologie*, ed. from the literary estate by Carl Albrecht Bernoulli (Basel, 1919).

6. This posthumous text by Overbeck has remained untranslated.

7. JT: Eberhard Vischer, "Overbeck Redivivus (Der neuentdeckte Overbeck)," *Die Christliche Welt* 36 (1922): 110f.

8. JT: Ernst Troeltsch, Review of Christianity and Culture, *Historische Zeitschrift* 3, no. 26 (1920): 279ff.

9. JT: *Christianity and Culture*, p. 289.

10. This citation is all the German text provides. But see Karl Barth, "Unerledigte Anfragen an die heutige Theologie," in *Zur inneren Lage des Christentums*, ed. Karl Barth and Eduard Thurneysen (Munich: Kaiser, 1920), pp. 3–24. This text is cited again on p. 5 in this essay.

11. JT: Karl Barth, "Unerledigte Anfragen an die heutige Theologie" [Ch. F.: Unanswered Questions for Contemporary Theology], in K. B. Thurneysen and Eduard Thurneysen, *Zur Inneren Lage des Christentums* [*On the Inner Situation of Christianity*] (Munich: Kaiser, 1920).

12. JT: Overbeck, *Das Johannesevangelium: Studien zur Kritik seiner Erforschung* [*The Gospel of John: Studies Toward a Critique of Its Investigation*], ed. Bernoulli from the literary estate (Tübingen, 1911), p. 391.

13. Darmstadt: Wissenschaftliche Buchgesellschaft, 1966 (reprinted).

14. JT: *On the Christianity*, p. 107.

15. The reference here is to Overbeck's early work *Über die Anfänge des Mönchthums* (1867). It is republished in the first volume of his *Werke und Nachlaß* (Stuttgart: Metzler, 1994).

16. JT: Ibid., p. 94.
17. JT: *Christianity and Culture*, p. 33.
18. JT: Ibid., p. 34.
19. JT: Ibid., p. 279.
20. JT: *On the Christianity*, p. 94.
21. JT: Ibid., p. 95.
22. JT: Ibid.
23. Taubes text indicates elision here, but there is none.
24. The omitted subclause is the following: . . . the expectation of the return of Christ . . . "which brightened the prospect of the end of the present form of the world with all sorts of Judaistic hopes . . . "; see Wilson, p. 95.
25. The source for this statement in Overbeck is Heinrich Spörri, *Der alte und der neue Glaube* (Hamburg, 1873), p. 36.
26. JT: Ibid., p. 95 [with two minor emendations by the current translator].
27. JT: Ibid., p. 108.
28. JT: Ibid.
29. JT: Ibid., p. 110.
30. JT: Ibid.
31. JT: Ibid., p. 108.
32. JT: Ibid., p. 111.
33. JT: *Christianity and Culture*, p. 190.
34. JT: Carl Albrecht Bernoulli, *Franz Overbeck and Friedrich Nietzsche: A Friendship*, 2 vols. (1908), vol. 1, pp. 365f.
35. JT: *On the Christianity*, p. 88.
36. JT: Ibid., p. 81.
37. JT: Ibid., p. 92.
38. JT: Ibid., p. 152.
39. JT: *Christianity and Culture*, pp. 198f.
40. JT: Ibid., pp. 208f.
41. JT: Ibid., p. 242.
42. JT: Ibid., p. 9.
43. JT: Ibid., p. 242.
44. JT: Ibid., p. 70.
45. JT: Ibid., p. 8.
46. JT: Ibid., pp. 268f.
47. JT: Ibid., p. 9.
48. JT: Ibid., p. 7.
49. JT: Ibid., p. 72.

50. JT: Ibid., p. 73.
51. JT: Ibid., p. 7.
52. JT: Ibid., p. 297.
53. JT: Ibid., p. 293.
54. JT: Ibid., p. 13.
55. JT: *On the Christianity*, p. 111.
56. JT: *Christianity and Culture*, p. 77.
57. JT: Ibid., p. 270.
58. JT: Ibid., p. 77.
59. JT: Ibid.
60. JT: Ibid., p. 136.
61. JT: *On the Christianity*, p. 62.
62. JT: Ibid., p. 62.
63. JT: Ibid., p. 64.
64. JT: Ibid., p. 63.
65. JT: *Friedrich Nietzsche's Correspondence with Franz Overbeck*, ed. Richard Oehler and Carl Albrecht Bernoulli (1916), p. 296.
66. JT: *Correspondence*, pp. 230, 185, 158.
67. JT: Ibid., p. 238.
68. JT: Franz Overbeck, *Confessions*, with an introduction by Jacob Taubes (Frankfurt: Inselverlag, 1966), p. 104.
69. JT: Ibid., p. 105.
70. JT: Ibid.
71. JT: Ibid., p. 139.
72. JT: Ibid., p. 117.
73. JT: *Christianity and Culture*, p. 250.
74. JT: *Confessions*, p. 141.

CHAPTER 11

1. Eds.: This article originally appeared in English as an essay in the *Journal of Religion* 34, no. 2 (April 1954): 11–19. The chapter in VKK presents a close translation of that article. The English article is introduced with the following bio: "Jacob Taubes, Ph.D., a Fellow in Philosophy in the Hebrew University of Jerusalem, is now in this country on a Rockefeller grant working on the problem of political theology. He originally studied and taught in Switzerland, where he published in 1948 a work on *Abendländische Eschatologie*. Several of his papers on ontology and theology and on the philosophy of history have appeared in philosophical journals, including *The Proceedings of the XIth International Congress of Philosophy* (1953). An article of his on the theology of Paul Tillich recently appeared in the *Journal of Religion*."

2. JT: See his Preface to the second edition.

3. Eds.: Taubes here points to the discussion in German Protestant theological circles that were launched by the New Testament theologian Rudolf Bultmann and his essay on "Neues Testament und Mythologie" (New Testament and Mythology), in which he draws a distinction between the mythological view of the world to which the New Testament writers are beholden, which can be historicized, and the message of the Gospel itself (the "*kerygma*"). The debate entered the public arena in the edition of Hans-Werner Bartsch, ed., *Kerygma und Mythos: Ein theologisches Gespräch*, 3 vols. (Hamburg: Reich und Heidrich Evangelischer Verlag, 1948), with contributions by Rudolf Bultmann, Fritz Buri, Karl Jaspers, and Hans-Werner Bartsch.

4. JT: See his essay on Anaximander in *Holzwege* (1950), pp. 296ff. [Ch. F.: "Der Spruch des Anaximander," in *Holzwege*, Gesamtausgabe, Bd. 5, 2d ed. (Frankfurt: Vittorio Kaufmann, 2003), pp. 321–73; in the meantime this essay was translated into English by Julian Young and Kenneth Haynes as "Anaximander's Saying" in Martin Heidegger, *Off the Beaten Track* (New York: Cambridge University Press, 2002), pp. 242–82.]

5. JT: See J. Taubes, *Abendländische Eschatologie* (1947), pp. 79ff.; and Karl Löwith, *Meaning in History* (1949), pp. 160ff.

6. See the chapter on "Joachimitische Prophetie und Hegelsche Philosophie" (pp. 122–32) in his *Abendländische Eschatologie* (2007).

7. JT: Cf. E. Reisner, *Die christliche Botschaft im Wandel der Zeiten* (1935), pp. 99–100; and Taubes, op. cit., p. 88. [Ch. F.: Correct title of Reisner, as cited in *Abendländische Eschatologie*, would be *Die christliche Botschaft im Wandel der Epochen*.]

8. JT: Leo Strauss, *Philosophie und Gesetz* (1935), pp. 13–14. [Ch. F.: Translated twice, first by Fred Baumann as *Philosophy and Law: Contributions to the Understanding of Maimonides and His Predecessors* (Philadelphia, PA: Jewish Publication Society, 1987), a translation that is dismissed and redone by Eve Adler, *Philosophy and Law: Contributions to the Understanding of Maimonides and His Predecessors* (Albany: State University of New York Press, 1995).]

9. JT: *Kirchliche Dogmatik*, vol. I (1932), Introduction, p. viii. [Ch. F.: Translated by Geoffrey W. Bromiley as *Barth's Church Dogmatics: The Word of God as the Criterion of Dogmatics* (London and New York: T. & T. Clark, 2004).]

10. *The Education of Humankind*.

CHAPTER 12

1. Eds.: This essay was published first in English in *The Journal of Religion* 34, no. 3 (Oct. 1954): 231–43, on which VKK bases its German translation. The biographical sketch that is included in the published essay reads: "Jacob Taubes con-

tributed an article on the theology of Paul Tillich, 'On the Nature of Theological Method,' in the first issue of the *Journal* for 1954. He continued his discussion of theological method in the next issue by presentation of the article, 'Dialectic and Analogy.' The present article forms a unity with these and completes a trilogy. Dr. Taubes, who is well known for his *Abendländische Eschatologie*, is a Fellow in Philosophy in the Hebrew University of Jerusalem. He is in this country on a grant from the Rockefeller Foundation to work on the problem of political theology." Hence, the sequence of the three essays of Taubes's 1954 trilogy would be Tillich, Dialectic, and then Barth, while the editors of VKK decided to rearrange the trilogy in the order we are following here qua edited translation of that volume. The essay appears without any endnotes in the English original.

2. Hans Urs von Balthasar, *The Theology of Karl Barth: Exposition and Interpretation*, trans. Edward T. Oakes (San Francisco: Ignatius Press, 1992).

3. Throughout the essay Taubes spells Barth's title as *Roemerbrief*, rather than with the umlaut, so I am leaving it as such. As it will become clear from what follows, Barth wrote two substantially different versions of his *Römerbrief*, the commentary to Paul's "Epistle to the Romans."

CHAPTER 13

1. Eds.: This essay was published originally in English in *The Journal of Religion* 34, no. 1 (Jan. 1954): 12–25. It forms part of the trilogy of articles that appeared during that year in *The Journal of Religion*. The essay is subscribed with the following bio—in line with the other two (Chapters 11–13 in our edition): "Jacob Taubes, Ph.D., of Zurich, Switzerland, and Research Fellow for Philosophy in the Hebrew University, Jerusalem, is now on a Rockefeller Fellowship in the United States for a study of the relation of philosophy and political theology. His publications include *Abendländische Eschatologie* (1948), an analysis of the theology and philosophy of history with special emphasis on the eschatological interpretation of history throughout the Christian Era. Several of his articles on the problem of theology and philosophy have appeared in philosophical journals. In 1949 Mr. Taubes studied with Paul Tillich in New York and in the same year published his 'Notes on the Ontological Interpretation of Theology' in the *Review of Metaphysics* which complements the analysis of Tillich's theology in the present article by a systematic interpretation." Taubes's notes to the article are minimal, and as usual, we preserve them as footnotes in his essay, supplemented by our bibliographical endnotes. VKK's translation into German is based on this English version, while our edition again is based on the English original.

2. The quest for the "historical Jesus."

3. Ferdinand Christian Baur, *Lehrbuch der christlichen Dogmengeschichte* (Stuttgart, 1847); and *Vorlesungen über die christliche Dogmengeschichte* (Leipzig, 1865–67).

4. Adolf von Harnack, *Das Wesen des Christentums* (1900). As opposed to Baur's work, Harnack's book has been republished many times since its original publication, most recently *Das Wesen des Christentums: sechzehn Vorlesungen vor Studierenden aller Fakultäten im Wintersemester 1899/1900 an der Universität Berlin*, ed. by Claus-Dieter Osthövener (Tübingen: Mohr Siebeck, 2005). It has been translated by Thomas Bailey Saunders (with an Introduction by Rudolf Bultmann) as *What Is Christianity?* (New York: Harper, 1957).

5. Paul Tillich, *Systematic Theology* (Chicago: University of Chicago Press, 1951–63). The English publication preceded the German one. Cp. *Systematische Theologie*, 3 vols. (Stuttgart: Evangelisches Verlagswerk, 1955/58/66). Taubes had volume one of the English edition at his disposal when he wrote this essay and all the page numbers refer to that edition.

6. Karl Heim, *Der christliche Gottesglaube und die Naturwissenschaft. Grundlegung des Gesprächs zwischen dem Christentum und den Naturwissenschaften*, 1949 (2d ed. 1953), also translated into English by N. Horton Smith as *Christian Faith and Natural Science* (New York: Harper, 1953).

7. JT: All page references, unless otherwise indicated, refer to Tillich's *Systematic Theology*, vol. I (Chicago, 1954).

8. JT: Leo Strauss, *Die Religionskritik Spinozas* (Berlin, 1930). [Ch. F.: Since published in translation by E. M. Sinclair as *Spinoza's Critique of Religion* (New York: Schocken Books, 1965).]

9. JT: Erwin Reisner, *Die Geschichte als Sündenfall und Weg zum Gericht* (Munich, 1929).

10. Richard Rothe, *Zur Dogmatik* (Gotha 1863, 2. Aufl. 1869).

11. JT: Published for private circulation (Zurich, 1952). [Ch. F.: Published meanwhile as "Zürcher Seminar, Aussprache am 6. November 1951," in Martin Heidegger, *Seminare*, Gesamtausgabe, vol. 15 (Frankfurt, 1986), p. 437.]

12. Ludwig Klages (1872–1956).

13. Hermann Graf Keyserling (1880–1946).

14. Friedrich Wilhelm Joseph Schelling, *Philosophie der Mythologie* (1842) and *Philosophie der Offenbarung* (1854). The lectures have been only partially translated, as *Historical-Critical Introduction to the Philosophy of Mythology*, by Mason Richey and Markus Zisselsberger (Albany: State University of New York Press, 2007).

15. JT: Ludwig Feuerbach, *Grundsätze der Philosophie der Zukunft*, p. 2.

16. Ludwig Feuerbach, *Grundsätze der Philosophie der Zukunft* (Zürich und Winterthur 1843), p. 2. Cp. Manfred H. Vogel's translation, *Principles of the Philosophy of the Future* (Indianapolis, IN: Hackett Pub. Co., 1986).

CHAPTER 14

1. Eds.: This essay was published originally in English, in *The Review of Metaphysics* 2, no. 8 (1949): 97–104. It is, therefore, the oldest essay in this volume and

among the earliest that Taubes published at all (he finished and published his dissertation in 1947); it is also the first one to be published outside of Switzerland. VKK translated the essay for their volume, while we replicate Taubes's English publication.

2. The paraphrasing reference seems to be to Gerhardt Kuhlmann, "Zum theologischen Problem der Existenz: Fragen an R. Bultmann," *Zeitschrift für Theologie und Kirche* 10 (1929): 28–57.

3. Left in German in the English version. The connotations of the term range from something like excessive enthusiasm to sentimentality.

4. Cp. Karl Barth, "An Introductory Essay," in Ludwig Feuerbach, *The Essence of Christianity*, trans. George Eliot (New York: Harper/Torchbooks, 1957).

CHAPTER 15

1. Eds.: This essay was published originally in English in *Social Theory* 22 (1955): 57–68, and presumably it was translated from there into German by VKK. Our text is based on the English original.

2. See Donoso Cortés, *Versuch über den Katholizismus, den Liberalismus und Socialismus*; translated from the French by Carl B. Reiching (Tübingen: H. Laupp, 1854).

3. VKK provides a precise citation here for the German translation of *De Nobilitate* from which it cites the text. Taubes refers to the chapter only, without textual reference. The full title of the pamphlet is *Declamatio de nobilitate e praecellentia foeminei sexus*, which Henricus Cornelius Agrippa wrote in 1509, but presented to the Margaret of Habsburg only in 1529, presumably to gain favors from her. The work, a treatise in defense of women's equality, gained considerable literary success with several reprints in Latin and translations into vernacular languages, among them English (1542). For information on the history of the declamation, see the recent translation and edition by Albert Rabil, *Declamation on the Nobility and Preeminence of the Female Sex* (Chicago: University of Chicago Press, 1996). It is not clear from where Taubes is citing the text.

4. Georges Sorel, *Réflexions sur la violence* (Paris: Seuil, 1990; reprint of 11th edition of 1950). Cp. translated by Jeremy Jennings, *Reflections on Violence* (New York: Cambridge University Press, 1999).

CHAPTER 16

1. Eds.: Taubes published this essay in English originally for the *Partisan Review* 21 (1954): 304–5. VKK translates the essay from that version. The present edition is Taubes's original English version, provided with a few editorial notes. In German literature Oskar Goldberg, the subject of this essay, has retained some presence through his critical reception by Thomas Mann, especially in his repre-

sentation in the figure of Dr. Chaim Breisacher in *Dr. Faustus*, a connection discussed by Taubes in the first section of this essay. In the Anglophone world, by contrast, Goldberg was and has remained virtually unknown. Taubes was the first to devote a critical discussion to Goldberg's oeuvre in this essay of 1954. Taubes's essay has been discussed by Manfred Voigts, in his contribution to the volume dedicated to the fiftieth anniversary of the publication of Taubes's *Occidental Eschatology*, and to the tenth anniversary of his death, edited by Richard Faber, Eveline Goodman-Thau, and Thomas Macho as *Abendländische Eschatologie. Ad Jacob Taubes* (Würzburg: Königshausen and Neumann, 2001). Voigts's contribution is "Jacob Taubes und Oskar Goldberg: Eine problematische Beziehung, dargestellt anhand der erhaltenen Briefe," pp. 447–65. See also the earlier version of this essay: "Jacob Taubes und Oskar Goldberg," in *Zeitschrift für Religions- und Geistesgeschichte* 43 (1991): 76–83, based on Taubes's English essay. Both are invaluable resources for placing Taubes's essay in his overall intellectual development, as Voigts presentation of Taubes's occupation with Goldberg reaches beyond the essay of 1954 and draws on the broad correspondence that Taubes's conducted with Goldberg's students on their master's work. As to the publication of Taubes's essay for the *Partisan Review*, Voigts notes that Taubes himself mentioned that for that periodical he emphasized mostly the more general aspects of Goldberg's work, and he had intended to follow up on this essay with one on the "Goldberg's 'Hebrew' philosophy" for *Commentary*, which he never did. See Voigts 2001, p. 456, and Voigts 1991, p. 81.

2. The quotation is left without specific reference in Taubes's text, as in general there are no notes provided in the English original of the essay. The passage can be found in Thomas Mann's *Dr. Faustus*, trans. H.T. Lowe-Porter (New York, 1965), p. 282. Voigts notes the poor referencing in the essay (on which more significantly see below, n10), which Taubes attributes in a letter to the fact that the editors of the *Partisan Review* shortened the essay, a fact Taubes excused with the poor working conditions of the periodical. See Voigts 1991, p. 81.

3. Again, Taubes neglected to provide a precise reference, which is I Kings 8:27.

4. Psalms 50:13.

5. On the connection between Thomas Mann and Oskar Goldberg as reflected in Taubes essay, see Voigts 1991, p. 80; and more recently also Christian Hülshörster's *Thomas Mann und Oskar Goldbergs "Wirklichkeit der Hebräer"* (Frankfurt: V. Klostermann, 1999).

6. I have not been able to locate the precise quote. But see Thomas Mann, *Selected Essays* (New York: F.S. Crofts & Co., 1941).

7. The general reference to Philip Rahv (1908–73) is not entirely arbitrary, as Taubes wrote his essay for the *Partisan Review*, of which Rahv was a cofounder.

8. In fact, Goldberg contributed altogether four essays to Mann's antifascist periodical; according to Voigts, Taubes was familiar with this material and had planned to translate it into English and publish it with an introduction.

9. In August 1952. See Voigts 2001, p. 452.

10. This is one of the passages that Voigts notes as representing an exact paraphrase from Goldberg's essays, which Taubes neglects to mention (see above, n1), Voigts 2001, p. 448. For this articulation, Taubes also refers to Kleist's *Über das Marionettentheater*, in one of his letters, namely, that "in order to regain our innocence, we have to eat from the tree of knowledge—again," see Voigts 1991, p. 80.

11. Lit., "rock of bronze/ iron," that is, it is set in stone.

12. VKK has "gods of the people" instead.

13. VKK italicizes "because Babylon . . . the incarnation of 'culture,'" without noting why.

CHAPTER 17

1. Eds.: This essay was originally published in German, in *Spaetkapitalismus oder Industriegesellschaft? Verhandlungen des 16. Deutschen Soziologentages vom 8.-11. April 1968 in Frankfurt*, ed. by Thodor W. Adorno (Stuttgart, 1969), pp. 117–38.

2. Chartism is considered to be the first working-class social and political movement. It was active in Britian in the mid-nineteenth century and worked to reform the political system in order to allow younger, working-class citizens political influence. For more on this movement, see Frank F. Rosenblatt, *The Chartist Movement* (New York: Taylor & Francis, 2006).

3. JT: Karl Marx and Friedrich Engels, *Werke*, vol. 12 (Berlin: Dietz, 1963), p. 3.

4. JT: Cf. Marx, *Introduction to a Critique of Political Economy*.

5. JT: Georg Lukács, *History and Class Consciousness: Studies in Marxist Dialectics*, trans. Rodney Livingstone (Cambridge, MA: MIT Press, 1971), p. 85.

6. JT: Marx, *Das Kapital*, vol. 1 (Berlin: Dietz, 1961), p. 77.

7. JT: Ibid.

8. JT: Walter Benjamin, *Briefe 2* (Frankfurt: Suhrkamp, 1966), p. 659.

9. In English this essay appears in Walter Benjamin, *The Arcades Project*, ed. Rolf Tiedemann, trans. Howard Eiland and Kevin McLaughlin (New York: Belknap Press, 2002).

10. JT: *Selected Writings Volume 3: 1935–1938* (Cambridge, MA: Harvard University Press, 2002), pp. 36–38.

11. JT: Ibid.

12. JT: Cf. Letter from Adorno to Benjamin, Aug. 2, 1935, in *The Complete Correspondence 1928–1940*, trans. Nicholas Walker (Cambridge, MA: Harvard University Press, 1999), p. 106.

13. JT: Ibid.
14. JT: *Charles Baudelaire*, trans. Harry Zohn (London: Verso, 1997), p. 175.
15. JT: Benjamin, "Eduard Fuchs: Collector and Historian," *The Essential Frankfurt School Reader* (Oxford: Blackwell, 1978), p. 233.
16. JT: Ibid.
17. JT: See Adorno, *Prisms* (Cambridge, MA: MIT Press, 1981), p. 65.
18. JT: Letter from Adorno to Benjamin, Aug. 2, 1935, p. 112.
19. JT: Letter from Adorno to Benjamin, Nov. 10, 1935, p. 282.
20. JT: Adorno, ibid., p. 284.
21. JT: See "The Work of Art in the Age of Mechanical Reproduction," *Illuminations* (New York: Schocken Books, 1969), p. 218.
22. JT: Letter from Adorno to Benjamin, Aug. 2, 1935, p. 105.
23. JT: Ibid., pp. 109, 113.
24. JT: Adorno, *Prisms* (Cambridge, MA: MIT Press, 1981), p. 30.
25. JT: Adorno, "Gesellschaft," in *Evangelischen Staatslexicon* (Stuttgart, 1966), p. 639.
26. JT: Ibid.
27. JT: Marx, *Grundrisse der Kritik der politischen Ökonomie* (Berlin: Dietz, 1953), p. 592.
28. JT: Ibid.
29. JT: *Aus dem Nachlass*, in *Werke*, Bd. 3, p. 505.
30. JT: *Beyond Good and Evil*, trans. R. J. Hollingdale (Harmondsworth, Eng.: Penguin, 1973), p. 173.
31. JT: *The Will to Power*, trans. Walter Kaufmann and R. J. Hollingdale (New York: Vintage, 1967), p. 501.
32. JT: Karl Marx, "A Contribution to the Critique . . . Introduction," in *Critique of Hegel's Philosophy of Right*, trans. Annette Jolin and Joseph O'Malley (Cambridge [Eng.], 1970), p. 134.
33. JT: "Parliament and Government in Reconstructed Germany," in *Economy and Society*, vol. 2 (Berkeley: University of California Press, 1978), p. 1402; and "Diskussionsrede auf den Tagungen des Vereins für Sozialpolitik," in *Gesammelte Aufsätze zur Soziologie und Sozialpolitik* (Tübingen: Mohr, 1924), p. 414.
34. JT: Trsl. by Talcott Parsons (Charles Scribner & Sons, 1958), p. 181. Weber, "*The Protestant Ethic and the Spirit of Capitalism.*"
35. JT: See n33.
36. JT: See n33.
37. JT: Weber, "Science as a Vocation," in *From Max Weber: Essays on Sociology* (New York: Oxford University Press, 1955), p. 155.
38. JT: Ibid., p. 149.
39. JT: Ibid.

40. JT: Weber in a letter to Robert Liefmann on Mar. 9, 1920, printed in *Max Weber und die Soziologie heute*. Verhandlungen des 15. deutschen Soziologentages (Tübingen, 1965), p. 137, n12.

41. JT: Arnold Gehlen, "Über kulturelle Evolutionen," in *Die Philosophie und die Frage nach dem Fortschritt* (Munich: Pustet, 1964), pp. 208, 211.

42. JT: Ibid., p. 208.

43. JT: Ibid.

44. JT: Ibid.

45. JT: Ibid., p. 217.

46. JT: Gehlen, *Urmensch und Spätkultur* (Bonn: Klostermann, 1956), p. 9.

47. JT: Ibid., pp. 233f.

48. JT: Gehlen, "Die Geburt der Freiheit aus der Entfremdung," *Archiv für Rechts- und Sozialphilosophie*, Bd. 40, 1952/1953.

49. JT: Ibid., p. 352.

50. JT: Cf. Theodor Adorno and Walter Benjamin, *The Complete Correspondence 1928–1940* (Polity Press, 1990), p. 111. Cf. Letter from Adorno to Benjamin, Aug. 2, 1935, p. 112.

51. JT: Gehlen, *Über kulturelle Evolutionen*, p. 218.

52. JT: Walter Benjamin, "Central Park," in *Selected Writings: Vol. 4, 1938–1940*, p. 34.

53. Here Taubes refers of course to the eight-thousand-mile-long retreat of the communist armies under the command of Mao Zedoung from the Koumintang national army. Above, however, the "long march of the institutions" is a reference to the parole of the student movement in Germany in the '60s, spread by Rudi Dutschke, calling for a longer term political-strategic perspective along the lines of left, socialist perspectives.

54. JT: Cf. Marx, *On the Jewish Question*.

55. JT: "The Work of Art in the Age of Mechanical Reproduction," *Illuminations*, p. 224.

56. JT: Ibid., p. 225.

57. JT: Gehlen, *Urmensch und Spätkultur*, p. 285.

58. JT: Marx, "Economic and Philosophic Manuscript of 1844," in Karl Marx and Friedrich Engels, *Economic and Philosophic Manuscripts of 1844 and the Communist Manifesto*, trans. Martin Milligam (Prometheus Books, 1988), p. 109.

59. JT: Gehlen, "Die Säkularisierung des Fortschritts," in *Säkularisation und Utopie*, Festschrift für Ernst Forsthoff (Stuttgart, 1967), pp. 65 and 70f.

60. JT: Cf. Marx, *On the Jewish Question*.

61. JT: Cf. Marx, *Critique of Hegel's Philosophy of Right*.

62. JT: *Illuminations*, p. 259.

63. JT: *Die Säkularisierung des Fortschritts*, pp. 69f.

382 Notes

64. JT: "Der Sozialismus," *Gesammelte Aufsätze zur Soziologie und Sozialpolitik*, p. 498.

65. JT: Karl Marx and Friedrich Engels, "Critique of Hegel's Philosophy of Law," Introduction in *Collected Works of Karl Marx and Friedrich Engels*, 1843–44, vol. 3, p. 17.

66. JT: Ibid.

67. JT: Ibid.

CHAPTER 18

1. Eds.: Taubes published this essay originally in English as "Four Ages of Reason," *Archiv für Rechts- und Sozialphilosophie* 42 (1956): 1–14. We are following the English edition. The essay is signed by Taubes as located at Princeton with the note that "a draft of this paper was delivered as a lecture at the Philosophy Club at Yale and at the Philosophy Club at Harvard in the Fall Term 1954/1955. I am indebted to Professor Walter Kaufmann for some valuable criticism."

2. JT: Theodor W. Adorno, "Kritik des Logischen Absolutimus," *Archiv für Philosophie* 2 (1954): 130ff.

3. JT: Max Horkheimer, *Eclipse of Reason* (New York, 1917), pp. 17ff.

4. The book to which Taubes refers was originally published in German in 1927, with a second edition in 1928 (*Kaiser Friedrich der Zweite* [Berlin: G. Bondi]). Taubes's reference on the next page, at the conclusion of his summarizing account of Kantorowicz, is to a 1931 edition. However, in 1931 an authorized English translation by E. O. Lorimer was published in London: *Frederick the Second, 1194–1250* (London: Constable & Co. Ltd., 1931), and simultaneously in New York (by R. R. Smith). This was republished in New York by F. Ungar Publishing Company in 1957.

5. Frederick II in 1231, also *Constitutiones Regni Siciliae*.

6. JT: Ernst Kantorowicz, *Kaiser Friedrich* (Berlin, 1931), pp. 207ff.

7. JT: Carl Schmitt, *Ex Captivitate Salus* (Köln, 1950), pp. 68ff.

8. JT: Francis Bacon, *Novum Organum*, ed. Basil Montague (London, 1825); *Summary of the II Part: On the Interpretation of Nature and the Empire of Man* XIV, p. 31.

9. Ostwald, who received the Nobel Prize for chemistry in 1909, published a little book during that same year, "Die energetischen Grundlagen der Kulturwissenschaft." Three years later he published another version, *Der energetische Imperativ* (Leipzig: Akademische Verlagsgesellschaft, 1912). The basic imperative is not to waste energy, but rather to utilize it.

10. JT: Herbert Marcuse, "Some Social Implications of Modern Technology," *Studies in Philosophy and Social Sciences* IX (1941): 421.

11. JT: Kant, *Critique of Pure Reason,* A 804f., B 832f.

CHAPTER 19

1. Eds.: This essay appeared originally in German as "Die Intellektuellen und die Universität," in *Universitätstage 1963: Universität und Universalität* (Berlin: Walter de Gruyter, 1963), pp. 36–55. In that 1963 volume Taubes is presented as "Prof. Dr. phil., Jewish Studies, Columbia University, New York, currently Visiting Professor at the Free Unversity of Berlin." We are translating into English for this edition.

2. JT: To understand Joachim's role in the development of the modern Weltanschauung, see H. Grundmann, *Studien über Joachim von Floris* (Leipzig, 1927); Alois Dempf, *Sacrum Imperium* (Munich, 1929); E. Benz, *Ecclesia Spiritualis* (Stuttgart, 1936); J. Taubes, *Abendländische Eschatologie* (Bern, 1947); K. Löwith, *Meaning in History* (Chicago, 1949); H. Grundmann, *Neue Forschungen über Joachim von Fiore* (Marburg, 1950); E. Voegelin, *The New Science of Politics* (Chicago, 1952).

3. JT: H. Grundmann, *Studien über Joachim von Floris* (Leipzig: Teubner, 1927), pp. 164ff.

4. JT: E. Voegelin (n1), pp. 109ff.

5. JT: For the emergence of the medieval university, see the extremely informative yet neglected lecture by Herbert Grundmann, *Vom Ursprung der Universität im Mittelalter* (Berichte über die Verhandlungen der Sächsischen Akademie der Wissenschaften, Philologisch-historisch Klasse, Bd. 103, Heft 2) Berlin 1957, which I gratefully follow in outline.

6. JT: Grundmann (n4), p. 11.

7. JT: F. Stein, *Die akademische Gerichtsbarkeit in Deutschland* (Berlin, 1981), pp. 11ff.

8. JT: G. Post, "*Parisian Masters as a Corporation*" (1200–1246), Speculum IX (1934): 421–45.

9. JT: Grundmann, op. cit., p. 16.

10. Eds.: The German term *Stände* is rendered throughout this essay as "estates," since that is the term that is still used in medieval history to describe the orders of the feudal division

11. JT: P. Kibre, *The Nations in the Medieval Universities* (Washington, DC: Medieval Academy of America, 1948).

12. JT: Grundmann, op. cit., p. 26.

13. JT: Grundmann, op. cit., p. 31; and H. Koeppler, "Friedrik Barbarossa and the Schools of Bologna," *English Historical Review* LIV (1939): 577–607.

14. JT: Scc the new and improved edition of *Historia calamitatum,* ed. J. T. Muckle, *Medieval Studies* XII (Toronto, 1950).

15. JT: See H. Grundmann, "Sacerdotium—Regnum—Studium. Zur Werung der Wissenschaft im 13. Jahrhundert," *Archiv für Kulturgeschichte* XXX IV (1951): 5–21.

16. JT: H. Grundmann, *Studien*, p. 168.

17. JT: P. Mandonnet, *Siger de Brabant et l'Averroisme latin au XIIIme siècle. Étude Critique et Documents inédits* (Fribourg, 1899). Second edition, vol. I: *Étude Critique* (Louvain, 1911); vol. II: *Textes Inédits* (Louvain, 1908) is still decisive for our understanding of Siger. Cf. E Voegelin, "Siger de Brabant," *Philosophy and Phenomenological Research IV* (1944): 505–25.

18. JT: Siger de Brabant, *Quaestiones de Anima Intellectiva* VII (Mandonett, ibid., vol. 2, pp. 164ff.).

19. JT: Mandonnet (n15), vol. 2, p. 171.

20. Ed.: The German term that Taubes uses here—Intelligenz or intelligence—is difficult to translate. The abstract noun mostly refers to the intellectual elite of the respective eras throughout this essay. "Intelligentsia" serves as a good equivalent, but Taubes discusses this term specifically further down, its etymology and its culturally specific valence, when analyzing the history of the university in Russia. With this in mind, we use the term interchangeably with intellectual elite.

21. JT: Cited following J. Habermas, *Stukturwandel der Öffentlichkeit* (Neuwied: Luchterhand, 1962), p. 83. [Translated by Thomas Burger, *The Structural Transformation of the Public Sphere: An Inquiry into a Category of Bourgeois Society* (Cambridge, MA: MIT Press, 1991).]

22. JT: Cf. Hunter van Duzer, *The Contribution of the Ideologues to French Revolutionary Thought* (Baltimore, 1935).

23. JT: A. Gouillois, *Le Salon de Madame Helvétius* (Paris, 1894), p. 206.

24. JT: See, for the following, Hans Barth, *Wahrheit und Ideologie* (Zürich: Eugen Rentsch, 1961), pp. 23ff.

25. JT: Ibid.

26. JT: E. Durkheim, *Le Socialisme*, ed. Marcel Mauss (Paris: Felix Alcan, 1928), p. 131.

27. JT: M. Barrès, *Scènes et Doctrines du Nationalisme* (Paris: F. Juven, 1902).

28. JT: Cf. A. Thibaudet, "Pour l'histoire du parti intellectuel," *Nouvelle Revue Française* (XXV): 132, 265–72.

29. JT: Cf. the essay "Matérialisme et Revolution," *Situations* III (Paris, 1949), pp. 172ff.

30. JT: M. Malia, "Was ist Intelligentsia?" in *Die Russische Intelligentsia*, ed. R. Pipes (Stuttgart: Kohlhammer, 1962), pp. 11–32.

31. JT: *My Past and Thoughts: The Memoirs of Alexander Herzen*, trans. Constance Garnett (New York: Alfred A. Knopf, 1973), p. 232.

32. JT: See L. Labedz, "The Structure of the Soviet Intelligentsia," in *Die Russische Intelligentsia*, p. 100.

33. JT: R. Hofstädter, *The American Political Tradition* (New York: Vintage, 1948).

34. A. M. Schlesinger Jr., *The Age of Jackson* (Boston: Little Brown and Company, 1945).

35. JT: R. K. Merton, "The Role of the Intellectual in Public Bureaucracy," in *Social Theory and Social Structure* (Glencoe, NY: Free Press, 1957).

36. JT: N. Birnbaum, "Die Intellektuellen in der gegenwärtigen Politik der Vereinigten Staaten," *Zeitschrift für Politik* II, N.F. (1955): 118–32.

37. JT: Cited from P. F. Lazarsfeld and Wagner Thielens Jr., *The Academic Mind* (Glencoe, NY: Free Press, 1958), p. 167.

38. JT: Ph. Rieff, "The Case of Dr. Oppenheimer," *The Twentieth Century* CLVI (1954): 113ff., 218ff.

39. JT: H. Rosenberg, *The Tradition of the New* (New York: Horizon Press, 1959), pp. 280ff.

40. JT: J. Habermas in the introduction to the study *Universität und Gesellschaft* (Studentenbefragung), Frankfurt 1955 (Manuskript) (Forschungsbericht im Archiv des Instituts für Sozialforschung).

41. JT: Cf. H. Marcuse, *Eros and Civilization* (New York: Vintage, 1955); and his essay "Idéologie et Société Industrielle Avancée," *Meditations* 5 (1962): 57–71.

42. JT: Ibid.

43. JT: E. Von Haler, *Der Beruf als Wissenschaft* (Berlin: Bondi, 1920), pp. 8ff. See E. Topitsch, *Sozialphilosophie zwischen Ideologie und Wissenschaft* (Neuwied: Luchterhand, 1962), pp. 79ff.

44. JT: Trans. William S. Lewis, in *The Heidegger Controversy*, ed. Richard Wolin (Cambridge, MA: MIT Press, 1991), p. 30.

45. JT: Ibid., p. 32.

46. JT: Ibid., p. 36.

47. JT: Habermas, *Universität und Gesellschaft*, n40 above.

48. Eds.: One of the many instances in which Taubes does not cite his source. We are using the English translation of Benjamin's "One-Way Street," published in *Reflections: Essays, Aphorisms, Autobiographical Writing*, trans. Edmund Jephcott, ed. Peter Demetz (New York: Schocken Books, 1986), see p. 93.

CHAPTER 20

1. Eds.: This essay was published originally in German, as "Zur Konjunktur des Polytheism," in Karl Heinz Bohrer, ed., *Mythos und Moderne: Begriff und Bild einer Rekonstruktion* (Frankfurt, 1983), pp. 457–70.

2. Eds.: The earliest program of German idealism was described in a short manuscript of 1796 in Hegel's handwriting, the Systemfragment, often rendered as System Programme, and was first published by Franz Rosenzweig in 1917. Au-

thorship cannot be determined unequivocally. However, it is certain that it was written in the Tübingen seminary during the time when Hegel, Schelling, and Hölderlin studied there. Different scholars attribute the writing of the text to all or one of these men. It therefore appears in the collected works of all three. The text discusses the form of the ideal future knowledge and is quite aptly titled.

3. Eds.: Taubes makes a pun. In German the word "hell" [*Hölle*] is phonetically similar to the word cave [*Höhle*]. The case no doubt invokes Plato's cave, of Plato's cave.

4. Eds.:. The war of all against all, which is, according to Hobbes, the natural state of human interaction.

5. Eds.: This is one of Taubes's favorite locutions in his German essays, so we are introducing it into the English translation.

6. Eds.: Theodor W. Adorno, Max Horkheimer, *Dialectic of Enlightenment* (London: Verso, 1997), p. 27

7. Eds.: Taubes does not provide a reference here. The statement can be traced back to an interview with Lévi-Strauss conducted by *Spiegel* ("Humanism Threatens Humanity," 53 [1971]: pp. 91ff.), which is one of Germany's prominently left, and more recently center-left, weeklies, on the political and philosophical implications of structuralism. Lévi-Strauss explains the attraction of structuralism to his contemporaries who were active in the student movement, by claiming that it does not separate science and art in its analyses of concrete phenomena.

8. Eds.: Appears in English as chapter 5, "In Praise of Ploytheism (On Monomythical and Polymythical Thinking)," in Odo Marquard, *Farewell to Matters of Principle: Philosophical Studies* (New York: Oxford University Press, 1989), pp. 87–111.

9. Eds.: An allusion to Hans Blumenberg's essay "Wirklichkeitsbegriff und Wirkungspotential des Mythos," in Manfred Fuhrmann, ed., *Terror und Spiel: Probleme der Mythenrezeption*, vol. IV, *Poetik und Hermeneutik* (Munich: Wilhelm Fink Verlag, 1971), pp. 23ff.

10. Eds.: An allusion to Leszek Kolakowski, *Die Gegenwärtigkeit des Mythos* (Munich: Piper, 1973), in the meantime translated by Adam Czerniawski as *The Presence of Myth* (Chicago: University of Chicago Press, 1989).

11. Eds.: This phrase stems from Kolakowski's essay, *Die Gegenwärtigkeit*, p. 90.

12. Eds.: The term *Geisteslage* is one that Taubes uses often, especially in this essay. It can be traced back to Paul Tillich's essay "Ideen zur Geisteslage der Gegenwart" in the volume *Kairos: Geisteslage und Geisteswendung* (Darmstadt, 1926), pp. 1–21. It implies situation of consciousness, intellectual situation, or episteme.

13. Eds.: Taube alludes to Paula Philipsson, *Genealogie als mythische Form: Studien zu Theogonie des Hesiod* (Osloae: A.W. Brogger, 1936).

14. Eds.: This is one of the most prominent verses to be recited in the liturgy of the Day of Atonement, which Taubes knew quite well.

15. Eds.: See Simon Kaplan's translation, *Religion of Reason Out of the Sources of Judaism* (New York: F. Ungar, 1972), pp. 191ff.

16. JT: Cohen, p. 193.

17. Eds.: Taubes's allusion to Robert Musil's *The Man Without Qualities* (1930–42), translated most recently by Sophie Wilkins (New York: Alfred A. Knopf, 1995).

18. Eds.: *Religion of Reason*, p. 194.

19. Eds.: Taubes refers to Marquard's treatise *Schwierigkeiten mit der Geschichtsphilosophie* (Frankfurt: Suhrkamp, 1973), to date untranslated.

20. Eds.: Allusion to Jesus, the "Galilean." Medieval legend had it that Julian's last words were *vicisti Galilaee*.

21. Eds.: This is Nietzsche's locution from his Preamble to the *Gay Science*.

22. Eds.: This catch phrase to capture the entire course of philosophy is Franz Rosenzweig's in his *Star of Redemption* (1921). Rosenzweig was incidentally also the one who discovered the *Systemfragment* with which Taubes starts his essay.

23. Eds.: Most recently translated by Rudolf A. Makkreel and Frithjof Rodi (Princeton, NJ: Princeton University Press, 1991).

CHAPTER 21

1. Eds.: This essay was produced in German originally, as a presentation on radio for the station Sender Freies Berlin, Dec. 11, 1963, and repeated on Mar. 24, 1988. We are translating this essay from the version presented in *Vom Kult zur Kultur*.

2. JT: S. Freud, *An Autobiographical Study* (New York: W. W. Norton, 1989), p. 52.

3. JT: S. Freud, "The Libido Theory," *General Psychological Theory* (New York: Collier, 1963), p. 228.

4. JT: E. Jones, *The Life and Work of Sigmund Freud* (New York: Basic Books, 1953–1957), vol. II, p. 109.

5. JT: M. Heidegger, *Kant and the Problem of Metaphysics* (Bloomington: Indiana University Press, 1990), p. 140.

6. JT: Ibid., p. 141.

7. JT: Ibid., p. 168.

8. JT: M. Heidegger, "What Is Metaphysics?" in *Basic Writings*, trans. David Farrell Krell (New York: HarperCollins, 1993).

9. JT: K. Jaspers, *Reason and Anti-Reason in Our Time*, trans. Stanley Goodman (Hamden, Eng.: Archon, 1971), p. 23.

10. JT: Ibid.

11. JT: Ibid., p. 22.

12. JT: F. Borkenau, "Atomphysik und Tiefenpsychologie," *Der Monat*, VII, vol. 83 (June 1955): 257–64.
13. JT: Ibid., p. 251.
14. JT: Ibid., p. 262.
15. JT: Ibid.
16. JT: K. Jaspers, *Reason and Anti-Reason in Our Time*, p. 23.
17. JT: *Archiv für Rechts- und Sozialphilosophie* XI (1952/1953): 338–53.
18. JT:. Gehlen, *Die Seele im technischen Zeitalter* (Frankfurt: Klostermann, 1957), p. 340
19. JT: Ibid., p. 100.
20. JT: Herbert Marcuse, *Eros and Civilization* (Boston: Beacon Press, 1965), p. 13.
21. JT: Ibid., p. 126.
22. JT: Ibid., p. 24.
23. JT: On the Depotentialization of Transcendental Philosophy.
24. JT: In *Literatur und Gesellschaft* (1963): 23–35.
25. JT: G. W. F. Hegel, *The Phenomenology of the Spirit*, trans. A. V. Miller (Banarsidass, 1998), p. 49.
26. JT: Ibid., p. 54.
27. JT: Ibid., p. 53.
28. JT: Freud, *The Ego and the Id* (New York: W. W. Norton, 1989).
29. JT: *New Introductory Lectures on Psycho-Analysis, Works*, vol. 22 (London: Hogarth Press, 1953–74), p. 68.
30. JT: Ibid., vol. 19, p. 236.
31. JT: "The Structure of the Unconscious," in *An Outline of Psychoanalysis* (London and New York: W. W. Norton, 1949), pp. 35–37.
32. JT: Hegel, *Phenomenology*, p. 492.
33. JT: Ibid., p. 493.
34. JT: "Economic and Philosophical Manuscripts of 1844," in *Early Writings*, trans. Rodney Livingstone (London: Penguin, 1994), p. 357.
35. JT: Marx, Grundrisse: *Foundations of the Critique of Political Economy*, trans. Martin Nicolaus (London: Penguin, 1996), p. 366.
36. JT: Ibid., p. 106.
37. JT: S. Freud, "Civilization and Its Discontents," in *Works*, vol. 21, p. 140.
38. JT: T. Adorno, *Minima Moralia* (London: Verso, 1996), p. 66.
39. JT: S. Freud, "Civilization and Its Discontents," in *Works*, vol. 21, p. 143.
40. JT: H. Marcuse, "Trieblehre und Freiheit," in *Freud in der Gegenwart* (Frankfurter Beiträge zur Soziologie Bd. 6) (1957): 411.
41. JT: S. Freud, "Civilization and Its Discontents," in *Works*, vol. 21, p. 180.
42. JT: "Group Psychology and the Analysis of the Ego," in *Works*, vol. 18, p. 103.

43. JT: Ibid., p. 6.

CHAPTER 22

1. Eds.: This essay was originally published in English, in *Psychoanalysis and the Future: A Centenary Commemoration of the Birth of Sigmund Freud* (*Psychoanalysis* 4, no. 45) (New York, 1957), pp. 136–42. The German translation in VKK is adapted from Volker Läpple's German translation in *Psychoanalyse und Religion*, ed. Eckart Nase and Joachim Scharfenberg (Darmstadt: Wissenschaftliche Buchgesellschaft), pp. 167–75. We are following the English original here.
2. Eds.: Cp. *Totem and Taboo*. Freud's reference is to William Robertson Smith, *Lectures on the Religion of the Semites,* first series: *The Fundamental Institutions* (Edinburgh: A. and C. Black, 1889).
3. JT: Freud.
4. JT: Freud.
5. Eds.: From "Moses and Monotheism," see *Standard Edition of the Complete Psychological Works of Sigmund Freud*, ed. and trans. James Strachey, vol. 23, p. 85. He deploys the same quote again in his final lectures on Paul; see *Political Theology of Paul*, trans. Dana Hollander (Stanford: Stanford University Press, 2003), p. 91. Cp. the whole section there, pp. 88–95.
6. Eds.: Ibid., pp. 86–87.
7. Eds.: Ibid., pp. 87–88.
8. *Moses and Monotheism.*
9. Nietzsche, *Will to Power.*
10. Eds.: Taubes seems to quote Karl Löwith's *Weltgeschichte und Heilsgeschehen: Die theologischen Voraussetzungen der Geschichtsphilosophie* (Stuttgart: Kohlhammer, 1956), p. 186. So VKK, p. 378. Löwith has precisely the same quote, without reference.

Index of Names

Abelard, Peter, 285
Abrams, Meyer Howard, 110, 365, 366
Abulafia, Abraham, xxix, 54
Adeimantus, 222
Adorno, Theodor W., xxi, xxix, xlvi, 250–54, 262, 303, 305–7, 313, 344, 347, 379–82, 386, 388
Agamben, Georgio, xvi
Akiva, Rabbi, 143
Aland, Barbara, 145, 370
Albertus Magnus, 286
Almarich of Bena, 285
Althizer, Thomas J. J., xxxviii, xli, 346
Aquilas, 143
Aragon, Louis, 99, 104
Aristotle, 30, 127, 285, 286
Auerbach, Erich, 76, 77, 85, 346, 360
Augustine, xlix, 37, 77, 85, 86, 153, 166, 167, 171, 172, 187, 218, 337, 354

Baader, Franz von, 107
Bach, Johann Sebastian, 236
Bachofen, Johann Jakob, 238, 314
Bacon, Francis, 99, 106, 121, 274, 382
Badiou, Alain, xx
Bakunin, Mikhail, 15, 230, 231
Balthasar, Hans Urs von, xl, 182, 183, 186, 187, 193, 375
Barrès, Maurice, 389, 290, 384
Barth, Hans, 384
Barth, Karl, xix, xxii, xxxvii–xli, 51, 148, 149, 171, 174, 178, 179, 177–94, 207, 213, 218, 371, 375
Basilides, 87, 360

Baudelaire, Charles, 100–102, 105–7, 110–12, 114, 121, 122, 365–67, 380
Bauer, Bruno, 16, 292
Bauer, Walter, 361
Bäumler, Alfred, 314
Baur, Ferdinand Christian, 187, 197, 369, 375, 376
Bayle, Pierre, 224
Beauvoir, Simone de, 290
Beda, 131
Belinsky, Vissarion, 15
Benjamin, Walter, xix, xxi, xxxiii, xlvi, 105, 109, 110, 112, 120, 249, 250–53, 262, 264, 266, 301, 347, 358, 366, 379, 380, 381, 385
Benz, Ernst, 383
Berdyaev, Nikolai, 168
Berger, Klaus, 346
Bergson, Henri, 176, 183, 231, 239
Bernoulli, Carl Albrecht, 147, 155, 371–73
Birnbaum, Norman, 385
Blake, William, 108, 121
Blass, Friedrich, 79
Bloch, Ernst, 120, 140–42, 370
Bloom, Harold, 346
Bloy, Leon, 341
Blüher, Hans, 46, 34
Blumenberg, Hans, xvii, xxiii, xxxi, xxxvi, xlvii, 61, 63, 115, 119–23, 138, 313, 358, 359, 365, 369, 386
Bohatec, Josef, 360
Böhme, Jacob, xxxv, 133, 209, 369
Bolz, Norbert, 344
Bonald, L. G. A. Vicomte de, 289

Bonhoeffer, Dietrich, xix
Borkenau, Franz, 318, 319, 388
Bosch, Hieronymus, 228
Bousset, Wilhelm, 89, 361
Breton, André, 110, 114, 120, 366
Breughel, Pieter, 228
Bruno, Giordano, 170
Buber, Martin, xxiv, xxv–xxvii, xxx, xxxvi, 10–27, 46, 52, 53, 141–46, 345, 350, 351–54, 370
Bulgakov, Mikhail, 168
Bultmann, Rudolf, xxxvii, 47, 73, 216, 314, 374, 376, 377

Camus, Albert, 290
Cardozo, 7
Carnap, Rudolf, xxxv, 124, 127, 368
Celsus, 77, 80, 91, 92
Cieszkowski, Earl, 15
Clemenceau, 289
Clemens of Alexandria, 65, 91, 366
Cohen, Hermann, 66, 307, 314, 355
Colpe, Carsten, 359
Comte, Auguste, 224, 283, 389
Constantine, 95, 156, 201
Copernicus, Nicolaus, 29, 196
Cornelius Agrippa, 337
Couliano, Joan P., 345
Cousin, Victor, 355

da Costa, Uriel, 7
Dadisho, 16
Däubler, Theodor, 107
David of Dinand, 285
Davies, William David, 5
de Benoist, Alain, 313
de Leon, Moses, 54
de Lubac, Henri, 175
de Maistre, 123, 289, 292
de Vries, Jan, 314
Dempf, Alois, 383
Descartes, René, xxii, 16, 99, 106, 181, 273, 324–26, 353, 356
Deutero-Isaiah, xxvi, 19–23

Dilthey, Wilhelm, 166, 176, 310
Dölger, Joseph, 89
Donne, John, 121, 367
Donoso Cortés, Juan, 223, 377
Dostoyevsky Fyodor, 15, 121, 193, 293
Dreyfus, Alfred, 289–91
Dürer, Albrecht, 228
Durkheim, Emile, 276, 384

Ebertz, Michael N., 346
Eckhart, 133, 172
Einstein, Albert, 295
Eliade, Mircea, 305
Eliot, T. S., 122
Elisha ben Abuya, 145, 370
Engels, Friedrich, 16, 310, 349, 379, 381, 382
Epiphanius, 74
Eusebius of Caesarea, xxxvii, 97, 156
Ezekiel, xlvii, 18, 19, 306, 307, 356
Ezra, 53

Falke, Konrad, 239
Faye, Jean Pierre, 136
Festinger, Leon, 146, 349, 370
Feuerbach, Ludwig, 16, 181, 198, 206, 211, 218, 291, 330, 376, 377
Fichte, Johann Gottlieb, 168, 173, 262, 291, 321
Flaubert, Gustave, 110, 111
Franck, Sebastian, 168
Frank, Jacob, xiiii, 8
Fränkel, Herrmann, 128, 368
Franklin, Benjamin, 229
Freud, Sigmund, xix, xxii, xlii, xliii, xlix, 231, 238, 239, 315–33, 334–41, 348, 387, 388
Frederick II, of Hohenstaufen, 382
Friedrich, Hugo, 98, 102
Fuhrmann, Manfred, 313
Funkenstein, Amos, 345

Gadamer, Hans-Georg, xviii
Galilei, Galileo, 29

Index of Names   393

Gamaliel, Rabban, 53
Gehlen, Arnold, xlv, xlvi, 260–67, 321, 322, 332, 347, 381, 388
Geiger, Abraham, 57
George, Stefan, xxiii, 344
Gerke, Friedrich, 363
Glatzer, Nahum N., 32
Goethe, Johann Wolfgang, 28
Goldberg, Oskar, xx–xxii, xlii–xlv, 238–47, 347, 377–79
Goppelt, Leonhard, 346
Gouillois, Alois, 384
Grabar, André, 96, 364
Grandville, 250
Grant, Robert. M., 359
Grass, Günter, 136, 362
Grillmeier, Aloys, 96
Grundmann, Herbert, 383–84
Guttman, Julius, 34, 35, 355

Haardt, Robert, 359
Habermas, Jürgen, 384, 385
Ha-Levi of Marvege, Jacob, xxix, 54
Ha-Levi, Yehuda, 33
Hamann, Johann Georg, 77
Harnack, Adolf von, xxxvii, 140, 141, 143, 155, 156, 194, 197, 199, 370, 376
Harrington, Sir John, 228
Haussmann, Georges-Eugène, 251
Hayim, Hafetz, 99
Hegel, Georg Wilhelm Friedrich, xxi, xxii, xxv–xli, xlvi, x,viii, 6, 10–12, 14–18, 25, 27, 28, 30, 31, 34–39, 42, 44, 50, 52, 77, 114, 115, 124, 125, 128, 131, 137, 168, 173, 174, 176, 180, 181, 184, 185, 187–94, 197, 202, 209–13, 218, 219, 224, 230–32, 241, 262, 280, 281, 283, 286, 287, 291–93, 302, 304, 310, 323–33, 349, 351, 353, 354, 374, 380–82, 385, 386, 388
Heidegger, Martin, xi, xxxv, xlvii, 17, 73, 77, 124–36, 137, 166, 181, 183, 207, 218, 247, 276, 299, 300, 316, 317, 320, 353, 358, 368, 369, 376, 385, 387

Heim, Karl, 200, 216, 376
Heisenberg, Werner, 260
Helvétius, Madame, 288, 384
Hennecke, Edgar, 361
Henrich, Dieter, 104
Heraclitus, 179
Herberg, Will, xxx, 46, 50, 51, 357
Herder, Johann Gottfried, xlv, 28, 311, 361, 364
Herzen, Alexander, 293, 384
Heselhaus, Clemens, 107, 366
Hesiod, 242, 386
Hess, Moses, 16–17
Hippolyt, 63, 64, 70
Hitler, Adolf, 5, 142
Hobbes, Thomas, 244, 386
Hoffmann, Ernst Theodor Amadeus, 113–14
Hofmannsthal, Hugo von, 261
Hofstädter, R., 385
Hölderlin, Friedrich, 302, 386
Horkheimer, Max, 268, 303, 305–7, 313, 344, 382, 386
Hübener, Wolfgang, 130, 136
Humboldt, Wilhelm von, 287, 291, 293, 298
Hume, David, 277
Hunter van Duzer, Ch., 384
Husserl, Edmund, 73, 176, 325
Huxley, Aldous, 296

Ibn Ezra, xxviii, 34, 35
Ignatius, 87, 375
Imdahl, Max, 363
Irenaeus, 68, 70, 74, 92, 94, 152, 359–62
Isaac, Jacob, 23, 24
Iser, Wolfgang, 108, 109, 364

Jackson, Andrew, 294, 385
Jacobsen, J. P., 158
Jaspers, Karl, xlvii, 317–20, 329, 374, 387, 388,
Jauss, Hans Robert, 85, 110, 359, 365–67

Index of Names

Jefferson, Thomas, 229
Jesus, xxxiv, xxxv, 23, 25, 26, 47–56, 71, 78, 80, 81, 84, 85, 91, 92, 95, 96, 150, 167, 191, 192, 197, 202, 204, 351, 352, 357, 360, 261, 364, 365, 387
Joachim of Fiore, xxviii, xlvi, 167, 181, 202, 210, 282, 383
Johannes Scotus Eriugena, xxv, 133
Jonas, Hans, xxxii, 73, 101, 105, 109, 112, 115, 137, 145, 358, 359, 365, 366, 369, 370
Jones, Ernest, 387
Julian, 63, 309, 387
Jung, Carl Gustav, 104, 253, 276
Justin, 88–90, 361–63
Justinian, 272, 285

Kahler, Erich von, 385
Kant, Immanuel, xxi, 30, 58, 165, 176, 179, 181, 184, 272, 274, 277, 280, 281, 290, 302, 311, 312, 324, 382, 383, 387
Kantorowicz, Ernst, 272, 382,
Kerényi, Karl, 238, 305
Keyserling, Hermann Graf, 210, 376
Kibre, Pearl, 383
Kierkegaard, Søren, xxii, xxxvii, xxxix, 114, 156, 171, 174, 180, 181, 185, 188–90, 193, 207, 211, 213, 218, 223
Kireyevski, Ivan, 15
Kirk, Geoffrey Stephen, 314
Klages, Ludwig, 210, 276, 376
Kleist, Heinrich von, xx, 379
Koepp, Wilhelm, 177
Koeppler, H., 383
Kracauer, Siegfried, 112, 359, 367
Kramer, Fritz, 314
Krochmal, Nachman, xxvii–xxviii, 28–44, 345, 355
Kuhlmann, Gerhardt, 217, 377

Labedz, Leopold, 384
Lautréamont, 122
Leibniz, Gottfried Wilhelm, 38, 134, 135, 181, 273
Leiris, Michel, 112

Lenin, Vladimir, 310
Lessing, Gotthold Ephraim, xxvii–xxxix, 33, 173, 184, 283
Lévi-Strauss, Claude, 304–5, 386
Liefmann, Robert, 260, 381
Lilla, Mark, xv
Locke, John, 224, 228
Loerke, Oscar, 107
Lohmeyer, Ernst, 85, 381
Löwith, Karl, xxxvii, 346, 354, 374, 383, 389
Luhmann, Niklas, 130, 136
Lukács, Georg, 111 249, 367, 379
Luria, Isaac, xxix, xxxii, 54, 109
Luther, Martin, xxxvii, 170, 171, 186, 192, 207, 211, 218

Macho, Thomas, 344, 345, 348, 378
MacLachlan, Wilson R., 346
Maimonides, xxvii, xxix, 32, 54, 55, 133
Malia, Martin, 384
Malthus, Thomas Robert, 116
Mandonnet, P., 384
Mann, Thomas, xlii, xliii, xlvii, 235, 237–40, 377–78
Marcion, xxxvi–xxxix, 93, 137–46, 187, 362, 369, 370
Marcuse, Herbert, xxi, 321, 322, 332, 344, 382, 385, 388
Marquard, Odo, xvii, xxxi, xlvii, 135, 302, 314, 323, 386, 387
Marx, Karl, 10 f., 15xi, xxi, xxii, xxv, xlvi, xlvii, 6, 15–17, 20, 24, 172, 298, 219, 224, 230, 231, 248–50, 255–67, 283, 292, 293, 304, 309–11, 313, 314, 321, 323, 325, 326, 329, 330, 331, 335, 349, 379–82, 388
McCarthy, Joseph, xlvii, 295
Meinecke, Friedrich, 28, 354
Mendelssohn, Moses, xxvii, 33, 355
Merton, Robert K., 385
Milton, John, xlvi
Mohammed, 50
Mombert, Alfred, 107
Montaigne, Michel Eyquem de, 158

Index of Names 395

Montesquieu, Charles de, 228
Morey, Charles, 96
Mozart, Wolfgang Amadeus, xxxix, 189–90

Napoleon, 288–89
Nathan of Gaza, 6
Naville, Pierre, 109–10, 366
Necker, Jacques, 287
Nerval, Gérard de, 120, 367
Nestle, Walter, 314
Newton, Isaac, 273
Nietzsche, Friedrich, xii, xix, xxxiv, 46, 52, 76–77, 85–86, 95, 97, 107, 121, 122, 134, 148, 151–52, 159, 160, 165, 181, 184, 189, 193, 194, 197, 198, 206, 208, 209, 224, 231, 239, 257, 258, 261, 302, 307, 323, 325, 335, 339–41, 359, 360, 364, 372, 373, 387, 389
Nock, Arthur D., 347
Novalis, 100

Oepke, Albrecht, 186–87
Offenbach, Jacques, 351
Oppenheimer, Robert, xlvii, 295–96, 385
Origen, xxxix, xli, 80, 81, 92, 184, 202, 212, 362
Orwell, George, 296
Ostwald, Wilhelm, 277, 382
Otto, Walter F., 305
Overbeck, Franz, xix, xxii, xxxvii, 46, 147–61, 181, 193, 370–73

Pannenberg, Wolfhart, xxxi
Parmenides, xxxv, 124–30, 134–36, 368
Pascal, Blaise, xxxvii, 121, 171
Paul the Apostle, xi, xvi, xviii, xix, xx, xxiv, xxvi, xxxiv, xxxv, xxxvii, xlix, 4–6, 11–13, 18, 20, 21, 47, 49, 51, 53–58, 76–88, 94, 140, 142, 183–85, 187, 189, 192–94, 198, 199, 306, 312, 337–39, 341, 343, 344, 347, 351, 352, 354, 359, 363, 375
Péret, Benjamin, 110
Peter, 87, 89, 71, 361

Peterson, Erik, xix, 364
Petrarch, Francesco, 282
Philippson, Paula, 306
Plato, 16, 30, 88, 127, 131, 144, 196, 222, 223, 226, 232, 361, 386
Plotinus, 131
Pokorny, P., 358
Polycarp, 87
Porphyr, 77
Post, Gaines, 383
Pound, Ezra, 247
Preisendanz, Wolfgang, 114, 367
Proclus, xxvii, 35, 355
Proudhon, Pierre Joseph, 223, 230, 231
Przywara, Erich, 175, 186, 187
Pugachev, Yemelyan, 292

Rahner, Hugo, 89
Rahv, Philip, 238, 378
Ranke, Leopold von, 311
Rawidowicz, Simon, 39, 355
Reinhardt, Karl, 129
Reisner, Erwin, 204, 374, 376
Rieff, Philip, 385
Riesman, David, 296
Rimbaud, Arthur, 122
Robespierre, Maximilien de, 287
Roes, Alexander von, 285
Rohde, Erwin, 248
Roosevelt, Franklin Delano, 294
Rosenberg, Harold, 385
Rosenstock, Eugen, 46, 52
Rosenzweig, Franz, xxiv, xxx, 28, 46, 48–52, 345, 355, 357, 385, 387
Rotenstreich, Nathan, 33, 355
Rothe, Richard, 376
Rousseau, Jean-Jacques, 181, 228, 262
Ruge, Arnold, 291

Saadia Gaon, 54, 133
Sabbatai Zvi, 3, 6–8, 55, 349, 357
Saint-Simon, Claude Henri de, 250, 251, 289
Sallust, 63
Sandkühler, Hans Jörg, 314

Index of Names

Sartre, Jean Paul, 181, 290, 291
Schaeder, Hans Heinrich, xlvii, 359
Scheler, Max, 173
Schelling, Friedrich Wilhelm Joseph, xxxv, 133, 135, 137, 168, 173, 209, 211, 241, 291, 302, 307–11, 313, 314, 323, 369, 376, 386
Schiller, Friedrich, xxxii, 333
Schleiermacher, Friedrich E. D., 137
Schlesinger, Arthur M., 385
Schlier, Heinrich, 361
Schmidt, Hans Wilhelm, 187
Schmidt, Karl Ludwig, 46, 52, 345
Schmithals, Walter, 77, 360, 361
Schmitt, Carl, xiii, xvi, xix, xxiii, 252, 261, 345, 369, 382
Schoeps, Hans Joachim, xxx, 46, 50, 51, 345
Scholem, Gershom, xxiv, xxv, xxvi, xxvii, xxxii, xl, 3–8, 55, 66, 68, 133, 344–49, 355, 357–59, 369
Schopenhauer, Arthur, 61, 107
Schubert, Gotthilf Heinrich, 114
Schürer, Emil, 357
Schwarz, Hermann, 173
Schwarzschild, Steven, 355
Schweitzer, Albert, 5, 349
Sedlmayr, Hans, 363
Segal, Alan. F., 145
Sewell, Elizabeth, 122, 377
Shaftesbury, Anthony, 28
Shakespeare, William, 335
Siger von Brabant, 286, 384
Simmel, Georg, 275, 322
Simon Magnus, 91
Sloterdijk, Peter, 345
Smith, Robertson, 337, 389
Socrates, 114, 179, 222, 239, 247, 289
Solger, Karl Wilhelm Ferdinand, 113, 114
Sorel, Georges, 231, 239, 289, 377
Spencer Brown, George, xxiii
Spengler, Oswald, 112
Spinoza, Baruch de, xxxvii, 7, 41, 99, 106, 135, 158, 170, 184, 204, 273, 308, 376

Steding, Christoph, 252
Stein, David, 345
Stein, Friedrich, 383
Steiner, George, xxi
Steinschneider, Moritz, 41
Strabo, xliv
Strauss, David Friedrich, 107, 151–53, 189, 292, 308
Strauss, Leo, 204, 374, 376
Stroumsa, Gedalyahu G.145, 370

Taubes, Susan A., 343, 347
Tertullian, 92, 359, 362
Thales von Milet, 16
Theissen, Gerd, 346
Thibaudet, Albert, 384
Thoby, Paul, 363
Thomas Aquinas, 131, 132, 171, 175, 176, 286, 368
Thurneysen, Eduard, 371
Tillich, Paul, xxxix–xli, 195–213, 347, 373, 375, 376, 383
Tönnies, Ferdinand, 257
Topitsch, Ernst, 385
Treitschke, Heinrich von, 153
Troeltsch, Ernst, 28, 29, 148, 173, 194, 205, 371
Tugendhat, Ernst, xxxv, 124, 125, 127, 129, 131, 135, 368
Turgenev, Ivan, 293
Turgot, Anne Robert de, 283

Valentinus, 81, 87
Valery, Paul, 122
Vico, Giambattista, 309
Vischer, Eberhard, 147, 149, 371
Voegelin, Eric, xxiv, xxxvi, 137, 138, 386, 384
Voigts, Manfred, xliv, 347, 378, 379
Volkelt, Johannes, 173
Voltaire, 230
Voss, Johann Heinrich, 61

Wagner, Richard, 189, 224, 385
Weber, Max, xxiii, xxv, xxxiv, xlv, xlvi,

50, 539, 172, 257–61, 266, 267, 271,
  275, 277, 278, 299, 303, 322, 345, 357,
  380, 381
Weil, Simone, xxxvi, xli, 144, 145
Weiss, Joseph, 360
Weisse, Hermann, 173
Wellhausen, xliv, 347
Whytes, William H., 296
Wilckens, Ulrich, 77, 86, 360, 361
Wilson, Thomas Woodrow, 294
Winckelmann, Johann Joachim, 61

Wittgenstein, Ludwig, 144, 303
Wolfson, Harry A., 132

Yamauchi, Ewin A., 349
Yeats, William Butler, 108
Yehuda Ha-Nassi, Rabbi, 9
Yerushalmi, Yosef Hayim, 345

Ziegler, Leopold, 173
Zunz, Leopold, 41–42

Cultural Memory in the Present

Jacob Taubes, *Occidental Eschatology*

Roberto Esposito, *Communitas: The Origin and Destiny of Community*

Peter Hitchcock, *The Long Space: Transnationalism and Postcolonial Form*

Vilashini Cooppan, *Worlds Within: National Narratives and Global Connections in Postcolonial Writing*

Josef Früchtl, *The Impertinent Self: A Heroic History of Modernity*

Michael Rothberg, *Multidirectional Memory: Remembering the Holocaust in the Age of Decolonization*

Jean-François Lyotard, *Enthusiasm: The Kantian Critique of History*

Frank Ankersmit, Ewa Domanska, and Hans Kellner, eds., *Re-Figuring Hayden White*

Stéphane Mosès, *The Angel of History: Rosenzweig, Benjamin, Scholem*

Ernst van Alphen, Mieke Bal, and Carel Smith, eds., *The Rhetoric of Sincerity*

Alexandre Lefebvre, *The Image of the Law: Deleuze, Bergson, Spinoza*

Samira Haj, *Reconfiguring Islamic Tradition: Reform, Rationality, and Modernity*

Diane Perpich, *The Ethics of Emmanuel Levinas*

Marcel Detienne, *Comparing the Incomparable*

François Delaporte, *Anatomy of the Passions*

René Girard, *Mimesis and Theory: Essays on Literature and Criticism, 1959–2005*

Richard Baxstrom, *Houses in Motion: The Experience of Place and the Problem of Belief in Urban Malaysia*

Jennifer L. Culbert, *Dead Certainty: The Death Penalty and the Problem of Judgment*

Samantha Frost, *Lessons from a Materialist Thinker: Hobbesian Reflections on Ethics and Politics*

Regina Mara Schwartz, *Sacramental Poetics at the Dawn of Secularism: When God Left the World*

Gil Anidjar, *Semites: Race, Religion, Literature*

Ranjana Khanna, *Algeria Cuts: Women and Representation, 1830 to the Present*

Esther Peeren, *Intersubjectivities and Popular Culture: Bakhtin and Beyond*

Eyal Peretz, *Becoming Visionary: Brian De Palma's Cinematic Education of the Senses*

Diana Sorensen, *A Turbulent Decade Remembered: Scenes from the Latin American Sixties*

Hubert Damisch, *A Childhood Memory by Piero della Francesca*

Dana Hollander, *Exemplarity and Chosenness: Rosenzweig and Derrida on the Nation of Philosophy*

Asja Szafraniec, *Beckett, Derrida, and the Event of Literature*

Sara Guyer, *Romanticism After Auschwitz*

Alison Ross, *The Aesthetic Paths of Philosophy: Presentation in Kant, Heidegger, Lacoue-Labarthe, and Nancy*

Gerhard Richter, *Thought-Images: Frankfurt School Writers' Reflections from Damaged Life*

Bella Brodzki, *Can These Bones Live? Translation, Survival, and Cultural Memory*

Rodolphe Gasché, *The Honor of Thinking: Critique, Theory, Philosophy*

Brigitte Peucker, *The Material Image: Art and the Real in Film*

Natalie Melas, *All the Difference in the World: Postcoloniality and the Ends of Comparison*

Jonathan Culler, *The Literary in Theory*

Michael G. Levine, *The Belated Witness: Literature, Testimony, and the Question of Holocaust Survival*

Jennifer A. Jordan, *Structures of Memory: Understanding German Change in Berlin and Beyond*

Christoph Menke, *Reflections of Equality*

Marlène Zarader, *The Unthought Debt: Heidegger and the Hebraic Heritage*

Jan Assmann, *Religion and Cultural Memory: Ten Studies*

David Scott and Charles Hirschkind, *Powers of the Secular Modern: Talal Asad and His Interlocutors*

Gyanendra Pandey, *Routine Violence: Nations, Fragments, Histories*

James Siegel, *Naming the Witch*

J. M. Bernstein, *Against Voluptuous Bodies: Late Modernism and the Meaning of Painting*

Theodore W. Jennings, Jr., *Reading Derrida / Thinking Paul: On Justice*

Richard Rorty and Eduardo Mendieta, *Take Care of Freedom and Truth Will Take Care of Itself: Interviews with Richard Rorty*

Jacques Derrida, *Paper Machine*

Renaud Barbaras, *Desire and Distance: Introduction to a Phenomenology of Perception*

Jill Bennett, *Empathic Vision: Affect, Trauma, and Contemporary Art*

Ban Wang, *Illuminations from the Past: Trauma, Memory, and History in Modern China*

James Phillips, *Heidegger's Volk: Between National Socialism and Poetry*

Frank Ankersmit, *Sublime Historical Experience*

István Rév, *Retroactive Justice: Prehistory of Post-Communism*

Paola Marrati, *Genesis and Trace: Derrida Reading Husserl and Heidegger*

Krzysztof Ziarek, *The Force of Art*

Marie-José Mondzain, *Image, Icon, Economy: The Byzantine Origins of the Contemporary Imaginary*

Cecilia Sjöholm, *The Antigone Complex: Ethics and the Invention of Feminine Desire*

Jacques Derrida and Elisabeth Roudinesco, *For What Tomorrow . . . : A Dialogue*

Elisabeth Weber, *Questioning Judaism: Interviews by Elisabeth Weber*

Jacques Derrida and Catherine Malabou, *Counterpath: Traveling with Jacques Derrida*

Martin Seel, *Aesthetics of Appearing*

Nanette Salomon, *Shifting Priorities: Gender and Genre in Seventeenth-Century Dutch Painting*

Jacob Taubes, *The Political Theology of Paul*

Jean-Luc Marion, *The Crossing of the Visible*

Eric Michaud, *An Art for Eternity: The Cult of Art in Nazi Germany*

Anne Freadman, *The Machinery of Talk: Charles Peirce and the Sign Hypothesis*

Stanley Cavell, *Emerson's Transcendental Etudes*

Stuart McLean, *The Event and Its Terrors: Ireland, Famine, Modernity*

Beate Rössler, ed., *Privacies: Philosophical Evaluations*

Bernard Faure, *Double Exposure: Cutting Across Buddhist and Western Discourses*

Alessia Ricciardi, *The Ends of Mourning: Psychoanalysis, Literature, Film*

Alain Badiou, *Saint Paul: The Foundation of Universalism*

Gil Anidjar, *The Jew, The Arab: A History of the Enemy*

Jonathan Culler and Kevin Lamb, eds., *Just Being Difficult? Academic Writing in the Public Arena*

Jean-Luc Nancy, *A Finite Thinking*, edited by Simon Sparks

Theodor W. Adorno, *Can One Live after Auschwitz? A Philosophical Reader*, edited by Rolf Tiedemann

Patricia Pisters, *The Matrix of Visual Culture: Working with Deleuze in Film Theory*

Talal Asad, *Formations of the Secular: Christianity, Islam, Modernity*

Dorothea von Mücke, *The Rise of the Fantastic Tale*

Marc Redfield, *The Politics of Aesthetics: Nationalism, Gender, Romanticism*

Emmanuel Levinas, *On Escape*

Dan Zahavi, *Husserl's Phenomenology*

Rodolphe Gasché, *The Idea of Form: Rethinking Kant's Aesthetics*

Michael Naas, *Taking on the Tradition: Jacques Derrida and the Legacies of Deconstruction*

Herlinde Pauer-Studer, ed., *Constructions of Practical Reason: Interviews on Moral and Political Philosophy*

Jean-Luc Marion, *Being Given: Toward a Phenomenology of Givenness*

Theodor W. Adorno and Max Horkheimer, *Dialectic of Enlightenment*

Ian Balfour, *The Rhetoric of Romantic Prophecy*

Martin Stokhof, *World and Life as One: Ethics and Ontology in Wittgenstein's Early Thought*

Gianni Vattimo, *Nietzsche: An Introduction*

Jacques Derrida, *Negotiations: Interventions and Interviews, 1971–1998*, editd by Elizabeth Rottenberg

Brett Levinson, *The Ends of Literature: Post-transition and Neoliberalism in the Wake of the "Boom"*

Timothy J. Reiss, *Against Autonomy: Global Dialectics of Cultural Exchange*

Hent de Vries and Samuel Weber, eds., *Religion and Media*

Niklas Luhmann, *Theories of Distinction: Redescribing the Descriptions of Modernity*, edited and introduction by William Rasch

Johannes Fabian, *Anthropology with an Attitude: Critical Essays*

Michel Henry, *I Am the Truth: Toward a Philosophy of Christianity*

Gil Anidjar, *"Our Place in Al-Andalus": Kabbalah, Philosophy, Literature in Arab-Jewish Letters*

Hélène Cixous and Jacques Derrida, *Veils*

F. R. Ankersmit, *Historical Representation*

F. R. Ankersmit, *Political Representation*

Elissa Marder, *Dead Time: Temporal Disorders in the Wake of Modernity (Baudelaire and Flaubert)*

Reinhart Koselleck, *The Practice of Conceptual History: Timing History, Spacing Concepts*

Niklas Luhmann, *The Reality of the Mass Media*

Hubert Damisch, *A Childhood Memory by Piero della Francesca*

Hubert Damisch, *A Theory of /Cloud/: Toward a History of Painting*

Jean-Luc Nancy, *The Speculative Remark (One of Hegel's Bons Mots)*

Jean-François Lyotard, *Soundproof Room: Malraux's Anti-Aesthetics*

Jan Patočka, *Plato and Europe*

Hubert Damisch, *Skyline: The Narcissistic City*

Isabel Hoving, *In Praise of New Travelers: Reading Caribbean Migrant Women Writers*

Richard Rand, ed., *Futures: Of Derrida*

William Rasch, *Niklas Luhmann's Modernity: The Paradox of System Differentiation*

Jacques Derrida and Anne Dufourmantelle, *Of Hospitality*

Jean-François Lyotard, *The Confession of Augustine*

Kaja Silverman, *World Spectators*

Samuel Weber, *Institution and Interpretation: Expanded Edition*

Jeffrey S. Librett, *The Rhetoric of Cultural Dialogue: Jews and Germans in the Epoch of Emancipation*

Ulrich Baer, *Remnants of Song: Trauma and the Experience of Modernity in Charles Baudelaire and Paul Celan*

Samuel C. Wheeler III, *Deconstruction as Analytic Philosophy*

David S. Ferris, *Silent Urns: Romanticism, Hellenism, Modernity*

Rodolphe Gasché, *Of Minimal Things: Studies on the Notion of Relation*

Sarah Winter, *Freud and the Institution of Psychoanalytic Knowledge*

Samuel Weber, *The Legend of Freud: Expanded Edition*

Aris Fioretos, ed., *The Solid Letter: Readings of Friedrich Hölderlin*

J. Hillis Miller / Manuel Asensi, *Black Holes / J. Hillis Miller; or, Boustrophedonic Reading*

Miryam Sas, *Fault Lines: Cultural Memory and Japanese Surrealism*

Peter Schwenger, *Fantasm and Fiction: On Textual Envisioning*

Didier Maleuvre, *Museum Memories: History, Technology, Art*

Jacques Derrida, *Monolingualism of the Other; or, The Prosthesis of Origin*

Andrew Baruch Wachtel, *Making a Nation, Breaking a Nation: Literature and Cultural Politics in Yugoslavia*

Niklas Luhmann, *Love as Passion: The Codification of Intimacy*

Mieke Bal, ed., *The Practice of Cultural Analysis: Exposing Interdisciplinary Interpretation*

Jacques Derrida and Gianni Vattimo, eds., *Religion*